The Virtuoso Conductors

The Virtuoso Conductors

The Central European Tradition from Wagner to Karajan

RAYMOND HOLDEN

Yale University Press
New Haven and London

For information about this and other Yale University Press publications please contact:
U.S. Office: sales.press@yale.edu   yalebooks.com
Europe Office: sales@yaleup.co.uk   www.yalebooks.co.uk

Set in Sabon by J&L Composition, Filey, North Yorkshire
Printed in Great Britain by St Edmundsbury Press Ltd, Bury St Edmunds

Library of Congress Control Number 2005930977

ISBN 0–300–09326–8

A catalogue record for this book is available from the British Library

10 9 8 7 6 5 4 3 2 1

For Mary
and in memory of
Sir John Pritchard and Professor Cyril Ehrlich

Contents

Illustrations

Preface

To write a book about virtuoso conductors from Central Europe is a daunting task. The topic is vast and the possibilities are manifold. Because of the sheer volume of material available, I limited the scope of this book by applying strict criteria to each chapter. First, the principal subject had to be an important figure who wielded considerable artistic power, rather than just a jobbing conductor; second, the greater part of his career had to be based in Europe; third, his rise to fame had to have taken place in the German-speaking countries, and, fourth, he had to have interacted regularly with at least one previous generation of Central European conductors. As these criteria presented structural problems, I decided against a continuous chronological narrative and focused instead on individual artists. By devoting chapters to single conductors, I was better able to explore their influences, practices and principles, programme policies, relationships with other artists and place in the historical continuum.

Accessing and interpreting original source material relating to conductors is often a difficult task. Their scores, diaries and orchestral parts have in many cases been sold, lost or given away by their heirs. Artefacts belonging to conductors are scattered across the globe and often prove difficult, if not impossible, to authenticate. Late nineteenth- and early twentieth-century opera programmes and posters rarely contain the names of conductors, and theatre reviews of the period mention conductors only when discussing either a new production or a première. Although concert programmes, posters and reviews are less problematic because they place the conductor more prominently, performance information belonging to opera houses, concerts halls, orchestras and record companies is often either incomplete or riddled with errors. There is nevertheless a wealth of source material available, and that which the scholar has the privilege of examining allows a fascinating insight into the thoughts and practices of artists who dominated music performance from the middle of the nineteenth century.

I would like to thank my editor, Malcolm Gerratt, for his unswerving support, patience and advice during the preparation of this book. I would also like to thank Dr Robert Baldock, Dr and Mrs Kenneth Birkin, Professor Chris Walton, Albert Landa, Alexander Negrin and the late Professor Cyril Ehrlich for their generous help and counsel, and Polly Fallows for her contribution as copy-editor. But my greatest debt of gratitude is to my wife, Mary, for her unfailing optimism and encouragement. She sustained me throughout this project, and without her support this book would not have been written.

Richard Wagner, *Zukunftsdirigent*

For more than 150 years, conducting has been dominated by artists from Central Europe. Their homogeneity of approach, their sense of purpose and their unique relationship with the music that they performed set them apart from the other schools of conducting that emerged during the same period. Unlike the Italian, Russian, British and American schools, that of Central Europe grew out of the music itself. Many of the conductors either were composers or aspired to composition and saw the recreative process as a direct consequence of their creative activities. This meant that throughout the school's history its conductors had a special relationship with, and understanding of, new music. As each of the artists from the school was the product of German cultural practices, they also felt a particular affinity with the developing Austro-German canon of compositions. They considered that their ethnicity predetermined their ability to perform masterworks from that tradition and that their interpretations of those works had a greater authority than those by artists from other racial groups. Their socioeconomic backgrounds, their musical education, their career paths, their approach to programming, their theories and practices and their professional relationships all had much in common. As time progressed, those commonalities became increasingly important to them as individuals and were the basis for a special bond that eventually united them as a group.

While conducting in the German-speaking countries can be traced back to Louis Spohr, Carl Maria von Weber and Felix Mendelssohn, the modern school of Central European conductors was influenced principally by the thoughts and practices of Richard Wagner.[1] Although his name is generally associated today with stage works, or, at the very least, extracts from stage works of his own creation, he was also an interpreter of importance, whose experiences on the podium led to a set of practices and principles that coloured the interpretations of future generations of artists. While some of Wagner's ideas on performance have fallen from favour in recent years, they were of seminal importance between the late nineteenth and mid twentieth centuries. The application of those ideas was a defining feature of the Central European school and their effect can still be heard in the interpretations of some artists from that tradition today.

Like most other German conductors, Wagner rose through the ranks of the opera-house system.[2] His first professional post was at the Würzburg theatre, where he was appointed répétiteur and chorus master in January 1833. As a mediocre pianist, Wagner must have found his duties at Würzburg daunting. Nevertheless, he continued to pursue a career in the theatre when he accepted the post of Musikdirektor at Magdeburg in 1834. After making his conducting début with Mozart's *Don Giovanni* that August,[3] he conducted a repertoire with the Magdeburg company that included stage works by Bellini, Rossini, Weber, Boieldieu, Spohr, Marschner and Cherubini[4] and the first performance of his second opera, *Das Liebesverbot*. For the première of the last named on 29 March 1836, Wagner was given the luxury of ten days of rehearsal. During that preparation period, he worked closely with the singers and attempted to make them more secure in their roles by 'continual prompting, loud singing along, and shouting drastic directions concerning the necessary movements'.[5] Although Wagner was tireless in his effort to achieve the highest standard possible, 'the singers, especially the men, were so exceptionally unsure of themselves that from beginning to end their embarrassment crippled the effect of every one of their roles'.[6]

Wagner left Magdeburg at the end of March 1836 and joined the staff of the Königsberg theatre on 1 April 1837. Although the Königsberg company had much in common with that of Magdeburg, he was able to gain new experiences by conducting symphonic music for the first time.[7] His stay in Königsberg was brief, however, and from July 1837 to March 1839 he worked at the Stadttheater in Riga. From his description of the theatre and its orchestra, it seems that his working conditions were grim. The theatre was small, with a stage that could accommodate only modest scenery, and the orchestra pit was tiny, with seating for only two first violins, two second violins, two violas and one double bass. Although Wagner introduced 'substantial reinforcements into [the] pit',[8] the instrumental forces at his disposal remained meagre and must have sounded something akin to a modern-day amateur orchestra. Nevertheless, he continued to expand his musical horizons there by conducting fifteen operas in his first season and twenty-four in his second.[9]

After Riga, Wagner spent time in Paris before being appointed 'Kapellmeister to His Majesty [the King of Saxony]' at Dresden on 2 February 1843.[10] The Dresden theatre was of a superior kind to those that had engaged him previously and his duties included the conducting of operas and, later, a few concerts. Among the stage works that he performed were Gluck's *Armida* and Mozart's *Don Giovanni* in 1843. His tempi for the latter seem to have been particular contentious, prompting one critic to write:

> In Paris it is a consistently prevailing error in the performance of German compositions that the slow tempos are taken far too slowly, the quick too quickly; and yesterday, . . . Herr Wagner fell into the same basic error . . . in the A-major duet of Don Giovanni and Zerlina, or Zerlina's F-major aria, or the A-major trio in the second act, yesterday's tempos were so far too slow for them to have kept to the most correct as four is to three, i.e., in the period which would have been used for three beats, at least four would have had to be completed. Other [places] were the opposite, e.g., the entrance of the 4/4 time in C Major in the first finale [was] by the same ratio too quick. . . . Of course, I must add that the *Kapellmeister* in many instances could not do as he wished; that he gave one tempo, but the singers took another, and there was nothing left for him but to give in.[11]

During the winter of 1846, Wagner prepared a performance of Beethoven's Symphony No. 9 ('Choral'). According to him, the work was hardly known in Dresden and had failed to impress at a charity concert given there some years earlier. In an effort to make the work more appealing to the public, Wagner wrote a series of short preliminary articles in the local newspaper and drew up an extra-musical programme for the symphony based on Goethe's *Faust*. The programme was not only welcomed by some local listeners but was later issued by Wagner's protégé, Hans von Bülow, at his double performance of the work at Meiningen on 19 December 1880.[12]

For the 1846 performance, Wagner borrowed the orchestral material from the Leipzig Concert Society, and marked it according to his own musical demands. Central to those demands was the balance of the orchestra. Traditionally, in late Classical and early Romantic music, woodwind and brass instruments were doubled in the loud passages.[13]

Although Wagner was not completely opposed to that approach, he felt that it needed to be refined and extended. In his influential article of 1873, *Zum Vortrage der neunten Symphonie Beethoven's* (*Performing Beethoven's Ninth Symphony*), he set out his ideas about how that could be achieved and his reasons for modifying the work's existing orchestration.[14] For Wagner, Beethoven's deafness and the more primitive instruments available to him meant the certain passages lacked clarity and brilliance. Wagner's aim was to rectify these shortcomings by retouching Beethoven's original text. Those adjustments then became popular with subsequent generations of Central European conductors, who later interpolated them into their interpretations.

Wagner also altered the regular disposition of the chorus and orchestra for his Dresden performance of Symphony No. 9. To achieve his musical objectives, he undertook a complete reconstruction of the stage area, so that the orchestra could be seated in the centre. For the chorus, he obtained permission to construct a semicircular, terraced seating area that partially surrounded the orchestra. The building of this terrace was costly and Wagner was required to argue strongly in its favour.[15] Today his seating plan might seem obvious, but at the time it was revolutionary. Previously, when concerts involving choirs were given in the Dresden theatre, the chorus and vocal soloists were placed in front of the orchestra. By seating the orchestra in front of the singers, Wagner ensured that he was in closer contact with orchestral players throughout the performance and that the balance between chorus and orchestra in the fourth movement could be adjusted according to the needs of the music and the theatre's acoustics. It seems, then, that Wagner's modified plan literally set the stage for future performances of Beethoven's Symphony No. 9.

While Wagner's Dresden period was the last in which he held a titular post as a conductor, he appeared in a number of cities as a guest conductor from 1850. His activities in Zürich and London were of particular significance. Having accepted an invitation in late 1849 to conduct at a concert given by the Allgemeine Musikgesellschaft of Zürich, Wagner made his début with its orchestra on 15 January 1850 with Beethoven's Symphony No. 7.[16] As he considered the orchestra to be 'rather weak',[17] the experience must have been disappointing. Nevertheless, he respected the ability of individual players and decided to instigate a number of reforms to improve the orchestra's overall standard. He suggested that the strings should be strengthened and that more experienced players should be brought in from neighbouring towns. He also insisted upon at least three rehearsals for each symphony, which, he argued, resulted in 'a freedom of execution which had previously eluded me'.[18]

The 'freedom' that Wagner gained from those reforms probably benefited the other performances he gave at Zürich between 1850 and 1855. His repertoire was relatively wide and, at the eight operatic performances and twenty-nine public and private concerts that he conducted, he gave music by six and nine composers respectively.[19] While three of his public concerts were devoted to his music and a further seven contained worksone or more either composed or edited by him, the composer whose music he performed most at Zürich was Beethoven. Twenty-two concerts contained a work by the composer and, apart from Nos. 1, 2 and 9, Wagner conducted all the Beethoven symphonies at the public concerts.[20] In view of its importance to him, the absence of Symphony No. 9 from the public concerts might seem strange, but the cost of performance, along with the poor standard of the orchestra, possibly precluded him from giving a complete performance of the work at Zürich.

While resident in Switzerland, Wagner was approached by the Philharmonic Society of London to conduct eight concerts between March and June 1855.[21] In November 1854, Michael Costa resigned as the Society's conductor and a replacement was needed urgently.[22] The Philharmonic's first choice was Louis Spohr but he declined its invitation. Shortly thereafter, on 24 December 1854 letters were sent to Hector Berlioz and Wagner; Cyril Ehrlich argues convincingly that, by sending the letters on the same day, the Society have intended that both artists should share the season.[23] This hypothesis is given greater weight when one considers that Berlioz had already conducted for the organization in 1853[24] and therefore was familiar to the Society. In contrast, Wagner's abilities were known only by personal recommendation.[25] Unfortunately, Berlioz was unable to accept the offer as the Philharmonic's rival, the New Philharmonic Society, had already engaged him. Wagner, on the other hand, was willing to accept, with two stipulations: he needed an assistant conductor to perform some of the more minor works and he was to be given sufficient rehearsal time to meet his needs. As the new season was approaching and greater clarification was needed, the Society decided that a representative should travel to Zürich to discuss the details of the arrangement with Wagner in person. George Anderson, the treasurer, was dispatched and was empowered to offer a fee of 200 guineas. If he was unable to secure the services of Wagner, he was to proceed first to Liszt in Weimar and, if that should fail, to Franz Paul Lachner in Munich.[26]

These contingency plans proved unnecessary, however, as Anderson's discussions with Wagner were successful.[27]

Given Wagner's love of rehearsing, his first encounter with the Philharmonic's orchestra must have been unsettling.[28] Unlike their colleagues in mainland Europe, London musicians were in the habit of presenting concerts after one rehearsal only.[29] Nevertheless, Wagner was able to rise to the challenge and to give a wide repertoire that included fourteen symphonies, twenty-three vocal works, six concerts and seventeen overtures.[30] At the heart of that repertoire were the symphonies of Beethoven, which were performed at seven of his eight Philharmonic concerts.[31] Although Wagner's rehearsal time in London was limited and he was able to communicate only in French, he seems to have imposed his will on the orchestra successfully. That said, the critics for *The Times* and the *Spectator* were unimpressed by him both as a composer and as an interpreter. Central to their concerns was Wagner's manipulation of tempo. Although many of the reviews dealt with his approach in general terms, Henry Smart's critique in the *Sunday Times* was more specific and recorded that Wagner reduced 'the speed of an allegro – say in an overture or the first movement – fully one-third, immediately on the entrance of its cantabile phrases'.[32] Despite its brevity, Smart's analysis is of vital importance, because it raises issues that Wagner would later address at length in his influential treatise, *Über das Dirigiren (On Conducting)*.

Few of Wagner's prose works were as significant as *On Conducting*.[33] For later generations of conductors, many of the practices and principles enshrined therein were fundamental to their interpretations of works from the Austro-German canon. The treatise's style is highly personal, with Wagner expressing his ideas, both explicitly and implicitly, in an outspoken and occasionally racist manner. Much of his wrath is focused on his conducting colleagues, some of whom he considered ill-equipped executants because they were not from the opera-house system or the orchestra. Wagner was also scathing about the lack of leadership shown by the 'older conductors', the outdated system of orchestral tenure and the inadequate string strength of most orchestras when performing 'modern orchestral music'.[34] Although Wagner states at the outset that he '[did] not mean to set up a system [with his treatise], but simply [wanted] to . . . record a number of practical observations',[35] the didactic tone of the piece and the points that it raises have ensured its central place in the history of Central European conducting.

The two areas of Wagner's treatise that influenced future generations of conductors most were those concerning melos and tempo manipulation. For him, the 'whole duty of a conductor is comprised in his ability always to indicate the right *tempo*'. He particularly admired François-Antoine Habeneck's 1839 performance of Beethoven's Symphony No. 9 at Paris where 'the right tempo [was found because the conductor] persistently fix[ed] the attention of his orchestra upon the melos of the symphony'.[36] It was self-evident to Wagner from Habeneck's approach that 'The right comprehension of the melos is the sole guide to the right tempo' and that 'conductors so frequently fail to find the true tempo because they are ignorant of singing'.[37] This simple guide to tempo soon influenced not only conductors from Central European but also those from other backgrounds. The French composer and conductor Pierre Boulez, for example, later recorded that he had read 'with great interest what Wagner thought about conducting' and concurred with it. Like Wagner, Boulez argued 'Until one finds the right speed – not necessarily a constant speed, but one that fits the moment, and can vary with the context – until one finds that tempo, then even in one's own compositions the interpretation remains weak and prevents the music from swelling forth'.[38] Similarly, the British conductor Sir John Barbirolli wrote: 'Wagner laid it down that the two fundamental principles underlying the art [of conducting] were: (1) giving the true tempo to the orchestra; (2) finding the "melos," by which he means the unifying thread of line that gives a work its form and shape. Given these two qualities, of course, we have the conductor *in excelsis*, and most of our lives must be spent in trying to obtain these qualities, the more especially the first.'[39]

Concerning tempo modification, Wagner argued: 'since Beethoven there has been a very considerable change in the treatment and the execution of instrumental music'.[40] And, where 'Things which formerly existed in separate and opposite forms, each complete in itself, are now placed in juxtaposition, and further developed, one from the other, so as to form a whole[,] . . .[w]e may consider it established that in classical music written in the later style *modification* of *tempo* is a *sine qua non*'.[41] Central to Wagner's understanding of tempo modification were the speeds of the first and second subjects in sonata form movements. Of Weber's overture to *Oberon*, for example, he wrote: 'The second theme . . . does not in the least partake of the character of the allegro . . . but, as soon as the true character of the theme is brought out, it becomes apparent that a composer must think such a scheme capable of considerable modification if it is to combine both principles (*Hauptcharactere*).'[42] When performing the second theme of Weber's overture to *Der Freischütz*, Wagner also took into account the character of the passage and performed it at a slightly slower speed than the first. Similarly, when interpreting Beethoven's overture to *Egmont*, Wagner argued in favour of a reduced tempo at the second subject (bar 82). He considered that a *meno mosso* was particularly effective at that juncture and that when his protégé, Hans von Bülow, followed his suggestion and 'firmly arrested and very slightly modified' the speed at that point, it 'brought about a new reading of the overture – the *correct* reading'.[43]

Wagner's influence on subsequent generations of Central European conductors cannot be stressed enough. He was a giant figure to whom they all looked for inspiration and guidance. His stage works were at the heart of their programme policies and his thoughts on conducting were seminal to their performance styles. Many of the conductors to whom a chapter is devoted in this book either openly acknowledged Wagner's importance in their own treatises on conducting or applied his principles in their marked scores and recordings. The need to retouch the orchestrations of established masterpieces, the notion of melos as the basis for a correct tempo and the need to modify tempo at structurally important passages were practices common to all of Wagner's successors in Central Europe. For them, his ideas formed the nucleus of a style of conducting that was representative of the artistic culture from which they emerged. That culture nurtured them as young musicians as they rose through the opera-house system, provided them with a repertoire of works that was the basis for their programme policies and gave them a sense of belonging that was unique in the history of performance. As curators of that culture, they were aware of their artistic responsibilities and ensured that what they had learned, either directly or indirectly, from Wagner was passed from one generation to the next.

HANS von BUELOW

CHAPTER 1

'The master-conductor Hans von Bülow'[1]

Hans von Bülow was one of the most dynamic and versatile musicians of the nineteenth century. A protégé of Richard Wagner, Bülow was an outstanding teacher, pianist, editor, journalist, composer and conductor.[2] Although his unpredictable personality meant that his career path was sometimes rocky, he overcame many of the difficulties he faced during his often colourful and sometimes traumatic life to become the idol of the next generation. He was admired particularly by Gustav Mahler and Richard Strauss for his strict personal discipline, his integrity as an artist, his elegant podium style and his penetrating interpretations. But he was not without his critics, and he was accused by some of giving eccentric performances that were perversions of the printed text. While the exact nature of his performance style might never be known fully, his stature as an artist has rarely been doubted.

Born at Dresden on 8 January 1830, Hans was the first of Eduard and Franziska von Bülow's two children.[3] Like many of the other conductors discussed in this book, Hans came from a secure middle-class background.[4] Although serious music had a relatively broad appeal during the nineteenth century, the cost of music lessons meant that, as a rule, only children from the middle class and above could aspire to a career in the arts. Ironically, however, music tended to be considered an undesirable profession by the bourgeoisie and was often shunned as a job by those who benefited from it most. While the Bülows were disciplined intellectually and placed great importance on a broad knowledge of the arts in general, they too were not keen for Hans to pursue a career in music. Nevertheless, the family considered a good practical understanding of music to be desirable socially, so they sent Hans for his first piano lessons when he was aged seven. After two years with his first teacher, a chamber music partner of his mother, Hans became a pupil of Cäcilie Schmiedel, with whom he studied for five years; later, he was a student of Friedrich Wieck and Louis Plaidy.[5]

As domestic music-making was a common feature of middle-class life during the nineteenth century, it is unsurprising that Bülow's first performing experiences were in the home. Having developed quickly as a pianist, Hans was encouraged to accompany family performances of Lieder and to perform four-hand piano arrangements of symphonies and chamber music. For the rigorously disciplined Bülows, domestic performances of art music were only part of a wider set of experiences that they had planned for their children. Eduard and Franziska considered a good general education to be of vital importance, and when the family moved to Stuttgart, Hans was encouraged to complete his schooling there. But music continued to fascinate him, and although he had no formal piano teacher during that period, he benefited artistically from his encounters with the local conductor, Bernhard Molique, with whom he played chamber music, and the composer Joachim Raff, whose friendship and music he valued for the rest of his life.[6]

At Stuttgart, Bülow's outstanding abilities as a pianist were soon recognized. The quality of his musicianship and the sureness of his technique led to his being invited to perform at the local Hofkapelle's Fifth Abonnement (subscription) Concert on 1 January 1848. At that concert, he played Raff's *Pianoforte-Fantasie über Themen aus Kükens Prätendenten*,[7] the first of 390 performances that he gave of his boyhood friend's works during his career. His début must have been a considerable success, because he was invited to perform Mendelssohn's D minor Piano Concerto with the Hofkapelle three months later.[8] Again, the performance was a triumph, an achievement made more remarkable because it took place only weeks before Bülow completed his Abitur, the qualification gained by young Germans after successfully finishing their secondary education.

After completing his schooling, Bülow attended university at Leipzig, where he studied legal history, philosophy, religious history and literature.[9] His parents hoped that he would pursue a career in law,[10] but music remained his overriding passion and he continued his piano and theory studies at Leipzig with Moritz Hauptmann.[11] To supplement his formal music lessons, Bülow attended concerts and operas regularly and, after his parents divorced in the autumn of 1849,[12] he followed his mother and sister to Berlin,[13] where he wrote an article for the *Berliner Abendpost* about Richard Wagner's essay, *Das Kunstwerk der Zukunft* (*The Art Work of the Future*).[14] Bülow's interest in Wagner's music stemmed from his youth in Dresden, where he attended performances of

Rienzi, *Tannhäuser* and Beethoven's Symphony No. 9 ('Choral') under the composer-conductor. Those performances were milestones in Bülow's musical development and, after he attended the première of Wagner's *Lohengrin* conducted by Franz Liszt at Weimar on 28 August 1850, it became clear to him that the music of the future was also to be his destiny.

A chance for Bülow to further his ambitions occurred shortly after the première of *Lohengrin*, when an opportunity arose for him to work closely with Wagner at Zürich. The composer had taken refuge in the Swiss city after the political disturbances of 1849 and had begun to conduct opera and concerts there. Against the wishes of his parents, Bülow decided to accept an engagement at the Zürich Stadttheater, where he was able to work under the guidance of Wagner. It seemed that Bülow, like his mentor, would take the accepted route to national and international prominence as a conductor by rising through the ranks of the Central European opera-house system. Of course, that meant that he should have been restricted to coaching singers, to rehearsing the chorus and the orchestra, and to directing off-stage bands before taking charge of performances at the Stadttheater. But because his talent was precocious and the theatre's music staff was small, he was allowed to conduct operas in public shortly after his arrival there in the middle of October 1850.

After making his début with Donizetti's *La Fille du régiment*, he conducted at least six other operas – Lortzing's *Zar und Zimmermann*, Rossini's *Il barbiere di Siviglia*, Auber's *Fra Diavolo* and *La Muette de Portici*, Cherubini's *Les Deux Journées* and Méhul's *Joseph* – and the farce *100,000 Taler* at the Zürich Stadttheater. From the list of works performed, it is clear that Bülow's ambition to explore new German music failed to materialize at the Swiss city, because the operas that he performed there had been premièred between 1800 and 1840, and only *Zar und Zimmermann* was written for the German stage. As a young conductor at a commercial theatre, Bülow's repertoire was in keeping with his junior rank, and the operas that he was allocated were typical fare for a repertory opera house of the period. For a young idealist, however, the local theatre's need to mount with popular appeal works that did little to challenge the conductor, the musician, the singers or the audience either musically or intellectually must have been frustrating, but that was the price he had to pay to work closely with his hero, Richard Wagner.

While some of the operas that Bülow conducted failed to tax him mentally, others challenged him professionally. In a letter to his sister,

Isidora,[15] dated 26 October 1850, he noted that his duties were not as simple as they appeared and that the singers and orchestra were intriguing against him because of his youth.[16] He did manage to make a few friends, however, and he was able to report that a local paper, the *Eidgenössische Zeitung*, considered his performance of *La Fille du régiment*, to be a verification of his worth as a very talented conductor. Paradoxically, the newspaper also mentioned that the orchestra lacked confidence in him because he made occasional errors.[17] His uneasy relationship with the musicians and the singers was a theme that appeared regularly in his letters to his family during his Zürich period, and, after a stormy encounter with a singer who refused to work under his direction, he left the Stadttheater in the middle of December 1850.

From Zürich, Bülow moved directly to the local theatre at nearby St Gallen. Although Wagner had recommended him for the job, he was no longer under the direct supervision of the composer. Nevertheless, Wagner continued to take an active interest in Bülow's development and visited him during his stay there. In later years, Wagner recalled that the St Gallen troupe was very poor, that the orchestra was 'dreadful' and that the theatre was 'shabby'.[18] For a town of 15,000 inhabitants, however, the size and type of theatre that Bülow encountered was common for the period. The company was managed as a commercial enterprise and the orchestra was a mixture of professional and amateur musicians. When programming, the theatre's director, Carl Herbort, was concerned principally with providing an entertaining and popular blend of works for a mixed and often undiscerning audience. It was almost inevitable, therefore, that the repertoire that Bülow conducted at St Gallen was conservative and populist and included Lortzing's *Der Waffenschmied von Worms*[19] and *Zar und Zimmermann*, Donizetti's *La Fille du régiment*, Kreutzer's *Das Nachtlager von Granada*, Weber's *Der Freischütz*, Boieldieu's *La Dame blanche* and Flotow's *Martha* and *Stradella*.

Two of the operas that Bülow conducted at Zürich – *Zar und Zimmermann* and *La Fille du régiment* – were also included in his St Gallen repertoire. Nevertheless, his task was not easy and he was soon introduced to the problems of provincial theatre life. Of particular concern was the orchestra. As it drew heavily upon the support of local amateurs, its size and personnel shifted from performance to performance. This meant that Bülow had to reorchestrate some of the works to suit the forces available. His reworking of the performance material, however, was only part of a punishing schedule that began with a chorus rehearsal at 10 a.m. and ended with either an orchestral rehearsal or a performance in the theatre at night. Living conditions were also diffi-

cult at St Gallen, and when learning a score he often remained at his
lodgings, where, to stay warm, he would study his scores in bed.[20]

Of the works that Bülow conducted during his period in Switzerland,
his performance of *Der Freischütz* in the middle of January 1851 was of
particular personal and musical importance. Bülow was aware that the
opera was a pivotal work in the history of early Romantic German
opera and that it was his first attempt at conducting a work of national
significance.[21] He was also aware that his father would be attending his
performance at St Gallen and that his decision to pursue a career in
music would be examined critically. From Eduard's correspondence, it
seems that any fears that Hans might have harboured were groundless.
Eduard reported proudly to a family member that Hans commanded the
respect of the sixty members of the orchestra, attracted a full house, was
meticulous in bringing out nuances and details, acquitted himself in
every respect as a master ('Meister') and performed without the aid of a
score,[22] a practice that he continued throughout his career.[23]

Any sense of euphoria that Bülow might have felt following his success with *Der Freischütz*, however, soon turned to disillusionment. After
being involved in a series of farces and vaudevilles that included
Nestroy's *Lumpazivagabundus* and Raimund's *Alpenkönig und
Menschenfeind*, Bülow hoped to supplement his meagre income with a
benefit performance of *La Dame blanche*. But his choice of opera was
unacceptable to the theatre's director and he was eventually allocated a
performance of *Martha* instead. With his expenses mounting, Bülow
needed to be paid promptly after the performance. After waiting in vain
for the money, he eventually demanded that he be paid immediately. His
demand did little to impress Herbort and he had to settle for only part
payment of the proceeds. Disillusioned and angry, Bülow decided to cut
his losses and leave St Gallen.

After leaving Switzerland at the end of April 1851, Bülow moved to
Weimar. There he became a piano student of Liszt, under whose influence his interest in the compositions of Beethoven blossomed. In 1852,
he gave his first public performances of that composer's music,[24] – the
first of at least 2333 Beethoven performances that Bülow gave during
his career.[25] Of those, 1386 were of works for solo piano, 831 were of
orchestral music,[26] 98 were of pieces for chamber groups, 13 were of the
opera, *Fidelio*, and 5 were of the incidental music to Goethe's *Egmont*.
When Bülow's career is examined as a whole, Beethoven's works are
found to constitute a quarter of all performances given, a statistical divi-
sion that indicates clearly the importance of the composer's music
within Bülow's overall performance aesthetic.

In April 1855, Bülow accepted an appointment at the Stern Conservatory in Berlin. Although he was employed to teach piano he was also able to give concerts regularly, and on 14 January 1858 he conducted a programme of new music with the Liebig'sche Kapelle[27] at the Berliner Singakademie. The works performed were Berlioz's overture to *Benvenuto Cellini*, Wagner's duet from the *Der fliegende Holländer*,[28] Liszt's *Festklänge* and Piano Concerto No. 2[29] and Bülow's own overture to Shakespeare's *Julius Caesar*. While the programme was a homage to new music in general and the works of Liszt and Wagner in particular,[30] Bülow also hoped to use the concert as a vehicle for promoting his own work. Although his abilities as pianist and conductor were acknowledged increasingly by the time of the concert, his skills as a composer were undervalued. Having performed his overture at Hamburg on 20 November 1855, Bülow hoped that the work would gain wider recognition from exposure in Berlin. That, however, was not the case and it failed to ignite the interest of either the public or the press. The indifference that Bülow's music faced in Berlin was typical of the reception that it received in general, and that experience may explain his reluctance to programme his works regularly at his concerts in later life.[31]

On 14 January 1859, Bülow returned to the Liebig'sche Kapelle and conducted a programme of mainly new music that included works by Beethoven, Berlioz, Wagner, Liszt and Raff.[32] Aware that his first concert with the orchestra had attracted little critical or public interest, Bülow was keen to make a greater impact at his second appearance with the ensemble by opting to act as soloist in a reading of Beethoven's Piano Concerto No. 4.[33] His ploy worked: the concert was better attended and his performance of the concerto drew a storm of applause. The response to the concerto, however, was in sharp contrast to the reaction that followed his reading of *Die Ideale*, which resulted in noisy protests from some members of the audience. But the outburst did not deter Bülow from organizing a third concert of new music with the Liebig'sche Kapelle[34] that included his own *Symphonischer Prolog zu Byrons Kain*, later renamed *Nirwana*, Berlioz's overture *Le Carnaval romain*, Wagner's *Faust Overture*, Schubert's 'Wanderer' Fantasy (arr. Liszt) and Liszt's *Fantasie über Motive aus Beethovens 'Ruinen von Athen'* and *Die Ideale*.[35] This time the audience responded enthusiastically to Liszt's symphonic poem and Bülow was able to report proudly to Wagner that:

February 27 (Sunday) was a memorable day. The opposition was silenced. The *Ideale*, with Liszt conducting, made an overwhelming impression and roused undivided enthusiasm. . . . Not one of the opposition dared to protest. . . . The *Ideale* positively drew sparks and we have at least something to take our stand on now. . . . The programme opened with my orchestral fantasia. . . . The audience listened attentively, the orchestra showed its mettle, friends behaved discreetly, but clapped enough to drown two or three fairly timid hissers, who did not feel justified in depriving me of the honour of their ill will. I had really expected this in a more intense form, and that is why I sent my unpopular piece into the flames.[36]

In the period immediately following his concerts with the Liebig'sche Kapelle, Bülow was occupied mostly by his work as a teacher and pianist. Nevertheless, he did conduct the first concert performance of Wagner's Prelude to *Tristan und Isolde* at Prague on 23 March 1859,[37] his initial reading of Liszt's *Eine Faust-Symphonie* at Weimar on 6 August 1861, the première of his own orchestral ballad *Des Sängers Fluch* at Berlin on 30 January 1863 and the Funeral March from Beethoven's Symphony No. 3 ('Eroica') at Frankfurt on 8 January 1864. At those concerts, Bülow used a conducting technique that resembled those of Wagner and Liszt. By adopting his mentors' dramatic and demonstrative methods, Bülow attracted the wrath of some commentators. The critic Richard Wuerst was particular aggrieved by Bülow's approach and argued that his 'eccentric gestures', which included 'sinking low and then quickly raising his hands high with accompanying dramatic facial expressions', were unacceptable and not the method of a good conductor.[38]

On 31 October 1863, Bülow performed Beethoven's Symphony No. 9 ('Choral') for the first time. The work was part of a concert for the Gesellschaft der Musikfreunde at the Berlin Singakademie that also included Beethoven's cantata *Meeresstille und glückliche Fahrt*, Liszt's Piano Concerto No. 2 and Gade's overture *Hamlet*.[39] Bülow's interpretation of Symphony No. 9 was influenced heavily by Wagner's thoughts on the work. The application of his mentor's ideas on tempo and reorchestration, along with his exaggerated physical gestures, elicited a mixed response from the critics. His slow speed in the first movement, his tendency to rush in the Trio, his excessive use of rubato, his habit of making stringendi and ritardandi before structurally important passages and his overstated and inconsistent approach to pauses were all attacked by the reviewers and were to become familiar criticisms of his Beethoven style in later years. What the critics failed to remark upon, however, was the structure of the concert. Previously, Bülow's programmes had been dominated by new music, but at that concert he balanced cutting-edge works with established masterpieces, a juxtaposition that would later become his preferred method when programming.

While Bülow's approach to Beethoven's Symphony No. 9 divided the critics, the Gesellschaft der Musikfreunde continued to support him and on 28 November 1863, four weeks after his first concert for the organization, he conducted his second. At that performance he gave Liszt's *Les Préludes*, Gluck's overture to *Paride ed Elena* (ed. Bülow), Beethoven's overture *Zur Namensfeier* and Violin Concerto and another reading of his own orchestral ballad, *Des Sängers Fluch*.[40] With the exception of the overtures by Gluck and Beethoven, the works he performed at that concert were all familiar to him.[41] But his increasing familiarity with orchestral music in general did not make his interpretations any less controversial, and when he gave Beethoven's Symphonies Nos. 3 and 8 for the first time, on 24 January and 6 March 1864 respectively, he continued to draw the wrath of the Berlin critics. The critical storm that raged around him did little to harm his career, however, and at the end of March 1864 he made his début at St Petersburg, where he extended his repertoire with performances of Beethoven's Symphony No. 6 ('Pastoral'), Meyerbeer's *Fest-Ouvertüre zur Eröffnung der Weltausstellung London 1862* and Mozart's Symphony No. 41 ('Jupiter').[42]

In November 1864, King Ludwig II of Bavaria engaged Bülow to assist Richard Wagner at Munich. After moving there with his wife Cosima,[43] Bülow found his duties often less than inspiring. The tedium of copying material for Wagner and playing the piano for him changed, however, when he was entrusted with the première of Wagner's *Tristan und Isolde*. Although excited by the prospect of conducting an important operatic world première for the first time, he was aware that he was also making his début at a major court theatre before a new and potentially hostile audience. Any fears that Bülow may have had were soon realized because of his relationship with Wagner. As the composer treated the Hoftheater's incumbent Generalmusikdirektor, Franz Lachner, shabbily and was engaged in a controversial relationship with King Ludwig, Bülow was swept along in the maelstrom of bad publicity and ill feeling that accompanied Wagner's every move. The press were merciless with Wagner and Bülow, often demanding that they leave Munich, but Bülow was no stranger to controversy and he was determined to do justice to his hero's score.

Having worked under Wagner's direction at the preparatory piano rehearsals for *Tristan und Isolde*, Bülow conducted the first orchestral rehearsal of the opera at the Residenztheater on 10 April 1865.[44] It then became his practice to rehearse the orchestra in the mornings and the singers in the evenings. After completing eighteen orchestral rehearsals by the beginning of May,[45] Bülow conducted the dress rehearsal in front of an invited audience of 600 guests on 11 May, took a correction rehearsal on 13 May and gave the first performance on 10 June.[46] Throughout, Bülow strove tirelessly to draw the highest standards from the singers and the orchestra and, as the Hofoper was not subjected to the rigorous financial restraints imposed by commercial theatres, he was able to achieve that goal by rehearsing systematically and meticulously. But his part in bringing the opera before the public was more than an exercise in logistics: it was a labour of love, because for him *Tristan und Isolde* was 'as beautiful as the most beautiful of dreams . . . [and] simply indescribable . . . [because of the] dreadful fascination it exerts[;] . . . an experience beyond time and place'.[47]

In the period immediately preceding the première of *Tristan und Isolde*, Bülow's wife Cosima became involved in a spectacular affair with Wagner. As the liaison was reported widely in the press, the public soon revelled in the conductor's misery. The affair quickly became a personal tragedy and a public humiliation for Bülow, who attempted to defuse the situation by taking his wife to Pest after the last performance of *Tristan und Isolde*[48] for the world première of Liszt's oratorio *Die Legende von der heiligen Elisabeth*.[49] Bülow was smitten immediately by the work and conducted the first of his six performances of it at Munich on 24 February 1866. After the second performance at the Bavarian capital the following month, Bülow reported with satisfaction to his friend Karl Bechstein,[50] 'the gallery roared at the repetition of *St. Elisabeth* the other day! You should have heard them! And these are the very people who were ready to stone me less than a year ago!'.[51]

In May 1867, Bülow returned to the Munich Hofoper as Hofkapellmeister. During his tenure there, he gave thirty-four performances of eighteen operas between May 1867 and August 1869. Of the operas performed, only a handful remained in his repertoire and, of those, nine were performed only once by him during his career.[52] Although Bülow's approach to programming at Munich was wide-ranging, it seems that many of the operas he conducted were a reaction to the needs of the wider musical community rather than an expression of his performance aesthetic. The inclusion of Franz Lachner's *Catharina Cornaro*, for example, appears to confirm that hypothesis, because neither Bülow nor Wagner held Lachner in high esteem. Bülow's performance of Lachner's opera was probably a response to his popularity at

Munich rather than his abilities as a composer. Similarly, *La Juive, Die lustigen Weiber von Windsor* and *Il trovatore* were all popular works that had limited appeal for Bülow and were included in his programme only to fulfil his obligations as Hofkapellmeister.

To suggest, however, that Bülow was occupied solely with routine duties after his return to Munich in 1867 would be to create a false impression. Although he had little to thank Wagner for personally, he remained a devoted champion of the composer's music and, when he was entrusted with the world première of *Die Meistersinger von Nürnberg* in 1868, he tackled his task with a missionary's zeal. As for the first performance of *Tristan und Isolde*, Bülow's approach to rehearsal was detailed and methodical. The singers were coached individually by the répétiteurs, the orchestra was rehearsed in sections, the company united for *Sitzproben*[53] and the production was drawn together for stage and dress rehearsals.[54]

To assist him during the long and complicated rehearsal period, Bülow enlisted the help of the young Hungarian conductor Hans Richter,[55] a former student of the Vienna Conservatory. After working for a period as Wagner's assistant at Tribschen, Richter was appointed to the music staff of the Munich Hofoper in December 1867.[56] Like Bülow, Richter was later considered a leading conductor of Beethoven's works and a champion of new music. He was recognized quickly as a versatile and reliable conductor and was influential in Vienna, Bayreuth and Britain from the late 1870s.[57] As a devoted Wagnerian who was capable of withstanding the attacks of those who opposed the composer both artistically and morally, Richter was a much valued assistant to Bülow at Munich. Even so, the mounting of *Die Meistersinger von Nürnberg* must have been extremely taxing logistically for him, because the première was the last of a series of three new productions that he conducted there during the first half of 1868.[58] Nevertheless, he was able to devote much of his time to Wagner's new work, resulting in a meticulously rehearsed première that was considered by some to be Wagner's greatest critical success since *Rienzi*. Bülow's part in bringing the opera to the stage was commented upon widely in the press and, after the première on 21 June 1868, he gave eight more performances of the work during the second half of that year.[59]

On the retirement of Lachner, Bülow took charge of the Munich Hofkapelle's Abonnement Concerts.[60] His previous experience as a concert conductor was limited to a mere handful of concerts . Moreover, the performances that he had given in Berlin and elsewhere were largely vehicles for new music. He realized quickly that, as the permanent con-

ductor of a major Abonnement series, he needed to expand his repertoire and to be more catholic in his approach. Along with the
Hofkapelle's main subscription series at the Odeon, Bülow also conducted public concerts at the Residenztheater, the Nationaltheater and
the newly established Musikschule. In an effort to meet the demands of
those engagements, Bülow increased his repertoire with performances of
twenty-eight works by thirteen composers between March 1867 and
April 1869.[61] That period also witnessed both a consolidation and an
expansion of his Beethoven repertoire, and at least two concerts were
devoted to that composer's music. At the first, on 29 March 1867,
Bülow included Symphony No. 6, excerpts from *Fidelio*, the overture
Die Weihe des Hauses and Piano Concerto No. 4 (Frl. Marstrand,
piano), and at the second, on 1 November 1868, he programmed the
overture *Leonore* No. 1, the Terzett for soprano, tenor and bass Op.
116, Piano Concerto No. 5 ('Emperor') (Hans von Bülow, piano and
conductor), some unidentified Lieder (Eduard Bachmann, soloist),
Romance for violin in F major (Joseph Venzl, violin) and Symphony No.
7. To modern listeners the length of Bülow's Munich concerts might
seem extreme, but they were typical of the period and the inclusion of
Lieder was not uncommon. Conversely, the programming of extracts
from *Fidelio* at the second concert was unusual for Bülow, who generally did not include large excerpts from operas in his concert
programmes.

From the beginning of his career, Bülow was known as a champion
of new music. At Munich, however, he became increasingly interested
in the symphonic compositions of Schubert, Schumann and
Mendelssohn,[62] a development that was greeted sceptically by some fellow Wagnerians. Although Bülow was passionate about *Zukunftsmusik*
during the early part of his career, he was soon aware that those works
could form only part of his repertoire as a jobbing conductor. As most
nineteenth-century German-speaking orchestras drew heavily upon the
emerging Austro-German canon as the basis for their concert series,
Bülow quickly realized that the music of early Romantic composers had
to be included in his programmes. But his decision to extend his conducting repertoire to include symphonic music by Schubert, Schumann
and Mendelssohn was not simply a consequence of his duties as a
Hofkapellmeister. He had always been keen to investigate unfamiliar
musical avenues, and his exploration of the early Romantic orchestral
repertoire during his Munich period was a natural extension of that
artistic journey. Consequently, he gave sixty-five performances of
orchestral works by Mendelssohn, fifty-one by Schumann and thirteen

by Schubert between 1868 and 1892. While those statistics appear comprehensive, Bülow was highly selective when adding works to his repertoire and, of those composers' symphonies, he conducted only Symphonies Nos. 2 ('Lobgesang') and 3 ('Scottish') by Mendelssohn, Symphonies Nos. 1 ('Spring'), 2 and 3 ('Rhenish') by Schumann and Symphonies Nos. 7 in B minor and 8 in C major ('Great') by Schubert during his career.

While his tenure at Munich might have satisfied Bülow musically, it did little to please him personally. Throughout the late 1860s, the affair between Cosima and Wagner continued to be a source of public humiliation and, by the summer of 1869, Bülow had decided to separate permanently from his wife. The effect of the separation was devastating for the conductor, and, in a letter to his friend Karl Klindworth[63] at the end of July 1869, he wrote that his 'health [was] ruined, physically and morally' and that he could 'hardly pull [himself] together to carry on with [his] official duties until the holidays'.[64] Two days after that note, he asked Karl Bechstein to recommend a *'thoroughly enlightened* attorney' because he intended to dissolve his marriage. He also mentioned to his friend that he had submitted his resignation for a second time and ensured that 'care has been taken not to have it refused in high quarters this time'.[65] By the end of the summer, Bülow's wish had been granted and Ludwig had released him from his contract. Ironically, the last opera that he conducted during his Munich tenure was Wagner's *Tristan und Isolde*, on 20 June 1869, and although he was adamant that he would never return to the Bavarian capital, he was persuaded by the King to conduct *Der fliegende Holländer* and *Tristan und Isolde* there in 1872. But Bülow neither forgot nor forgave the Munich public for the way in which he was treated during his tenure there and, in later life, the city and its inhabitants became his *bête noire*.

Having left Munich, Bülow worked mainly as a pianist until 1877, when he was appointed Hofkapellmeister at the Hanover Hoftheater with an annual salary of 6000 marks.[66] Part of his duties at Hanover included conducting the Hofkapelle's Abonnement Concerts, which he used as a vehicle to promote the music of Johannes Brahms.[67] After being introduced to the composer by the Hungarian violinist Joseph Joachim in 1854,[68] Bülow became increasingly interested in Brahms's music and gave no fewer than 488 performances of the composer's works during his career.[69] At Hanover, Bülow was able to explore Brahms's orchestral music for the first time with performances of Symphonies Nos. 1 and 2 and the 'Haydn' Variations on 20 October 1877, 26 April 1879 and 16 February 1878 respectively. But the Hofkapelle's

Abonnement Concerts were not simply a showcase for Brahms's works, they were also a platform for Bülow's wider performance aesthetic. In keeping with his concerts at Berlin and Munich, Bülow's first concert with the Hanover Hofkapelle was a mixture of new and established works. The programme on 29 September 1877 included Weber's overture to *Euryanthe*, an aria from Scholz's opera *Golo* (Gustav Gunz, bass), Lalo's *Symphonie espagnole* (Pablo de Sarasate, violin), Lieder by Schumann, Eduard Lassen and O. H. Lange, Sarasate's *Zigeunerweisen* (Pablo de Sarasate, violin) and Beethoven's Symphony No. 5.[70] Bülow's practice of balancing new music with familiar masterpieces was a feature of his Hanover period as a whole and, of the forty-five works by twenty-nine composers that he added to his orchestral repertoire between 29 September 1877 and 30 September 1879,[71] nineteen were composed by twelve of his contemporaries.[72] Bülow's enthusiasm for new music was not shared universally at Hanover, however, and his programme policy was criticized sharply by some members of the public who felt that they were expected to digest too many modern works. But when he planned to perform all nine Beethoven symphonies over three evenings in October 1879, the audience also reacted unfavourably, and the series had to be abandoned after the first concert.[73]

As Hofkapellmeister at Hanover, Bülow's principal duties were those of an opera conductor. Although the theatre there was less prestigious than that of Munich, it did have a long and rich tradition. After the composer Heinrich Marschner was appointed Hofkapellmeister at Hanover in 1832, he remained there for nearly thirty years, during which time he built a formidable ensemble and an excellent orchestra. As the creator of popular operatic favourites such as *Der Vampyr* and *Hans Heiling*, Marschner had little interest in promoting the early operas of Wagner at Hanover. With the appointment of his successor, Karl Ludwig Fischer, however, that situation changed, and *Tannhäuser*, *Lohengrin*, *Der fliegende Holländer* and *Rienzi* were soon heard regularly.[74] As in Munich, Bülow used the existing repertoire as the basis for his own programme policy and built upon it where necessary. During his period in Hanover, he conducted no fewer than 110 operatic performances of twenty-six works by fifteen composers.[75] Some operas, like Marschner's *Der Holzdieb*, *Der Vampyr* and *Hans Heiling* and Meyerbeer's *Robert le diable*, *Le Prophète* and *Le Pardon de Ploërmel*,[76] were obviously included to appease local audiences and to cater for popular tastes, while others, like Beethoven's *Fidelio*, Mozart's *Die Entführung aus dem Serail*, *Le nozze di Figaro*, *Don Giovanni* and *La clemenza di Tito*, Wagner's *Rienzi*, *Der fliegende Holländer*,

Tannhäuser and *Lohengrin*, Glinka's *A Life for the Tsar* and Berlioz's *Benvenuto Cellini*, were clearly designed to expand and consolidate Bülow's personal repertoire.[77]

As in Munich, Bülow set in place a series of innovations and practices at Hanover that had a direct bearing on the way his interpretations were perceived and received. Of the modifications that he made there, the disposition of the orchestra was the most visible. When conducting the Abonnement Concerts in Munich, he seated the first violins on the left, the second violins and the violas on the right, and the cellos in the middle. He then placed the winds and the horns behind the first violins, the brass and the percussion behind the second violins and violas, and the double basses behind the cellos.[78] At Hanover, Bülow continued to apply this plan at the Abonnement Concerts but used a different seating arrangement when performing in the theatre. After the orchestra pit was extended to accommodate more musicians during the summer holidays in 1879, he placed the winds to his left and the strings to his right, creating a more substantial and rounder sound.[79]

Another highly visible innovation that Bülow made at the Hofoper was his approach to the continuo in Mozart operas. During his tenure at Hanover, Bülow became increasingly interested in the composer's stage works[80] and conducted a total of nineteen performances of *Die Entführung aus dem Serail*, *Le nozze di Figaro*, *Don Giovanni* and *La clemenza di Tito* between 25 January 1878 and 23 October 1879. With the exception of *Die Entführung aus dem Serail*, a Singspiel with dialogue, the other Mozart operas contained secco recitatives and needed a continuo. In the mid to late nineteenth century, these passages were often cut heavily, abandoned in favour of spoken dialogue or reorchestrated according to the whim of the producer or the conductor. Less common in German theatres of the period was the conductor-continuo player, a practice adopted by Bülow for his interpretation of *Don Giovanni* at Hanover. Today, conductor–continuo players are increasingly common in period performance. In Bülow's case, however, where it is likely that a piano rather than a harpsichord or a fortepiano was used, artistic control, rather than an attempt at historical correctness, was probably the motivating factor. This hypothesis is confirmed partially by Bülow's cavalier attitude to the printed text. Like many of his contemporaries, Bülow was influenced heavily by Wagner's thoughts on textual fidelity. At Hanover he regularly adjusted and manipulated the scores that he performed in accordance with the ideas of his former mentor, and by inserting Prosper Pascal's orchestral arrangement of Mozart's 'Rondo alla turca' from the Piano Sonata K. 331 as a kind of

Entr'acte before Act 2 of Die Entführung aus dem Serail[81] and beginning Beethoven's opera, Fidelio, with the overture Leonore No. 3,[82] Bülow left the listener in no doubt that he was a child of his time rather than a slave to authenticity.

As in Zürich, St Gallen and Munich, Bülow's tenure at Hanover ended unhappily. Throughout his career, his tempestuous personality often affected his relationships with colleagues adversely. A perfectionist by nature, he was unwilling to make concessions easily and he expected of others the same sense of rigour that he applied personally. Of course, that expectation was doomed to failure from the outset at a provincial opera house, and while some musicians and singers were prepared to tolerate Bülow's high-handed approach, others found it unpalatable. Tension was particularly high during the preparation of Lohengrin in September 1879, when Bülow fell out with the tenor, Anton Schott.[83] Bülow's sarcasm was often biting and could be particularly offensive. After a series of rhythmic inaccuracies by Schott at a Lohengrin rehearsal, Bülow reportedly remarked in a loud voice 'das ist kein Schwanenritter, das ist ein Schweineritter!' ('that is no swan knight, that is a pig knight!'). The situation worsened at the subsequent performance when Schott was unable to control his tempi and Bülow responded by racing through the last scene. The following day the Intendant, Hans von Bronsart,[84] was confronted by Schott who refused to sing the remaining performances under the conductor and by Bülow who demanded to be released from the production. Matters then ran out of control when Schott took the matter to a higher authority in Berlin, resulting in Bülow being formally disciplined. Any hope of conciliation had faded by that point and the conductor tendered his resignation at the end of 1879.

In 1873, Bülow met Herzog Georg II von Sachsen-Meiningen,[85] whose wife, the actress Ellen Franz,[86] was a former piano pupil of Bülow. Georg was passionately interested in theatre and music and was keen to utilize fully the artistic institutions at his ducal seat, the Grand Duchy of Meiningen. To achieve that aim, he instigated a series of reforms that revolutionized the way in which theatre and concert performances were organized and perceived. His first innovations were to shift the emphasis of the Hoftheater from opera to the spoken word and to establish a theatre company of some seventy actors whom he organized personally. He then mounted productions that strove for the highest possible standards of ensemble acting and historical accuracy, ceded artistic control to the director and commissioned costumes and sets that reflected the period being portrayed. By 1874, the standard of the company had risen substantially and Georg decided to allow the troupe to tour for the first time. The Hoftheater was soon celebrated internationally and, by 1890, the company had given 2591 guest performances from London in the west to Moscow in the east.[87]

Having raised the profile of the Hoftheater, Georg was keen to transform the Hofkapelle similarly. To achieve that metamorphosis, he needed a conductor who shared his passion for excellence. Bülow was the obvious choice, but, was initially unwilling to work permanently at Meiningen. Georg was reluctant to accept Bülow's position and, after several unsuccessful attempts at engaging him, finally tempted Bülow to the Grand Duchy in 1880.[88] Crucial to Bülow's acceptance was artistic sovereignty. Although Georg could offer a salary of only 5000 Marks, considerably less than Bülow had received in Hanover, the conductor had been promised a free hand concerning all things musical and the rank of Intendant. He was also attracted by the prospect of rehearsing and performing new and established music with an orchestra that was not hindered by duties in the opera pit, the chance to explore and to disseminate his chosen repertoire systematically and didactically, the opportunity to prepare model performances of works by Beethoven and others over extended periods and the option of performing chamber music in a series that was linked programmatically to his work with the Hofkapelle. To realize those goals, Bülow increased the orchestra's strength from thirty-six to forty-nine players, engaged members of the orchestra as soloists and as chamber musicians at the subscription concerts, introduced the Ritter viola, the pedal tympani and the five-string double bass into the orchestra, insisted that the Hofkapelle stand while performing and trained the strings to play his arrangement of Beethoven's *Grosse Fuge* Op. 133 from memory.[89]

Crucial to Bülow's reforms at Meiningen was his systematic approach to programming. As a pianist, he championed the piano sonatas of Beethoven and created a sensation by performing the last five sonatas in a single evening. While he did not perform all thirty-two sonatas, he gave twenty-nine of them regularly,[90] arguing that a true understanding of the works could be achieved only through familiarity. That approach was also the basis for his method when programming Beethoven's orchestral music at Meiningen,[91] where he devoted a series of six Abonnement Concerts to the composer's music in 1880 and conducted four all-Beethoven evenings between 19 December 1880 and 16 December 1883.[92] The 1880 series, the first of two Abonnement Cycles with the Hofkapelle at Meiningen during the 1880–1 season, was given between 7 November and 12 December 1880. At those concerts, Bülow performed a comprehensive overview of the composer's orchestral out-put.[93] Curiously, Symphony No. 9 was not given as part of the First Abonnement Cycle, but was heard at a discrete concert on 19 December 1880. On that occasion, Bülow performed the symphony twice on the same evening, a practice that he repeated with the Hofkapelle on 2 April 1881 and 2 April 1884[94] and with the Berlin Philharmonic on 6 March 1889. Bülow's bizarre habit of conducting Symphony No. 9 twice at the same concert was taxing for listeners and musicians alike. The Meiningen audience, however, was warned of the conductor's intentions in advance: the programme for the 1880 performance, which contained a copy of Wagner's pamphlet about the work, and the posters for the 1881 and 1884 readings, stated clearly that the work would be heard twice. Bülow's double performances of the symphony soon became an accepted part of his performance style in the Grand Duchy and only a handful of listeners ever left the auditorium after the first reading of the work.

The impact of Bülow's interpretations of Beethoven at Meiningen was often profound. The young Richard Strauss, engaged as Bülow's assis-tant in 1885,[95] was particularly impressed by his approach to Beethoven's music. In later life, Strauss stated: 'The exactitude of his phrasing, his intellectual penetration of the score combined with almost pedantic observation of the latter, his analyses of the period structure and above all, his understanding of the psychological content of Beethoven symphonies ... have been a shining example to me to this day.' Strauss 'found particularly memorable [Bülow's] ... rigid slow temp[o] ... in the *Coriolan* overture, the slow beginning of various scherzi (*Eroica*: bridge passage leading to the funeral march ... [and] the great working up to the *fortissimo furioso*) ... [in the Ninth Sym-phony]'. Strauss also recalled that Bülow 'took the three repetitions of the scherzo of the 7th Symphony a little faster each time, not reaching full *prestissimo* until the third time[;] ... started the finale of the A major symphony like a peasants' dance with minor modifications, [and] took the coda [of the Seventh Symphony] as a tremendously exciting *stretta*'.[96]

Strauss's description of Bülow's Beethoven style was not simply the rose-tinted reminiscences of a former assistant. As a young musician, he was also impressed by his mentor's approach and reported to his father at the end of January 1886:

The performance of the 'Eroica',[97] without rehearsal, was the most splendid that you can imagine. Although our orchestra lacks the shine of the Munich orchestra, although our hall has a poor acoustic, although the Finale contained a small error in the violins, it was a performance that I will scarcely encounter again. In the Funeral March every note contained a spirit and a soul that I did not think possible from an orchestra, and the Finale: concerning the Finale, I can say that it was the first time that I encountered the full brilliance of Beethoven's Sun. . . . I was so moved after the last movement that I wept like a child in the artist's room. I was alone there with Bülow, who embraced me and gave me a kiss which I will not forget for the rest of my life.[98]

Bülow's systematic approach to programming at Meiningen also applied to other composers. Although the only cycle of works that he conducted in the Grand Duchy was that of the Beethoven symphonies, he did devote two concerts to the works of Mozart and one each to those of Mendelssohn, Brahms, Haydn and Schumann during the 1881–2 season,[99] one concert to the music of his recently deceased friend Joachim Raff during the 1882–3 season,[100] and one concert each to the music of Brahms, France and Russia during the 1884–5 season.[101] Of the living composers, Johannes Brahms benefited most from Bülow's comprehensive programme policy, and, with the exception of the 1882–3 and the 1883–4 seasons, at least one work by him was programmed every year. In all, seventeen performances of his music were heard at Bülow's concerts between 13 March 1881 and 25 October 1885,[102] including those given at the two all-Brahms concerts mentioned above. The composer was a regular visitor to the Grand Duchy and participated either as a soloist or as a conductor in four of those concerts.[103] Because of Brahms's involvement, those performances have been cited as model performances, but the concerts were given under exceptional conditions and were not typical of the period as a whole. The unrepeatable readings should therefore be regarded as divergences rather than models, and any attempt to build a tradition based on them should be treated with caution.

Part of Bülow's duties as Intendant at Meiningen involved regular tours with the Hofkapelle. Georg had already been using the emerging railway and telegraph networks to plan and implement national and international tours with the Hoftheater since 1874 and, with the arrival of Bülow in the Grand Duchy, he was keen to send the Hofkapelle on similar journeys. Some performance historians have suggested incorrectly that the Meiningen orchestra was the world's first touring orchestra. That distinction, however, probably belongs to the American conductor Theodore Thomas,[104] and his eponymous orchestra, who had already undertaken extensive tours of the USA from 1869.[105] Thomas needed to tour with his musicians to ensure the orchestra's survival, but that was not the case for the Meininger Hofkapelle and, although Georg tried to avoid making a financial loss, monetary gain was not his primary motivation. Nevertheless, he was aware of his limitations as a music impresario, so he engaged the services of the agent Hermann Wolff,[106] '[a]n efficient, enterprising, sensible, and witty man . . . [who was] a sincere friend and adviser of the artists [whom] he managed',[107] to help plan some of the Hofkapelle's tours.

Bülow toured extensively with the Meininger Hofkapelle between 27 December 1880 and 24 November 1885, directing 162 concerts from Poland in the east to the Netherlands in the west. By performing Beethoven's *Grosse Fuge* from memory, by playing while standing and by merging the roles of conductor and soloist in piano concertos by Beethoven and Brahms, Bülow and the orchestra created a sensation wherever they played. With the exception of 1883 Bülow toured annually with the orchestra, and the longest tour that they undertook together was in the autumn of 1884, when they performed thirty-two concerts in thirty-six days in seventeen cities. Because rehearsal time was limited when travelling, the main preparation for the tours happened at Meiningen. As Bülow's performances of Beethoven's works in the Grand Duchy had acquired a near iconic status, it was almost inevitable that 139 touring concerts contained music by that composer and, of those, seventy-two were devoted to his works.[108]

Another composer whose music was heard frequently during the Hofkapelle's tours was Johannes Brahms, whose works were performed at seventy concerts.[109] Brahms participated either as a pianist or as a conductor at sixteen touring concerts during Bülow's tenure and was involved heavily in the conductor's final tour with the orchestra in November 1885.[110] During that series, Brahms was engaged to perform his recent Symphony No. 4, which he had conducted first at Meiningen the previous month.[111] The work was given on nine occasions during the course of the tour and eight of the nine performances were under his direction.[112] Towards the end of the trip it emerged that Brahms had received, and accepted, an invitation to perform the work at the prestigious Frankfurt Museum Concerts. Bülow had intended to perform the symphony at that series on 24 November 1885 with the Hofkapelle, but had to abandon the work in favour of Beethoven's Symphony No. 7 because of the organizers' invitation to the composer. Ever quick to take offence, Bülow was incensed by Brahms's decision to accept the invitation and a rift between composer and conductor soon emerged. Bülow's anger also affected his relationship with the Hofkapelle and Georg, whom he informed that the Frankfurt concert was to be his last with the orchestra. Although Bülow's resignation was the end of an era, it had little effect on the performing habits of the Hofkapelle, which continued to tour extensively under its conductors, Fritz Steinbach, Wilhelm Berger and Max Reger, until Georg's death in 1914.[113]

Having left the Hofkapelle in haste, Bülow soon longed for an ensemble of a similar standard with which to work. Of course, his experiences at Meiningen were exceptional, and it was unlikely that he would be able to recreate easily the conditions that had prevailed there. His friend Hermann Wolff was aware of his dilemma and soon proposed a viable alternative. Wolff hoped to trade on Bülow's fame and experience by establishing a new concert series for him at Hamburg. The series would provide the conductor with the orchestra that he desired and the impresario with an exciting new business venture. To implement this plan, Wolff needed an ensemble that could compete musically with that of the long-established Philharmonische Gesellschaft.[114] The obvious choice was the orchestra of the Hamburg Stadttheater, which was managed by the well-known impresarios Bernhard Pollini and Chéri Maurice.[115] For Pollini and Maurice, the chance to lease their orchestra to a successful concert agent and fellow impresario made financial sense, and, for Wolff, the use of an existing ensemble meant that his initial costs could be kept to a minimum.[116] Publicity, however, was a preliminary expense that Wolff was willing to meet, and when the first advertisements for the 1886–7 season appeared in the Hamburg newspapers, the name 'Herrn Dr. Hans von Bülow' appeared in large print. To whet the public's appetite further, Wolff stated that the orchestra would consist of eighty to a hundred musicians, would use soloists of the front rank, and would perform established masterpieces and the best works by new composers.[117]

The new Abonnement series at Hamburg initially consisted of six concerts annually but rose to ten from the 1889–90 season. As it was a commercial enterprise, extreme caution might have been expected when programming, but Wolff's approach was adventurous, capitalizing on Bülow's dual reputation as a leading conductor of Beethoven's works and a champion of new music. Most of the concerts that Bülow gave at Hamburg, therefore, pitted works from the crystallizing Austro-German canon against those of the avant-garde and, of the fifty-three Abonnement Concerts that he conducted at Hamburg, eighty-six per cent contained a work by a living composer.[118] As his taste was catholic, the new works were drawn from cultures ranging from Russia to Ireland. He took particular delight in performing works by Anton Rubinstein and Alexander Borodin from Russia, Ignacy Jan Paderewski from Poland, Antonín Dvořák from Bohemia, Charles Villiers Stanford from Ireland, and Jules Massenet, Camille Saint-Saëns and Léo Delibes from France. Of the living Austro-German composers, he continued to champion the music of Johannes Brahms and Richard Strauss, of whose Horn Concerto No. 1 he had given the première at Meiningen,[119] and took up the causes of Felix Draeseke, Max Bruch and the Scottish-born Germanophile Eugen d'Albert. He was also keen to promote the music of the Prussian Moritz Moszkowski and the Hungarian-born Joseph Joachim. In general, the critics welcomed Bülow's interest in new and colourful music, but they did object to the works of d'Albert, a protégé of Liszt and Bülow, whom they considered a superior pianist but an inferior composer.

By the time of his Hamburg concerts, Bülow was arguably German's leading Beethoven conductor. His touring activities with the Meininger Hofkapelle had ensured that his individual approach to the composer's music was known widely but, unlike his concerts with that orchestra, where programmes devoted to Beethoven's works were common, Bülow conducted two all-Beethoven concerts only at Hamburg.[120] Moreover, he never performed a cycle of the symphonies there, conducting no more than four performances of any of them in a single season. A curiosity of his Hamburg concerts was his rejection of the last movement of Symphony No. 9 from 1892. When on tour with the Meininger Hofkapelle, he conducted performances without the finale for practical reasons, but he gave the work in its entirety at Hamburg during his first season there.[121] By the time of his second performance of the symphony at Hamburg,[122] however, he lacked sympathy with the last movement and refused to include it in the concert. Although the press and the public might have been alerted to his truncated approach by the absence of soloists and choir from the pre-concert advertising, they were still understandably baffled by his stance, and one critic likened his reading to that of a body without a head.[123]

At Hamburg, Bülow returned to the opera pit for the first time since leaving Hanover. In September 1887, Pollini tempted him back to the theatre by offering him a production of Spohr's *Jessonda*.[124] The management had hoped to introduce Bülow at the Stadttheater with a work by Wagner, but he was wary of performing the composer's early operas since the debacle at Hanover and had little sympathy with Wagner's works after *Die Meistersinger von Nürnberg*. He was keen, however, to consolidate his Mozart repertoire at Hamburg and planned a Mozart cycle that was to include *Idomeneo, Die Entführung aus dem Serail, Così fan tutte, Don Giovanni, La clemenza di Tito, Der Schauspieldirektor, Die Zauberflöte* and *Le nozze di Figaro*. After a performance of *Don Giovanni* on 29 October 1887 to mark the hundredth anniversary of its première at Prague, the cycle began with *Idomeneo* on 31 October 1887. The critics and the public responded enthusiastically to the production and were surprised when the cycle was abandoned after only a handful of performances. It transpired that Bülow was dissatisfied with the standard of the orchestra and refused to continue with the project after a performance of *La clemenza di Tito* on 11 November 1887.[125]

Along with the operas of Spohr and Mozart, Bülow conducted Cherubini's *Les Deux Journées* and Bizet's *Les Pêcheurs de perles* and *Carmen* at the Hamburg Stadttheater. His reading of *Carmen* was particularly controversial and was later criticized heavily by Felix von Weingartner. Weingartner was a member of the Stadttheater's music staff at the time of the production[126] and recalled, 'The first performance of *Carmen* under Bülow induced in me a feeling of acute discomfort, almost of horror. . . . Why these incongruities in such a natural piece of work? Why these tricks, these pauses, these discriminations for which there is no warrant either in the instructions given by the composer or in the music itself? Why that positively ridiculous procrastination over the opening and many other parts of this sparkling opera?'[127] Ostensibly, Weingartner's concerns related solely to Bülow's idiosyncratic approach to tempi, an area of his performing style that remained highly controversial throughout his career. Less obvious, however, was the wider basis for Weingartner's comments. In 1885, Weingartner was one of number of young conductors who were being considered for the post of Bülow's assistant at Meiningen.[128] Bülow overlooked him for the job and Weingartner never forgave him for the perceived snub. That said, there was a clear difference of artistic opinion between Bülow and Weingartner concerning *Carmen*, for when Weingartner conducted a performance of the same production at the Altona Theatre, a subsidiary of the Hamburg Stadttheater, Bülow described his reading as 'absolutely disgusting'.[129]

After the success of Bülow's Abonnement Concerts at Hamburg, Wolff was keen to exploit the conductor's reputation at other North German centres. Along with the Hamburg series, the agent managed the affairs of the Bremen and Berlin Philharmonics, and in 1887 he engaged Bülow as the conductor of the Abonnement series of those orchestras.

But the number of performances that he had to give each season soon became unmanageable, and he resigned from the Bremen series in March 1889.[130] He remained at Berlin until the end of the 1891–2 season, however, and conducted fifty Philharmonic Concerts there.[131] The content and structre of his Berlin concerts resembled those of Hamburg, with the music of Beethoven being common to both. In Berlin, he continued to avoid performing the symphonies in cycles, did not perform any all-Beethoven concerts and never performed Symphony No. 9 as part of the Abonnement series.[132] As in Hamburg, modern music featured prominently, with ninety-two per cent of his Berlin concerts containing at least one work by a living composer.[133] For logistical and financial reasons, most of the new or recent compositions performed were heard in both cities. There were, however, some exceptions, including Leopold Damrosch's Violin Concerto No. 2,[134] Robert Kahn's Serenade, Anton Rubinstein's overture Antony and Cleopatra, Ernst Rudorff's Symphony No. 2, Richard Strauss's Burleske and Robert Radecke's Capriccio for large orchestra, which were given only at Berlin.[135] At his Hamburg and Berlin concerts, Bülow regularly performed solo works and Lieder alongside symphonic music. While he applied that policy more commonly in Hamburg, he occasionally employed it in Berlin and, at a marathon concert on 6 April 1888, he conducted Beethoven's overture to Egmont, Moszkowski's Fantastischer Zug, Taubert's Lustspiel-Ouvertüre, Brahms's Symphony No. 1 and Wagner's prelude to Die Meistersinger von Nürnberg, was the soloist in Hummel's Piano Concerto in B minor (Gustav Kogel, conductor) and played Schubert's Impromptu Op. 90 No. 3 and Beethoven's Thirty-Two Variations in C minor.

During his years at Hamburg and Berlin, Bülow's health declined sharply. He had been attending sanatoria and clinics regularly in the years following his Munich tenure and suffered greatly from bouts of anxiety and severe headaches. Having resigned as conductor of the Philharmonic Concerts in Berlin at the end of the 1891–2 season, Bülow intended to concentrate his efforts on his Abonnement series in Hamburg, but by December 1892 his health had deteriorated to such an extent that he had to abandon the series after the fourth concert.[136] By March 1893, however, he had recovered his strength sufficiently to return to the podium for concerts at Berlin and Hamburg,[137] but his sense of well-being was only fleeting and those engagements were his last as a conductor. In an attempt to restore what remained of his health, he attended more sanatoria in Germany and later travelled to Cairo, where he died of a stroke on 12 February 1894.

Bülow's death shocked the music world. He was an artistic colossus whose wide-ranging interests spanned all aspects of musical life. Although few could imagine concert life without him, he remained for many an enigmatic figure, whose personal and professional lives were a series of paradoxes. His balancing of Wagner's artistic principles with those of Brahms, his juxtaposition of new music and the works of established masters within a single performance aesthetic, and his ability to gain the respect and the admiration of some while engendering loathing in others, all contributed to a larger-than-life image that defined his public persona. While his private life was often tempestuous, his artistic integrity never wavered, and '[t]o anyone who ever heard him play Beethoven or conduct Wagner, or who attended his music lessons or listened to him during orchestral rehearsals, he was bound to be the example of all the shining virtues of the reproductive artist'. [138]

CHAPTER 2

The Magician of the Podium: Arthur Nikisch

Hans von Bülow's death robbed the musical world of one of its great figures. It seemed to many that the void created by his passing would be difficult to fill. His loss particularly affected Hermann Wolff and the Berlin Philharmonic, who needed a dynamic personality to replace the charismatic Bülow and to lead the orchestra into the new century. Some members of the younger generation of conductors, like Gustav Mahler and Richard Strauss, were successful in the opera house but had failed to distinguish themselves in the concert hall, while others, such as Felix Weingartner, had proved able in the symphonic repertoire but lacked the stature necessary to lead Germany's premier orchestra. Of the artists available to Wolff, only Arthur Nikisch seemed to fit the bill. For many, he was the quintessential conductor. Orchestral musicians identified with him as a former colleague, solo artists considered him a sympathetic accompanist and audiences were enthralled by his stage presence. With his appointment to the Berlin Philharmonic in 1895, he soon became the idol of the German concert-going public and quickly consolidated a career that had begun less than two decades earlier.

Born at Lébényi Szent Miklós in Hungary on 12 October 1855, Arthur was the third of a string of children born to August and Luise Nikisch.[1] Although Hungarian by birth, Arthur was influenced by German cultural and educational practices during his childhood. His father was a senior clerical officer of German descent and his mother was an ethnic Hungarian. In keeping with lower-middle-class *mores*, the Nikischs were keen for their children to have an understanding of the arts. For a family from that socio-economic group, educating their children musically was an indication of social standing, and it was with some pride that August and Luise arranged for Arthur to attend music lessons after they settled at Butschowitz in Moravia. Having begun piano and theory lessons with Franz Prochazka in 1861, Nikisch was taken to his first orchestral concert in 1862 by his parents. Whether by design or by chance, the concert contained music that was both attractive and familiar to younger listeners of the period and included Rossini's overtures to *Guillaume Tell* and *Il barbiere di Siviglia* and an orchestral fantasy on Meyerbeer's *Robert le diable*.

By the time of the concert, Nikisch's abilities had developed into a precocious talent and he astounded his parents by transcribing the music that he had heard from memory.[2] Described by some commentators as an act of genius comparable to that of Mozart's transcription of Gregorio Allegri's *Miserere* in 1770,[3] Nikisch's feat of memory and musicianship was not only an indication of his ability but also a reminder that his gifts needed careful nurturing. It was clear to his parents that he had outgrown his provincial music education and that a more sophisticated environment was necessary if he were to fulfil his potential. It was decided therefore that he should enter the Vienna Conservatory in 1866. For an eleven-year-old boy, attending classes with students who were often aged between eighteen and twenty must have been daunting. Nevertheless, he joined the master classes of leading musicians and studied violin with Joseph Hellmesberger,[4] piano with Schenners and composition with Otto Dessof.[5] Nikisch's progress at the Conservatory was quick and his talents were recognized formally at the age of thirteen, when he was awarded the Gold Medal for his String Sextet and won prizes for his piano and violin playing.

During his student years, Nikisch was keen to develop his talents both as a creative and as a performing artist. As an executant, he was particularly active as a chamber musician and played the second violin in Schumann's Piano Quintet in November 1872 and the first violin in Beethoven's F major Quartet the following month. But it was his interest in composition that dominated his activities at the Conservatory, where he wrote a variety of works, including a sonata for violin and piano, a string quartet and a cantata for soloists, chorus and orchestra. Nikisch also composed a symphony in D minor during his student years, the opening movement of which he performed in 1873, his first appearance as a conductor. It was, however, as a violinist that Nikisch made his greatest impact at the Conservatory, and Hellmesberger soon recommended him to the Vienna Hofkapelle and the Vienna Philharmonic.

Deputizing on a regular basis for indisposed members of the violin sections of both orchestras, Nikisch was able to learn much of the standard repertoire at first hand. But for an aspiring composer with an interest in *Zukunftsmusik*, engagements as an orchestral violinist could not be fully satisfying. As the Hofoper and the Conservatory were bastions of the old, Nikisch spent his nights studying Wagner's revolutionary scores by candlelight. Although largely restricted to vocal scores because of his limited income, he did have an opportunity to expand his knowledge of Wagner's music when the composer conducted excerpts from his compositions at Vienna on 12 May 1872. Fortunately for Nikisch, a member of the orchestra's violin section had fallen ill and he was asked to substitute at short notice. Enthralled by the composer-conductor's approach to Beethoven's Symphony No. 3 ('Eroica'), the 'Bacchanale' from *Tannhäuser* and 'Wotan's Farewell' and the 'Magic Fire Music' from *Die Walküre*, Nikisch was determined to work with Wagner again and to explore his performance style more fully.

On 22 May 1872, Wagner laid the foundation stone at the Bayreuth Theatre. To mark the occasion, he conducted a performance of Beethoven's Symphony No. 9 ('Choral') with an orchestra consisting of musicians from the Hofkapellen of Vienna, Munich, Berlin and Dresden.[6] The contingent from Vienna consisted originally of twenty players, but, with the help of Hellmesberger, that number was increased to twenty-one, with Nikisch supplementing the second violin section. Again, the impact of Wagner's approach on Nikisch was profound, and in later life he recalled: 'What I learnt in the four rehearsals with Wagner influenced my whole artistic career immensely. ... I can say that Wagner's "Eroica" in Vienna and then the Ninth at Bayreuth was, for my conception of Beethoven as a whole and for my orchestral interpretation in general, decisive.'[7] Of the two interpretations, that of Symphony No. 9 made the deepest impression on Nikisch, who was fascinated by the way in which Wagner achieved the music's melos through bodily gestures. Nikisch argued that Wagner was not a routine Kapellmeister, and that his stick technique was not that of a dry 'Taktschläger', but, rather, of a musician who spoke from the soul, lifting the listener to a higher artistic plane through gestures that were pure music.[8]

Having worked with the Vienna Hofoper orchestra as a deputy for two years, Nikisch became a permanent member of the ensemble from 1 January 1874. While much of the work involved the performance of routine operas, he occasionally had the chance of working with some of the leading musicians of the age. Significantly, he worked under Anton Rubinstein, Franz Liszt and Johannes Brahms, composers whose works he performed regularly later in his career. He also had an opportunity to play under Giuseppe Verdi in June 1875, when the composer visited Vienna to conduct his Requiem and *Aida*.[9] Those interpretations were a revelation for Nikisch, who noted the composer's tempi and nuances in detail and who drew upon them when performing those works later in his career.

Keen to put into practice all that he had observed, Nikisch began to look for work as a professional conductor. Although he had had some success as composer, pianist and violinist, his practical experience of conducting was minimal. Nevertheless, when the post of chorus master at the Leipzig Stadttheater fell vacant in December 1877, Otto Dessof recommended him for the job. The Stadttheater boasted a formidable troupe of performers that included Josef Sucher,[10] 'a strikingly good and temperamental conductor, particularly of Wagner',[11] and a renowned director, Angelo Neumann. Seemingly undaunted by the responsibility of preparing material for some of the leading figures in German theatre, Nikisch began work on 15 January 1878 with a spirited chorus rehearsal of Beethoven's *Fidelio*. It soon became clear to Neumann that he had engaged a musician of talent, and, keen to exploit Nikisch's potential to the full, he decided to allow the young conductor to make his professional début with Paul Lacôme's operetta *Jeanne, Jeannette et Jeanneton* on 11 February 1878. The evening was a resounding success, and Neumann was encouraged to promote Nikisch to the post of temporary First Kapellmeister later that year.

Neumann was a devoted Wagnerian who had sung in the composer's productions of *Tannhäuser* and *Lohengrin* before taking up his post at the Stadttheater. As a disciple of the Master, he was delighted to learn of Nikisch's enthusiasm for Wagner's works and allowed him to conduct *Tannhäuser* and *Lohengrin* in the period directly following *Jeanne, Jeannette et Jeanneton*. The performances were a triumph, with Nikisch impressing Neumann not only with his command of the music but also by his management of the orchestra. Unlike many of his colleagues, Nikisch's preferred persuasion to intimidation and used his experiences as an orchestral violinist as the basis for his podium manner. By being on good terms with the players, he managed to draw the best from them and, as a result, secured impressive playing for both *Tannhäuser* and *Lohengrin*. Nikisch approach to the orchestra was central to his activities and was much discussed by the music profession. The violinist Carl Flesch was particularly impressed by his method and later recalled that orchestras:

> went with him through thick and thin, and submitted willingly to the influence of his personality, since the orchestral musicians regarded him as one of themselves. . . . As a former violinist he understood the

practical side of orchestral playing down to the last detail, and his criticism never took the form of those aesthetic and metaphysical considerations detested by orchestral musicians; every one of his remarks started out first and foremost from a practical mistake. . . . As he never indulged in hot air or general twaddle, always mentioned what was necessary and never the superfluous, his rehearsals were of a comforting brevity, a circumstance that made him even more popular with the orchestra: there is nothing to which the orchestral musician is more responsive.[12]

As a direct result of his management of the orchestra and his impressive interpretations of *Tannhäuser* and *Lohengrin*, Nikisch was entrusted with a cycle of *Der Ring des Nibelungen* in 1878, the first complete performance of the tetralogy outside Bayreuth.[13] The commitment with which he tackled the cycle, and his clear affinity with the music that he was performing, encouraged Neumann both to ratify Nikisch's appointment as First Kapellmeister in 1879 and to allocate him his first performance of *Tristan und Isolde* the following year.

Nikisch's interest in new music was not restricted to the operas of Wagner; he also conducted new productions of Verdi's *Aida* and Goldmark's *Die Königin von Saba* at Leipzig. Having heard and noted Verdi's approach to *Aïda* in detail during his Vienna period, Nikisch was able to offer an interpretation that was both colourful and authoritative. Like his performances of Wagner's operas, his reading of Verdi's masterpiece was a critical and popular success. But with the departure of Neumann in 1882,[14] Nikisch was concerned that his well-trained ensemble might be under threat and that his ability to explore new and obscure works might be curtailed. Fortunately for Nikisch, Neumann's successor, Max Staegemann,[15] shared some of his predecessor's interests and was an impresario of sound musical and financial judgement. Staegemann, like Neumann, realized quickly that Nikisch's was an outstanding talent and allowed him free reign over all matters musical and the authority to programme with audacity. New works that Nikisch conducted at the Stadttheater under Staegemann's management included Rubinstein's *The Demon* and *Die Makkabäer*, Brüll's *Königin Mariette*, Bungert's *Die Studenten von Salamanka* and the world première of Nessler's *Der Trompeter von Säkkingen* on 4 May 1884. Dedicated to Nikisch, the opera was an instant success and quickly became extremely popular throughout the German-speaking world during the late nineteenth and early twentieth centuries. In response to Nessler's dedication, Nikisch wrote a fantasy on some of the opera's themes. Although competent as a composer, he decided that the fantasy was to be his last composition, because he felt that by comparison with the music that he was interpreting, his was simply 'Kapellmeistermusik'.

On 12 February 1880, Nikisch conducted a concert with the Gewandhaus Orchestra of Leipzig for the first time. Deputizing for an indisposed Karl Reinecke,[16] he gave a programme that included works by Hauptmann, Volkmann, Mendelssohn, Gade and Schumann.[17] The performance was a triumph, and when Reinecke was unable to take charge of the orchestra's 15th Abonnement Concert of the 1880–1 season on 3 February 1881, Nikisch returned to conduct music by Haydn, Mozart, Beethoven, Mendelssohn and Schumann.[18] Again, the performance was a success and Nikisch was then engaged to conduct Beethoven's Symphony No. 9 at the Theater auf dem Augustusplatz.[19] The juxtaposition of new and familiar works at his first Gewandhaus Orchestra concerts later became a feature of Nikisch's programme policy. His interest in Schumann's music was lifelong, and the inclusion of a composition by Volkmann was an expression of the growing attraction of that composer's music. Although rarely heard today, Volkmann's works held some appeal for Nikisch, who included them regularly in his programmes with both the Berlin Philharmonic and Leipzig Gewandhaus Orchestra.

Nikisch continued to signal his interest in new music when he conducted for the Allgemeiner deutscher Musikverein at Leipzig on 4 May 1883. At that concert, he conducted Borodin's Symphony in E flat major, his first performance of a modern Russian symphony.[20] It was, however, his direction of the world première of Bruckner's Symphony No. 7 with the Gewandhaus Orchestra at Leipzig on 30 December 1884 that secured his reputation as a champion of the moderns. Nikisch's interest in Bruckner's music had begun at Vienna during his student years, when he was a member of the second violins for a performance of Symphony No. 2 under the composer's baton. Much to Nikisch's chagrin, his passion for the symphonies of Bruckner was not shared universally and the première of Symphony No. 7 nearly failed to take place at Leipzig because of Staegemann's attitude towards the composer's music. Although a committed Wagnerian and supporter of new music, Staegemann was unconvinced by Bruckner's symphonies and was reluctant to sanction the performance. But when confronted by a passionate First Kapellmeister who was determined to give the work at all costs, Staegemann finally relented and gave his permission for the Gewandhaus Orchestra to perform the symphony at the Stadttheater.[21] Having secured Staegemann's agreement, Nikisch was then faced with a paucity of rehearsal time, a lack of Wagner tubas and a change of performance date. Working tirelessly, he soon overcame those problems and ensured that the work was given under the most favourable circumstances possible. His interest in the symphony was not purely altruistic, however, for the première also fulfilled three important personal ambitions: to give the first performance of a major new orchestral work; to be the first conductor to perform Bruckner's music outside Austria, and to be recognized internationally as an executant.[22]

In 1889, the Boston Symphony Orchestra needed a new Music Director. In keeping with the contemporary trend of looking to musicians from Central Europe rather than native talent to lead American orchestras, the Boston Symphony Orchestra had engaged Georg Henschel as its first conductor in 1884 and Wilhelm Gericke as its second in 1889.[23] With the departure of Gericke, Henry Lee Higginson, the philanthropist and driving force behind the orchestra, again turned to Central Europe for a replacement. Ideally, he wanted a musician who would exercise a strong influence over the day-to-day management of the orchestra, who would make decisions concerning its repertoire and who would be willing to engage and to dismiss players. He was happy to allow the conductor to be 'free and unfettered in all these matters, . . . [and, with] no government officer, inspector, or director to bother him[, he] . . . [would be] as free as a man can well be in this world – any man who has much work and considerable responsibilities on his shoulders'.[24] To find the right man for the job, Higginson cast his net wide and, after the seeking the opinions of the pianists Julius Epstein and Otto Dresel,[25] he appointed Nikisch Music Director of the Boston Symphony Orchestra from the beginning of the 1889–90 season.[26]

For Nikisch apologists his Boston period is an embarrassment, and in the encomia that followed his death, many commentators minimized the problems that he faced there. From the start, he attracted unwelcome controversy and comment. On entering America in the autumn of 1889, the Musicians' Protective Union challenged his right to perform in the USA, arguing that 'his admission to the United States was a violation of the Contract Labour Law'.[27] Although the objection was dismissed, it not only soured Nikisch's introduction to America but also alerted him to the complex labour relations that existed in American orchestras. Those relations also extended to the day-to-day management of the Boston Symphony Orchestra, which was manned by non-union labour. In a country with egalitarian aspirations, Higginson's objection to organized labour might seem strange, but as an expression of the commercial imperatives that dominated the behaviour patterns of America's bourgeois elite during the late nineteenth and early twentieth centuries, it was not uncommon. Nikisch, however, must have felt uncomfortable with Higginson's methods, because he believed that a good working relationship between players, management and conductor was essential if art was to flourish. Faced with a situation that ran contrary to his own ideals, his tenure was soon fraught with difficulty.

Nevertheless, Nikisch quickly overcame his initial problems and became the talk of Boston. For those interested in style rather than content, 'His hands, his hair, his bearing and manner – all his personal attributes, became at once the subjects of written and spoken comment'.[28] Of course, a detailed discussion of Nikisch's merits as an interpreter would have been preferable, but most audience members were preoccupied with puerilities rather than dialectics. That said, Nikisch might have unwittingly fuelled this superficial debate because, on hearing the orchestra for the first time, he was reported to have commented: '"All I have to do is to poetize".'[29] While Nikisch probably intended this remark as fodder for the popular press, his critics took it as a statement of policy, and, when the orchestra's standards began to drop, the comment returned to haunt him. Some linked the orchestra's difficulties to Nikisch's habit of conducting without a score, while others argued that his catholic programmes were to blame. More worrying, many felt that Nikisch lacked Gericke's discipline and that there were fundamental problems in his relationship with the Boston Symphony Orchestra. But the increasing atmosphere of dissatisfaction was not restricted to Nikisch's critics, for he too was disillusioned. Specifically, he objected to the extensive tours that were a feature of the Boston orchestra's calendar. Travelling mainly by rail, Nikisch and the orchestra toured regularly throughout the USA, covering some 50,000 miles during his tenure. The combination of vast distances, lack of rehearsal and often poor concert facilities failed to recommend touring to Nikisch, whose previous experiences as a German Kapellmeister did little to prepare him for his more demanding duties as an American Music Director.

Central to Nikisch's role with the Boston Symphony Orchestra were the Subscription Concerts that he performed at the Boston Music Hall between October and April each season.[30] With no fewer than 190 concerts of ninety-five programmes between 11 October 1889 and 29 April 1893, Nikisch was faced with a wide and varied repertoire that was often new to him professionally.[31] In keeping with contemporary practice, two thirds of the works performed were by Austro-German composers, with fifty concerts devoted to music by that group. Beethoven's compositions were particularly common, with Nikisch conducting at least eighty performances of works by the composer, approximately a quarter of all music heard. While he never gave a cycle of Beethoven's symphonies at the Subscription Concerts, he did conduct forty-four performances of those works during his tenure, including eight of Symphony No. 8, six each of Symphonies Nos. 3, 4, 5 and 7, four each of Symphonies Nos. 2 and 6 and two each of Symphonies Nos. 1 and 9. Although those works dominated Nikisch's programmes statistically, he ensured that they were integrated musically, and conducted only four all-Beethoven concerts at the Boston Music Hall.[32]

The other established Austro-German composers whose music Nikisch performed regularly at Boston were Mozart, Wagner, Liszt, Schubert, Mendelssohn, Haydn and Weber. Although he conducted two all-Mozart concerts on 18 and 19 December 1891 to mark the centenary of the composer's death,[33] Nikisch's Mozart repertoire was in keeping with late-nineteenth-century trends and was restricted to excerpts from operas, the Flute and Harp Concerto, the *Maurerische Trauermusik*, the first movement of the Sinfonia concertante K. 364 and Symphonies Nos. 31, 39, 40 and 41. Similarly, when performing orchestral music by Schubert, Nikisch also followed contemporary practice by conducting only Symphonies Nos. 7 in B minor ('Unfinished') and 8 in C major ('Great'). His Haydn repertoire, however, was more adventurous and included Symphonies Nos. 82, 88, 95, 102, 103 ('Drum Roll') and 104 ('London'). When performing Wagner, Nikisch adapted quickly to the Anglo-American fashion of devoting whole concerts to that composer's music. The all-Wagner programmes that he conducted in 1891 and 1893 were typical of those that were popular in Britain and North America during the late nineteenth and early twentieth centuries and included vocal and orchestral excerpts from some of the composer's more popular works.[34] Largely unknown in Central Europe where full-time opera houses were common, subscription concerts devoted to Wagner's music were a regular feature of concert life in the English-speaking countries. As there was a relative paucity of lyric theatres in those countries, all-Wagner programmes were an attempt at compensating for the shortage while trying to satisfy audiences' seemingly unquenchable thirst for the composer's music.

A prominent feature of Nikisch's Boston concerts was his emphasis on modern music. As a champion of the new for much of his career, he was keen to use his tenured positions as showcases for contemporary composers. That was particularly true of Boston where, of the 724 performances of individual works that he gave at the Subscription Concerts, 324 were of new or recent compositions. While the Boston public was probably better educated and more open-minded than most other American audiences, the sheer volume of new music challenged even the most adventurous concert-goer. Nikisch presented recent compositions by Austro-German, American, Franco-Belgian, Russian, Italian, Polish, Hungarian, Czech, Scandinavian and British composers, led at least six all-contemporary concerts, conducted four world premières and gave the first work by a woman composer to be performed by the Boston Symphony Orchestra.[35] All the works premièred were by Americans and were four of only thirty performances of works by composers from that fledgling tradition. Curiously, Nikisch programmed no symphonies by Bruckner at the Subscription Concerts. As he had given the first performance of his Symphony No. 7 at Leipzig and was a devotee of the composer for much of his career, their omission seems uncharacteristic. Given that nearly half of all works programmed were new and that he had a first-class orchestra of more than eighty musicians at his disposal, the absence of Bruckner's symphonies is a conundrum that is not easily solved.

Nikisch left Boston in the spring of 1893 and was appointed Director of the Königliches Opernhaus in Budapest from the beginning of the 1893–4 season.[36] Having been Music Director of an American orchestra, Nikisch had grown accustomed to exercising considerable authority, but in Budapest he no longer enjoyed that degree of power and soon became dissatisfied. The unhappy atmosphere that pervaded the Budapest theatre made work both unpleasant and arduous, and his inability to modify the behaviour patterns and the working habits of his colleagues distressed Nikisch considerably. Nevertheless, he put aside his feelings of dissatisfaction and pursued his responsibilities with vigour, conducting at least eight new productions of operas by Smetana, Bizet, Mozart, Lortzing, Puccini, Massenet, Wagner and Humperdinck in eighteen months.[37] As in Boston, the emphasis was on new music and the inclusion of *Manon Lescaut*, *Hänsel und Gretel* and *La Navarraise*, all recent compositions, was typical of Nikisch's programming in general.[38] By performing those works, Nikisch not only continued to develop his interest in new music, but also provided Budapest's operagoing public with an overview of both the standard and the emerging operatic repertoires.

Although Nikisch's principal responsibility in Budapest was the performance of opera, he was also active as an orchestral conductor. As for his concerts with the Leipzig Gewandhaus and the Boston Symphony Orchestras, he was concerned that his programmes with the Budapest Philharmonic should reflect his catholic approach. Unlike many of his contemporaries, he did not actively cultivate an image as a Beethoven specialist and performed only three of the composer's works at Budapest between 8 November 1893 and 16 January 1895.[39] Given the overwhelming public interest in Beethoven's music during the late nineteenth and early twentieth centuries, its relative absence from the nine concerts that Nikisch conducted in the Hungarian capital must have been disappointing for some members of his audience.[40] Nevertheless, Nikisch was determined to pursue his typically wide-ranging approach to programming with the Philharmonic and added spice to his concerts by including works by Erkel, Liszt, Moszkowski, Berlioz, Goldmark, d'Albert, Scharwenka and Volkmann, composers who had little appeal for the notoriously conservative Budapest public.[41]

Aware that the Budapest theatre had limited status internationally, Nikisch was keen to accept engagements as a guest conductor abroad and, on 15 June 1895, he made his London début at the Queen's Hall with a concert that included familiar works by Beethoven, Wagner, Dvořák and Grieg.[42] Hoping for success with a popular programme, Nikisch must have been disappointed by the response of the London press. While the critic for *The Musical Times* was quick to acknowledge Nikisch's 'great reputation abroad', he found his interpretations unorthodox and felt unable to pass judgement on his ability in general. When Nikisch returned to the Queen's Hall podium on 22 June 1895 to conduct works by Schubert, Smetana, Wagner and Mendelssohn, he again failed totally to impress the critics.[43] Of 'the orchestral part of Mendelssohn's Violin Concerto', the *Musical Times* reviewer found it 'quite devoid of distinction'. Moreover, he argued, 'We have plenty of Conductors without a tithe of Mr. Nikisch's reputation who could do as well as this, and several others who can – and are accustomed to – do much better'. To make matters worse, 'Mr. Nikisch . . . brought his own oboe player from Buda-Pesth' and until the critic had 'heard this gentleman', 'had no idea that so disagreeable a tone could be produced from the instrument'.[44] But the critic was impressed by the conductor's ability to obtain 'perfect clearness, and the gradations of speed and power . . . [indicating] a mind with the sense of form strongly developed and acting in every case with consciousness of the end in view'.[45] Concerning Nikisch's podium manner, he observed that the 'audience naturally came prepared to find in [Nikisch] the qualities which distinguish great leaders of men, and they were not disappointed'. He also sensed that '[Nikisch's] *bâton* [was] employed . . . to indicate effects of accent, phrasing, and expression [rather] than to beat "time" in the ordinary acceptance of the term, and the way in which its complicated but highly significant suggestions were carried out by the orchestra spoke volumes'.[46]

While in London, Nikisch received a letter from the management of the Leipzig Gewandhaus Orchestra. Unhappy with Reinecke's conservative methods, the orchestra's management was hoping to replace the ageing conductor with the vibrant Hungarian. Although Nikisch was contracted to the Budapest opera for a further three years, he was keen to accept the Leipzig offer and managed to secure an early release from his existing responsibilities. After beginning work at the Gewandhaus on 10 October 1895, Nikisch gave no fewer than 569 Abonnement Concerts at Leipzig over the next twenty-seven years.[47] Given the importance of that orchestra's position in German concert life, it might seem odd that Nikisch decided that his role at Leipzig should be that of conductor, educator and musical evangelist. Although the orchestra had a distinguished history and was held in high regard locally and internationally, he was eager to ensure that it was relevant to the community as a whole. In achieving that aim, he programmed works that not only entertained and edified his audiences but also reflected his interests and abilities. He regularly juxtaposed symphonic works with chamber music and often performed as both conductor and piano accompanist. A typical programme was that of 24 October 1895, when orchestral music by Tchaikovsky, Goldmark and Schumann was pitted against an operatic aria by Mozart and Lieder by Schubert, Grieg, Brahms and Strauss.[48] Although not unknown at Abonnement Concerts at other major artistic centres, the composite programmes that Nikisch offered at Leipzig became a regular feature of his programme policy there and were an opportunity for him to explore repertoire that might otherwise have been unavailable to him as a guest or tenured conductor elsewhere.

As in Budapest, Beethoven's works were an integral, rather than a dominant, part of his Leipzig programme policy.[49] Of the Abonnement Concerts performed, 219 contained a composition by Beethoven. While that appears a large number, the ratio of works to concerts given was considerably lower than in the case of other colleagues holding similar positions.[50] Moreover, during his twenty-seven seasons at Leipzig, Nikisch conducted only two complete cycles of Beethoven symphonies.[51] When performing those works individually, he gave Symphonies Nos. 3, 5, 7 and 9 most frequently, with Symphony No. 9 being heard usually at the last concert of each season.[52] When programming Beethoven's other orchestral compositions, Nikisch was again highly selective and seems to have chosen such works as the overtures *Leonore* Nos. 2 and 3, *Coriolan* and *Egmont*, the Violin Concerto

and Piano Concertos Nos. 3, 4 and 5 ('Emperor') as much for their popular appeal as for their musical worth.[53] By restricting the number of
performances of Beethoven's works given and by emphasizing the more
populist elements of the composer's oeuvre, Nikisch not only satisfied
the public's insatiable thirst for those compositions but ensured that
they were heard as part of well-balanced concert seasons.

Central to Nikisch's activities at Leipzig were the works of Schumann,
Brahms and Bruckner. In contrast to some conductors who expressed
doubts about Schumann's abilities as an orchestrator and who programmed his symphonies sparingly,[54] Nikisch featured the composer's
orchestral works prominently.[55] In a spirit unlike that of his approach
to Beethoven, Nikisch was keen to explore all aspects of the Schumann
repertoire and programmed the more popular symphonies side by side
with the less well-known stage works, choral music and overtures.[56] His
approach to Brahms's music was also comprehensive and, along with
eighty-seven performances of the symphonies, he performed the four
concertos, the two overtures, the two serenades, the 'Haydn' Variations
and four of the choral works regularly.[57] But of the composers that
Nikisch performed at Leipzig, Bruckner benefited most from his patronage. Although admired by many musicians, the composer's works have
never fully ignited the public's interest, and Nikisch's advocacy of them
throughout his Leipzig period was a brave act of faith. Performing all
the numbered symphonies and the Te Deum, he conducted thirty complete performances of these works between 1896 and 1919 and a cycle
of the nine symphonies in numerical order in the 1919–20 season.[58]

Nikisch's passion for the music of his contemporaries was not
restricted to Brahms and Bruckner; he also championed the cause of
other leading living composers at Leipzig. He was well-known as an
admirer of Russia and Russian music, and his interpretations of
Tchaikovsky's mature works were acclaimed by critics and public
alike.[59] While he programmed those compositions regularly with the
Gewandhaus Orchestra, he did not overlook Tchaikovsky's fellow
countrymen and gave regular performances of music by Rimsky-
Korsakov, Glazunov and Rachmaninov. Although Nikisch's interest in
modern Slavic music is commonly known, his regard for contemporary
French, Scandinavian and English composers is less well documented.
With works by Franck, d'Indy, Sibelius and Elgar, Nikisch extended the
repertoire of the Leipzig orchestra and introduced new artistic worlds to
local audiences who had been previously fed on Reinecke's reactionary
diet. But it was with the new music of Central Europe that Nikisch led
his attack on conservatism at the Gewandhaus and, along with regular

performances of works by Strauss, he challenged listeners with readings of music by Mahler, Reger, Pfitzner, Busoni, Korngold and Schoenberg.[60]

A striking feature of Nikisch's Leipzig concerts was the type, sex and experience of the soloists with whom he worked. A musician of seemingly few prejudices, Nikisch was able to include a work by a living female composer at his subscription concerts in Boston. Although no works by women composers were performed by him at the Abonnement Concerts in Leipzig, he did engage female soloists when and where possible. Of the concerts given with the Gewandhaus Orchestra, two thirds had at least one woman soloist. That figure would be unremarkable if it were restricted to performances of music for voice and orchestra, but Nikisch seems to have applied his policy universally and actively sought out women as soloists for other genres. Along with female artists of stature, like the South American pianist Teresa Carreño, whom he engaged at Leipzig, Nikisch also invited novice performers such as the soprano Elena Gerhardt to perform at the Abonnement Concerts.[61] Young male artists also benefited from Nikisch's patronage, and the pianist Artur Schnabel was particularly grateful for his interest. In later life, Schnabel recalled that it was through Nikisch's positive intervention that his first performance of Brahms's Piano Concerto No. 2 was a success. Responding to the question, 'Was the Brahms concerto well received the first time you played it?', Schnabel replied:

Oh, yes, it was, and my performance was very well received too – thanks to Nikisch. I believe he told the Press beforehand to be friendly towards me. I did not fare so well, however, when a little later I played the first Brahms concerto in Berlin, also with Nikisch. The leading newspaper attacked him for allowing me to play the slow movement too slow (as the paper thought). They did not understand how a man like him could participate in such a distortion of a grand work. Years later I was told that Nikisch had written a letter to the offended journalist, telling him that a young artist is entitled to do things wrong and so he did not stop me.[62]

With the death of Hans von Bülow in February 1894, Hermann Wolff and the Berlin Philharmonic faced a crisis. Bülow's demise left Wolff and the orchestra in urgent need of a charismatic conductor to take over the Philharmonic Concerts series. The engagement of guest artists for the 1892–3 and 1893–4 seasons and the appointment of Richard Strauss as conductor of the 1894–5 season was less than satisfactory and had proved disappointing both artistically and commercially.[63] Filling Bülow's shoes at Berlin had proved more difficult than Wolff had expected, and Nikisch's appointment as conductor of the Philharmonic Concerts from October 1895 was both a brave act and an inspired move. As Nikisch's tenure with the Boston Symphony Orchestra had not been wholly trouble-free, Wolff had no guarantee that the conductor would be any more successful in Berlin than he was in Boston. But Wolff had a knack for appointing the right man to the right job at the right time and was confident that Nikisch had the ability to be Bülow's rightful heir. It was clear from the start that Wolff's instincts had proved correct and, with his appointment as conductor of the subscription series in both Leipzig and Berlin, Nikisch achieved a level of authority and notoriety that was unprecedented in the history of conducting.

Between 14 October 1895 and 9 January 1922, Nikisch gave 258 Philharmonic Concerts in Berlin. Along with these, he conducted some of the popular, soloist, pension fund and people's concerts that constituted the majority of the Berlin Philharmonic's calendar. He also performed with the orchestra in Hamburg, where he conducted 132 of the 148 subscription concerts that the orchestra gave in Germany's second city. Seemingly indefatigable, he regularly supplemented his Berlin and Hamburg concerts with engagements in other provincial centres such as Hanover, Stettin, Magdeburg and Görlitz. Those national trips were only part of Nikisch's touring calendar with the orchestra, which also included extensive journeys abroad. It seems strange that a conductor who had objected to the rigours of professional travel in the USA should be willing to accept similar engagements with the Berlin Philharmonic. But Nikisch appears not to have objected to touring widely as an independent guest conductor in Europe, and it can only be assumed that when travelling with his new orchestra there, he found that the physical conditions of touring suited him better than those in North America.

Nikisch's first tour with the Berlin Philharmonic was to Copenhagen, where he shared a series of three concerts with Victor Bendix and Karl Muck[64] in December 1896. The following April, Nikisch joined Felix Weingartner, Felix Mottl and Ferdinand Löwe for two cycles of concerts with the orchestra in Vienna and, after returning to Berlin briefly, he travelled with it through Germany and Belgium to France.[65] Part of that tour was spent in Paris, where orchestra and conductor performed five concerts in May 1897.[66] For Hermann Wolff, the Paris concerts were the realization of a long-standing ambition that had materialized only after a series of extended negotiations with the German Ambassador to France, the French Minister for Culture and the Prefect of Police for

Paris.[67] This extraordinary series of meetings was necessary as the French were reluctant to sanction the tour because of lingering public hostility towards Germany after their defeat in the 1871 war. To smooth the way, the Prefect of Police urged Wolff to drop the name 'Orchestre de Berlin' from the billboards, a suggestion that was unacceptable to the impresario. Drawing upon all his skills as a negotiator, Wolff finally managed to secure an agreement from the French authorities to allow the orchestra to perform in Paris at the Salle du Cirque d'Hiver on 9 May 1897. Although still concerned about the public's response to the orchestra's concerts, the French softened their attitude after Nikisch altered the programme of the first concert to conclude with Beethoven's Symphony No. 3. The change was prompted by a disastrous fire at a bazaar in the Rue Jean Goujon, five days before the first concert, that resulted in 200 deaths. By dedicating the performance of the symphony's slow movement – Marcia funebre – to the memory of those who lost their lives, Nikisch did much to change the image of Germans from that of hostile ogres to sympathetic fellow human beings.[68]

Having triumphed in Paris, Nikisch and the orchestra hoped to repeat their success when they visited Russia in 1899. Performing at Königsberg (Kaliningrad) on their outward journey and at Warsaw on their return, they gave concerts in St Petersburg, Riga, Dorpat, Reval (Tallinn), Moscow, Kiev and Odessa.[69] With a taxing schedule that included eighteen concerts in nine cities in twenty-four days, Nikisch was able to confirm his affection for both Russia and its music and to continue to establish his credentials as one of Central Europe's most versatile and travelled musicians. After touring much of Western Europe in the spring of 1901,[70] Nikisch and the orchestra returned to Russia in 1904, when they revisited many of the cities that had been included on their 1899 itinerary.[71] The 1904 trip to Russia was the last that Nikisch undertook with the Berlin Philharmonic for thirteen years, and although the outbreak of World War I in 1914 meant that the orchestra had to reduce its international commitments sharply, it was able to travel to neutral countries, to tour domestically and to visit some of Germany's allies. It was within those reduced parameters that Nikisch and the Philharmonic visited Scandinavia in May 1917[72] and undertook a tour of Germany and Austro-Hungary in May 1918.[73] The 1918 trip was their penultimate journey together, with their last tour abroad being to Scandinavia in May 1920, when they gave concerts in Copenhagen and Malmö.[74]

Although the number of subscription concerts that Nikisch conducted in Berlin was less than half that of Leipzig, his repertoire was similar in both centres. With only 113 of his Berlin concerts containing a work by Beethoven, Nikisch again rationed his performances of that composer's music strictly. Further, of the concerts that included a work by Beethoven, more than half were heard in the first decade of his tenure.[75] That did not mean, however, that Beethoven had lost his iconic status, because Nikisch regularly performed a work by him at either the first or the last concert of the season.[76] Given the statistics for Leipzig, it is understandable that Symphonies Nos. 3, 5 and 7 were performed most frequently in Berlin, with fifteen, fourteen and twelve readings respectively. In contrast, Nikisch gave proportionately fewer performances of the Symphony No. 9 at Berlin than at Leipzig, and that symphony was not the climax of the Philharmonic season as it had been in his concerts with the Gewandhaus Orchestra. Although the three performances that Nikisch conducted of the work were all given close to the anniversary of Beethoven's birth,[77] any special significance that the symphony had for the conductor seems to have soon evaporated, his last performance of it in Berlin was in 1902, some twenty years before his final concert with the Philharmonic.

As in Leipzig, Nikisch drew heavily upon the music of Brahms, Schumann, Liszt and Wagner when performing in Berlin. Of the concerts given, fifty-six contained at least one work by Wagner. Nikisch's interest in Liszt also continued to flourish in Berlin and, along with his performances of the piano concertos, *Totentanz* and the arrangement for piano and orchestra of Schubert's 'Wanderer' Fantasy, he gave *Orpheus, Mazeppa, Die Ideale, Tasso, Festklänge* and the 'Faust' and 'Dante' Symphonies. His interest in *Zukunftsmusik* also extended to Richard Strauss, of whose tone poems he gave at least twenty-eight performances.[78] Although his enthusiasm for works from music's cutting edge was clear, his interest in the new was not restricted to programme music. Nikisch continued to champion the symphonies of Bruckner and Mahler in Berlin, and although the number of concerts available to him in Berlin was limited, he gave multiple performances of Bruckner's Symphonies Nos. 2, 3, 4, 5, 7, 8 and 9 and readings of Mahler's Symphonies Nos. 1, 2, 4, 5, 7 and *Das Lied von der Erde*.[79] But it seems that Nikisch's efforts on behalf of Mahler were not appreciated fully, because after the performance of Symphony No. 5 on 20 February 1905, the work's Berlin Philharmonic première, Richard Strauss wrote to Mahler:

> Your Fifth Symphony again gave me great pleasure in the full rehearsal, a pleasure only slightly dimmed by the little Adagietto. But as this was what pleased the audience most, you are getting what you

deserve. The first two movements, especially, are quite magnificent; the Scherzo has a quality of genius but seemed rather too long; how far the somewhat inadequate performance was responsible, I was unable to judge. At the final rehearsal your work had a great and unclouded success. The concert audience, by contrast, showed themselves somewhat more indolent intellectually, which is nothing new to you or me. Nikisch set to work with much zeal and, as far as German music suits him at all, in my opinion acquitted himself very well.[80]

Strauss's opinion of Nikisch as a conductor of 'German music' was probably coloured by the latter's interest in music from other cultures. While it is clear that much of his Berlin repertoire was given over to Austro-German composers, his enthusiasm for music from other ethnic groups was obvious to musicians and public alike. Keen to perform works from his beloved Russia, Nikisch gave acclaimed performances of music by many of that country's leading composers, including Tchaikovsky, Glazunov, Rubinstein and Rachmaninov. But his interest in foreign music was not restricted to Russia; he also performed compositions from France, Scandinavia and England. Nikisch had a particular fondness for the music of Saint-Saëns and Elgar and, at his Berlin concerts, he gave seventeen performances of works by the former and four by the latter.[81]

Having taken an interest in English music, Nikisch soon became regularly involved with English orchestras. Although his début at the Queen's Hall in June 1895 elicited a mixed response from the critics, it quickly became clear to London audiences that Nikisch was a musician of stature. His performances with the Philharmonic Society and the London Symphony Orchestra were of particular importance and are a guide to his practices as a conductor outside Germany.[82] At his first concert with the Philharmonic Society on 14 May 1908, he performed Schumann's Symphony No. 2, Tchaikovsky's Violin Concerto, Wagner's 'Waldweben' from Siegfried, Liszt's Les Préludes and Lieder by Wolf, Strauss and Liszt. Efrem Zimbalist was engaged as the soloist for the concerto and Nikisch accompanied Elena Gerhardt in the songs. As Gerhardt was making her first appearance with the Society at the request of Nikisch, he told the Directors that she would not insist on the honorarium to which she was normally 'accustomed' but, instead, would leave the matter to their discretion.[83] Of course, such a suggestion was too tempting for the notoriously thrifty Philharmonic Directors to resist and she received no fee. In contrast, the Honorary Secretary of the Society, Francesco Berger, offered Nikisch a payment of £50.[84]

Aware that the sum offered was small, Berger attempted to placate the conductor in typical Philharmonic fashion by writing, 'to such an artist as yourself [the Directors] feel sure that money is not a primary consideration'.[85] As the concert was an overwhelming success, Berger was keen to ensure that Nikisch remained favourably disposed towards the Society and, in a letter overflowing with praise, he wrote: 'Your appearance in our midst will ever remain a red-letter day in the annals of this old Society and your complete artistic triumph will form one among the greatest and most brilliant of its many such.'[86] Although the fees that Nikisch received from the Philharmonic Society were not the largest of his career, he did return to perform for it regularly and gave concerts with its orchestra between 1909 and 1912.[87] Nikisch was then made an Honorary Member of the Society in 1913, a distinction that he had been offered initially in 1906.[88]

Nikisch performed with the London Symphony Orchestra for the first time in 1904. Impressed by his easy manner and his ability to shape the orchestra's sound, Wyn Reeves, a Director of the orchestra and its sub-principal violin, recalled: 'The Orchestra gloried in playing for him! He was the only conductor I can remember who was asked by them to continue the rehearsal after the time was up. . . . He had a wonderful sense of phrase and also a grasp of a symphony or any great work he was conducting; in fact he gave a revealing performance of practically everything he touched.'[89] From the start, the orchestra and Nikisch worked with mutual respect. Having conducted the second concert of its inaugural season on 17 November 1904,[90] Nikisch conducted a further 116 concerts with the orchestra in London and on tour.[91] Although they gave the majority of their performances outside the capital, their partnership soon became a highlight of the city's concert calendar, and their thirty-five performances at the Queen's Hall, five at the Royal Albert Hall and two at the Royal Opera House, Covent Garden, quickly became the benchmark against which all other London orchestral concerts were judged.

With its heavy emphasis on what was becoming established as the Austro-German canon, the repertoire that Nikisch performed with the London Symphony Orchestra was representative of the British capital's concert life in general. Of the concerts performed, twenty-one contained a work by Beethoven, and of these, two were all-Beethoven concerts. Symphonies Nos. 3, 5, 7 and 9 were heard most frequently, and the regular inclusion of those works underlined the need for Nikisch and the orchestra's Directors to programme carefully and with the box office in mind.[92] The Russian repertoire was largely restricted to performances of works by Tchaikovsky, with Symphony No. 5 being given most often.[93] No Schumann symphonies were heard, only six performances of symphonies by Brahms were given, and Bruckner was restricted to a single performance of Symphony No. 2.[94] While it might appear that Nikisch and the London Symphony Orchestra set out to cultivate a popular image, nothing could be further from the truth, because during his ten years with the orchestra, he performed music by a variety of contemporary composers, including Ethel Smyth, Elgar, Strauss, Goldmark, Delafosse, Sinigaglia and Adam Carse.

In addition to performing with the London Symphony Orchestra in the capital, Nikisch toured with it domestically and internationally. Together, conductor and orchestra made seven regional trips, the most extensive of which were to the north of England and Scotland between 1908 and 1910. But the journey of greatest importance historically was to the USA and Canada in 1912. Asked repeatedly to tour North America with a European ensemble, Nikisch finally decided to make the journey with the London Symphony Orchestra. Travelling under the patronage of King George V, the touring party left Euston Station on 28 March 1912 and embarked from Liverpool for the New World on the White Star liner *Baltic*. This represented a last-minute change to their existing travel arrangements, which had originally scheduled the orchestra to sail on White Star's new liner, *Titanic*. Having learned of the ship's loss only after their arrival in New York on 6 April 1912, the musicians were thankful that they had not been victims of the disaster and agreed to join members of six other orchestras at a memorial concert for those who had perished with the *Titanic* at the Royal Albert Hall after their return to London.[95]

Visiting many of North America's major centres, Nikisch and the orchestra gave thirty-one concerts in twenty-one days. For the tour, they prepared four programmes that included works by Beethoven, Tchaikovsky, Wagner, Brahms, Strauss, Weber and Liszt. Nikisch wanted to include Elgar's 'Enigma' Variations and Symphony No. 1, but was dissuaded from doing so by the tour's American sponsors, who argued that those works lacked popular appeal outside Britain and could not be justified commercially. It is ironic, then, that the seats for their first concert at Carnegie Hall and the concert at Cincinnati were not sold completely. But the situation soon changed and all subsequent performances played to full houses. Having impressed the public and critics with their musicianship and virtuosity, the touring party travelled back to the United Kingdom on the Dutch vessel *Potsdam*.

As the North American tour was an outstanding success, the potential for marketing both orchestra and conductor increased considerably. With the advent of sound recording, the profits from combining international success with modern technology were potentially huge. For the record producer Fred Gaisberg, the chance to record Nikisch and the London Symphony Orchestra for HMV was an opportunity not to be missed.[96] In his autobiography, Gaisberg recalls his encounter with Nikisch and some of the conductor's methods:

My first experience with a great symphonic conductor was in 1912, when Artur [sic] Nikisch and the London Symphony Orchestra, fresh from a grand concert tour . . . recorded a part of their touring programme. It was virtuoso playing which was unique at that time. . . . Nikisch, a trim, dapper little man, exuded a magic which made the players anxious to obey his slightest behest. He set about his rehearsals in a quiet yet whimsical way. The men nevertheless knew that sooner or later he would let fall one of those steely, satirical remarks for which he was famous. . . . Nikisch used to explain to his men, when he attempted an extremely extenuated *rubato*, that he permitted unlimited licence, but always within the framework of the bar, and he insisted on maintaining throughout the strictest rhythm. . . . With few words and motions, he studied with them only the more difficult parts of a score. He always conducted from memory. He would commence the *Oberon* Overture by merely raising his eyebrows and frequently gave directions by a nod. It was not his custom to carry his own orchestral parts and he usually doubled up the brass section.[97]

The repertoire from the North American tour that Gaisberg documented was limited. As sound recording was in its infancy, the works chosen needed to be associated closely with Nikisch and to be viable commercially. Apart from the overture to *Le nozze di Figaro*, HMV's recordings of Liszt's Hungarian Rhapsody No. 1, Beethoven's overture to *Egmont* and Weber's overtures to *Der Freischütz* and *Oberon* were all standard Nikisch fare. Encouraged by the success of these interpretations, Deutsche Grammophon then recorded Liszt's Hungarian Rhapsody No. 1 with Nikisch and the Berlin Philharmonic in 1921. That year, conductor and orchestra also recorded Berlioz's overture *Le Carnaval romain* for the German company, but it was Nikisch's recording of Beethoven's Symphony No. 5 that was of greatest significance. Made with the Berlin Philharmonic in November 1913, it was the first complete recording of a symphony.[98] Given the acoustical problems that the performers had to overcome, the speeds heard indicate a highly organized approach on the part of Nikisch, who systematically adjusted his tempi throughout the course of the reading to underline the symphony's structural integrity.

In 1913, Nikisch allowed himself to be filmed conducting.[99] The film, made in Berlin, is silent and of little value musically. But the gestures shown do suggest a conducting technique that might have been the basis for the mythology surrounding his famously 'mesmeric' approach. In the film, his arms are held high, with the beat placed firmly at the point of the baton. By having the end of the stick function at eye level, the player is brought into closer contact with the conductor. This, the composer-conductor Oliver Knussen suggests, may have been the source of Nikisch's mesmerism.[100] But his approach on the film could have been influenced by the height of the music stand. In photographs of Nikisch conducting the Berlin Philharmonic, the music stand is considerably lower than that seen on the film. As the height of the stand would have affected the position of the baton and its relationship with the conductor's line of sight, the film can be considered only a rough guide to Nikisch's technique in general.

Shortly after Nikisch's death, the issue of his podium style was addressed by the British conductor Sir Adrian Boult. In an article written in 1922, Boult argued that Nikisch's ability to 'mesmerize' was a consequence of sound musical practices, rather than some form of sorcery:

> . . . at the time when Nikisch first came to London a great deal was said about his mesmerising the orchestra, and the press contained quotations from statements of orchestral musicians to the effect that they 'felt unlike themselves' when playing under his direction. Such things are difficult to discuss and even more difficult to gauge, but it may be possible to think of certain causes contributory to this impression . . . his long experience as an orchestral player, coupled with a remarkable sympathy which also showed itself in his conducting of concertos and opera, made it easy for him to do things that would never occur to most people. . . . The curious slow gaze with which he seemed to take in the whole orchestra at the beginning of most rehearsals and of every concert gave him an opportunity of noticing everything and at the same time of getting on terms with everyone. Under such conducting it is easy for players to 'feel unlike themselves' and for observers to think they are being mesmerised.[101]

After a severe bought of influenza, Nikisch died from heart disease at Leipzig on 23 January 1922.[102] As with the death of Hans von Bülow, the world of music was quick to mourn his passing. Although less influential than Bülow professionally, Nikisch was held in higher regard personally. A likeable man who used his charm to achieve his musical ends, Nikisch was the darling of audiences and musicians alike. But with his links to the great composers of the past, his interest in new music, his early involvement with sound recording and his charismatic podium manner, Nikisch was also a pivotal figure who bestrode the nineteenth and twentieth centuries like a musical colossus. His dedicated and caring approach was a revelation for many musicians and few would have argued with Carl Flesch when he wrote:

With Nikisch began a new era of the art of conducting. . . . [his] technique . . . seemed unprecedented and completely individual . . . [because he] was the first conductor to beat in advance, i.e. to give the note value a fraction of a second early, a style that was later adopted, and somewhat exaggerated, by Furtwängler. . . . His early death left a painful gap in European musical life. The memory of this lovable and outstanding artist has remained alive among all who were close to him as men and musicians.[103]

CHAPTER 3

The Distiller's Son: Gustav Mahler

Gustav Mahler once lamented that he was 'a Bohemian among Austrians, an Austrian among Germans, and a Jew among all the nations on earth'.[1] Mahler's laconic self-assessment of his ethno-religious status is a poignant simplification of an often complex life that juxtaposed creative activities with duties as an executant musician. Although born into a society that was riddled with prejudices, he rose through the ranks of the Central European opera-house system to become one of the most respected and influential artists of his time. An acerbic individual whose podium manner had more in common with that of Hans von Bülow than that of Arthur Nikisch, Mahler was often offensive to singers, players and impresarios alike. But while some found him difficult personally, none doubted him artistically. His immaculate musicianship, his strict personal discipline and his artistic integrity meant that even those who had fallen foul of his notoriously volatile temper had nothing but respect for him. Considered during his lifetime to be a conductor who composed rather than a composer who conducted, Mahler lacked the universal appeal of Richard Strauss. Nevertheless, he was one of the leading interpretative musicians of his age whose model performances were widely emulated but rarely equalled.

Born on 7 July 1860 at Kalischt in Bohemia (now Kaliště, Czech Republic), Mahler was the product of an assimilated lower middle-class Jewish family. Although he was the second of fourteen children born to Bernhard and Marie Mahler, Gustav was one of only six to survive childhood.[2] His father worked initially as a carter at Kalischt and, later, as a distiller of liquor at Iglau, now known as Jihlava, the town to which the family moved in December 1860.[3] Mahler's mother, Marie, was from a higher social class than Bernhard, and it was at her family home at Ledeč that Gustav encountered a piano for the first time.[4] His interest in the instrument was immediate, and the Mahlers' sitting room soon boasted a Vopaterny grand piano.[5] A string of teachers were then engaged to instruct Gustav, of whom the local conductors Franz Victorin and Heinrich Fischer were of particular importance.[6] Gustav progressed quickly under their tutelage and he made his début as a pianist at the Iglau Stadttheater on 13 October 1870. The performance was well attended and a review in the local paper recorded that the quality of playing was higher than that of the instrument played.[7]

Shortly after his first concert, Mahler was sent to Prague to further both his musical and his general education. But his experiences in the capital were not good and he failed to realize his academic potential. Bernhard decided, therefore, that the boy should return to Iglau where he would continue his schooling at the local Gymnasium. He gained little from the formal environment of that institution, however, and began to use his father's small but diverse library as the basis for his studies. Although passionate about literature, Mahler's interest in music dominated his activities as a youth at Iglau and the local lending library soon became a valuable source of musical scores. The town also had an active artistic life during Mahler's childhood and the local theatre regularly presented works from the popular operatic repertoire. Unlike many of the other conductors considered in this book, Mahler's parents were not particularly musical and it is unclear whether he attended operatic performances during his early years.

In the summer of 1875, the young Mahler was engaged by Gustav Schwarz, a local estate manager at Čáslav, to play through a series of unpublished manuscripts by the pianist Sigismund Thalberg.[8] Schwarz had discovered the autographs by chance in an attic and Mahler had been recommended to him by a friend because of his ability to read difficult scores at sight. Schwarz was impressed immediately by Mahler's pianism and suggested that he should consider a career in music. It was clear to Schwarz that provincial Iglau was unsuitable for a young pianist of potential, so he also recommended that Mahler should continue his studies in Vienna. Keen to act on Schwarz's suggestion, but doubtful of his father's response, Mahler appealed to Schwarz to visit his father and to help persuade him of the benefits of the imperial capital. Although Bernhard was determined that Gustav should complete his general education at Iglau before pursuing his musical studies elsewhere, he eventually relented and Schwarz accompanied Mahler to Vienna, where he played to the eminent teacher and editor Julius Epstein.[9] Although initially unimpressed by Mahler's pianism, Epstein was enthusiastic about his compositions, which he considered to be 'in direct descent from Wagner'.[10] With Epstein's recommendation, Mahler enrolled at the

Vienna Conservatory in September 1875, studying piano with him, harmony with Robert Fuchs and composition with Franz Krenn.[11]

Having had the 'the doors to the habitation of the Muses' opened for him by Schwarz,[12] Mahler soon realized that he had been 'introduced . . . into the land of [his] desires'.[13] Inspired by an environment that encouraged artistic excellence, he progressed quickly and, at the end of his first academic year, he won first prize for both piano and composition.[14] Although his potential as a creative and as an executant musician was clearly apparent from the start, his future at the Conservatory was not assured and, by the beginning of his second year in Vienna, it was obvious to Mahler that his father was either unwilling or unable to support him financially and that his fees would have to be deferred if he was to continue his studies. In a letter to the Governing Board of the Conservatory the teenager asked, therefore, for his fees to be waived, arguing that his father was in no 'position to support' him and that he was unable to support himself.[15] His plea was successful, at least in part, and some of his fees were reduced by half for his second year.[16] The following academic year,[17] Mahler left Epstein's piano class to concentrate on composition and graduated from the Conservatory in the summer of 1878 with the first prize for composition.[18]

As Mahler had spent his student years living and studying in a city with a vibrant cultural life, it might be assumed that he supplemented his music education by regularly attending concert and operatic performances. This, however, was not the case, and, according to his friend the distinguished musicologist Guido Adler,[19] '[Mahler's] means were more than limited . . . [and] [a]lmost all of the operas that in the course of time he later had to direct, to "bring out" as best he could, he first became acquainted with through individual study'.[20] Nevertheless, it is inconceivable that he was unaware of the excitement that gripped Vienna in November and December 1875 when the recently appointed First Hofkapellmeister of the Hofoper, Hans Richter,[21] conducted *Tannhäuser* and *Lohengrin* under the direct supervision of the composer.[22] It is unclear whether Mahler attended either those or the seventeen other new productions and local premières that were given at the Hofoper during his student years,[23] but what is clear is that he was affected by Wagner's music and ideas from an early age, as he not only joined the Academic Wagner Society in 1877 but also devoured the composer's essay *Religion und Kunst* (*Religion and Art*) shortly after it was published in 1880.

After leaving the Vienna Conservatory, Mahler supported his composing activities by working as a piano teacher. As the genesis of his first major work, *Das klagende Lied*, was interrupted constantly by his teaching duties, Mahler was advised by the publisher Theodor Rättig to consult a theatrical agent so that he could secure a post as a conductor. But as he had received no formal lessons in conducting at the Conservatory[24] and had attended only a handful of operatic and theatrical performances during his student years, Mahler's formal music education did little to prepare him practically for life in the theatre. Nevertheless, the agent Gustav Löwy[25] was willing to act on Mahler's behalf and, within weeks of a contract being signed on 12 May 1880,[26] Mahler was sent to the small spa town of Hall in Upper Austria.

Today, Hall is known as Bad Hall and has a population of 4200 inhabitants. Situated near Linz at the relatively modest elevation of 380 metres, Hall continues to offer many of the attractions that Mahler would have enjoyed in 1880. Boasting an iodine salt-water spring that claims to benefit those who suffer from circulatory, respiratory and orthopaedic disorders, the town continues to stage operas, operettas and musicals at its small theatre. The present theatre, however, barely resembles the wooden construction that was managed by the actor-producer Karl Ludwig Zwerenz some 120 years ago, where performances were given at five o'clock in the afternoon because of the fire hazard caused by the theatre's gas and candle lighting systems. Mahler's conditions of service were also primitive and, with a monthly salary of 30 gulden that was supplemented by 50 kreuzer for each performance he conducted,[27] he was expected to direct an orchestra of fifteen musicians and a troupe of approximately two dozen actors and singers.[28] The repertoire that he performed is unknown, but, would almost certainly have been the usual mixture of opera, operetta and farce that was heard commonly at spas of the period. Mahler's duties were often menial, and his wife Alma later recalled that he also had 'to put out the music on the music-stands before each performance, to dust the piano and to collect the music again after the performance'. Moreover, 'he had to wheel the baby [of the theatre manager] round the theatre in her pram . . . [but he] drew the line . . . when he was required to deputize on the stage . . . [a decision that he] regretted later . . . [because it was a] lost opportunity [that] would have taught him much that was never likely to come his way again'.[29]

After being dismissed within weeks of taking up his post at Hall for missing the start of a performance after returning late from a walk with friends,[30] Mahler returned to Vienna in July 1880.[31] Throughout the winter of 1880–1, his living conditions in Vienna resembled those of his student years and he often took cheap lodgings that were unheated. His situation altered sharply, however, when he was offered the post of First Kapellmeister at Landschaftliches Theater in Laibach from September 1881. Laibach, now known as Ljubljana, was situated in the southern part of the Austrian empire and was the capital of the Duchy of Krain. The population of the city in 1881 was approximately 26,000, of whom some sixty per cent were German and forty per cent were Slovene. The Landschaftliches Theater, though primitive by international standards, was of a higher status than that of Hall and was directed by the comedian and stage producer Alexander Mondheim-Schneider.[32] The company was typically small and consisted of an orchestra of eighteen musicians, a chorus of fourteen singers and a troupe of principals who were mainly singer-actors.

The 1881–2 season at Laibach opened on 24 September 1881 with a gala performance of Bauernfeld's play *Bürgerlich und romantisch*. Before the play commenced, however, Mahler conducted Beethoven's overture to *Egmont*. Although it was an important milestone in his career as a conductor, the local German-language newspaper, the *Laibacher Zeitung*, failed to recognize the personal significance of the performance for him and reported simply: 'The gala evening was introduced by Beethoven's *Egmont* overture, played with precision by the orchestra under the Conductor, G. Mahler.'[33] Nine days later, on 3 October 1881, he conducted Verdi's *Il trovatore* for the first time.[34] Again, the performance was an important event for Mahler, because it was probably his first of a major opera. Although a novice by professional standards, Mahler soon learned to be adaptable and, between 24 September 1881 and 2 April 1882, he gave eighty-four complete performances of stage works by sixteen composers at Laibach.[35] Mahler's ability to study and to absorb scores quickly was formidable and he soon gained the respect of colleagues. His impact at Laibach was both immediate and profound, and some years later the concert master of the orchestra recalled that, although '[a]s a pianist he did not impress us, . . . his performance of Mozart's [*Die Zauberflöte*], for which he had only operetta resources at his disposal, made us realize that he was a very gifted conductor of opera'.[36]

Having completed his season at Laibach successfully, Mahler returned to Vienna by way of Trieste. From there, he wrote to Löwy on 4 April 1882 reminding him that he would 'be coming to Vienna next week' and hoped that he would 'call [him] to mind'.[37] But Löwy was unable to offer Mahler any work in the short term and it seemed that the benefits that he gained both financially and musically at Laibach were in danger of being lost. At the beginning of the 1882–3 season, however, the former director of the Hall theatre, Karl Ludwig Zwerenz, invited Mahler to perform Suppé's *Boccaccio* at the Iglau Stadttheater on 19 September 1882. Zwerenz had recently taken over the management of the Iglau theatre and was keen to engage his former conductor. For Mahler, performing before a home-town audience for an impresario who had dismissed him from his first post must have been both ironic and unsettling, but the performance was a success and the *Iglauer Grenzbote* reported proudly on 21 September that the 'ensembles were perfect, bearing witness to the spirited and crisp direction by our towns-fellow Herr Mahler, who was on the podium, and who recently initiated his career as *Kapellmeister* with such marked success at Laibach'.[38] Although praised for his interpretation and happy to visit his family at Iglau, Mahler was unwilling to accept a permanent post in his home-town and remained unemployed as a conductor until he was appointed Kapellmeister at the Olmütz Theatre in January 1883.

Situated some eighty kilometres north-east of Brno, Olmütz, now known as Olomouc, was a German-speaking enclave of some 20,000 inhabitants in east Moravia. Throughout the late 1870s the town's theatre had been failing financially, and by the beginning of 1883 it was having trouble meeting its debts. The theatre's director, Emanuel Raul, was partly responsible for the situation, as he insisted on staging productions that were both expensive to mount and unattractive to local audiences. On 10 January 1883, the theatre's troubles reached crisis point when the First Kapellmeister, Emil Kaiser,[39] confronted Raul over his inadequate salary. During a performance of Meyerbeer's *L'Africaine*, conductor and director became embroiled in a fierce altercation that resulted in the police being called. The incident soon turned into a public scandal and the conductor was removed from his post. Aware that his theatre was unable to function fully without a First Kapellmeister, Raul quickly set about finding a replacement. Although the exact circumstances of Mahler's appointment are unclear, Löwy must have been among the agents approached by Raul and must have recommended the young conductor for the vacant position.

On arrival at Olmütz, Mahler was confronted with a near bankrupt theatre that employed an orchestra of thirty musicians, a chorus of twenty singers and a troupe of mediocre actors and singers. Mahler's introduction to that motley crew was as bizarre as it was gauche. At his first rehearsal with the chorus, he failed to introduce himself and set about rehearsing them until they were hoarse. At the following soloist rehearsal, he again failed to introduce himself and demanded simply that they follow his instructions. And, at his local début with

Meyerbeer's *Les Huguenots*, the bass singing Marcel protested after the first act that he was unable to continue because he could not decipher Mahler's erratic conducting technique.[40] Mahler was also uncommunicative and eccentric on a personal level: he refused to introduce himself in public, avoided social contact with colleagues, insisted that local restaurants prepare him a vegetarian diet and abstained from drinking alcohol at the local bars.[41] His peculiar behaviour seems to have peaked on 13 February 1883, when one of the theatre's singers found Mahler 'running demented . . . and weeping loudly . . . through the streets'. Aware that the conductor's father was unwell, the singer enquired whether he had died. In reply, Mahler 'howled' '[w]orse, worse, much worse . . . [t]he worst has happened. The Master [Wagner] has died!' The news of Wagner's death left Mahler distraught for days and although he 'came to rehearsals and performances . . . he remained inaccessible to everyone for a long time'.[42]

The repertoire that Mahler conducted at Olmütz was both challenging and varied. After making his local début with Meyerbeer's *Les Huguenots* on 15 January 1883, he conducted that composer's *Robert le diable*, Auber's *La Muette de Portici*, Verdi's *Un ballo in maschera*, *Rigoletto* and *Il trovatore*, Méhul's *Joseph* and Bizet's *Carmen*.[43] The type and character of the operas heard at Olmütz during Mahler's period reflect Raul's interest in grand opera and his need to produce popular entertainment that would guarantee revenue. Nevertheless, it seems that Mahler was able to have some effect on Raul's programming, and, in a letter to his friend Friedrich Löhr, he sets out the way in which he influenced the choice of works performed, his impressions of his colleagues and his reaction to the Olmütz Theatre as a whole:

I am paralysed, like one who has been cast forth from heaven. Since the moment I crossed the threshold of the theatre in Olmütz, I have felt like a man about to face the Day of Judgement. Take a thoroughbred horse and yoke it to a cart with oxen – all it can do is to pull and sweat along with them . . . I feel so besmirched. . . . I have been conducting . . . almost exclusively Meyerbeer and Verdi. By dogged scheming I have succeeded in getting Wagner and Mozart out of the repertory; – for I could not endure rattling off, say, *Lohengrin* or *Don Giovanni* – in this place here. – Tomorrow we are doing *Joseph in Aegypten*. An extremely charming work, with something of Mozart's grace. – I really did get great enjoyment out of rehearsing it. And I must say – despite their incredible lack of sensibility, these people I have to work with here do now and then pull themselves together a bit for my sake, and this time they have tried somewhat harder – though I'm afraid it's only a way of showing they're sorry for this 'idealist' – a very contemptuous epithet, this – for the idea that an artist can become utterly absorbed in a work of art is quite beyond them.[44]

Mahler's conducting technique presented problems at Olmütz. When he first arrived, he had a habit of passing his baton from his right hand to his left and covering his face with his free hand, thus obscuring his cues.[45] Aware that the cast had trouble following him, Mahler tried to modify his approach and was later found practising his gestures in a local café with a billiard cue. His technique continued to be problematic for much of his career but, as time passed, he gradually altered his method. Towards the end of his life, his gestures were more restrained and he adopted a simpler beat that required very little body movement.[46] His quieter approach, however, was no easier for the musicians and the singers to follow, because, in an attempt to stress the music's important melodic and rhythmic content, he often minimized the first beat of the bar, stressing instead either the second or third. Mahler argued that by applying that method the players 'had to help produce the music themselves, instead of merely following someone else thoughtlessly and relying on him'.[47] He also recognized that the musicians found him hard to follow because he altered his tempi from performance to performance, a habit that he adopted because he would have been 'bored to death if [he] constantly had to take a work down the same monotonous beaten track'.[48]

On 18 March 1883, Mahler left Olmütz and returned to Vienna, where he worked as a chorus master for a season of Italian opera at the Carl-Theater. In early May 1883, Löwy learned of a vacancy at the Hoftheater in Kassel and wrote immediately to the Intendant, Adolph Freiherr von und zu Gilsa, on Mahler's behalf. In his letter of 12 May, Löwy mentions that Mahler had gained experience in Laibach and Olmütz, had received a thorough music education and had dedicated himself to his art.[49] Löwy also mentioned that Mahler's application would be supported by a letter of recommendation from the Régisseur (stage director) of the Königliche Oper Dresden, Karl Ueberhorst.[50] Ueberhorst had attended Mahler's benefit performance of Méhul's *Joseph* in Olmütz and commented later that a 'man who can bring off a performance like that is something astonishing'.[51] Ueberhorst's testimonial of 14 May 1883 was glowing and mentioned Mahler's attention to detail, his sense of good taste, his precision when conducting and his ability to achieve a sense of unity in performance.[52] Impressed by the testimonials that Mahler received, Gilsa invited the young conductor to Kassel for a set of trials that included directing Rossini's overture to *Guillaume Tell*, taking a series of chorus and solo rehearsals, and conducting the general rehearsal of Marschner's *Hans Heiling*. Mahler completed the tasks successfully and he was offered the post of Musik und Chordirektor on 31 May 1883 with a salary of 2100 marks.

The Hoftheater at Kassel was one of a group of Royal Prussian theatres that was managed from Berlin. As part of that network, it enjoyed greater funding than the theatres in Hall, Laibach and Olmütz and was of a higher status than many privately managed theatres in Germany. The Kassel company consisted of fifteen principal artists, a chorus of thirty-eight singers and an orchestra of forty-nine musicians.[53] As Musikdirektor, Mahler was subordinate to the Intendant, Gilsa, who undertook the day-to-day management of the theatre, the First Kapellmeister, Wilhelm Treiber, and the Oberrégisseur (head producer), Jacob Wohlstadt. Mahler's duties included coaching the singers, rehearsing the chorus, arranging and modifying works, composing additional music where necessary,[54] directing stage bands and conducting performances. His contract also specified that he was not allowed to excise material from a score without the prior permission of his superiors, was to prevent singers from cutting material, was to ensure the discipline of the chorus and the orchestra, was to write regular reports on the progress of singers and choristers and was to consult the management if he needed to employ extra musicians. As the member of a Prussian court theatre, he was also subject to a lengthy list of regulations concerning punctuality and behaviour, any breach of which would result in punishments being applied.[55]

Although Mahler's contract was scheduled to begin on 1 October 1883, he was asked by the Kassel management if he was willing to report for work during the summer. Mahler agreed happily and began his duties with a chorus rehearsal on 21 August. By mid September, however, his tempestuous personality had brought him into conflict with his superiors and, on the nineteenth of that month, the day that he was scheduled to conduct Meyerbeer's *Robert le diable*, he reported to Friedrich Löhr: 'the Herr Hofkapellmeister [Treiber] has an option on all the classics [and] he is the cheerfullest 4/4–beat man ever to come my way. I, of course, am the "most stiff-necked young man in the world", who absolutely refuses to be initiated into the mysteries of art by him'.[56] While Mahler was right to claim that Treiber withheld many of the 'classics', he was allocated a wide, varied and interesting repertoire that included operas and operettas by Adam, Auber, Bizet, Boieldieu, Delibes, Donizetti, Flotow, Gounod, Kreutzer, Lortzing, Maillart, Marschner, Meyerbeer, Nessler, Nicolai, Offenbach, Pillwitz, Rossini, Schubert and Verdi.[57] The absence of works by Beethoven, Mozart and Wagner from Mahler's allocated operas must have been frustrating for the fledgling conductor, but he was young and lacked experience. Nevertheless, he was entrusted with a number of local premières and new productions, which compensated, at least in part, for the seemingly unending stream of repertory performances that constituted the majority of his duties.

On 24 and 25 January 1884, Hans von Bülow and the Meininger Hofkapelle performed in Kassel.[58] Mahler was keen to meet the legendary conductor and, before the first concert, attempted to visit him at his hotel. Barred from entering by the concierge, Mahler remained undeterred and penned a letter to the conductor the day after the first concert. Still reeling from the impact of the all-Beethoven programme, Mahler wrote:

> When I asked you for an interview, I did not yet know what a flame your incomparable art would kindle in my soul. . . . I am a musician who is wandering without a guiding light. . . . At the concert yesterday, when I beheld the fulfilment of my utmost intimations and hopes of beauty, it became clear to me that I had found my spiritual home and my master, and that my wanderings would come to an end now or never. . . . [I] beg you to take me along in any capacity you like – let me become your *pupil*, even if I had to pay my tuition fees with my blood. . . . I give myself to you heart and soul, and if you will accept the gift, I cannot think of anything that could make me happier. . . . I am ready for anything you have in mind.[59]

While Mahler was prepared to throw caution to the wind, Bülow was more circumspect and was not prepared to become involved with an unknown musician who was clearly unhappy with his current situation. To avoid becoming embroiled in the petty politics of a small court theatre, Bülow followed protocol and passed the letter directly to Treiber, who handed it to Gilsa, who placed it in Mahler's personal file where it remains today.

In October 1884, a local choral group, the Mündener Chorverein, asked Mahler to be its conductor. Because his contract with the Hoftheater prevented him from taking additional work without the prior permission of the management, Mahler needed the consent of the

Intendant before he could accept the post. As the choir rehearsed on a Monday evening, the night on which no performances were given at the Hoftheater, Gilsa approved the request. Mahler seems to have been popular with the choristers and was able to communicate well with both the younger and older members of the group.[60] The first work that he tackled with the choir was Haydn's *Die Jahreszeiten* (*The Seasons*), which he performed at Münden on 14 February 1885 with an orchestra and soloists drawn from the Hoftheater.[61] The concert was a popular and critical success and Mahler was praised for his abilities as both choirmaster and conductor.

Having successfully conducted *Die Jahreszeiten*, Mahler's next major task with the Chorverein was to prepare the group for a festival performance of Mendelssohn's *St Paul* at Münden on 29 June 1885. The choir was to be joined by choral societies from neighbouring districts and the orchestra of the Kassel Hoftheater. As the Hoftheater orchestra was to be engaged as a unit, protocol dictated that its senior conductor, Treiber, should be invited to conduct the performance. This, however, was unacceptable to some of the festival's organizers, and when he was rejected as conductor the orchestra withdrew in solidarity.[62] Treiber's rejection then prompted a bitter public debate over who should lead the performance. For some, Mahler was the obvious choice, but for others he proved unacceptable. His supporters cited his outstanding musicianship, while his detractors argued that his Jewish heritage precluded him from conducting a Christian work. Of course, the irony of their objection would not have been lost on his supporters, who were probably aware that Mendelssohn had been both a practising Christian and an ethnic Jew. The faction in favour of Mahler eventually prevailed and he was invited to conduct the performance. By accepting the engagement, however, he brought himself into direct conflict with his superiors at the Hoftheater, who considered his acceptance to be an act of gross disloyalty. But Mahler cared little about the feelings of his colleagues and, in a letter to Friedrich Löhr in April 1885, wrote that his 'appointment caused terrible strife among the various parties. . . . [The] orchestra is on strike because the Herr Hofkapellmeister feels he has been made to look a fool, and the Herr Intendant has even had the brazenness to appeal to the nobility of my feelings in the hope of {persuading} [*sic*] me to withdraw. Of course I let him have a piece of my mind, and now I am a dead man so far as the theatre here is concerned'.[63]

Mahler's analysis of his situation in April 1885 was correct and, within days of his successful performance of *St Paul* on 29 June, his contract with the Hoftheater was terminated. For Mahler, his dismissal was neither unexpected nor unwelcome, as he had wanted to leave Kassel for some time and had taken steps to find alternative employment in December 1884. That month, he wrote to a number of leading impresarios, including Angelo Neumann at Bremen, Bernhard Pollini at Hamburg and Max Staegemann at Leipzig, about the possibility of work. While Pollini and Neumann were unable to offer Mahler a job in the short term, Staegemann did respond positively, and, in January 1885, engaged him as Arthur Nikisch's Second Kapellmeister at the Leipzig Stadttheater from the summer of 1886.[64] Although Mahler's negotiations were conducted covertly, Gilsa soon learned of his new contract and was displeased by his secrecy. Mahler's position at Kassel quickly became untenable and matters soon reached crisis point. As he had been a thorn in the side of the management throughout much of his tenure, had been disciplined on a number of occasions for breach of contract[65] and was publicly disloyal to Treiber over the planned performance of St Paul, his unauthorized absence from the pit for a performance at the Hoftheater on 10 April 1885 was the excuse that Gilsa needed to cancel his contract. When confronted by Gilsa over his absence, Mahler argued that, while he was not actually conducting the performance he was scheduled to lead, he had been in the auditorium throughout the evening and was able to superintend the performance from there.[66] Incensed by Mahler's cavalier attitude, Gilsa informed him on 13 April that his contract would be terminated on 1 September.[67] But, as Mahler was keen to leave, and Gilsa was eager for him to go, the termination date was brought forward to 1 July 1885.[68]

In the spring of that year, Angelo Neumann was appointed Director of the failing Deutsches Königliches Landestheater in Prague. The theatre had been the undisputed heart of Prague's cultural life until 1862, when its dominance was challenged by the Czech Interim Provincial Theatre.[69] That theatre's establishment and its subsequent popularity was a direct consequence of the granting of greater ethnic freedom to the non German-speaking communities within the Austrian Empire by the Emperor, Franz Joseph, in 1860. With their greater independence, Prague's Czech speakers took the opportunity to support their newly established theatre increasingly during the 1860s and 1870s, and by the mid 1880s, when it moved into the National Theatre (Národní Divadlo), its policy of programming interesting and colourful works by Smetana, Dvořák and other Slavonic composers attracted not only Czech-speaking patrons but also those from the German-speaking community.[70] Neumann had been engaged by the Deutsches Landestheater to reverse that trend and was given a free hand to make whatever innovations and appointments he felt were necessary. One of his first acts was to offer Mahler the post of First Kapellmeister in June 1885, a proposal that the conductor accepted, even though he was contracted to the Leipzig Stadttheater from mid 1886. Tempted by the status of the Prague position, Mahler tried to free himself from his agreement with Staegemann, but the Leipzig director refused to release him and Mahler was available to Neumann for one year only. Having faced the possibility of a lengthy spell of unemployment, Mahler now enjoyed the attention of two leading managers and was able to report to Löhr, 'it's all to the good to have the Herren Direktoren fighting over me!'[71]

Although Neumann was keen to have Mahler as his First Kapellmeister, it seems that his appointment was conditional. After arriving in Prague in July 1885, Mahler's first task was to take a rehearsal of Wagner's *Lohengrin* for his fellow First Kapellmeister, Anton Seidl, a long-standing and trusted colleague of Neumann.[72] As Neumann had never seen Mahler conduct and had only 'engaged the young musician after talking things over with him',[73] his rehearsal of *Lohengrin* was the first opportunity that the impresario had to assess the conductor's abilities personally. Seidl and Neumann were impressed by Mahler's skill and enthusiasm throughout the opera's preparation period and, the day after its première, the impresario decided 'to allow the young hothead to conduct Cherubini's *Les Deux Journées*, the performance in honour of the Emperor's birthday'.[74] Mahler's Prague début was set, therefore, for 18 August 1885. The evening was a triumph and Neumann later recalled that the 'new conductor . . . put all his available energy into [the] task . . . [and although he] seemed . . . to move about too much when he was conducting, . . . remind[ing] us strongly of Bülow[,] . . . [h]is début was a success, and resulted in the young man being given a contract at the German Theatre for a year'.[75] So impressed was Neumann by Mahler's performance that when he 'came to consider the cast and allotment of parts for the programme [he] was planning for the season, [he] entrusted the young conductor with *Rhinegold* and *Valkyrie* which were to be in the repertory for the first time'.[76]

Before conducting the local premières of *Das Rheingold* and *Die Walküre*, however, Mahler was allocated a revival of Mozart's *Don Giovanni*. Mahler's senior colleague, Ludwig Slansky, an established figure at the Deutsches Landestheater whose readings of Wagner's operas were held in high esteem by local musicians and audiences alike, had been scheduled to conduct the opera but had rejected it because he felt that it lacked local appeal. Mahler took a different stance and leaped at the opportunity of conducting Mozart's Prague masterpiece in the city in which it had first been performed. Working closely with Neumann as producer, Mahler conducted *Don Giovanni* for the first time on 6 September 1885. The interpretation captured the attention of the press, with the critics commenting upon Mahler's tempi, the virtuosity of the singers and the use of a keyboard as the accompanying instrument in the secco recitatives. Formerly in Prague, the accompaniments of such recitatives had been arranged for strings,[77] but Neumann and Mahler rejected that practice and entrusted Slansky with the responsibility of realizing the passages on a piano. In general, the critics welcomed the production and Neumann later recalled with pride that the 'young fire-brand took on *Don Giovanni* with great enthusiasm, I directed it, and the public and critics were delighted'.[78]

After *Don Giovanni*, Mahler took charge of Nessler's popular opera *Der Trompeter von Säkkingen* for an indisposed Slansky on 12 September 1885.[79] The performance was a success and, on 27 September, he conducted Wagner's *Tannhäuser*. Having lost Seidl to the Metropolitan Opera, New York, that month, Neumann turned increasingly to Mahler when mounting productions of Wagner's works. Although his performance of *Tannhäuser* was his first of an opera by that composer, his approach was convincing and, on 25 October, he was allocated *Die Meistersinger von Nürnberg*. Performed for the first time in Prague uncut, the opera aroused the interest of the critics, who praised Mahler's control of the orchestra and his ability to shape both the drama and the music. Within weeks of conducting *Die Meistersinger von Nürnberg*, Mahler began preparations for the local premières of *Das Rheingold* and *Die Walküre*. Both works had been advertised heavily in the local press, and by the time of the performances public interest was at fever pitch. On the morning of 19 December 1885, the day of the first performance of *Das Rheingold*, a queue for tickets encircled the theatre. Those lucky enough to obtain a seat were not disappointed by what they saw and heard and were rewarded by a performance that was described by one critic as 'brilliant'.[80]

As Mahler's fame as an opera conductor had risen sharply during the first half of his year at Prague, Neumann was keen to build on his local success by allowing him to perform as a concert conductor. Mahler's first opportunity to act in that capacity for Neumann took place on 13 February 1886, when he was one of three conductors who took part in a commemorative concert marking the third anniversary of Wagner's death. With the orchestra of the Deutsches Landestheater and the choirs of the Deutscher Männergesangverein and the Gesangverein St Veit, Slansky conducted extracts from *Götterdämmerung*, Mahler performed the 'Verwandlungsmusik' and the closing scene of Act 1 from *Parsifal*, and Karl Muck,[81] whom Neumann engaged later that year as a conductor in Prague, gave Beethoven's Symphony No. 9 ('Choral'). When the programme was repeated on 21 February, Mahler was given the responsibility of conducting not only the excerpts from *Parsifal* and but also the symphony by Beethoven. Having never performed a major symphony before, Mahler was faced with the prospect of interpreting a staple of the emerging Austro-German canon at very short notice. Undaunted by the task, he committed the works to memory and gave a performance of the symphony that was commended for its subtleties and its contrasts. On 18 April, Mahler conducted his third concert at Prague at which he performed various Lieder, songs and arias, Boccherini's Minuet for String Orchestra, Raff's Violin Concerto No. 2 (Karl Halir,[82] violin), Wagner's *Kaisermarsch*, Bruckner's Scherzo from Symphony No. 3 and Mozart's Symphony No. 40.[83] Although the audience and the critics found the length of the marathon concert taxing, Mahler's performance of the Mozart Symphony was praised widely.[84]

Mahler's tenure at Prague was an important milestone in his career. With the help and support of Neumann, he was able to perform for the first time some major Austro-German works that were acquiring canonic status. Because of Seidl's departure for America, Mahler dominated the conducting roster at the Deutsches Landestheater from September 1885 and eclipsed the activities of his more senior colleague, Ludwig Slansky. Aware that his move to Leipzig at the end of the 1885–6 season meant that he would be working with Arthur Nikisch, a conductor who was unlikely to concede the works of Wagner, Mozart and Beethoven to him, Mahler was keen to remain in Prague. Neumann was also eager for him to stay, so he offered to extend his tenure and to increase his salary in the autumn of 1885. Keen to accept Neumann's proposal, Mahler tried in vain to free himself from his contract with Staegemann. But Staegemann was a shrewd theatre director with a knack for spotting talent and was unwilling to forgo the opportunity of engaging a conductor of Mahler's talent. When it became clear that Staegemann was not going to release him, Mahler contacted the director in June 1886 to discuss the details of his forthcoming début at Leipzig.

Eager to establish his credentials as an interpreter of Wagner from the start, Mahler suggested to Staegemann that *Tannhäuser* might be a suitable work with which to begin his tenure at Leipzig. The conductor argued that the opera offered the 'opportunity . . . [for him] to introduce [himself] as an orchestral conductor and to prove [his] control of massed voices and of the structure of operatic ensembles'.[85] But Staege-mann rejected Mahler's suggestion and, on 3 August 1886, he made his début at the Leipzig Stadttheater with Wagner's *Lohengrin*. Within weeks of that performance, Mahler was given a wide and varied reper-toire to conduct and was allocated Wagner's *Rienzi* and *Tannhäuser*, Weber's *Der Freischütz*, Halévy's *La Juive*, Meyerbeer's *Le Prophète*, *Les Huguenots* and *Robert le diable* and Mozart's *Die Zauberflöte*. With the exceptions of *Rienzi* and *La Juive*, which he described as a 'wonderful, magnificent work . . . [that] rank[s] . . . among the greatest ever created',[86] all the operas that Mahler conducted during the first weeks of his tenure were familiar to him, allowing him time to prepare fully for his first performances of Meyerbeer's *L'Africaine*, Weber's *Oberon*, Auber's *Le Maçon*, Wagner's *Der fliegende Holländer* and Gluck's *Armida* between September and December 1886.

In November, Mahler came into conflict with the Staegemann over Wagner's *Der Ring des Nibelungen*. The director had recently obtained permission to perform the tetralogy and Mahler considered it appropri-ate that he should share the conducting of the cycle with Nikisch. Staegemann took a different stance and reserved the right to offer the whole of the tetralogy to his First Kapellmeister, who had conducted it first in 1878.[87] Mahler was so incensed by Staegemann's behaviour that he asked to be released from his contract and applied for work else-where. The Director, however, was not intimidated by his Second Kapellmeister's threats to leave and, in January 1887, offered to release him from his contract. In February, however, Mahler's fortunes changed for the better at Leipzig, because Nikisch had fallen ill and he was able to take over much of his indisposed colleague's repertoire. Among the works that Nikisch had been scheduled to conduct was *Die Walküre*, which Mahler performed in his stead on 9 February 1887. The per-formance was an outstanding success and, by April, Mahler was able to report that he was again on good terms with Staegemann.[88] Other works that Mahler conducted during Nikisch's absence included Wagner's *Das Rheingold*, *Siegfried* and *Lohengrin*, Mozart's *Così fan tutte* and *Le nozze di Figaro*, Bizet's *Carmen*, Beethoven's *Fidelio* and Offenbach's *Les Contes d'Hoffmann*. When Nikisch returned to work in the spring, Mahler's credentials as a Wagner conductor were firmly established, and in the summer of 1887 he shared the direction of a cycle of *Der Ring des Nibelungen* with his senior colleague.[89]

Nikisch was not the only thorn in Mahler's side at Leipzig. The orchestra of the Stadttheater also proved problematic and rebelled against his authoritarian manner during Nikisch's indisposition. Mahler had often taken a high-handed approach with the orchestras that he conducted in the past, but, unlike the theatres at Hall, Laibach, Olmütz and Prague, the Leipzig Stadttheater benefited from having members of the Gewandhaus Orchestra in its pit. As the orchestra had a long and distinguished history and had worked with many of the leading conductors of the period, the players objected strongly to Mahler's schoolmasterly manner and soon contacted the town council about his behaviour. In their formal letter of complaint against the conductor, the players asked the council for its 'protection and support owing to the unworthy way in which it [had been] treated by . . . Mahler'. They argued that he was 'hardly . . . [ever] satisfied with a single member of the Orchestra during rehearsals and . . . frequently demand[ed] what [was] absolutely impossible'. Moreover, when the players were unable to achieve the effect that Mahler wanted 'the member of the Orchestra involved [was] accused of malice and stubbornness'. They were concerned, therefore, that '[i]f the artistic standards of the Orchestra' were to be maintained 'the self-respect of individual members . . . [was] not [to] be trifled with in [that] way'.[90] Having set aside his differences with Mahler after the success of *Die Walküre*, Staegemann came to the defence of his Second Kapellmeister and, in a letter to the town council, 'reject[ed] categorically' the notion that Mahler was hot-headed, arguing, 'as he is always objective, his zeal can be insulting only to those who are disposed to be insulted'.[91]

Nevertheless, Mahler's approach to musicians and singers was often acerbic and, some years after leaving Leipzig, he raised the issue of his caustic manner with his friend the violist Natalie Bauer-Lechner. During that conversation, he argued that, for some musicians, 'art is only the cow which they milk so as to live their everyday lives undisturbed'. He conceded, however, that 'one ought to have more patience with them than [he was] able to manage', but 'if one of them [did not] immediately give [him] what [was] on the page, [he would] kill him on the spot'. Even so, he recognized that he 'often demand[ed] more of them than they [were] capable of actually giving . . .[and that it was] no wonder [that] they [did not] forgive [him] for it'. He observed that his relations with orchestras were worse 'towards the end of [each] season, when everybody [was] played-out and exhausted'. Although he, too, was tired by that part of the year, he believed that he had 'to test [his] own strength to the limit and [to] make even greater demands on the orchestra, in order to achieve the kind of perfection which alone [could] satisfy [him]'. Yet he felt that, as his career progressed, his manner became calmer and no longer resembled his approach in Kassel, where 'a real revolution threatened to break out in [the] orchestra' and where a 'friend warned [him] that all the orchestral players and choristers [intended] to come to the rehearsal armed with sticks and cudgels in order to beat [him] soundly'.[92] But Mahler's self-assessment of his manner in later years would have been challenged sharply by those with whom he worked, because he continued to be a severe taskmaster until the end of his career and was often in conflict with singers, musicians and administrators wherever he was employed.

The beginning of Mahler's second season at Leipzig was dominated by his involvement with Weber's unfinished opera, *Die drei Pintos*. The composer's grandson, Baron Karl von Weber, had met Mahler during the 1886–7 season and later invited him to complete the work. As Mahler was an admirer of Weber's music, he accepted the challenge willingly and completed the opera by juxtaposing some newly composed inserts with Weber's existing sketches and other music. The opera was performed for the first time under Mahler's direction at the Stadttheater on 20 January 1888 and was a resounding success. His publishers, C. F. Kahnt, had offered him 20,000 marks for the rights to the opera and had paid him half in advance of the première. The work was accepted immediately by other theatres and Mahler's fame soon spread throughout the operatic world. Although his commitments at the Stadttheater were reduced during the composition and editing of *Die drei Pintos*, he remained active as a conductor and prepared and performed works by Bruch, Weber, Nessler, Wagner, Gounod, Donizetti, Rossini, Gluck, Verdi and Mozart between September 1887 and the end of January 1888.[93] His busy conducting schedule continued into the spring but was interrupted in May 1888 when he suddenly resigned his post after his authority had been challenged at a rehearsal of Spontini's *Fernand Cortez* by the chief stage manager, Albert Goldberg.

Having conducted 214 performances of fifty-four works during the 1887–8 season at the Leipzig Stadttheater,[94] Mahler suddenly found himself unemployed. He was not idle for long, however, because his former employer, Angelo Neumann, engaged him to conduct and to prepare *Die drei Pintos* and Cornelius's *Der Barbier von Bagdad* at Prague in August 1888. Although the five performances of *Die drei Pintos* that Mahler led in the Czech city were a popular and critical success, his difficult personality soon caused problems and, during a rehearsal of *Der Barbier von Bagdad*, he was involved in a spectacular row with Neumann that resulted in his dismissal. Again, Mahler's period of unemployment was short because he was already being considered for the post of Director of the Königliches Opernhaus, Budapest. David

Popper,[95] the renowned Czech cellist and professor at the Budapest Academy of Music, had asked Guido Adler if he considered Mahler a suitable candidate for the post. Adler endorsed his friend strongly and, in August 1888, Popper attended one of Mahler's performances of *Die drei Pintos* in Prague. Impressed by what he heard, the cellist met the conductor after the performance and subsequently recommended him to the Budapest company's Intendant, Franz von Beniczky. As Arthur Nikisch and Felix Mottl had already refused the job, Beniczky needed to act quickly to fill the vacant post and, on 28 September, he engaged Mahler for a period of ten years from the beginning of the 1888–9 season with a salary of 10,000 gulden.[96]

The news of Mahler's Budapest appointment was a sensation. The local press and public were astonished by the selection of a relatively unknown Moravian Jewish conductor as director of Hungary's foremost opera house. They considered his salary exorbitantly high, his ethnicity a problem, his youth a worry and his lack of administrative experience a concern. Beniczky, however, was untroubled by those criticisms and allowed Mahler free reign over all things musical. But when Mahler arrived in Budapest to begin work, he soon realized that he had inherited an opera house that was troubled musically, financially and politically. The former director, Sándor Erkel, the son of Ferenc Erkel,[97] a founder of Hungarian national opera, was a poor administrator who was unable to maintain standards. By the time of Mahler's appointment, the level of singing and orchestral playing had declined badly, attendance figures had dropped sharply and finances were affected critically. As the theatre was facing financial and artistic chaos, it was hoped that the new director would be able to reverse those trends by raising standards and by turning the theatre into a national opera house.

When Mahler arrived at the Königliches Opernhaus, the custom was to perform individual operas in more than one language, resulting in a 'cosmopolitan babel of tongues . . . in which every foreigner who sang without a prompter had difficulty in keeping true to his language'.[98] That practice was clearly unacceptable, so to secure the ethnic character of the Opernhaus and to improve performance standards, Mahler announced that Hungarian would be the universal language of the theatre.[99] While the use of the vernacular as the sole performing language was logical, it also had its problems. Mahler, for example, was unable to speak Hungarian and, although he vowed to learn the language (a promise he failed to keep), he eventually had to engage a linguist to translate for him. Nevertheless, he attempted to fulfil his ambition of unifying the theatre by conducting Hungarian-language productions of

Das Rheingold and *Die Walküre* in January 1889. As those works were new to the Opernhaus in that format, Mahler devoted himself entirely to their preparation,[100] commissioned a new Hungarian translation, coached the singers personally, rehearsed the orchestra meticulously, lowered the pit for better balance between the orchestra and the singers, had a temporary bridge built over the pit so that he could superintend all aspects of the production by moving easily and quickly throughout the theatre, and insisted that audience attend both operas in the correct order by selling them tickets only in pairs. Press and public interest in the productions was high and Budapest was buzzing with talk of Mahler and his methods by the time the productions opened. Those who attended the first nights of *Das Rheingold* and *Die Walküre*, on 26 and 27 January 1889 respectively, were not disappointed and were thrilled by what they saw and heard. Mahler's success was such that Beniczky was prompted to publish an open letter to the conductor in the press, in which he congratulated Mahler for showing 'what one is capable of achieving through sheer hard work' and for demonstrating 'that it is possible to produce the greatest artistic creations of the present day . . . in the Hungarian language'.[101]

The success of Wagner's music dramas at the Opernhaus encouraged Mahler to extend the taste of the Budapest public further. Eager to shift the emphasis of the repertoire from Italian operas to a broader mix of works, Mahler conducted a series of new productions over the next two years that included Maillart's *Les Dragons de Villars*, Wagner's *Lohengrin*, Nicolai's *Die lustigen Weiber von Windsor*, Marschner's *Der Templer und die Jüdin*, Mozart's *Don Giovanni*,[102] Franchetti's *Asraël*, Mascagni's *Cavalleria rusticana*, Lortzing's *Der Waffenschmied* and Mendelssohn's *Die Loreley*.[103] Those productions were only nine of at least thirty-three operas, operettas and ballets either premièred or given new productions by French, German, Austrian, Italian and Hungarian composers that Mahler superintended or conducted during his tenure at Budapest.[104] Surprisingly, some contemporary commentators argued that the repertoire that he programmed was too narrow and that he placed too great an emphasis on works from the Austro-German canon as it took shape. While it is true that his preference was for those works, his sense of duty as director precluded him from programming in a partisan manner.

Mahler's career took on a new dimension during his second season at Budapest when he appeared for the first time as a composer-conductor.[105] On 1 October 1889, it was announced in the press that he would be conducting one of his 'Symphonic Poems' at the Philharmonic

Orchestra's second subscription concert on 20 November 1889.[106] Although Mahler had ample rehearsal time and was delighted by the performance of the orchestra at the dress rehearsal, the work failed to capture fully the imagination of either the press or the public. His performance with the Philharmonic Orchestra also marked his début as a concert conductor in Hungary and was the first of seven orchestral performances in which he participated at Budapest between 20 November 1889 and 6 December 1890.[107] With the exception of Mozart's Symphony No. 40, the works that he conducted were new to his symphonic repertoire and included his first performances of Beethoven's overture *Leonore* No. 3 and Symphony No. 5 and Liszt's *Festklänge*.[108]

During the latter part of his tenure at Budapest, Mahler came increasingly under attack for his policies and practices. His critics were unhappy about the repertoire that he presented, the quality of the voices he engaged, the way he treated the orchestra and his championing of Hungarian nationalism. By the beginning of his third season, his situation had become critical and a demand for his resignation appeared in the local press in November 1890.[109] Aware that Beniczky was to be replaced in 1891 by Count Géza von Zichy,[110] a composer and one-armed pianist whose views differed sharply from his, Mahler entered into negotiations with the Director of the Hamburg Stadttheater, Bernhard Pollini, who sent him a contract on 2 November 1890. When Zichy took up his appointment in January 1891, Mahler's position worsened, because the new Intendant was given the power to override his artistic decisions and was keen to remove him from office. In an attempt to replace him, Zichy secretly offered Mahler's job to Felix Mottl. Mottl, however, was unwilling to accept the position under those circumstances and informed Mahler of Zichy's offer. Aware that his situation at Budapest was untenable, but secure in the knowledge that Pollini was ready and willing to employ him, Mahler agreed to terminate his tenure at the Opernhaus in March 1891 with a severance payment of 25,000 gulden.

For much of his time at Budapest, Mahler was able to programme at will, but, as First Kapellmeister of the Hamburg Stadttheater, he re-entered the world of commercial theatre and was answerable artistically to Pollini.[111] As the principal theatre of Germany's second biggest city, the Stadttheater boasted excellent facilities and a company of singers and conductors of the front rank. Under the direction of Pollini, the company had developed a reputation for its performances of Wagner's stage works and it was with *Tannhäuser* that Mahler made his début at Hamburg on 29 March 1891. The evening was an overwhelming success and, within days, Mahler was back in the pit of the Stadttheater for a performance of *Siegfried*. Again, his interpretation was a triumph, prompting the critic Josef Sittard to write in the *Hamburgischer Correspondent*:

In the Conductor Herr Gustav Mahler our Opera has gained a motive force of the first order. If the great reputation that preceded him made us expect a superb achievement, then Herr Mahler exceeded even these expectations and, a thing which only happens in the rarest of cases, electrified the audience on the very first evening by his brilliant conducting. . . . Herr Mahler is a conductor who has in his command not only the notes in the score but, what is more, the spirit of the artistic work . . . [and has] the gift of transmitting this spirit to the entire cast and carrying them along with him. There is no entry that is not cued by him, no dynamic shading that remains unobserved; Herr Mahler holds the reins in his hand with an energy which binds the individual firmly to him [and] draws him . . . with magical force into his own world of thought. . . . How clearly, rhythmically defined, carefully nuanced and phrased everything seemed. . . . If Herr Mahler displays the same qualities in classical opera as in Wagner's music dramas, then our Opera may count itself fortunate to have a brilliant conductor at its head.[112]

Sittard's opinion was shared by Hamburg's most celebrated resident musician and 'the undisputed ruler of German orchestral music',[113] Hans von Bülow, who also attended a performance of *Siegfried* under Mahler. Bülow was impressed by what he heard and wrote in a letter to his daughter, Daniela, 'Hamburg has now secured a really excellent opera-conductor in Herr Gustav Mahler (a serious, energetic Jew from Budapest), who in my opinion equals the very best: Mottl, Richter'. As a strict orchestral disciplinarian, Bülow was 'filled with honest admiration for [Mahler], for he made – no forced – the orchestra to pipe to his measure, without having had a rehearsal'.[114] Mahler soon became personally acquainted with Bülow and regularly attended many of his Hamburg Abonnement Concerts. At those performances, Bülow reserved a seat for Mahler directly behind the podium and, when Bülow entered the auditorium, he would hurry down the steps of the platform and offer Mahler his baton. After inviting him to mount the podium in his stead, which Mahler would invariably decline, Bülow would take his place on the rostrum and begin the concert.[115] While Bülow's overt gestures of respect for Mahler might have been excessive, they were meant sincerely. Mahler was deeply touched by Bülow's interest and he retained for many years a presentation wreath inscribed 'To the Pygmalion of the Hamburg Opera – Hans von Bülow'.

Mahler's schedule of performances as First Kapellmeister of the Hamburg Stadttheater was formidable. During his tenure, the theatre presented in excess of 270 performances annually and, between 29 March 1891 to 24 April 1897, the dates of Mahler's début and farewell performances, it mounted more than seventy new productions or premières. As the company presented a variety of entertainments, not all of its performances were operas. Nevertheless, a high proportion of the works given were from that genre and it was Mahler's responsibility to superintend their musical execution. While he was able to delegate some conducting to other members of the music staff, which later included Bruno Walter and Wilhelm Kienzl,[116] he was expected to lead important premières and new productions. Of the operas that were either heard for the first time or staged afresh at Hamburg during his tenure, Mahler conducted twenty-three and, of those, eighteen were by living composers.[117] Curiously, only eight were by Austro-Germans, the majority being by either French or Italian artists. No new restaging of works by Mozart and Wagner were conducted by Mahler at Hamburg and the only Classical opera that was produced afresh was Haydn's little-known *Der Apotheker*. But to infer that either Mahler's interests or the taste of the Hamburg public had shifted away from the crystallizing Austro-German canon would be wrong, because during the 1894–5 season he gave 144 performances at the Stadttheater and at its subsidiary venue in Altona,[118] of which 107 were of works by composers from that tradition and, of those, thirty-five were of compositions by Wagner.[119]

At Hamburg, Mahler began to conduct concerts regularly for the first time. For a musician whose fame now rests largely on his symphonic creations, it is perhaps surprising that his experiences as a concert conductor were largely restricted to the last two decades of his life. Until his appointment at the Stadttheater, Mahler had worked mainly in the opera theatre and had conducted only a handful of symphonic and choral works. That changed, however, from November 1891, when Pollini widened Mahler's responsibilities to include the direction of the theatre's annual Good Friday and Day of Penance concerts.[120] At those performances, Mahler invariably conducted a programme of choral music that included variously Mozart's Requiem, Haydn's *Die Schöpfung* (*The Creation*) and Bruckner's Te Deum and Mass No. 1 in D minor.[121] As Mahler had admired Bruckner's music since his student days in Vienna, he took particular pleasure in presenting that composer's Te Deum and Mass to the Hamburg public, and, after his performance of the 'glorious and powerful *Te Deum*' on 15 April 1892, he reported proudly to Bruckner: 'Both the *performers* and the *whole audience* were deeply affected by the overwhelming form and truly sublime conception; and at the end of the performance I experienced what I consider to be the greatest triumph for any work – the audience remained sitting without a sound, without stirring; and not until the conductor and the performers had left their places did the storm of applause break out.'[122] Along with his choral concerts for Pollini, Mahler also conducted a series of memorial and benefit performances at the Stadttheater. At the latter, he generally performed Beethoven's Symphony No. 3 ('Eroica'), 5, 6 (*'Pastoral'*) or 7 before conducting a performance of *Fidelio*.[123] Symphonies Nos. 3, 6 and 7 were new to Mahler's repertoire and were the first of eleven, sixteen and thirteen performances respectively that he gave of those works during his career.[124]

With the death of Hans von Bülow, Hermann Wolff engaged Mahler as conductor of the Hamburg Abonnement Concerts from the 1894–5 season. Mahler appeared first at that series in place of an indisposed Bülow on 12 December 1892[125] and returned for the performance of Beethoven's Symphony No. 3 on 26 February 1894.[126] Although Mahler was responsible for conducting the eight concerts that made up the 1894–5 season, Wolff retained overall control of the series and continued to influence programme policy. With the death of Bülow, Wolff had lost his star attraction and he was increasingly cautious when programming unfamiliar works with less popular conductors. As Mahler's reputation as a concert conductor was far from established, Wolff took steps to ensure that the concerts remained attractive musically and viable financially. A popular feature of the series since its inception was the inclusion of instrumental and vocal solos and chamber music. Wolff realized the commercial importance of those works and continued to programme them during Mahler's tenure.[127] Wolff's caution also extended to the symphonic repertoire and, with the exception of Bruckner's Symphony No. 4 ('Romantic'),[128] all the major symphonies and concertos that Mahler presented were familiar to local audiences.

Central to Wolff's programme policy for the 1894–5 season were Beethoven's Symphonies Nos. 6, 7 and 9 and Schubert's Symphony No. 8 in C major ('Great'),[129] which he placed strategically in the fourth, first, eighth and second concerts respectively. It was hoped that Mahler's interpretations of those works would be attractive to press and public alike. The conductor's unconventional approach, however, soon alienated critics and audiences, and attendance figures dropped sharply from the third concert onwards. Mahler's erratic tempi, his extensive retouching of the original orchestration and his placement of musicians off-stage for part of the last movement in Beethoven's Symphony No. 9 all contributed to the critics' disquiet. With a deficit of 13,000 marks by the end of the season, Wolff refused to re-engage Mahler for the following year, arguing that while he might be suited to the opera house, he was unsuited to the concert hall.

During his tenure at the Stadttheater, Mahler began to promote his own works in earnest. Undaunted by the response of the critics and the audience to his symphonic poem at Budapest, Mahler decided to include it in a concert that he organized with the augmented Laube Orchestra at the Ludwig Konzerthaus in Hamburg on 27 October 1893. Presented as *Titan, a Tone Poem in Symphonic Form*, the work was given in a programme that also included the premières of six of Mahler's Lieder from *Des Knaben Wunderhorn*, arias by Marschner and Adam and overtures by Beethoven and Mendelssohn.[130] The public's response to Mahler's music was good but the reaction of the critics was generally unfavourable. Undeterred, Mahler performed three of his Lieder again at Wiesbaden on 17 November 1893.[131] The response of the public to his music on that occasion was cool, and when he performed *Titan* for the Allgemeiner deutscher Musikverein at Weimar on 3 June 1894, his work was again the subject of derision. Although Mahler gained little comfort from the reaction to his music in general, he was supported throughout that difficult period by his friend and colleague Richard Strauss.[132] Strauss had been appointed conductor of the Berlin Philharmonic's subscription series for the 1894–5 season and had asked Mahler to share the podium with him at a concert with that orchestra on 4 March 1895. Strauss's invitation provided Mahler with an opportunity to perform three movements of his new Symphony No. 2 ('Resurrection')[133] and the chance to make his début as conductor with the Berlin Philharmonic. Again, the reaction to Mahler's music was mixed, but he did return to the orchestra to conduct the first complete performance of his Symphony No. 2 on 13 December 1895 and a programme of his works on 16 March 1896.[134]

Although Mahler gave performances of his works at Hamburg, Wiesbaden, Leipzig, Weimar and Berlin during his tenure as Pollini's First Kapellmeister, opportunities to perform elsewhere were limited because of his commitments at the Stadttheater. An opportunity did arise, however, in the summer of 1892, when the English impresario Sir Augustus Harris collaborated with Pollini to mount a series of German operas in London. Along with a cast that drew heavily from the

Hamburg Stadttheater, the Berlin Hofoper and the Bayreuth Festival,[135] Mahler was sent to London by Pollini to conduct Wagner's *Der Ring des Nibelungen*, *Tristan und Isolde* and *Tannhäuser* and Beethoven's *Fidelio* at Covent Garden.[136] The press quickly took an interest in the enterprise and demand for tickets soon outstripped supply. Keen to capitalize on the public's enthusiasm, Harris responded to the increased demand and scheduled extra performances at the Drury Lane Theatre. Inevitably, Mahler's readings were examined in detail by the press and were praised widely. Some critics, however, were concerned by his cuts in Act 2 of Wagner's *Die Walküre*, his speeds in *Fidelio* and his approach to tempo manipulation and tempo integration in the overture *Leonore* No. 3, which he performed before Act 2 of Beethoven's opera. The critics also mentioned his habit of conducting surrounded by the musicians from the middle of the pit, a placement that was common in Germany and Austria during the late nineteenth and the early twentieth centuries.[137] While Mahler's London performances were an undisputed success, they were the last that he gave as a guest conductor outside central and north Germany until March 1897.[138] That month, he performed at Moscow, Munich and Budapest on the fifteenth, twenty-fourth and thirty-first respectively.[139] Common to all those performances was Beethoven's Symphony No. 5, a work that was central to Mahler's repertoire throughout his career and of which he conducted seventeen performances, the most of any symphony in his repertoire.

By the mid 1890s, Mahler had become disillusioned by the commercial character of the Stadttheater and wanted to leave. He had longed for some time to return to Vienna and hoped to secure a place at the city's Hofoper. Although he had begun to make enquiries about a job there as early as the summer of 1895, it was not until the end of 1896 that a post became vacant. By December that year it had become apparent that the health of the Hofoper's Director, Wilhelm Jahn,[140] had begun to fail badly and that he would need the assistance of an able and energetic junior colleague. Mahler seized upon the opportunity and applied formally for the post on 21 December 1896. Aware that his application would be hindered because of his ethnicity and his reputation for being eccentric and irritable, he converted to Roman Catholicism on 23 February 1897 and called upon his friends and supporters to lobby on his behalf. With the help of leading artistic personalities and some members of the aristocracy, Mahler was able to overcome any existing obstacles and was appointed Kapellmeister in April 1897. As Jahn's health deteriorated quickly over the following months, it was clear that promotion for Mahler was inevitable and, in October, he replaced Jahn as Director of the Hofoper.

Mahler made his début as Jahn's subordinate with Wagner's *Lohengrin* and as Director with Smetana's *Dalibor* on 11 May and 4 October 1897 respectively. As Kapellmeister, Mahler conducted sixteen operas at the Hofoper, of which seven were by Wagner.[141] The flurry of Wagner performances that Mahler gave during his first months in Vienna might have been a reaction to the presence of the eminent Wagnerian Hans Richter, who was still a member of the Hofoper's conducting staff.[142] Mahler was obviously keen to make an early impact as an interpreter of Wagner's music and he made local history by conducting the Hofoper's first uncut cycle of *Der Ring des Nibelungen* in August. Although *Der Ring des Nibelungen*, *Lohengrin*, *Tannhäuser*, *Die Meistersinger von Nürnberg*, *Der fliegende Holländer*, *Tristan und Isolde* and *Rienzi* were performed frequently by Mahler between the beginning of the 1897–8 and the end of the 1901–2 seasons,[143] only *Das Rheingold*, *Die Walküre* and *Tristan und Isolde* remained in his Hofoper repertoire during the second half of his tenure. *Das Rheingold*, *Die Walküre* and *Tristan und Isolde* were also three of forty-two new productions that Mahler conducted in Vienna.[144] Of those, probably the most revolutionary was that of *Tristan und Isolde* on 21 February 1903.[145] For that reading, Mahler, acting as producer and conductor, a dual function that he adopted throughout his period in Vienna, engaged the Secessionist artist Alfred Roller[146] to design the scenery and the costumes. Roller rejected the naturalism of earlier productions in favour of new sets, costumes and lighting effects that were 'truly overpowering in [their] effect, without in any way impairing [their] function through obtrusiveness'.[147]

Of the other new productions on which Mahler and Roller collaborated, probably the most influential were those of Beethoven's *Fidelio* and Mozart's *Così fan tutte*, *Don Giovanni*, *Le nozze di Figaro*, *Die Zauberflöte* and *Die Entführung aus dem Serail*.[148] Their new production of *Fidelio* on 7 October 1904 caused a local sensation by using colour and light in a spectacular and atmospheric manner and by placing the overture *Leonore* No. 3 between the opera's penultimate and last scenes. At the Hofoper, the overture had been heard traditionally at the beginning of the opera. Mahler, however, considered the E major overture (*Fidelio*) to be more in keeping with the action of the first act and the C major overture to be a natural introduction to the last scene. By placing *Leonore* No. 3 before the finale, he argued that the overture 'compresse[d] the drama's whole gamut of emotions into a great climax . . . [and] thus . . . the triumph of good over the forces of evil [would] seem overwhelming'.[149] There was also a practical reason for placing the longer overture between the last two scenes: Roller needed more time to change the sets before the finale, and the extra minutes gained allowed him to erect an imposing structure that reinforced the conductor's ethical and musical interpretations of the opera. Mahler's placement of the overture soon proved influential, and it was later adopted by subsequent generations of conductors including Otto Klemperer and Lorin Maazel.[150]

Mahler's and Roller's new productions of Mozart's *Così fan tutte*, *Don Giovanni*, *Die Entführung aus dem Serail*, *Le nozze di Figaro* and *Die Zauberflöte* were staged during the 1905–6 season to mark the 150th anniversary of the composer's birth.[151] Although it would be an overstatement to suggest that the cycle ['brought] about the Mozart renaissance' as Guido Adler claimed[152] – that honour belongs to the productions of Richard Strauss and Ernst von Possart at Munich in the 1890s – Mahler's and Roller's readings were influential, innovative and controversial. Of Roller's sets, Bruno Walter argued that, while 'his relation to Mozart . . . was uncertain and groping[,] . . . [his] two stationary towers [in *Don Giovanni*], one on each side of the stage, between which the various changes of scenery took place[,] . . . [was] a determining factor in the future development of the scenic picture'.[153] Of Mahler's Mozart style, Walter claimed that the conductor 'saved Mozart from the lie of daintiness as well as from the boredom of academic dryness'.[154] But the approach that Mahler adopted during the Vienna cycle was already dated, and his habit of setting additional text to music, adding new recitatives to supplement the originals, altering the orchestration and dynamics, inserting and omitting passages, using parts of the overtures and other works as intermezzi, cutting and altering articulation and dynamic marks in the overtures, arias and ensembles, and retouching the orchestration[155] had more in common with the principles of Wagner and the mid nineteenth century rather than the leaner and more historically aware style of Richard Strauss and the early twentieth century.[156]

Mahler replaced Hans Richter as a conductor of the Vienna Philharmonic's Abonnement and Nicolai Concerts from the beginning of the 1898–9 season.[157] Unlike the concerts that Mahler conducted for Hermann Wolff in Hamburg, those that he gave with the Vienna Philharmonic included no songs with piano, instrumental solos or chamber music. Concertos and songs with orchestra were also heard rarely and, of the twenty-two Abonnement Concerts that Mahler performed with the orchestra between 6 November 1898 and 24 February 1901, only six involved either an instrumental or a vocal soloist.[158] In contrast, the four Nicolai Concerts that he conducted all included vocal soloists because the programmes contained either his Symphony No. 2 or Beethoven's Symphony No. 9.[159] In general, Mahler's programmes at the Abonnement Concerts were conservative and, apart from the two programmes that contained some of his songs with orchestra and his Symphony No. 1, he included works by living composers at only seven concerts.[160] The composer whose works appeared most frequently was Beethoven and, of the twenty-six Abonnement and Nicolai Concerts that Mahler conducted, fifteen contained a work by that composer.[161] While he never conducted a cycle of all nine symphonies during his time with the Vienna Philharmonic, he did conduct five all-Beethoven programmes.[162] As in Hamburg, his extensive alterations and amendments to Symphony No. 9 were greeted with anger and amazement.[163] The sense of outrage felt by the critics and the public after his performance of the work on 18 February 1900 was such that he was compelled to issue a printed justification of his approach at the repeat concert four days later. In that pamphlet, he actively underplays the type, quantity and nature of the changes that he made, and argues that they went no further than those of Wagner. By the time that the pamphlet was issued, however, Mahler's reputation as a Beethoven interpreter was being questioned widely, and his retouching of Symphony No. 9 was damned as 'a regrettable example of this aberration, this barbarism'.[164]

As with other orchestras with which he worked, Mahler's approach to the Vienna Philharmonic was often domineering and demanding. Because the orchestra was a self-governing organization whose members were drawn from the Hofoper orchestra,[165] the players gradually began to resent having to work under Mahler in both the concert hall and the opera house and were relieved when he resigned as the orchestra's conductor on 1 April 1901. Although he cited ill health and pressure of work at the theatre as his reasons for resigning, Mahler continued to accept engagements as a guest conductor at home and abroad throughout the remainder of his Hofoper tenure. The majority of the engagements that he accepted, however, were showcases for his compositions and, of the fifty-three concerts that he gave in centres other than Vienna between March 1898 and 24 November 1907, his last concert in Europe before conducting in America for the first time, forty-four contained a work by him.[166] At those fifty-three concerts, forty-eight of which were given between 25 November 1901 and 9 November 1907, Mahler conducted seven, five, thirteen, six, eight and two performances of his Symphonies Nos. 1, 2, 3, 4, 5 and 6 respectively, two performances of groups of songs with orchestra and one performance each of *Das klagende Lied*, *Kindertotenlieder*, the Adagietto from Symphony No. 5 and *Ich bin der Welt abhanden gekommen*.[167] While the critical response to his music was often mixed, his eight concerts with the Concertgebouw Orchestra of Amsterdam during that period[168] were more favourably received than the concerts he gave elsewhere and were the basis for his close professional relationship with the Dutch conductor Willem Mengelberg.[169]

Mahler was attacked regularly by the critics during his tenure at the Hofoper. The anti-Semitic elements of the Vienna press were particularly venomous in their approach and were scathing when reviewing his work in both the opera theatre and the concert hall. His regular absences from the Hofoper to conduct and to promote his music elsewhere from 1903 were also greeted poorly and they fuelled the campaign against him. Although he continued to have the support of some of his superiors throughout much of that period, his dealings with court officials deteriorated sharply by the summer of 1907, and by June that year he had decided to leave the Hofoper. Among the offers that he received at that time was one from Heinrich Conried,[170] the Director of the Metropolitan Opera, New York. Conried had been pursuing Mahler for some time and was willing to offer him a lucrative four-year contract from 1908. After a period of intense negotiation, Conried and Mahler reached an agreement on 21 June 1907 whereby Mahler would conduct an annual three-month season at the Metropolitan Opera for a fee of 75,000 crowns.[171] While Mahler's decision to accept Conried's offer was principally financial, he was also 'no longer able to endure the rabble' in Vienna.[172] Nevertheless, there were many in the Austrian capital who had supported Mahler throughout his tenure at the Hofoper and he was keen to reward them with farewell performances that reflected his work both as a conductor and as a composer. For his Vienna swansongs, therefore, he conducted Beethoven's *Fidelio* and his own Symphony No. 2 to capacity houses at the Hofoper and the Musikverein on 15 October and 24 November 1907 respectively. On 9 December, some 200 members of Vienna's pro-Mahler faction were present for his departure for America from the West Railway Station and, with emotions running high, few would have guessed that he would never conduct in Vienna again.

Mahler made his New York début with Wagner's *Tristan und Isolde* on 1 January 1908. That performance was the first of fifty-four that he gave of eight works over three seasons with the Metropolitan Opera in

New York and on tour. The operas that he performed during his American period – Mozart's *Don Giovanni* and *Le nozze di Figaro*, Beethoven's *Fidelio*, Tchaikovsky's *The Queen of Spades*, Smetana's *The Bartered Bride* and Wagner's *Tristan und Isolde, Siegfried* and *Die Walküre*[173] – were drawn from his existing repertoire and were sure to appeal to the conservative taste of New York's opera-going public. All five works that Mahler performed during his first season at the Metropolitan Opera – *Tristan und Isolde, Don Giovanni, Die Walküre, Siegfried* and *Fidelio*[174] – were drawn from the Austro-German canon and, of those, three were by Wagner.[175] Mahler's arrival had been the source of considerable copy in the New York press, and his abilities as a Wagner, Mozart and Beethoven conductor were of particular interest to critics and audiences alike. Mahler's interpretations of works by those composers during his first season were generally greeted favourably, and his ability to draw the best from the singers and the orchestra was commented upon widely. Some critics were concerned by the way in which he altered and retouched parts of the orchestration in *Fidelio* and his decision to place the overture *Leonore* No. 3 between the penultimate and final scenes of the opera.[176] Any reservations that the reviewers had, however, were minor and it was felt generally that Mahler 'brought a new spirit into [the five operas that he conducted] and revealed a kind of beauty that [had] not been enjoyed in [those] works for a long time'.[177]

After completing his first season at New York, Mahler returned to Europe for concerts in Wiesbaden, Prague, Munich and Hamburg between 8 May and 9 November 1908. At the second of his two Prague concerts,[178] Mahler gave the world première of his Symphony No. 7, after which he gave a further performance of the work at Munich on 27 October 1908. On his return to New York for the 1908–9 season, he was greeted by a new management team at the Metropolitan Opera that consisted of Giulio Gatti-Casazza as artistic director and Andreas Dippel as administrative director.[179] Gatti-Casazza had been Director of the Teatro alla Scala, Milan, and was instrumental in bringing the former Principal Conductor of that theatre, Arturo Toscanini,[180] with him to New York. Toscanini's engagement at the Metropolitan Opera triggered a barrage of press speculation that pitted the Italian conductor against Mahler. The New York critics had commented widely upon Toscanini's outstanding abilities as a Wagner conductor and it came as no surprise to some that he was keen to conduct *Tristan und Isolde* during his first season at the Metropolitan Opera. But as Mahler was intent on preserving his interpretation of the work, it was agreed that

Toscanini would not perform the opera during that period and that he would tackle another work by Wagner instead.[181]

Under the new regime at the Metropolitan Opera, Mahler was able to conduct symphonic concerts with other American organizations for the first time.[182] Keen to take advantage of the new situation, he gave three performances with the New York Symphony Orchestra at Carnegie Hall between 29 November and 13 December 1908[183] and two with the New York Philharmonic Orchestra at the same venue on 31 March and 6 April 1909. Those five concerts marked an important turning point in Mahler's activities in America, because, thereafter, the majority of the engagements that he gave there were as a concert conductor. With exception of four performances of Tchaikovsky's *The Queen of Spades* at the Metropolitan Opera House in March 1910, Mahler's attention was focused firmly on the New York Philharmonic Orchestra from the beginning of the 1909–10 season.[184] Having been appointed the new permanent conductor of the orchestra from the start of that season, Mahler was able to exercise considerable power over programming and personnel, and, under his leadership, the number of concerts increased sharply[185] and the membership of the orchestra altered radically.[186]

As permanent conductor of the New York Philharmonic, Mahler gave no fewer than ninety-five concerts at fifteen towns and cities.[187] Of those, the majority were performed at Carnegie Hall New York, where he conducted sixty-seven concerts between 4 November 1909 and 21 February 1911. During his first season with the orchestra at that hall, Mahler conducted sixteen Subscription Series Concerts, six Historical Concerts, six Beethoven Cycle concerts, six Sunday Afternoon Concerts and one Pension Fund Concert. The composer who dominated Mahler's Carnegie Hall programmes during his first season was Beethoven, whose works were heard at eighteen concerts. Of those, six were devoted to the composer's music and, as in many European series, Symphony No. 9 was heard at the penultimate and final concerts of the season.[188] Unlike European concert series, however, Mahler's first season also contained an all-Wagner concert.[189] As that type of programme was rare in the German-speaking countries but popular in North America and Great Britain, Mahler's inclusion of it at that concert can be viewed as a response to local taste rather than an expression of his performance style in general.[190]

After the 1909–10 season, the Historical Concerts and the Beethoven Cycles were dropped from the orchestra's Carnegie Hall programme and, consequently, Beethoven's works were heard at five concerts only during the 1910–11 season.[191] Wagner's music was more prominent during Mahler's second season and, of the nine concerts that contained a work by him at Carnegie Hall, four were all-Wagner programmes. While works by established composers dominated Mahler's Manhattan programmes, he was able to include works by some of his contemporaries and, during the 1909–10 and 1910–11 seasons, he performed music by living composers at seventeen and nineteen Carnegie Hall concerts respectively. As Mahler was principal conductor of the New York Philharmonic Orchestra, it might be assumed that he was able to programme his music regularly. This, however, would be a false assumption because at Carnegie Hall only seven concerts during his two seasons with the orchestra contained a work by him.[192] In contrast, fourteen concerts at that hall contained a composition by his friend Richard Strauss, a statistic that reflects not only the relative popularity of both composers during the first decade of the twentieth century but also Mahler's interest in Strauss's music in general.[193] Less attractive to Mahler was the music of American composers, whose works were heard at only three Carnegie Hall concerts during his two seasons with the Philharmonic. Two of those concerts were devoted to living or recently deceased composers from Britain and the US and were two of only four concerts that focused solely on contemporary artists that Mahler conducted at Carnegie Hall during his Philharmonic tenure.[194]

Mahler's health had been troubling him for some time. In July 1907, he had been diagnosed as suffering from heart disease and, in February 1911, it was discovered that he had contracted bacterial endocarditis. After further investigation, the presence of streptococci in his blood was confirmed and it was clear to his American physicians that his situation was grave. Having abandoned his concerts with the New York Philharmonic Orchestra after their performance on 21 March 1911,[195] he took his doctors' advice and attended a clinic at Neuilly near Paris. There, his condition continued to deteriorate and it was decided to move him to Vienna in early May. His painful journey across Europe soon caught the imagination of the press, and accounts of his failing health were published widely in both the New and Old Worlds. After arriving at the Loew Sanatorium in Vienna on 12 May, reports of his condition were issued frequently to journalists by his doctors. With a local press that cared more for circulation figures than good taste, some of the stories that appeared in Vienna's newspapers during his last days verged on the ghoulish, and it was a relief for those close to him when his struggle for life ended shortly after 11 p.m. on 18 May 1911.[196] As

Mahler's relationship with critics on both sides of the Atlantic was often uneasy, the press entered a period of intense artistic soul-searching after his death. While some questioned the quality of his creative output, few doubted his abilities as a conductor. Many would have agreed, therefore, with Julius Korngold's view that Mahler was 'the Bülow of the post-Wagner period'.[197]

Felix Weingartner.

CHAPTER 4

'An unrecognised genius'? Felix Weingartner[1]

'An exceptionally handsome man, well-proportioned in his figure and features like a Greek sculpture',[2] Felix Weingartner was an enigmatic individual who could be difficult professionally but often charming personally.[3] A musician of outstanding ability who was plagued with insecurities, he married five wives and engaged in relationships with colleagues and administrators that were often strained and at times openly hostile. Remembered today primarily as a Beethoven interpreter, Weingartner was an artist of wide and varied interests, and although he was in constant demand as a conductor, pianist, editor, teacher and author, his greatest desire was to be recognized as a composer of standing.[4] Deeply envious of Richard Strauss's success as a creative artist, Weingartner harboured a festering resentment towards his celebrated colleague for much of his career. The feeling that he was an 'unrecognised genius' remained with him throughout his life and coloured his dealings with not only Strauss but also other successful composers. Nevertheless, Weingartner had a long and distinguished career as a performing artist, rising to Director of the Opera in Vienna on two occasions and establishing a relationship with the Vienna Philharmonic that was the envy of many of his contemporaries.

Born into a lower middle-class Austrian Catholic family at Zara in Dalmatia on 2 June 1863,[5] Weingartner was blessed with a supportive family who valued his musical abilities. After the death of his father, Guido, a local telegraph inspector,[6] Felix's mother, Karoline, a good amateur pianist, undertook Felix's upbringing and supervised his early education. Impoverished by Guido's early and unexpected death, Karoline and Felix were forced to rely financially on the help of relatives to make ends meet. Unable to remain in Zara, they led an itinerant life for a period, lodging first with various family members in Voitsberg, Baden and Vienna, before settling in Graz, where Karoline began to teach Felix piano. Although not a particularly keen student, he developed fast and soon took part in family musical evenings, at which he performed standard Classical sonatas, played four-hand arrangements of the symphonic repertoire and accompanied many Schubert songs.[7] When it was discovered that he had absolute pitch, his mother decided that formal music lessons were appropriate and, in 1873, she sent him to study with their neighbour, Wilhelm Mayer, a former director of the Styrian Musical Association. Under Mayer's supervision, Weingartner's piano playing continued to progress quickly and, from 1876, his studies were extended to include the rudiments of harmony and counterpoint.

Central to Weingartner's early education were his visits to the local orchestra and theatre. After attending Weber's *Oberon* and Mozart's *Don Giovanni* at the Stadttheater in Graz, Weingartner returned to hear Gounod's *Faust*, Beethoven's *Fidelio*, Wagner's *Tannhäuser*, *Lohengrin* and *Die Meistersinger von Nürnberg* and Meyerbeer's *Les Huguenots*. Unimpressed by *Oberon* and confused by *Die Meistersinger von Nürnberg*, Weingartner's youthful taste was challenged by some of the operas that he attended. But on hearing *Fidelio*, he was 'held . . . by bonds fashioned of awe and reverence'[8] and, after receiving a piano-duet score of *Don Giovanni*, which he played with his mother, he decided to become a musician.[9] Weingartner was also exposed to symphonic music from an early age, and at a concert given by the Styrian Musical Association under Ferdinand Thieriot, he heard a performance of Beethoven's Symphony No. 4. '[F]ired . . . with enthusiasm' from '[t]he very first notes of the [work's] introduction',[10] he immediately set about studying all the Beethoven symphonies with Mayer in piano-duet form. While the cycle as a whole made a deep impression, the work that made the greatest impact was Symphony No. 3 ('Eroica'), which he considered 'the climax of the series'.[11]

After completing his secondary education at the Graz Gymnasium in 1881, Weingartner entered the Leipzig Conservatory. There he studied piano and composition with Karl Reinecke, counterpoint with Salomon Jadassohn,[12] and keyboard and orchestral technique with Oskar Paul. As a member of Paul's class, Weingartner also had rudimentary lessons in conducting. For those sessions he would alternate with other members of the class to play orchestral transcriptions on the piano while fellow classmates conducted. Although that method did little to prepare Weingartner professionally, it did encourage him to study orchestral and operatic scores in earnest. A chance to put into practice that which he had learned in the classroom occurred when he was invited to perform one of his own compositions with a military band. In later life,

Weingartner recalled, 'instinctively I gave the signal to begin. Everything swam before my eyes, but after a few bars I recovered – it all sounded as I had wished it to sound. Not a note of the score had to be altered – now I knew that I was capable of achieving something. I repeated a few difficult passages, then we played the whole piece straight through. The audience praised the composition and Jahrow [the band's conductor] asked where I had a post as conductor. "Nowhere," I said, "I am still a pupil at the Conservatorium and have just conducted a full orchestra for the first time in my life".'[13]

While at the Conservatory, Weingartner regularly attended performances at the Stadttheater, the Bayreuth Festival and the Gewandhaus. At the Leipzig Stadttheater, Weingartner heard and met Arthur Nikisch, whose readings of works from the standard operatic repertoire made an immediate impression. Similarly, Anton Seidl's interpretation of Wagner's *Tristan und Isolde* at the Stadttheater amazed Weingartner with its sense of construction and dramatic flair, while at the Bayreuth Festival, which he attended in 1882, he was able to hear Wagner's *Parsifal* conducted by Hermann Levi.[14] Weingartner was also a regular member of the audience at the Gewandhaus, where he attended, among others, concerts by Hans von Bülow and the Meininger Hofkapelle. As part of their touring schedule in 1882, Bülow and the Hofkapelle visited Leipzig on 20 January and 13, 14 and 17 March. While it is probable that Weingartner attended all four concerts, it was the all-Brahms programme on 14 March that remained in his memory.[15] At that concert, Bülow launched a savage verbal attack against the Leipzig concert-going public for not responding more positively to Brahms's performance of his own Piano Concerto No. 2 at the Gewandhaus earlier that season. Weingartner was shocked by Bülow's behaviour and argued that his outburst did little to help Brahms's cause, serving only to alienate further the supporters of Wagner, who were already hostile towards the symphonist.

Dismayed by Bülow's tirade but impressed by his virtuosic conducting style, Weingartner applied Bülow's then controversial habit of conducting from memory at his final year examination. Having decided to leave the Conservatorium at Easter 1883, Weingartner was required to perform some of his own piano pieces and to conduct both his Serenade and Beethoven's Symphony No. 2 before being allowed to graduate. Among those present at the rehearsals for the symphony was the conductor Karl Reinecke, who objected strongly when Weingartner began to rehearse from memory. Angry that a student should adopt what he considered the modish habit of conducting without a score, Reinecke demanded that Weingartner either work from the music or be disallowed from taking part in the examination concert. Aware that Reinecke's comments were not simply directed against him but were also a jibe at Bülow, Weingartner leaped to Bülow's defence and ignored Reinecke's demands. But the incident seems to have been nothing more than a storm in a teacup, because Weingartner conducted the Beethoven symphony, received an excellent report and was rewarded with the Mozart Prize of 130 marks.[16]

Having graduated from the Leipzig Conservatory, Weingartner faced a summer of unemployment. Keen to establish himself professionally, he applied to various managers for work as a conductor but was rejected because of his age. It was clear to the twenty-year-old novice that a post at an established theatre was not likely in the immediate future, so he accepted a tour of the Low Countries and Germany as an accompanist and approached Franz Liszt in Weimar for help. Impressed by Weingartner's abilities both as a composer and as a pianist, Liszt asked the Hofkapellmeister of the Weimar Hoftheater, Eduard Lassen,[17] to listen to Weingartner's first opera, *Sakuntala*. The young composer demonstrated the score on the piano to Lassen and it was agreed that the work would be included in the Hoftheater's 1884 schedule. Eager to benefit as much as possible from this unexpected opportunity, Weingartner used the opera's preparatory period to broaden his musical horizons. As he had no first-hand experience of professional theatre life, he participated in *Sakuntala*'s rehearsals and attended performances and rehearsals of operas by other composers at the Hoftheater. By so doing, he was able to acquire some practical skills and to broaden his knowledge of the standard operatic repertoire.

Around the time of the *Sakuntala* première at Weimar, Weingartner received news from the tenor Anton Schott[18] of a conducting vacancy at the theatre in Königsberg. Schott suggested that, if Weingartner were interested, he should contact the theatre's director urgently, as the vacancy was for the 1884–5 season. Acting quickly, Weingartner wrote to the theatre's management and was pleasantly surprised when he was offered a one-year contract at a salary of 180 marks a month by return of post. With the arrogance of youth, Weingartner then demanded that he be allocated a fixed number of performances so as not to be eclipsed completely by the theatre's First Kapellmeister, one Herr Kriebel.[19] Astonishingly, the management agreed to his demand and, after a performance of *Fidelio* conducted by Kriebel, Weingartner made his local début with Verdi's *Il trovatore*.

With that performance of Verdi's masterpiece, Weingartner was introduced to the rigours of the Central European opera-house system for the first time. Like other talented young conductors before and since, he was eager to stamp his individuality on a work that had become routine fare. Predictably, his attempt to colour Verdi's score with subtle shadings caused the orchestra and the singers to react unfavourably.[20] Nevertheless, he considered the performance a success and looked forward to conducting his next work at Königsberg, Lortzing's *Zar und Zimmermann*. Unlike many of his colleagues, Weingartner did not consider operetta a task to be endured but, rather, an ideal training ground for young conductors, because it developed technical confidence and increased stage awareness. After *Zar und Zimmermann*, Weingartner conducted another popular opera, Weber's *Der Freischütz*. As a keen advocate of Wagner's theories on performance, Weingartner applied some of his hero's theories on tempo modification and melos in the overture. His interpretation proved controversial and he was soon concerned that the orchestra and local press had begun to plot against him. With a situation that moved swiftly from bad to worse, Weingartner was eager to leave Königsberg as quickly as possible. But opportunities for relatively inexperienced young conductors were small and even after contacting all the Berlin agents he failed to secure a new post.

Weingartner's fortunes changed, however, when he was offered a four-month contract with salary of 150 marks a month at the Danzig Stadttheater during the 1885–6 season.[21] Bizarrely, the theatre's director, Herr Jantsch, greeted Weingartner by stating that he had heard dreadful things about him. Undeterred, Weingartner replied that Jantsch should wait until he heard him conduct and, if dissatisfied, could give him four weeks' notice. The first opera that Weingartner tackled at Danzig was Anton Rubinstein's *Die Kinder der Heide*, a work that was new to him. Having accepted the opera in a fit of bravado, Weingartner studied the score overnight and began the next day's rehearsal fully prepared. Although the singers were acceptable, the orchestra was less than adequate and, as in Königsberg, he believed that the players were conspiring against him. Nevertheless, Rubinstein's opera was a triumph and Weingartner went on to conduct equally successful productions of Verdi's *Il trovatore* and Mozart's *Die Zauberflöte*. Impressed by Weingartner's ability, the theatre's new director, Herr Rosé, rewarded his success by extending his contract to include the 1886–7 season at an increased salary of 200 marks a month.

Weingartner's contract at Danzig was valid only for the winter season, however, and he desperately needed to find work during the summer months. His luck altered quickly when Hermann Levi introduced him to Cosima Wagner, who engaged him as a musical assistant at the 1886 Bayreuth Festival.[22] Weingartner had met Levi earlier that summer when the latter conducted the première of the former's second opera, *Malawika*, at the Munich Hofoper on 3 June 1886. Thrilled by having his new opera performed at one of Europe's most prestigious opera houses by one of the world's leading conductors, Weingartner wanted to exploit the opportunity fully. Levi's conducting style was of particular interest to Weingartner, who used the preparation period to study it in detail. Reflecting reverentially on Levi's personality and podium manner in later life, Weingartner recalled that, unlike Bülow, Levi was a pleasant and encouraging individual who reduced his stick technique to a minimum. His controlled but expressive use of the baton was a revelation for Weingartner, who later argued that Levi's method was the basis for his own approach. Weingartner was also impressed by Levi's catholic taste and his ability to perform a variety of musical styles with equal skill. For Weingartner, Levi was an inspiration and was an important figure in his development, both as a musician in general and as a conductor in particular.

Weingartner's second season at Danzig was something of an anticlimax after the summer of 1886. Having heard his new opera mounted at the Munich Hofoper and having been a member of the music staff at the Bayreuth Festival, Weingartner tackled his routine duties at Danzig with little enthusiasm. With a schedule that was dominated by operas from the standard repertoire and with productions that were given with a minimum of rehearsal, Weingartner became increasingly disillusioned and began to look for work elsewhere. Paid seasonally to conduct substandard performances, Weingartner was eager to find stable employment at a prestigious theatre. After making a number of discreet enquiries, he was introduced to the director of the Hamburg Stadttheater, Bernhard Pollini, by a Berlin agent. Although the Hamburg theatre was of a much higher status than that of Danzig, it was still a repertory company and Weingartner would be engaged only as Josef Sucher's Second Kapellmeister. Moreover, Weingartner was warned of Pollini's 'high-handed' management style and was concerned that his contract could be terminated with only four weeks' notice. Nevertheless, the chance to work at one of Germany's leading lyric theatres was both a daunting and an exhilarating prospect that Weingartner could ill afford to ignore.

Worried about his conditions of employment and Pollini's reaction to him as a musician, Weingartner made his Hamburg début with some

trepidation. He need not have worried, however, because his performance of Meyerbeer's *Les Huguenots* was a success. Weingartner then
went on to conduct equally well-regarded performances of Halévy's *La
Juive* and Wagner's *Lohengrin* and *Die Meistersinger von Nürnberg*.
Those performances, however, were high points of a tenure that had
quickly turned sour over questions of programming and repertoire.
Having had to endure on occasion more than twenty performances a
month during his first season at Hamburg, Weingartner was to be
rewarded for his efforts by Pollini by being allowed the honour of opening the 1888–9 season with Beethoven's *Fidelio*. But with the departure
of Sucher to Berlin, Pollini made an unexpected volte-face and gave that
distinction to the theatre's new First Kapellmeister, Karl Schröder.
Weingartner had to settle instead for a revival of a long-standing production of *Tristan und Isolde*. From that point forward, his relationship
with Pollini became increasingly fragile, with the impresario systematically relieving him of many of the duties that he had enjoyed during his
first season at Hamburg. Eager to escape from what had become an
insupportable situation, Weingartner wanted to accept the post of
Hofkapellmeister at the Mannheim Hofoper. The job had been offered
to him during his second year at the Stadttheater, but Pollini was reluctant to release him from his contract. Even though it was clear that conductor and manager had serious personal and professional differences,
it was only after a period of extreme acrimony on both sides that
Weingartner was finally given permission to leave Hamburg for
Mannheim.

Before Weingartner's contract at the Mannheim Hofoper could be
ratified, however, he had to conduct trial performances of Beethoven's
Fidelio and Wagner's *Der fliegende Holländer*. Neither opera presented
any major problems for Weingartner, and after conducting them successfully he was officially offered the post of Hofkapellmeister at a
salary of 4200 marks a year.[23] As the senior conductor at Mannheim,
Weingartner was also expected to direct the Hofkapelle's Academy
Concerts. As he had never taken charge of a concert series before, the
Mannheim Academy Concerts were important to him in at least three
ways: first, he was accorded an extra fee of 1200 marks as their director; second, when the local choir joined the Hofkapelle for performances of choral music, his salary was increased by 1000 marks,[24] and,
third, he was able to explore repertoire that would be the basis for his
emerging performance aesthetic. From the outset, Weingartner programmed music with which he would later be associated closely and, at
the first Academy Concert of the 1889–90 season, his first professional

concert, he signalled his advocacy of *Zukunftsmusik* by programming Wagner's *Faust Overture*, Liszt's *Hungaria* and Piano Concerto No. 1 (Alfred Reisenauer, piano) and his interest in Beethoven's works by including that composer's Symphony No. 8.

Weingartner's obvious abilities soon attracted the attention of the Generalintendant of the Berlin theatres, Graf Bolko von Hochberg.[25] As Weingartner's tenure at Mannheim had proved successful, Hochberg was keen to engage him at the Berlin Hofoper. An interview with the Intendant's emissary, Henry Pierson, was arranged, therefore, at the Hotel Schwann in Frankfurt on 9 March 1891. During that meeting, Weingartner was offered the post of Kapellmeister at the Berlin theatre with an annual salary of 9000 marks, more than twice that which he received in Mannheim.[26] Although he would again be subordinate to Josef Sucher,[27] the job offered at the Hofoper meant that Weingartner would be able to conduct important works under good conditions and be able to perform with some of the leading operatic artists of the age. Realizing that the post had the potential to secure his future as a performing musician, Weingartner accepted the Berlin offer eagerly. Keen to exploit the talents of his new, young Kapellmeister from the outset, Hochberg informed Weingartner shortly after he arrived in Berlin in April 1891 that he was to conduct a new production of Wagner's *Lohengrin*. Arranged to coincide with the composer's birthday, the production was given its première on 22 May 1891. As the performance was Weingartner's Berlin début, he was keen to ensure that his musical demands were understood clearly. Impressed by the chorus, 'which was full and good',[28] and generally pleased by the standard of the principal singers, Weingartner's greatest worry was the orchestra. Before accepting the post, he had been warned that the Hofkapelle's standards had been declining for some time. For Weingartner, the orchestra's habit of playing with 'an indeterminate mezzoforte, to which they seemed to have become addicted'[29] was distressing. He suggested, therefore, that by 'conscientiously following all the dynamic instructions and by rhythmical phrasing' an improvement could be achieved quickly.[30] Weingartner's meticulous approach quickly paid off and the orchestra's playing soon reached a standard that elicited positive comments not only from Bolko but also from Sucher.

Shortly after Weingartner took up his post at the Hofoper, his responsibilities were widened to include the shared direction of the Berlin Hofkapelle's Abonnement Concerts.[31] Some commentators have argued that Berlin audiences were drawn to Weingartner because of his podium manner and his temperament.[32] Those elements, however, were only part of his attraction, because he also performed programmes that were a crafty mix of the new, the familiar and the challenging. At his first concert with the Hofkapelle on 18 October 1891, for example, the works chosen were designed both to appeal and to challenge. The programme began with Mendelssohn's Overture Op. 26 (*The Hebrides*), continued with Berlioz's *Symphonie fantastique* and concluded with Beethoven's Symphony No. 5. While the Mendelssohn overture was sure to appeal to the audience, Berlioz's symphony was certain to be less attractive. The French composer's music struggled at the box office throughout the late nineteenth century and Weingartner's inclusion of it at his début concert with the Hofkapelle was a courageous act.[33] Nevertheless, he was unwilling to conclude his first concert in Berlin with a work that had only limited appeal, so he ended the evening with Beethoven's ever popular Symphony No. 5.

The inclusion of a work by Beethoven at Weingartner's first Hofkapelle concert was typical of his programming at Berlin as a whole. Between 18 October 1891 and 20 December 1907, Weingartner directed 160 of the 187 concerts given by the Hofkapelle and, at these, he gave 168 performances of works by Beethoven. Most frequently heard were the composer's symphonies, with six performances of Symphony No.1, ten of Symphonies Nos. 2, 4 and 7, eleven of Symphonies Nos. 6 ('Pastoral') and 8, twelve of Symphony No. 3, thirteen of Symphony No. 5 and seventeen of Symphony No. 9 ('Choral').[34] From those statistics, it might be assumed that Weingartner performed the works in cycles, but that was not the case. The only season in which all nine symphonies were given was 1906–7, and, even then, they were not heard in numerical order. Although unwilling to perform these works in cycles, Weingartner did give all-Beethoven concerts at regular intervals with the symphonies being programmed alongside a concerto and an overture. In keeping with late nineteenth- and early twentieth-century trends, the concertos that were heard most often were the last three for piano, with two performances of No. 4, three of No. 3 and five of No. 5 ('Emperor'). Weingartner also gave two performances each of the Triple Concerto and the Violin Concerto, for which the leader of the Hofkapelle, Karl Halir, was engaged as soloist. Along with those works, Weingartner conducted the three *Leonore overtures* and the overtures to *Egmont* and *Coriolan* regularly but performed the choral music only sparingly, with the Choral Fantasy, the Missa solemnis and *Christus am Ölberg* each being given once only.

Although the Hofkapelle's concerts allowed Weingartner to consolidate his growing reputation as a Beethoven conductor, he also performed music by other composers that he later edited and recorded. Among the works that he programmed regularly were Mozart's Symphonies Nos. 39, 40 and 41 ('Jupiter'), which he conducted on seven, nine and ten occasions respectively. As a direct result of those readings, Weingartner began to formulate a performance style that he later developed in his treatise on the interpretation of those symphonies[35] and in his four recordings of Symphony No. 39 for Columbia.[36] The music of Haydn and Berlioz also featured prominently at Weingartner's concerts with the Hofkapelle, and his involvement with Breitkopf & Härtel's editions of Haydn and Berlioz was an ideal complement to his work as a performing musician. It is tempting to think, therefore, that he employed some of the information gleaned from Haydn's autographs when preparing at least some of his twenty-three performances of that composer's late symphonies in Berlin.[37] Similarly, Weingartner's championing of the music of Berlioz was an important feature of his Berlin programmes and, again, it can be assumed that his editorial duties had an impact on his interpretations. The depth of his commitment to Berlioz was clear to all who attended his Hofkapelle concerts and along with five performances of the *Symphonie fantastique*, he conducted some of the overtures, *La Damnation de Faust*, *Harold en Italie*, *Roméo et Juliette*, *L'Enfance du Christ* and the *Symphonie funèbre et triomphale*.

Weingartner was keen to promote new music at Berlin and, as a composer-conductor, he had a personal stake in that area. On 22 March 1896, Weingartner introduced his music to local audiences, when he conducted *Die Wallfahrt nach Kaevelaar* and the intermezzo from his second opera, *Malawika*.[38] He then performed his Symphony No. 1 on 16 January 1899 and his tone poems, *Das Gefilde der Seligen* and *König Lear*, on 22 January 1900 and 22 March 1901 respectively. Apart from three performances of his arrangement of Beethoven's *Grosse Fuge*, the only other work of his own that he performed during his Berlin period was his Symphony No. 2.[39] Considered by many to be a conductor rather than a composer, Weingartner was distressed by the cool response of the public to his music. Nevertheless, he tirelessly championed the cause of new music and continued to challenge Berlin's atmosphere of artistic conservatism by regularly programming the music of other prominent contemporary composers. Although Weingartner gave only two works that were new to the German capital during his first full season as sole conductor of the Hofkapelle's Abonnement Concerts,[40] he soon built a reputation as a champion of the moderns by directing seventy-three Berlin premières during the course of his tenure.[41]

In 1898, Weingartner entered into an agreement with Franz Kaim[42] to become the permanent conductor of his Munich-based orchestra. The Kaim Orchestra, now known as the Munich Philharmonic, was founded in 1893 and was conceived as a foil to the Munich Hofkapelle. Kaim was eager to provide the Bavarian capital with a concert orchestra that could programme and perform unencumbered by operatic duties. Weingartner's first concert with the Kaim Orchestra was on 19 March 1898, during which he conducted the Munich première of his symphonic poem *König Lear*. After accepting the direction of the orchestra from October 1898, Weingartner continued to programme imaginatively, prompting many modern commentators to argue that his tenure was a high point in the history of the ensemble.[43] During his nine seasons as *Chefdirigent*, Weingartner gave thirty-two local premières, some of which he conducted in both Munich and Berlin.[44] From the start, he was able to programme his own compositions and, after conducting his Symphony No. 1 in the 1898–9 season, he performed *Das Gefilde der Seligen*, Symphony No. 2 and seven songs with orchestra between 1900 and 1905.[45]

Weingartner's period with the Kaim Orchestra was successful, but because of commitments with the Berlin Hofkapelle he resigned from the Munich orchestra in 1905. In a letter responding to Weingartner's resignation note,[46] Franz Kaim acknowledged the importance of his tenure and suggested that a permanent link between orchestra and conductor be forged by the latter accepting the post of 'Ehrendirigent' (Honorary Conductor).[47] The Munich public also expressed their appreciation for Weingartner at the end of his tenure and, after his final concert as *Chefdirigent* with the orchestra on 3 April 1905, for which he programmed Bach's Suite for Orchestra No. 3, Brahms's Piano Concerto No. 2 with the Scottish pianist and fellow-Liszt pupil Frederic Lamond[48] as soloist and Beethoven's Symphony No. 5, the audience erupted with a storm of applause. The ovation that Weingartner received not only confirmed the regard in which was held in the Bavarian capital but also his place amongst the front rank of concert conductors.

On 1 January 1908, Weingartner succeeded Gustav Mahler as Director of the Vienna Hofoper. Although impressed by Mahler,[49] Weingartner believed that the standards at the Hofoper had diminished under his leadership and that some of his practices were unacceptable.[50] For his local début on 23 January 1908, Weingartner conducted a production of *Fidelio* that differed sharply from Mahler's conception of the work. Unlike Mahler, Weingartner argued against the use of the overture *Leonore* No. 3 as a kind of entr'acte linking the penultimate and final scenes. In Mahler's production, the overture acted not only as a means by which to unify some of the musical content of the opera but also as a way of concealing the time-consuming scene change that was required at that juncture. For Weingartner, however, neither reason was sufficient to justify the inclusion of the overture, so his 'only alternative was to eliminate [Alfred] Roller's final scenery, with which otherwise [he] had no fault to find . . . [because] Beethoven was worth more in [his] eyes than any scenery'.[51] But having excised *Leonore* No. 3 from Act 2, Weingartner then decided to begin the opera with the overture *Leonore* No. 2, a modification that sparked a critical debate which was eclipsed only by his use of cuts in Wagner's operas, a practice that had been rejected by his predecessor. For those who continued to support the principles of Mahler, Weingartner's adjustments and excisions were unacceptable and were tantamount to sacrilege.

The music critic of the *Neue Freie Presse*, Julius Korngold, led the attack on Weingartner with damaging and often outspoken comments. Even so, the critic was unable to break the bond that had developed between the Vienna Philharmonic and Weingartner, who was unanimously elected Director of the orchestra's Abonnement Series after their first concert together on 26 January 1908.[52] While his tenure at the Hofoper ended in 1911,[53] his relationship with the Vienna Philharmonic lasted twenty-five years and, as Director of its Vienna series from the beginning of the 1908–9 season, he conducted no fewer than 247[54] of the orchestra's 273 Subscription and Nicolai concerts between 8 November 1908 and 20 March 1927.[55] That figure, however, understates his activities with the orchestra, because when his touring calendar, additional concerts and performances as guest conductor after 1927 are included, the total number of engagements that he undertook with the orchestra is at least 432.[56] As a sizeable chunk of that enormous number of concerts was given outside Vienna, not all of the performances benefited from the relatively good conditions of the Musikvereinsaal. One of their more strenuous undertakings was their tour of South America, during which Weingartner and the Philharmonic gave thirty-eight performances in Rio de Janeiro, Montevideo and Buenos Aires between 19 July and 31 August 1922.[57] Although much of the music performed was standard touring repertoire, they also gave the first complete cycle of Wagner's *Der Ring des Nibelungen* at the Teatro Colón in Buenos Aires.[58]

Weingartner's programme policy with the Vienna Philharmonic

resembled his earlier activities with the Berlin Hofkapelle. At the Subscription and Nicolai Concerts in Vienna, he, again, balanced the new with the familiar. The symphonies of Beethoven retained their central importance:[59] in each of the seasons directed he conducted at least two symphonies by that composer, and in the 1916–17 and 1926–7 seasons he performed all nine in numerical order.[60] As in Berlin, the two symphonies that were given most frequently were Nos. 5 and 9,[61] with eighteen and thirteen performances respectively. Curiously, Weingartner tended to avoid works that required soloists and there were no performances of the masses, the Triple Concerto, the Violin Concerto or Piano Concertos Nos. 1, 2 and 3. There were, however, performances of Piano Concertos Nos. 4 and 5, but even those were reduced to one and two readings respectively. A work that sparked a lively critical debate was Weingartner's arrangement for orchestra of Beethoven's Sonata Op. 106 ('Hammerklavier'). Performed as part of an all-Beethoven programme on 19 December 1926,[62] its inclusion was a serious error of judgement on Weingartner's part. At best the arrangement is a curiosity, but in a city that was about to commemorate the one hundredth anniversary of Beethoven's death its performance was considered close to blasphemy.

Weingartner's advocacy of the new was a hallmark of his Vienna programmes and, as in Berlin, his concerts in the Austro-Hungarian capital regularly contained works from music's cutting edge. Because of his unassailable position, Weingartner was able to present his compositions regularly with the Vienna Philharmonic. In contrast to his practice in Berlin, where his music was heard at only five of his seventeen seasons, at Vienna he marketed his music aggressively. With the exception of the 1913–14 season, Weingartner gave at least one performance of his music each year between 1910–11 and 1922–3. From the works performed, it is clear that he wanted to underline his abilities as a versatile composer of orchestral music. Along with performances of Symphonies Nos. 1 to 4, he also conducted his concertos, tone poems, variations for orchestra, orchestral suites, overtures, extracts from operas, arrangements and editions.[63] But his interest in new music was not restricted to his own compositions: he also performed music by Debussy, Goldmark, Korngold, Schreker, Sibelius, Stravinsky, Delius, Mahler and Strauss.[64] It would be wrong, however, to assume that Weingartner's activities in Vienna were dominated by either the symphonies of Beethoven or musical novelties, because there were also performances of works by Mozart, Weber, Schumann, Berlioz, Brahms, Wagner, Liszt, Haydn and Bruckner.

In 1919, Weingartner was appointed Director of Vienna's second lyric theatre, the Volksoper. Although the post lacked the lustre of his former job at the Hofoper, Weingartner approached it with professionalism. After making his house début with Wagner's *Die Meistersinger von Nürnberg* on 31 August 1919, he then programmed a series of Italian operas that soon proved controversial. Although not in complete sympathy with the operas of Puccini and Mascagni, Weingartner recognized their immense popularity and importance to a company like the Volksoper.[65] Having accepted the post at a time of financial uncertainty,[66] Weingartner's pragmatic approach was welcomed by many of his junior colleagues. Like Strauss and Schalk at the Staatsoper, Weingartner faced workers' organizations that were often hostile towards management. Although representatives from the chorus and orchestra made demands that were often hard to meet, he maintained that the majority of his junior colleagues worked in the best interests of the company. Weingartner was keen, therefore, to provide them with the best employment conditions possible and, after some tough discussions, he secured for them annual salaries, an important gesture at a time of political upheaval. Moreover, he was able to upgrade the infrastructure of the Volksoper and to improve and modernize much of its dilapidated scenery. It is unsurprising, therefore, that Clemens Höslinger's thesis that Weingartner's departure 'ended for a long time the last fairly stable phase of the house'[67] has been supported by other commentators.

After leaving the Volksoper in 1924,[68] Weingartner worked for a period as a guest conductor[69] before being approached by Otto Maag of Basel concerning the direction of the city's Allgemeine Musikgesellschaft and Conservatory. With the death of the institutions' former director, Herman Suter, both organizations needed a new head and Maag hoped to interest Weingartner in the positions. Attracted by the opportunity of working with students and by the city's geographic location, cultural heritage and international character, Weingartner agreed willingly to the proposal. After further correspondence and a meeting with representatives from the Allgemeine Musikgesellschaft, Weingartner conducted a preliminary concert for the organization on 15 January 1927. The concert was an outstanding success and he wrote immediately to the management of the Vienna Philharmonic informing them that he was no longer willing to conduct the orchestra's subscription concerts from the end of the 1926–7 season.[70] After honouring his final commitments in Vienna, Weingartner arrived in Basel on 17 May 1927 and started work at the Conservatory the next morning.

Later, Weingartner recollected, 'The eight years that I resided and worked [in Basel] were among the happiest of my rich and varied career.'[71] Much of his pleasure came from the conducting course that he taught at the Conservatory. The class was an outstanding success from the start, with no fewer than twenty students enrolling in the first year. The course was then given an international dimension each June when the weekly lessons were extended to include a master class at which students from eleven countries were brought together in Basel. Weingartner's concerts for the Allgemeine Musikgesellschaft were also a success and he later boasted with pride about the improvements that he made to the organization's orchestra.[72] Weingartner was also active as an opera conductor at Basel, where he conducted Mozart's *Le nozze di Figaro* and Wagner's *Tristan und Isolde* to both critical and popular acclaim at the Stadttheater. In 1930, Otto Maag founded an annual music festival at Basel, which was another source of pleasure for Weingartner. With programmes that highlighted his musical strengths and preferences, the festival performances retained a special place in the conductor's affections.[73]

Although happy at Basel, the lure of Vienna was ever present and, in 1935, he returned to the Staatsoper as Director. But the ghosts of his first period as Director returned to haunt him, and many commentators continued to be unconvinced by his abilities as a conductor of opera. Undeterred by the remarks of colleagues and critics, Weingartner took the course of greatest resistance. In view of the heavy criticism he had received for his interpretations of Wagner during his first period at the Opera, his programming of Wagner's *Der Ring des Nibelungen* in September 1935 was not a good choice.[74] Weingartner's detractors were relieved, therefore, when his tenure terminated after little more than a year.[75]

Throughout much of the second half of his career, Weingartner was active as a recording artist. Although remembered largely for his interpretations of Beethoven, he was a musician of catholic taste and was keen to promote his diverse interests in recorded sound. Like other major musicians of the period, his recording career began not on shellac but on piano rolls. Unlike the rolls that are associated with the standard domestic upright player-piano, those on which Weingartner recorded in 1905 were made for the new, sophisticated reproducing pianos. The new instruments could imitate the player's articulation, rhythm and dynamics more closely than pianolas, and one of the first and most important companies to record with them was the German firm Welte.[76] As the company was keen to promote the music of the artists whom it recorded, it might be assumed that Weingartner documented a wide selection of his works. But that was not the case, and he recorded only three of his compositions for the firm; the majority of his rolls were of keyboard works by Bach, Beethoven, Chopin, Schubert and Schumann.[77] Like the rolls of other major artists, those of Weingartner leave a distorted impression of his activities as an interpretative artist and it is fortunate, therefore, that he was an early advocate of the gramophone.

Recording for Columbia between 1910 and 1940, Weingartner amassed a considerable discography for the period.[78] With his third wife,[79] the soprano Lucille Marcel, and the orchestra of the Vienna Hofoper, Weingartner entered the recording studio for the first time in June 1910 and documented two of his songs with orchestra.[80] By securing the services of both the Director and the orchestra of the Vienna Hofoper, Columbia hoped for commercial success, but as relatively few homes had reproducing equipment, the popular appeal of these early recordings was limited. Even so, Weingartner continued to record for Columbia when he visited North America in 1913 and 1914. Travelling between Boston and New York, he arranged his time wisely and when not performing with the Boston Opera Company, he used his free days to record with the Columbia Symphony Orchestra in New York. Again, he was able to document his music and to use Marcel as soloist, a partnership that was profitable both musically and financially. Although keen to promote his wares, he also recorded music by other composers and, along with excerpts from Bizet's *L'Arlésienne* and *Carmen*, he documented music by Schumann, Tchaikovsky, Verdi, Wagner and Weber.[81]

After those early recordings, Weingartner did not enter the studio again for nearly a decade and it was only after 1923 that his career as a recording artist flourished. Although he had worked regularly with many leading orchestras in North America and Europe, he made recordings with only six established ensembles after that date: the orchestra of the Royal Philharmonic Society, the London Symphony Orchestra, the London Philharmonic Orchestra, the Vienna Philharmonic, the Paris Conservatoire Orchestra and the orchestra of the Basler Orchester-Gesellschaft.[82] Overwhelmingly – and, considering his 432 performances with the Vienna Philharmonic, perhaps surprisingly – Weingartner made more recordings with the London Symphony Orchestra than with any other ensemble. Of the eighty-seven commercial recordings that Weingartner made for Columbia, twenty-three were with that orchestra. Nevertheless, he did record with the Vienna Philharmonic, the Paris

Conservatoire and the London Philharmonic Orchestras regularly and made thirteen, fourteen and fifteen discs respectively with them. But he appeared less frequently on record with the orchestras of the Royal Philharmonic Society and the Basler Orchester-Gesellschaft and made only eight and seven recordings respectively with those orchestras.

From a close reading of his discography, it is clear that Columbia cultivated Weingartner's image as a leading interpreter of Beethoven, Brahms and Wagner[83] by engaging him to record with orchestras with which he had developed a relationship and with which his interpretations of a particular composer's works were closely associated. He made, for example, all his recordings of vocal excerpts from Wagner's operas with the Vienna Philharmonic and all his recordings of Brahms's orchestral works with London orchestras.[84] Of the eighteen recordings that he made of Beethoven's symphonies, thirteen were recorded with London orchestras, while five were with the Vienna Philharmonic. Columbia's preference for London orchestras when recording Weingartner's interpretations of Beethoven was most pronounced when documenting Symphony No. 5, which he recorded four times over a nine-year period solely with London orchestras.[85] Columbia's partiality for those ensembles was probably more commercial than interpretative. As the British capital was a centre of recording excellence, the city was able to provide Columbia with technicians of the highest quality. Moreover, London orchestras were renowned for their ability to sight-read efficiently and for their flexible working practices. More important, they were willing to link their concert programmes with the works to be recorded. For Weingartner's recordings of Brahms's Symphonies Nos. 1 and 4 with the London Symphony Orchestra, for example, the recording sessions were linked to concert performances of the works. Similarly, for his recording of Symphony No. 2 in February 1940 with the London Philharmonic Orchestra, he was again able to perform the work in concert. The advantages of this system are obvious. For Columbia and the London orchestras, rehearsal time could be maximized, while, for Weingartner, he was able to develop his ideas fully before documenting the work concerned. But the gramophone was not the only medium that Weingartner used to secure his ideas for future generations: he was also an indefatigable author, whose writings were both provocative and influential.

Like Wagner, Weingartner used the written word to good effect, and it is no coincidence that a number of his literary works bear a striking similarity to those of his musical hero. In general, his writings can be divided into three areas: fiction and the editing of fiction; dissertations on philosophy and life style, and musical treatises. For those interested in the life of Weingartner, his enthusiasm for the writings of the mystic Bô Yin Râ is relevant, but his book about the thinker, *Bô Yin Râ: Einführung in seine Lehre* (*Bô Yin Râ: Introduction to his Teachings*), is only eclipsed by his *Die Lehre von der Wiedergeburt und das musikalische Drama* (*Doctrine of Reincarnation and the Musical Drama*) as biographical ephemera. Similarly, his collected essays, published as *Akkorde*, and his five dramas, *Terra: ein Symbol*, are of little interest. But his thoughts on performance are important and, apart from his autobiography, *Lebenserinnerungen*, translated as *Buffets and Rewards*, his writings that are most often quoted are *Über das Dirigieren* (*On Conducting*), *Die Symphonie nach Beethoven* (*The Symphony after Beethoven*) and *Ratschläge für Aufführungen klassischer Symphonien* (*Advice for the Performance of Classical Symphonies*).

Weingartner published his *Ratschläge für Aufführungen klassischer Symphonien* in three parts and each section considers music that was central to his repertoire. Part 1 is an analysis of Beethoven's nine symphonies; Part 2 is a discussion of those by Schubert and Schumann, while Part 3 is devoted to Mozart. Although Weingartner's approach in the three sections is didactic, it is also an expression of his thoughts on performance at the time of publication. It seems that the popularity of the individual *Ratschläge* relates directly to Weingartner's discography. Of the three sections, the least known is that pertaining to Schubert and Schumann. As he recorded no symphonies by them, interest in that study has been minimal. Similarly, the volume on Mozart is yet to be exploited fully. In contrast, the longer and more detailed treatise on the performance of Beethoven has been quoted regularly. Generally, commentators consider it a tool, along with his commercial recordings, with which to compare and to contrast Weingartner's approach to Beethoven. As the treatise was originally published in 1906,[86] any comparison with his recordings is flawed. Rather than use the volume as a sophisticated form of checklist, commentators should view it as a complement to his recordings. By so doing, they can fully chart the development of Weingartner's Beethoven style between the 1890s and the 1930s.

While the *Ratschläge* are devoted to individual composers, Weingartner's treatise *Über das Dirigieren* is a general manifesto on conducting. It is no coincidence that this essay shares the name of that by Wagner on the same subject. For Weingartner, arguing that his hero 'laid the foundation for a new understanding of the function of the conductor', Wagner's thoughts were seminal.[87] In particular, it was Wagner's ability to capture the '*spirit of the artwork*' by carefully observing the work's '*melos*' that impressed Weingartner.[88] Although unconvinced by Wagner's adjustments to the vocal parts of Beethoven's Symphony No. 9, Weingartner argues that none of his contemporaries would consider performing the work without the former's amendments to the orchestration.[89] And by tackling important issues, 'Wagner's treatise combated the philistinism that suffocated every modification of tempo and therefore all vitality of phrasing in a rigid metronomism'. It is hardly surprising, then, that Weingartner considered his 'own book on the other hand [a means by which to combat] the errors that had arisen through exaggeration of these modifications'.[90]

In pursuing his war against excess, Weingartner targets Hans von Bülow. Much of the first half of Weingartner's treatise is given over to lambasting Bülow's interpretations. In particular, he objects to Bülow's exaggerated methods when manipulating tempo, phrasing and dynamics. Although Weingartner is negative in his approach, careful analysis of his comments not only illustrates Bülow's methods, but also his own. In Beethoven's overture to *Egmont*, for example, Weingartner objects to Bülow's marked reduction in tempo at the second subject, arguing that 'The proper expression can be obtained *without* any change of the main tempo' and can be achieved 'if the strings, who have the first two bars of the theme, are told to bring them out energetically and very precisely by a uniform down-bowing of the crotchets, thus preventing the last quaver of the first bar from being turned, as often happens, into a semiquaver'. While obvious to many string players, this bowing pattern is a rare example of Weingartner's published thoughts on string technique. Similarly, his castigation of Bülow's tempi in the overture as a whole allows an interesting insight into Weingartner's own. The latter argues that the Introduction's marking, 'sostenuto, ma non troppo', does not signify a slow tempo and that the allegro increases to an allegro con brio only at the coda. Like many of his colleagues from the Central European school of conducting, Weingartner is fond of linking and integrating his tempi in the course of a movement and throughout the work as a whole. To achieve a satisfactory relationship between the Introduction and the Allegro 'one bar of the 3/4 section is about equivalent to a minim, and so to a third of a bar in the 3/2 section, whereby the crotchets at the entry of the allegro do not become about half what they are in the introduction'. Again, for professional performers, tempo integration is no revelation but, by clarifying his approach, Weingartner's rule, that 'No slow tempo must be so slow that the melody of the piece is *not yet* recognisable, and no fast tempo so fast that the melody is *no longer* recognisable',[91] is given a practical context.

With much of the opening two thirds of the treatise devoted to the musical sins of Bülow and his followers, the remainder of the volume is given over to the conductor's art in general. Weingartner believed fully that a conductor's talent was '*inborn*' and that '*There is no performance of genius without temperament*'.[92] While his use of the word 'genius' is difficult to define accurately, his overall thesis is one that has been supported by most prominent performing artists. More important, he argues that a conductor must always be the faithful servant of the work and the composer, and any action that distracts the listener from the music must be avoided. Specifically, and somewhat curiously considering his approach as a student at Leipzig, he states that conductors should resist the temptation of performing without the score. But, when a score is used, it should act simply as an aide-mémoire, preventing the conductor from becoming 'a mere time-beater, a bungler, with no pretensions to the title of artist'.[93] For Weingartner, performing from memory was only part of the conductor's art and his views on stick technique were equally strong. While 'Some conductors are reproached with making too many gestures . . . [a] pose of assumed quiet is however just as repellent'. It is better, therefore, '*not to make any more movements than are necessary*. The expression of each passage will then generate an appropriately great or small motion of the baton.[94] . . . as a general thing it may be pointed out that short, quick motions ensure greater precision than very extensive ones'.[95] From the extant video footage of Weingartner conducting in Paris,[96] his thoughts on technique are a true representation of his practice in general. He was never given to unnecessary movements, and his gestures were always a model of concision.

When Weingartner died at Winterthur on 7 May 1942, his desire to be recognized as a leading composer remained unfulfilled. It was clear to all who had experienced him both as a creative and as a recreative artist that his strengths were overwhelmingly interpretative. The obituarist in *The Musical Times* considered this true and recalled that Weingartner:

> was liked because in an age when showmanship became more and more in the ascendant he employed none of its self-advertising tricks and mannerisms. His only objective was musical interpretation prompted by the composer's text and an intimate feeling for the composer's style. Though his gestures were restrained, he was visibly and audibly in control of all those niceties of phrase, rhythm and balance that make up true performance. . . . [Although] Weingartner was a prolific composer, . . . he lacked inventive genius, and the impression

he made was not commensurate with the importance he attached to this branch of his work.[97]

Nevertheless, at a time when record companies are releasing obscure works by marginal composers, Weingartner's compositions deserve to be heard. While his music might be no better than that of Hans Pfitzner, he was an artist of stature and an important historical figure. Moreover, by releasing Weingartner's works on CD, modern listeners will be better able to place his activities as an interpreter into the context of his work as a whole. Although Weingartner died without achieving his primary artistic goal, he did achieve a status that eluded many of his contemporaries. And while he never received the acclaim of Richard Strauss as a composer, he was invariably considered a conductor of the front rank whose interpretations are as fresh today as they were at the time of performance.

CHAPTER 5

Richard III: Richard Strauss[1]

Richard Strauss was the last great composer-conductor. Active professionally for more than seven decades, he enjoyed staggering success both as a creative and as an executant musician that was unsurpassed during his lifetime and has had no parallels since his death. Although remembered today largely as the composer of such works as *Der Rosenkavalier, Salome, Don Juan* and *Tod und Verklärung*, he was also an outstanding conductor who commanded the respect of musicians, audiences and critics alike. Inevitably, impresarios and orchestras were keen for him to perform works of his own creation, but those invitations often had little appeal for Strauss, who preferred instead to conduct the compositions of his musical heroes, Mozart, Beethoven and Wagner. A champion of new music, Strauss also regularly performed works by his contemporaries and did much to promote the music of his friend and colleague Gustav Mahler. Often misrepresented as a mercenary musician who was interested solely in the promotion of his own works, Strauss was an artist of catholic taste who invariably placed art before ambition.

Strauss was the son of Germany's most celebrated horn player, Franz Strauss.[2] Described by Hans von Bülow as 'the Joachim of the Waldhorn', Franz was a member of the Munich Hofkapelle for forty-two years. A notoriously conservative musician who abhorred the works of Wagner and his followers, he considered the great Classical composers to be iconic figures who were to be admired above all others. As the Hofkapelle's principal horn, he played under Wagner and his '*alter ego* . . . the master-conductor Hans von Bülow'[3] regularly in the 1860s and was constantly at loggerheads with them. He found their approach to music and music-making decadent and their unconventional marriage arrangements contemptible. He lobbied against them while they were active professionally in Munich and when it was announced at a

Hofkapelle rehearsal that Wagner had died, he alone refused to stand in respect.

Franz's dogmatic personality was probably the result of an unhappy early life. Born out of wedlock in 1822, he lost contact with his father at the age of five and as a boy was cared for largely by his uncles. He learned a variety of instruments during his childhood and began to play professionally at weddings and festivals as a youth. After marrying Elise Seiff in 1851, he had two children, a son and a daughter, but tragedy struck when his son died of tuberculosis at the age of ten months and his wife and daughter died shortly after of cholera. Those early experiences affected him badly and he became increasingly bitter with age. After being widowed at the age of thirty-two, he met Josepha Pschorr, the daughter of one of Munich's leading brewers, in 1856 and married her seven years later. Determined that their children should be raised according to his strict ethical and musical principles, Franz became the dominant parent and attempted to mould his offspring in his image.

As the first of Franz's and Josepha's two children,[4] Richard was born into a comfortable upper middle-class family at Munich on 11 June 1864. Having begun piano lessons at the age of four with the Munich Hofkapelle's harpist, August Tombo,[5] Richard progressed quickly and was soon able to sight-read with ease. He had little interest in practising the piano, however, and he later argued that his eagerness to play through orchestral and operatic scores at the keyboard meant that his technique was flawed for life.[6] At the age of five he began to compose, and three years later he attempted orchestration for the first time. After entering the Cathedral School in Munich in 1871, he attended his first opera and began violin lessons with his cousin, the Concertmaster of the Munich Hofkapelle, Benno Walter.[7] In 1874, Strauss progressed to the Ludwigs-Gymnasium, where his interest in all things Greek was awakened, and the following year he started harmony, counterpoint and composition lessons with the musically conservative conductor Friedrich Wilhelm Meyer.[8] When he was eighteen, Strauss matriculated to the University of Munich, where he attended lectures on art history, aesthetics, philosophy and Shakespeare. But he soon realized that university life was not for him and, in 1883, he left formal education to travel to Berlin and Dresden, where he visited art galleries and attended concerts and operas.

Because of his father's position with the Munich Hofkapelle, Strauss was able to attend rehearsals and performances at the Hofoper throughout his formative years. Influenced by Franz's conservatism, the young Strauss was unimpressed by the works of Wagner and preferred instead the operas of Auber. In his extensive correspondence with his boyhood friend, the theorist and composer Ludwig Thuille, Strauss railed against Wagner's music and reported that he 'was bored stiff' by *Siegfried*.[9] Nevertheless, Franz was happy to let leading Wagnerians champion Richard's early compositions and to support his career as a performer.

One of the first major conductors to recognize Strauss's talent publicly was Hermann Levi. Although Franz had an uneasy relationship with Levi because of his association with Wagner, the conductor set aside his feelings and gave the first professional performances of Strauss's Symphony in D minor and the Concert Overture in C minor at Munich in 1881 and 1883 respectively.[10] Levi was not the only conductor connected to Wagner to recognize Strauss's precocious gift; Hans von Bülow also took an interest in the young composer and performed his Serenade for Winds Op. 7 with the Meininger Hofkapelle in 1883. Impressed by Strauss's potential, Bülow then 'commissioned [Strauss] to write a similar piece for the Meiningen orchestra'.[11] The result of the commission was the Suite for Wind Op. 4, which the orchestra premièred at the Munich Odeonssaal on 18 November 1884 with the composer conducting.[12] As the Meininger Hofkapelle was on tour, Strauss had to perform his work without rehearsal. Never having conducted before, he was understandably nervous about his début and later recalled that he 'conducted [his] piece in a state of slight coma'.[13] At the end of the performance, Strauss's father attempted to thank Bülow for the allowing his son the opportunity to conduct his work but was set upon by his old enemy, who shouted: 'You have nothing to thank me for . . . I have not forgotten what you have done to me in this damned city of Munich. What I did to-day I did because your son has talent and not for you.'[14] Although Strauss's moment of glory was spoiled, Bülow more than compensated him for his vitriolic outburst by arranging Strauss's appointment as Hofmusikdirektor at the Grand Duchy of Meiningen in 1885.

Strauss's principal function at Meiningen was to act as Bülow's assistant with the Hofkapelle. Confident of the young man's abilities, Bülow decided to introduce him to the Grand Duchy by having him perform the solo part in Mozart's Piano Concerto No. 24[15] and conduct the local première of his Symphony in F minor on 18 October 1885. Strauss later recalled: 'Although I had practised busily all summer, the idea of playing the concerto with Bülow conducting filled me – by no means a fully-trained pianist – with fear and trembling. When we had negotiated the first movement quite creditably, the master encouraged me with the

words, "If you weren't something better, you might become a pianist."
Although I did not think that I fully deserved this compliment, my self-
confidence had been increased sufficiently to enable me to play the last
two movements a little less self-consciously'.[16] Nevertheless, Bülow's
praise was probably genuine, for two days after the performance he sent
a note to the publisher Eugen Spitzweg, stating '[Strauss's] playing – like
his conducting début – [was] downright breathtaking'.[17]

Having disposed of the Mozart concerto before the interval, Strauss
mounted the rostrum for a performance of his Symphony in F minor
after the break. In the audience was Johannes Brahms, who was at
Meiningen to conduct the première of his Symphony No. 4 with the
Hofkapelle.[18] Keen to hear Brahms's opinion, Strauss approached him
after the concert and was told that his symphony was '[q]uite nice'[19]
but was 'too full of thematic irrelevances'.[20] Brahms also felt that the
profusion of such themes was pointless when 'only contrasted rhythmically on one triad'. His advice was a revelation to the young
Strauss, who soon realized that 'counterpoint [was] only justified
when poetic necessity compel[led] a temporary union of two or several themes contrasted as sharply as possible, not only rhythmically
but especially harmonically'. Brahms also advised Strauss, 'take a
good look at Schubert's dances . . . and try your luck at the invention
of simple eight-bar melodies'. Strauss acted on Brahms's suggestion
and was subsequently unafraid of 'incorporating a popular melody in
[his] work'.[21]

As Hofmusikdirektor at Meiningen, Strauss was able to observe
Bülow's conducting style at first hand. Each morning, Strauss attended
the Hofkapelle's rehearsals, which Bülow directed solely, and was particularly impressed by his approach to the works of Beethoven and
Wagner. In later life, Strauss recalled that Bülow's interpretations were
compelling in their intensity and without any trace of arbitrariness, and
that they were the direct result of the work's form and poetic content.
As a teacher, Bülow insisted that Strauss should learn to read
Beethoven's scores accurately and to use that accuracy as the basis for
his interpretation. Strauss was also impressed by Bülow's painstaking
method in rehearsal, his eye for detail and his graceful baton technique.
The influence that Bülow exerted over the young Strauss was profound,
and he never forgot or betrayed what he had learned from his mentor
during his short stay at Meiningen. His reverence for Bülow was lifelong
and in maturity he wrote: 'The touching interest he took in me and his
influence on the development of my artistic talent were . . . the most
decisive factors in my career.'[22]

In general, Strauss's duties at the Grand Duchy were varied and interesting. In addition to occasional rehearsals and performances with the Hofkapelle, he taught piano to the Duke's sister, Princess Marie, performed as a chamber musician and directed the local choral society. When Bülow resigned unexpectedly from the Hofkapelle in November 1885, Strauss took sole charge of the orchestra and was responsible for its rehearsals and concerts. Although he inherited an orchestra that had been drilled by one of the world's most experienced conductors, he was a relative novice with little experience of the standard and emerging concert repertoires. In an attempt to expand his practical knowledge and to keep the musicians occupied, Strauss had the orchestra play 'the whole of their concert repertoire' to him at their daily morning rehearsals.[23]

Strauss's first opportunity to stamp his authority on the orchestra came on 6 December 1885, when he directed his first concert with the Hofkapelle as Bülow's successor. For that performance, he conducted Gluck's overture to *Iphigénie en Aulide*, Mozart's Requiem and Brahms's *Schicksalslied*. Typically, Strauss concluded the Gluck overture with Wagner's concert ending and revised Süßmayr's orchestration in the Requiem.[24] But with Bülow gone and the imminent reduction of the orchestra to thirty-nine players, Strauss soon began to lose interest in Meiningen. And even though he was offered an increased salary of 2000 marks to stay in the Grand Duchy,[25] he left the Hofkapelle in April 1886 to become Musikdirektor (Third Conductor) at the Munich Hofoper from the beginning of the 1886–7 season.

After an extended holiday in Italy, Strauss began work at Munich on 1 October 1886. Apart from the pleasure of directing a first-rate orchestra that included his father, the job proved disappointing. For much of the time, and in keeping with the rank of Musikdirektor, he was obliged to conduct operas from the standard repertoire. Along with a performance of Mendelssohn's incidental music to *Ein Sommernachtstraum* on 25 January 1887, Strauss took charge of twenty performances of nine operas by eight composers during his first season.[26] Statistically, the ratio of performances was 11 French : 8 Austro-German : 1 Italian. With the exception of Mozart's *Così fan tutte*,[27] an opera that he championed throughout his life and with which he would later be associated closely, all the operas that he performed held popular appeal and were in keeping with his junior rank. Strauss's second season at Munich bore a striking resemblance to his first, with four of the eight operas being carried over from the previous year.[28] His third season as Musikdirektor was again dominated by repeat performances and, of the nine performances of five operas by five composers that he performed during that period, only Donizetti's *La Favorite* and Verdi's *Un ballo in maschera* were new to his repertoire.[29]

During his stay at Meiningen, Strauss met and became friendly with the violinist and composer, Alexander Ritter.[30] The husband of Richard Wagner's niece, Franziska, Ritter was a passionate Wagnerian and a close friend of Hans von Bülow. Keen to initiate Strauss into the mysteries of *Zukunftsmusik* and German philosophy, Ritter bombarded the young musician with the writings of Schopenhauer and Wagner. Having been quickly converted into a fervent Wagnerian by Ritter, Strauss continued to explore his new-found passion when he returned to Munich and accepted with some excitement responsibility for the first ever production of Wagner's early opera, *Die Feen*, at the Hofoper in June 1888.[31] Preparations for the staging began in the spring of that year and Strauss continued to superintend the production until the final rehearsals. But at the eleventh hour, the Intendant, Baron Karl von Perfall, informed Strauss that his immediate superior, Franz Fischer,[32] was to take charge of both the dress rehearsal and the first performance. Strauss was devastated. Although he was granted an early and valuable insight into the machinations of operatic life, he felt nothing but contempt for his superiors at Munich and later described Perfall as 'a disgusting cad'[33] and Fischer as 'one of the most untalented musicians I have ever met and a real criminal at the rostrum'.[34] It was with some relief, therefore, that he was offered the post of Second Kapellmeister at the Weimar Hoftheater from the beginning of the 1889–90 season with a salary of 2100 marks.

Although Strauss argued that he had not been a particular effective third conductor at Munich, Bülow continued to take an interest in his career and brokered his appointment as Kapellmeister at the Grand Duchy of Saxe-Weimar-Eisenach.[35] For a German musician of Strauss's generation, Weimar was of particular significance. With its links to Bach, Goethe, Schiller and Liszt, it had a rich artistic heritage as the basis for a lively cultural environment that allowed Strauss to explore new musical avenues while discovering masterworks from the past. Working to a well-disposed Intendant, Hans Bronsart von Schellendorf,[36] and an amiable Hofkapellmeister, Eduard Lassen, Strauss was able to develop musically within a secure environment that valued his abilities both as a creative and as a recreative musician. His interest in *Zukunftsmusik* was nurtured at Weimar and, with the help of Bronsart and Lassen, he was also able to explore some important works by Mozart and Beethoven. As Strauss had to balance responsibilities in the opera theatre with duties in the concert hall for the first time, his exploration of those works included not only the operatic but also the symphonic repertoires.

Between 1889 and 1893, Strauss conducted sixteen Abonnement Concerts with the Weimar Hofkapelle. Of those, eleven contained a work by Beethoven, the composer that Strauss conducted most frequently at that series.[37] Although he never conducted an all-Beethoven concert at Weimar, he did perform five of the composer's nine symphonies at the Abonnement Series, including two performances of Symphony No. 3 ('Eroica') and one performance each of Symphonies Nos. 5, 6, 7 and 8.[38] The majority of his Beethoven performances were given over to the composer's other orchestral music, including Piano Concertos Nos. 3 and 4, the Violin Concerto, the Romance in F major, Clärchen's 'Die Trommel gerühret' and 'Freudvoll und leidvoll' from the music to *Egmont* and the overtures *König Stephan*, *Leonore* No. 1, *Egmont*, *Die Weihe des Hauses* and *Coriolan*.[39] Strauss's soloists were local musicians and included his future wife, the soprano Pauline de Ahna, the former Liszt pupils Bernhard Stavenhagen and Margarethe Stern, and the Concertmaster of the Weimar Hofkapelle, Karl Halir.

Less frequently performed by Strauss at the Abonnement Concerts were the orchestral works of Mozart, Wagner and Liszt, which were heard at three, five and seven concerts respectively. His performance of Mozart's Symphony No. 41 ('Jupiter') on 12 January 1891 was of particular significance, as it was his first of a symphony by that composer.[40] As a convert to the cause of *Zukunftsmusik*, Strauss ensured that the works of Wagner and Liszt occupied a central place in his Weimar repertoire, and although he never conducted an all-Wagner concert at the Grand Duchy, he did devote half an Abonnement Concert to the composer's works on 26 January 1891. Having given over the first part of the concert to works by Beethoven,[41] Strauss concluded the programme with Wagner's *Siegfried Idyll*, the Bacchanale from *Tannhäuser* (Paris version) and the Prelude and Liebestod from *Tristan und Isolde* (Pauline de Ahna, soprano). *Siegfried Idyll* was also heard on 9 December 1889 and 4 December 1893 and was the work by Wagner that Strauss conducted most frequently at the subscription concerts.[42] *Siegfried Idyll* also had the distinction of being the only work by either Wagner or Liszt that he gave more than once at that series. That said, Liszt's orchestral works appeared on Strauss's Weimar programmes more frequently than those of Wagner and included performances of *Die Ideale*, *Totentanz*, *A Faust Symphony*, *Ce qu'on entend sur la montagne*, *Les Préludes*, *Mazeppa* and *Festklänge*.[43] Strauss also peppered his programmes with

Liszt's Lieder and took part in three all-Liszt concerts for the local Liszt-Stiftung (Liszt Foundation) between April 1890 and October 1892.[44]

Keen to promote his own works and eager to be seen as a successor of Liszt and Wagner, Strauss included his own compositions in the Abonnement Concerts from the beginning of his tenure. After accompanying the tenor Hans Zeller in a performance of his *Ständchen* at his first Abonnement concert on 28 October 1889,[45] Strauss conducted the world première of his tone poem *Don Juan* at his second.[46] Composed with a virtuoso orchestra in mind, *Don Juan* tested the local Hofkapelle to its limits. Nevertheless, he was able to report to his parents on 8 November 1889 'Yesterday, I directed the first (part proof-reading) rehearsal of "Don Juan". . . . even though it is terribly difficult, everything sounded splendid and came across magnificently. I really felt sorry for the poor horns and trumpets. They blew themselves completely blue . . . it's fortunate that the piece is short. . . . the oboe's passage in G major, with the double-basses divided into four parts, sounded especially beautiful. The divided cellos and violas, who play with mutes, along with the horns, who also play with mutes, sounded absolutely magical.'[47] While the rehearsal on 9 November proved no less challenging for the orchestra, Strauss remained optimistic and was able to inform his parents: 'Yesterday's two-hour rehearsal of "Don Juan" went off splendidly; the piece sounded wonderful; Lassen was visibly moved. He felt that a work such as this will not be written again for another ten years. The orchestra puffed and gasped for breath but, nonetheless, did a wonderful job. A marvellous joke! After "Don Juan" one of the horn players, who was dripping with sweat and completely out of breath, asked: "Dear God, in what way have we sinned so as to cause you to send this scourge!" . . . We laughed till we cried.'[48] The orchestra's good will continued to the first performance on 11 November 1889 and Strauss was able to write that '"Don Juan" was a great success. The piece sounded enchanting and went wonderfully. For Weimar, it unleashed an unprecedented storm of applause.'[49]

With the success of *Don Juan*, Strauss took his first steps towards becoming the 'Leader of the Moderns', an appellation that he later disliked with intensity.[50] Nevertheless, his triumph with the tone poem meant that Bronsart and Lassen allowed him to perform his newly composed works at the Abonnement Concerts on a regular basis. Of the sixteen subscription and two pension fund concerts that he conducted, eight included a work or works by him. Along with performances of Lieder and the première of *Don Juan*,[51] Strauss conducted the first performances of his tone poems *Macbeth* (first version) and *Tod und*

Verklärung on 13 October 1890 and 12 January 1891 respectively, a second reading of *Don Juan* on 11 January 1892 and a performance of his symphonic fantasy, *Aus Italien*, on 4 December 1893. As the darling of the avant-garde, Strauss also worked actively on the behalf of other contemporary composers at Weimar, and although Bronsart was concerned that Strauss's first season was dominated by the music of Wagner, Liszt and Berlioz, he largely supported Strauss's interest in new music and allowed him to include recent works by his Weimar colleagues Eduard Lassen, Bernhard Stavenhagen and Karl Halir, his friends Alexander Ritter, Ludwig Thuille and Engelbert Humperdinck, his mentor Hans von Bülow and other living composers such as Max Bruch, Camille Saint-Saëns, Josef Weiss, Johannes Brahms and Felix Draeseke at the subscription and non-subscription concerts throughout his tenure.[52]

Although Strauss's concerts with the Hofkapelle did much to increase his public profile, his principal duty at Weimar was conducting operas at the Hoftheater. There, he gave 199 operatic performances between 22 September 1889 and 1 June 1894.[53] The red threads that ran through that fabric of performances were the operas of Mozart and Wagner. Of the former he gave thirty-three performances, while of the latter he directed fifty-two. Unsurprisingly, and in keeping with contemporary trends, his Mozart repertoire centred on *Don Giovanni, Le nozze di Figaro and Die Zauberflöte*. An exception, however, was *Bastien und Bastienne*, which was performed in a double bill with *Hänsel und Gretel* in the 1893–4 season.[54] Strauss did not perform *Così fan tutte* at Weimar, its absence having more to do with the regard in which it was held by musicians and the public in general than with Strauss in particular. Strauss's Wagner repertoire was also limited at the Grand Duchy because of his place in the conducting hierarchy. But he was allocated *Tannhäuser, Lohengrin, Rienzi* and *Die Meistersinger von Nürnberg* and created a local sensation when he challenged contemporary trends by conducting *Tristan und Isolde* without cuts.

Having made his Weimar début with *Die Zauberflöte* on 22 September 1889, Strauss then conducted fifty-four operatic performances of sixteen operas by nine composers during his first season.[55] Of those, only works by Méhul and Auber were not from the emerging Austro-German tradition. In contrast to the often tedious repertoire that he conducted at Munich, most of the operas that Strauss was allocated at Weimar were more substantial musically and more challenging technically. Keen to demonstrate his versatility and eager to underline his allegiance to new German music, he conducted Ritter's two one-act operas

Wem die Kron? and *Der faule Hans* in a double bill in June 1890.[56] A fiercely loyal musician, Strauss valued Ritter's ability and friendship highly and repaid his interest and help by giving a further five performances of *Wem die Kron?* and *Der faule Hans* during his Weimar tenure.[57] Strauss's first season at the Grand Duchy also saw him take his first steps as a Wagnerian, with performances of *Lohengrin* and *Tannhäuser*, works that he conducted annually at Weimar.[58] While operas by Mozart, Weber and Wagner accounted for nearly half of Strauss's operatic output during his first season, eighteen of the fifty-four performances that he gave were of operas and operettas by popular composers such as Lortzing, Marschner and Flotow.

The repertoire that Strauss conducted during his second and third seasons at Weimar was similar to that of his first. In 1890–1, he conducted forty-four performances of fifteen operas by nine composers, and in 1891–2 he conducted fifty performances of nineteen operas by ten composers.[59] The only works that were new to his Weimar repertoire during his second and third seasons were Wagner's *Rienzi* and *Tristan und Isolde*, Gluck's *Iphigénie en Aulide*, Kreutzer's *Das Nachtlager in Granada*, Auber's *La Muette de Portici*, Mozart's *Die Entführung aus dem Serail*, Beethoven's *Fidelio*, Cherubini's *Les Deux Journées* and Sommer's *Loreley*. Sensibly, Bronsart allowed Strauss to add only four operas in his second season and five in his third to his schedule, ensuring that the young conductor establish his personal repertoire in a systematic manner. As in his first season, the overwhelming majority of the works performed were finding their place in the Austro-German canon and the only operas not from that tradition were *Les Deux Journées* and *La Muette de Portici*, a work that was new to Strauss.

Having suffered a bout of pneumonia in 1891, Strauss was prone to infection and, in June 1892, had to abandon work for a period because of an attack of pleurisy. He resumed his duties briefly that autumn and conducted *Das Nachtlager in Granada* on 20 September and *Der Freischütz* on 27 October, but his health remained fragile and he was given leave to convalesce for the remainder of that season.[60] After returning to Weimar in the autumn of 1893, he began a busy period that included forty-nine performances of seventeen operas by ten composers.[61] As in previous years, the majority of the operas that he performed were already in his repertoire. He did, however, tackle seven operas that he had not conducted previously: Mozart's *Bastien und Bastienne*, Metzdorff's *Hagbart und Signe*, Wagner's *Die Meistersinger von Nürnberg*, Humperdinck's *Hänsel und Gretel*, Mottl's *Fürst und*

Sänger, Fiebach's *Bei frommen Hirten* and his own *Guntram*. Of those seven operas, four – *Hagbart und Signe*, *Hänsel und Gretel*, *Fürst und Sänger* and *Guntram* – were world premières. While the first performance of *Hänsel und Gretel* was probably of greatest importance historically, the première of Strauss's moribund first opera, *Guntram*, was most significant personally.[62]

In the spring of 1893, Strauss was headhunted by the Munich Hofoper. As Levi's health was failing, the theatre needed a dynamic young musician who could work alongside with him and absorb some of his duties. As a native of Munich and a former member of the Hofoper's music staff, Strauss seemed the logical choice. Levi approached Strauss's father in March 1893 and enquired whether his son's health would permit such an appointment and whether Richard could free himself from Weimar.[63] If so, he would be employed in Munich as Levi's peer and would have complete freedom in all matters artistic. While he had been given scope by Bronsart and Lassen to explore his interests at Weimar, Strauss was still a relatively junior member of the music staff there and was allocated operas that Lassen was either unwilling or unprepared to conduct. Under the conditions offered by Levi, Strauss would be able to programme freely, engage singers of his choice and work with an orchestra of the front rank. Moreover, as a senior conductor at one of Central Europe's premier theatres, his profile would increase internationally and the chance to promote his own works would improve substantially. With little reason to stay in Weimar, Strauss decided to accept the Munich offer, and he began work there at the beginning of the 1894–5 season.

As in Weimar, Strauss made his début as Kapellmeister with *Die Zauberflöte*. That reading was the first of 272 performances of thirty-five works by twenty-four composers that he conducted at the Hofoper between 7 October 1894 and 18 October 1898.[64] Unafraid of new challenges, Strauss continued to add works to his repertoire throughout his second Munich period and, of the operas performed, eighteen of the thirty-five had not been conducted previously by him. As a champion of the moderns, he continued to challenge audiences with new works, including the world premières of Thuille's *Theuerdank* and Hausegger's *Zinnober* on 12 March 1897 and 19 June 1898 respectively. Eager to introduce his *Guntram* to his fellow Müncheners, Strauss conducted the work at the Hofoper on 16 November 1895. In contrast to its reception at Weimar, *Guntram* provoked hostility from the start at Munich, causing the singers to rebel, the orchestra to demand to be freed of 'this scourge of God [Gottesgeißel]',[65] the critics to take a hostile stance and

Wagner's family to consider the opera a betrayal of the Master's principles.[66] *Guntram* never recovered fully from the blow that it received at
Munich and has remained on the periphery of the operatic repertoire
since that time.

Strauss consolidated his reputation as a Mozart and Wagner interpreter during his second Munich period by directing ninety-eight operatic performances of the former and eighty-five of the latter. Although
he had been a passionate advocate of those works from near the beginning of his operatic career, his senior position at Munich meant that he
was able to explore them more fully. With the producer Ernst von
Possart,[67] Strauss established in 1895 an annual series of Mozart and
Wagner performances that began each August and continued until
either the following autumn or winter. At the first of those discrete seasons, Possart and Strauss mounted thirteen performances of *Rienzi*,
Tannhäuser, *Tristan und Isolde* and *Die Meistersinger von Nürnberg*.
Those operas then formed the bases for the following three summer sea-
sons, during which twenty-nine further performances of operas by
Wagner were heard.[68]

When Strauss was promoted to the post of Hofkapellmeister on the
retirement of Levi in 1896, the content of the summer seasons was
extended to include operas by Mozart. That year, Strauss and Possart
staged a highly acclaimed new production of *Don Giovanni*, which was
followed by new productions of *Die Entführung aus dem Serail*, *Così
fan tutte* and *Die Zauberflöte* during the summers of 1897 and 1898.[69]
Those readings were influential in reawakening the interest of the public and the musical world in the operas of Mozart, with Munich soon
being recognized as a centre of Mozartian excellence.[70] When staging
those works, Strauss and Possart introduced a series of theatrical and
musical innovations that have since been called the 'Munich Reforms'.[71]
At the Residenztheater, Munich's ornate rococo theatre, they used an
orchestra of twenty-six, sets and costumes characteristic of the eighteenth century, Hermann Levi's revised translations of the libretti,
orchestral and vocal material based on Mozart's autographs, a revolving stage for the first time, the Prague version of *Don Giovanni*[72] and a
fortepiano for the recitatives, played by Strauss, who acted as both conductor and continuo player.[73] In later years, Strauss looked back on
those performances with affection and in 1928 he wrote that the
'Mozart Festivals, which I inaugurated together with Possart . . . stand
out among the truly wonderful memories of my life'.[74]

During his second Munich period, Strauss was also active as an
orchestral conductor and accepted the direction of the subscription con-

certs of both the Berlin Philharmonic and the Munich Hofkapelle in 1894. With the death of Hans von Bülow earlier that year, Hermann Wolff needed a conductor to lead the prestigious Philharmonic Concerts in Berlin. As Strauss had been Bülow's protégé and one of the most discussed musicians of the 1890s, he seemed the obvious choice for the job. With programmes that were catholic and pan-European, Strauss offered Berlin audiences a well-balanced series of concerts that regularly juxtaposed the new with the familiar. Central to his Berlin repertoire were the works of Beethoven, with seven of the ten concerts containing a work by him.[75] Modern music was also a regular feature of Strauss's concerts in the German capital, and he continued to signal his interest in the compositions of his contemporaries by including works by Saint-Saëns, Schillings, Rubinstein, d'Albert, Ritter, Gernsheim, Stenhammar, Sauret and Mahler.[76] Curiously, Strauss's orchestral works were not included in his Berlin programmes, with only extracts from *Guntram* being heard at his last Philharmonic Concert on 18 March 1895.[77] Although Wolff had allowed Strauss the opportunity to present interesting and colourful programmes in Berlin, his season with the Berlin Philharmonic was far from successful. Unable to fill Bülow's shoes, Strauss was not invited to return the following year and was replaced by the charismatic Hungarian Arthur Nikisch.[78]

Commuting between Prussia and Bavaria for much of the 1894–5 season, Strauss conducted the first of eight subscription concerts that year with the Munich Hofkapelle on 16 November 1894.[79] For practical reasons, some of the works that he performed in Berlin were also heard in Munich.[80] In general, however, the content and character of Strauss's concerts with the Hofkapelle were different from those that he directed with the Berlin Philharmonic. That said, he was no less demanding of the Munich public than he was of the Berlin audience, with six of his eight concerts containing a work by a contemporary composer.[81] While Strauss continued to programme new music with the Hofkapelle during the 1895–6 season,[82] the symphonies of Beethoven dominated his second year with the orchestra and, during that period, he gave his first cycle of those works, which he conducted in numerical order.[83] But as in Berlin, he failed to convince fully as an orchestral conductor, and after his second season as director of the Hofkapelle's Abonnement Concerts, he restricted his activities in Munich to the opera pit.

Although Strauss's success in the concert hall was conditional, his ability as an opera conductor was never in doubt and, in 1898, he was appointed Hofkapellmeister at the Berlin Hofoper. Understandably, Strauss wanted to incorporate the new theatrical techniques that he had pioneered in Munich into the Berlin theatre's productions, but his reforms were slow to be accepted. Nevertheless, the Prussian capital was soon alive with talk of Strauss's interpretations of Mozart and, in particular, his playing of the harpsichord for the accompaniment of the recitatives. Having made an immediate impact with his readings of Mozart and Wagner,[84] Strauss was able to pursue his interest in their operas and, of the 959 operatic performances that he directed at the Hofoper as either a tenured or a guest conductor between 1 November 1898 and 1 July 1939,[85] 131 were of Mozart and 253 were of Wagner.[86]

As Hofkapellmeister, Strauss was able to perform his operas on a regular basis. Previously, he had given five performances only of his opera *Guntram*.[87] While the opposition that the work met at Munich was an irritant that never fully left Strauss,[88] the extraordinary success of *Salome*, *Elektra* and *Der Rosenkavalier* meant that he was now Germany's leading operatic composer. Even though Kaiser Wilhelm II, to whom the Hofoper's music staff and administrators were directly answerable, was not an admirer of Strauss's music, the immense popularity of those works ensured their permanent place in the theatre's repertoire and it was with some satisfaction that the composer gave 200 performances of his operas there between 1902 and 1939.

After being promoted to Generalmusikdirektor in 1908, Strauss took charge of the Berlin Hofkapelle's subscription concerts.[89] Between 1908 and 1935, a period that includes his activities both as a staff and as a guest conductor, Strauss directed 130 concerts with the orchestra.[90] Although his repertoire was large, thirty-three concerts contained a work, or works, by him. It was the music of Beethoven and Mozart, however, that dominated his Hofkapelle programmes, with 116 of his concerts containing a work by the former and twenty-nine by the latter. Strauss also championed the cause of contemporary composers during his tenure with the orchestra by performing Mahler's Symphonies Nos. 1 ('Titan') to 4 and *Das Lied von der Erde* and the world premières of at least seventeen works by fourteen composers.[91] Some modern commentators have understated Strauss's interest in the music of his contemporaries and have accused him of being concerned solely with the promotion of his own compositions, but when his activities with the Berlin Tonkünstler-Orchester, an ensemble that he directed for two seasons between October 1901 and April 1903, and his work with the Berlin Hofkapelle are considered fully, that notion can be dismissed easily.[92]

Between 1919 and 1924, Strauss was Leiter (Director) of the Vienna Staatsoper, a post that he shared with the infamous Brucknerian Franz

Schalk.[93] Vienna had a special place in Strauss's affections. When the opportunity arose for him to occupy a titular post at what was then, and arguably still is, Europe's most prestigious opera house, the temptation to accept was overwhelming. In his correspondence with his operatic collaborator Hugo von Hofmannsthal, the question of his appointment was considered at length. Hofmannsthal advised Strauss that he was not the right man for the job, even though he 'would add outward lustre to the Opera'.[94] Specifically, the librettist was concerned that Strauss 'would put [his] own personal convenience, and above all the egoism of the creative musician, before the uphill struggle for the ultimate higher welfare of [the Staatsoper]'.[95] In response, Strauss accepted Hofmannsthal's objections and recognized that he 'neither could, nor would want to, accept this post today in the way Mahler filled it[,] [as] [t]hat would [only] have been possible fifteen or twenty years ago'.[96] Even so, he 'could well imagine' himself participating in 'the necessary new engagements of singers and young conductors' and 'the reorganisation and rejuvenation of the magnificent orchestra'.[97] Further, he argued 'Since I am generally regarded as a very good Mozartian and Wagnerian conductor, the works of these masters (in addition to Gluck and Weber) would be the first to be chosen for revival.'[98]

From the statistical evidence, it seems that Hofmannsthal's concerns were realized partially. Of the 187 operatic performances given by Strauss in Vienna between 1919 and 1924, six were of Weber, twelve were of Beethoven, thirty-five were of Mozart, forty-three were of Wagner and seventy-one were of Strauss. Because of these statistics, the composer-conductor was attacked from all sides. The press, who considered Strauss a foreigner, argued that he was often absent from Vienna and, when in attendance, was only interested in the performance of his own compositions. With the new republic replacing the Austrian Emperor as the driving force behind the Staatsoper, Schalk, who was responsible for the day-to-day running of the theatre, encountered trouble with both the unions and the workers' councils. For some, it seemed that Schalk shouldered the burden of responsibility, while Strauss basked in the glory. As the acrimony between the two Directors increased, politicians and civil servants were drawn into the dispute. By 1924, the crisis had reached its peak and, after unsuccessfully demanding Schalk's dismissal, Strauss resigned. Although his period as joint Director of the Staatsoper ended unhappily, he returned regularly in later years and his love of Vienna remained with him for the rest of his life.

Strauss was one of the first major composer-conductors to exploit the new medium of sound recording. Like many of his contemporaries, he was not totally convinced by the crude sound that early recordings produced. Even so, they provided a means by which to document and disseminate his methods, both as a creative and as an executant musician. It has been argued that Strauss undertook many of his recordings solely for financial gain. To a professional musician, the notion of profiting from art was not, and is not, unknown, but to suggest that money alone was his motivating force is naïve. From the works recorded in the early twentieth century, it is clear that such companies as Deutsche Grammophon were keen to document music that was both popular and profitable. As Strauss's tone poems were heard regularly in the concert hall and could be marketed easily, they were an attractive prospect for the fast-growing record industry. Moreover, as Strauss was a well-known interpreter of music by Mozart, Beethoven and Wagner, he was also the obvious choice to document works by those composers.

Performing on the popular medium of the piano-roll, Strauss made his recording début in 1905 with selections from *Salome* and *Feuersnot*, the love scene from *Ein Heldenleben* and four of his Lieder specially arranged for solo piano. The rolls were designed to be played on a reproducing piano and were recorded by Welte at the company's Freiburg studios. A publicity photo, released by the firm at the time of the recording, shows Strauss at the piano with the score of *Salome* in front of him and surrounded by members of the recording company. As the opera received its first performance the same year,[99] it is probable that the roll acted as a form of advance publicity. Nine years later, in 1914, Strauss recorded rolls of excerpts from the 1912 version of *Ariadne auf Naxos*, the love scene from *Ein Heldenleben* and an extract from his moribund ballet, *Josephslegende*, for Hupfeld. Unlike the Welte rolls, those for Hupfeld were made for the mass market and were designed to be played on ordinary player pianos.[100]

Strauss's first orchestral recordings were made for Deutsche Grammophon in 1916 with the Berlin Hofkapelle.[101] The works that he documented included *Don Juan*, *Till Eulenspiegel* and the suite from *Der Bürger als Edelmann*. The *Don Juan* recording had a particularly curious genesis because it involved not only Strauss but also his then assistant, George Szell. The exact extent of Szell's involvement in the recording remained unclear for decades and was made more confusing by an article in *The Gramophone* that stated:

> the recording of Strauss' *Don Juan* issued in either 1916 or 1917 and labelled as the work of the composer was in fact conducted by his young assistant. The great man had this session, and being busy had

asked young Szell to go down to the studios and prepare the orchestra and generally to make ready, which included the cutting of the music on to four sides. When all was prepared and there was still no sign of Strauss the recording director instructed Szell to take the session, since he was not prepared to waste his company's money. After much protest the young man launched the orchestra into the greatest manifestation of a young man ever written. After completing the third side he saw Strauss standing in the doorway in his overcoat, his face wreathed in smiles. Both he and the director were delighted with the way things were going 'and that is how my first records appeared under the name of Dr Richard Strauss'.[102]

Aware that the article in *The Gramophone* was misleading, Szell soon set the record straight by writing: 'I very definitely remember having conducted only sides 1 and 2 of that 1917 recording of "Don Juan" which came out under the name of Richard Strauss. He himself did sides 3 and 4. If *The Gramophone* writes that Strauss was in the recording studio at the end of side 3, it may be a misprint or a mistake. I very clearly remember that he had arrived when I was approaching the end of side 2.'[103]

In retrospect, it seems strange that Deutsche Grammophon should undertake a series of recordings during the last years of World War I, but when they are considered within the parameters of Berlin's concert life as a whole, their function is clear. Strauss and the Berlin Hofoper continued to present a full programme throughout the hostilities, with German audiences increasing during the war years and most forms of professional music-making being sought out by the general public. Although resources were scarce and only a few new productions could be mounted, people attended concerts and opera in unprecedented numbers, hoping perhaps to forget the rigours of their day-to-day existence. The new medium of sound recording also attracted the public's interest, and while gramophone records were too expensive for the average working-class German, they provided a further means of escape for the middle class and above. As Strauss's music was a regular feature of concert life in the German capital, and was considered by many to be the quintessence of German art, Deutsche Grammophon's decision to record these works at that time seems logical.

During his 1921–2 tour of the USA, Strauss recorded the dance from *Salome* and the Menuett and Intermezzo from *Der Bürger als Edelmann* with what was probably the Chicago Symphony Orchestra.[104] En route back to Germany, he gave four concerts in England, among which was a performance with the London Symphony Orchestra at the Royal Albert Hall on 17 January 1922. Although the programme included some of Strauss's more popular works and was his first visit to Britain after World War I,[105] the concert was poorly attended and the stalls remained half empty.[106] As Strauss was one of the first major German artists to visit Britain after the war, anti-German feeling, along with a programme that had become too familiar, dissuaded the public from attending. At least one critic was disappointed that the composer-conductor felt either unwilling or unable to perform any of his more recent works, such as *Eine Alpensinfonie*. But the inclusion of his latest tone poem in the concert would have needed considerable preparation and, as he was recording *Don Juan* for Columbia the following day, he organized the allocated time in favour of this early work. The 1922 recording of *Don Juan* is not totally representative of the previous day's concert, however, because it has a cut and various orchestral voices are doubled for clarity.[107] While those modifications were made so that the music could fit on to four sides of a 78–rpm gramophone set and to compensate for the aural shortcomings of the acoustic recording process, they are not typical of Strauss, who reverted to the original text when recording *Don Juan* electrically later in his career.

On arrival in London in 1922, Strauss was interviewed by *The Times*'s 'Special Correspondent', and was invited to comment upon the concept of accompanying 'cinematograph films with good music'. The interviewer asked Strauss whether he 'had ever considered the possibility of writing original music to accompany films'. The composer 'replied emphatically that he had never entertained such an idea, and declared that good music was quite able to stand on its own, without the adventitious help of the film producer'.[108] It is ironic that Strauss's next visit to London, in 1926, involved a performance, followed by a recording, of his specially adapted music for the film version of *Der Rosenkavalier*.[109] At first, Strauss was a reluctant participant in the project, but the librettist, Hugo von Hofmannsthal, convinced him of its potential and enticed him with the prospect of a large fee. The original music was rearranged substantially by the conductors Karl Alwin and Otto Singer and the première was given at the Dresden Staatsoper on 10 January 1926. Strauss then conducted a further performance at the Tivoli Theatre in London on 12 April 1926,[110] which the 'audience applauded enthusiastically' but which divided the critics sharply. Nevertheless, His Master's Voice records believed that the music had some commercial value and recorded excerpts from the score at the Queen's Hall on 13 and 14 April 1926.

Strauss's next series of recordings were made with the Berlin Staatskapelle and the Berlin Philharmonic. As he was one of the leading composers of the day, the greater body of Strauss's studio time was devoted to his own music. Fortunately, however, Deutsche Grammophon also recognized the importance of securing some of his interpretations of Mozart, Beethoven and Wagner. Of particular significance are his commercial recordings of Mozart's last three symphonies and the overture to *Die Zauberflöte*, which he made with the Berlin Staatskapelle between 1926 and 1928. Strauss was the first conductor to document Mozart's last three symphonies as a unit and those recordings, along with his discs of Beethoven's Symphonies Nos. 5 and 7,[111] were the only major symphonic recordings that he made of a composer other than himself. Strauss also documented Wagner's overture to *Der fliegende Holländer* and the Prelude to Act 1 of *Tristan und Isolde*, Weber's overture to *Euryanthe*, Gluck's overture to *Iphigénie en Aulide* (ed. R. Wagner) and Cornelius's overture to *Der Barbier von Bagdad* with the Berlin Philharmonic for Deutsche Grammophon in 1928. Those works, like the Mozart and Beethoven symphonies, were performed regularly by Strauss and his recordings of them provide a valuable insight into his interpretative process.

In 1929 and 1930, Strauss returned to the studio to record *Don Juan*, *Till Eulenspiegel* and *Der Bürger als Edelmann* with the Berlin Staatskapelle.[112] By the time of these sessions, Strauss had completed all his major tone poems but had made recordings only of *Don Juan*, *Till Eulenspiegel*, *Ein Heldenleben* and *Tod und Verklärung*.[113] The lack of interest shown by both composer and record industry in documenting works such as *Don Quixote*, *Symphonia domestica* and *Eine Alpensinfonie* during the 1920s is a conundrum. Although the public's interest in these tone poems had not diminished and the Berlin orchestra's expertise in realizing Strauss's intentions was not in question, Strauss failed to record them until the 1930s and the 1940s. It is possible that the record companies felt that the works were not viable commercially because of their length and complexity, but neither their length nor their complexity was substantially greater than that of *Ein Heldenleben* and the reason for their absence from Strauss's early discography remains a mystery.

Strauss conducted a revival of his performing version of Mozart's *Idomeneo* at the Vienna Staatsoper on 3 December 1941.[114] As this version contains new material specially composed by Strauss, his amendments, additions and revisions to the work stand in sharp contrast to his interpretations of Mozart's late operas. Although no commercial recording of the version exists with Strauss conducting, a member of the Staatsoper's staff, one Herr May, did make a private recording of the 1941 performance.[115] As May's machine was positioned behind the stage and was not designed for professional use, the stylus also recorded ambient theatre noise. Nonetheless, the incomplete recordings allow modern listeners an opportunity to hear Strauss conduct some of Mozart's operatic music and excerpts from his interpolations that are no longer common fare. May also documented four performances of *Salome* that Strauss conducted at the Vienna Staatsoper towards the end of the 1941–42 season.[116] As the role of Jochanaan was shared by Paul Schöffler and Hans Hotter that year,[117] May's recording is not only a valuable addition to Strauss's discography but an interesting insight into the way in which the composer-conductor responded to different singers performing the same role in the same season.

Vienna celebrated Strauss's eightieth birthday in June 1944 by mounting his important operas at the Staatsoper and a series of concerts and radio recordings with the Philharmonic.[118] Although the composer-conductor's association with the city began with the première of his Violin Concerto on 5 December 1882,[119] his début with the Vienna Philharmonic was delayed until 17 August 1906, when he deputized at short notice for an indisposed Karl Muck at Salzburg. As the performance was a success, he was invited to conduct four of the orchestra's subscription concerts at the Musikvereinsaal over the next two years.[120] He continued to work with the Philharmonic for a further forty years' and the 1944 radio recordings reflect the mutual understanding that had developed between them during that period.[121] The works that he recorded for Austrian Radio included *Also sprach Zarathustra*, the suite from *Der Bürger als Edelmann*, *Don Juan*, *Ein Heldenleben*, *Till Eulenspiegel*, *Tod und Verklärung* and Wagner's Prelude to *Die Meistersinger von Nürnberg*. Of these, only the Wagner Prelude had not been recorded previously by Strauss.

Like the 1917 recordings, those from 1944 had a wider social significance. The exact nature of Strauss's activities during the Third Reich has been a source of interest to historians and musicologists alike. Given his association with his librettist Stefan Zweig, along with his concern for the well-being of the Jewish members of his family throughout this period,[122] the hostile stance of some commentators seems difficult to justify. His letter to Zweig, written on 17 June 1935, with its characteristically blunt and sarcastic tone, sets out Strauss's feelings:

Dear Herr Zweig,
Your letter of the 15th is driving me to distraction! This Jewish obstinacy! Enough to make an anti-Semite of a man! This pride of race, this feeling of solidarity! Do you believe that I am ever, in any of my actions, guided by the thought that I am 'German' (perhaps, *qui le sait*)? Do you believe that Mozart composed as an 'Aryan'? I know only two types of people: those with and those without talent. 'Das Volk' exists for me only at the moment it becomes an audience. Whether they are Chinese, Bavarians, New Zealanders, or Berliners leaves me cold. What matters is that they pay full price for admission. . . . The comedy you sent me is charming. . . . I won't accept it under an assumed name. . . . Just keep the matter a secret on *your* part and let *me* worry about what I will do with the plays. Who told you that I have exposed myself politically? Because I have conducted a concert in place of that greasy rascal Bruno Walter? That I did for the orchestra's sake. Because I substituted for that other 'non-Aryan' Toscanini? That I did for the sake of Bayreuth. That has nothing to do with politics. It is none of my business how the gutter press interprets what I do, and it should not concern you either. Because I act the part of president of the Reich Music Chamber?[123] That I do only for good purposes and to prevent greater disasters! I would have accepted this troublesome honorary office under any government, but neither Kaiser Wilhelm nor Herr Rathenau offered it to me. . . . The show [*Die schweigsame Frau*] here will be terrific. Everybody is wildly enthusiastic. And with all this you ask me to forgo you? Never ever![124]

The letter was intercepted by the Gestapo and, because of Strauss's attitude, the Nazis actively set out to damage his credibility from 1935. Relations between composer and administration reached their lowest point in 1944, when on 24 January, six months before the composer's eightieth birthday celebrations, Martin Bormann announced:

The personal association of our leading men with Dr Strauss shall end. However, the Führer, to whom Reichsminister Dr Goebbels has referred the matter, has decided that the performance of his works should not be hindered.[125]

Although Strauss's works continued to be played, his inability to associate with some senior colleagues caused him concern. Even so, the Vienna Philharmonic was largely unaffected by the ban and fellow musicians continued to support him throughout this difficult period. Hitler's decision not to prohibit Strauss's music was shrewd, because the German authorities had become increasingly concerned by the decline in public morale. As Strauss was considered by many to be Germany's leading musician, the administration's decision to record these works for broadcast throughout the Reich supported the increasingly shaky illusion of social and artistic normality. More important, the 1943–4 recordings provide the modern listener with a means by which to compare and to contrast Strauss's evolving performing style over a period of some forty years.

No discussion of Strauss's activities as a conductor would be complete without mentioning his controversial podium manner. His critics have suggested that his economical method signalled a lack of interest in the music that he was performing, a notion that can be dismissed as naïve.[126] As a young conductor, his approach to stick technique differed sharply from that of his later years. At Meiningen, his gestures lacked sophistication, prompting his father to write, 'it is unattractive when conductors make such snake-like movements'.[127] Franz continued by suggesting that a conductor's left hand had no other function but to turn pages and, if no score was being used, should remain still. Because the advice of the battle-weary orchestral player whose war against podium incompetence was fought over a period of forty years had merit, Richard adopted the suggestions and modified his technique accordingly. His restrained approach then became a feature of his podium style and, in later life, he argued that:

> The left hand has nothing to do with conducting. Its proper place is the waistcoat pocket from which it should only emerge to restrain or to make some minor gesture for which in any case a scarcely perceptible glance would suffice. It is better to conduct with the ear instead of with the arm: the rest follows automatically.[128]

Strauss used a long, thin, tapered baton, believing that shorter movements of the arm, with a greater emphasis on the wrist, ensured the players' complete attention.[129] He also emphasized the need for the conductor to prepare the music with a decisive upbeat, followed by an 'extremely precise' downbeat. For Strauss, 'the second half of the bar [was] immaterial' because he 'frequently conduct[ed] it like an *alla breve*'.[130] Along with a judicious use of the eye, these techniques, wittily summarized in his tongue-in-cheek *Ten Golden Rules*, were the fundamental elements of Strauss's podium style:

Ten Golden Rules

For the Album of a Young Conductor[131]

1. Remember that you are making music not to amuse yourself but to delight your audience.
2. You should not perspire when conducting: only the audience should get warm.
3. Conduct 'Salome', and 'Elektra' as if they were by Mendelssohn: Fairy Music.
4. Never look encouragingly at the brass, except with a short glance to give an important cue.
5. But never let the horns and woodwind out of your sight: if you can hear them at all they are still too strong.
6. If you think that the brass is not blowing hard enough, tone it down another shade or two.
7. It is not enough that you yourself should hear every word the soloist sings – you know it off by heart anyway: the audience must be able to follow without effort. If they do not understand the words they will go to sleep.
8. Always accompany a singer in such a way that he can sing without effort.
9. When you think you have reached the limits of prestissimo, double the pace.*
10. If you follow these rules carefully you will, with your fine gifts and your great accomplishments, always be the darling of your listeners.

(*ca.* 1922)

* Today (1948) I should like to amend this as follows: Go twice as slowly (addressed to the conductors of Mozart!)

Strauss's death on 8 September 1949 ignited a debate that quickly proved divisive. While some lamented his passing as the end of the great Austro-German Romantic school of composition, others considered him no more than an artistic dinosaur whose contribution to music effectively ceased with the première of *Elektra*. Few, however, discussed his achievements as a conductor and the profound effect that his practices and principles had on subsequent generations of performers. His reforms at Munich during the 1890s influenced the Mozart styles of Fritz Busch, George Szell, Herbert von Karajan, Sir John Pritchard and

Wolfgang Sawallisch, his restrained podium style was adopted famously by the Hungarian-born conductor Fritz Reiner, and his advocacy of new music helped secure a place in the repertoire for some works that might otherwise have been overlooked. It is clear then that Strauss's achievements as a conductor were legion. The question must be asked, therefore, why have his activities as a performer failed to inspire serious research until relatively recently?[132] The answer of course lies in his phenomenal success as a composer. But to ignore his work as an executant artist is a mistake, because Strauss was proud of his achievements as a conductor and used his rich and varied experiences on the podium to inform his work as a creative musician.

CHAPTER 6

'That greasy rascal Bruno Walter'[1]

Bruno Walter is remembered primarily as a musician of great humanity. His *Weltanschauung* was the product of a turbulent life during which he endured not only the murder of his daughter and but also the distress of exile.[2] Having risen to prominence in the immediate post-World War I period, he suffered the privations of hyperinflation and the venom of Munich's anti-Semitic press. In the 1930s, he was displaced twice because of the Nazis and eventually had to move continents before finding peace in America. Although a passionate advocate of new music and a renowned interpreter of the Austro-German canon, he was eager to be considered a composer of talent. But when it was clear that he was unable to convince fully as a creative musician, he worked solely as an executant. Despite his failure as a composer, he acted tirelessly on behalf of others and ensured that their works were given under the best conditions possible. He associated closely with many of the leading composers of the late nineteenth and early twentieth centuries and developed a particularly deep relationship with Gustav Mahler. Walter was proud to have Mahler as his mentor and friend and honoured those bonds by championing the composer's music throughout his career.

A product of the lower-middle class, Bruno Walter was born Bruno Schlesinger in Berlin on 15 September 1876[3]. The second of three children to Joseph and Johanna Schlesinger, Bruno was a member of a 'modest Jewish family'[4] who considered the arts important and domestic music-making a regular feature of daily life.[5] The passion that his parents had for music was also evident in their three children. Bruno was the most talented of their progeny and, after initial piano lessons with his mother, he was taught by Konrad Kaiser. So rapid was his progress that Kaiser felt his abilities warranted further investigation. He soon suggested, therefore, that Walter be taken to Robert Radecke, a director of the Stern Conservatory, for tests to discover the true extent of his talents. Radecke assessed Walter for pitch recognition, sight-reading and improvising and had him perform prepared piano works that included a movement from a sonata by Mozart and two *Songs Without Words* by Mendelssohn. To the delight of Joseph and Johanna, it was established that their son had perfect pitch, was a musician of outstanding potential and was to be admitted to the Stern Conservatory at the age of eight.[6]

At the Conservatory, Walter studied piano with the conductor and former assistant to Hans von Bülow, Franz Manstädt, and theory with Ludwig Bussler. His piano studies progressed quickly and he was soon admitted to the class of the distinguished pianist, critic and music historian Heinrich Ehrlich. Ehrlich's influence was profound and, while still his pupil, Walter performed the first movement of Beethoven's Piano Concerto No. 2 at a student concert with the Berlin Philharmonic on 15 March 1889.[7] Encouraged by the success of the performance, Ehrlich made plans for Walter's official début and arranged for him to play for the impresario and agent Hermann Wolff. After performing Schumann's *Kreisleriana* for him, Walter was invited to play Moscheles's Concerto in E flat major with the Berlin Philharmonic on 12 February 1890.[8] Although the reviews of the performance were good, Walter remained unfulfilled; he was passionate about composition and aspired to be both a creative and a recreative artist. Having written his first work (a duo for violin and piano) at the age of nine, Walter began composition lessons with Radecke at thirteen and, although he later dismissed his activities as a composer, arguing that he was not gifted creatively, composition was important to him during his youth and early career.[9] Also of importance to him during his student years was Jenny Meyer, a director of the Stern Conservatory and a leading singing teacher. Walter acted as an accompanist at her classes and it was at these that he began to learn and to develop his interest in vocal music.

Formal studies are rarely fully satisfing for aspiring artists . In Vienna, Nikisch supplemented his lessons by attending performances conducted by Wagner, while, in Leipzig, the young Weingartner drew inspiration from performances given by Nikisch and Seidl at the Stadttheater. Walter also used his local opera houses educationally and attended performances of works by Lortzing, Mozart, Rossini and Verdi at the Kroll Theatre and the Hofoper.[10] Although impressed by opera, absolute music interested the young Walter more, and he soon became a regular member of the audience at Gustav Kogel's popular concerts with Berlin Philharmonic. But it was the orchestra's subscription concerts conducted by Hans von Bülow that made the greatest impression on Walter, who recalled in later life:

> seat[ed] high up on the platform behind the kettledrums, I heard and saw Hans von Bülow conduct the Philharmonic Orchestra in a classic programme. At the popular Philharmonic concerts under Kogel as well as at the operatic performances I had witnessed, I had paid hardly any attention to the conductor. Now, however, I saw in Bülow's face the glow of inspiration and the concentration of energy. I felt the compelling force of his gestures, noticed the attention and devotion of the players, and was conscious of the expressiveness and precision of their playing. . . . That evening decided my future. Now I knew what I was meant for. No musical activity but that of an orchestral conductor could any longer be considered by me. . . . the die had been cast. . . . I had recognized what I had been born for. I had decided to become a conductor.[11]

Walter's life-changing encounter with Bülow was soon followed by another: his first experience of Wagner's *Tristan und Isolde*. As a youth, Walter was discouraged from listening to Wagner's music by his parents, who considered the composer an anti-Semite who used Jewish money to achieve his own ends, and by his professors, who dismissed the composer's stage works as radical and contentious. Nevertheless, Walter wanted to experience Wagner's music personally, so he secretly attended a performance of *Tristan und Isolde* at the Hofoper.[12] Although his sense of expectation was high, he had not foreseen the strength of his reaction:

> Never before had my soul been so deluged with floods of sound and passion, never had my heart been consumed by such yearning and sublime bliss, never had I been transported from reality by such heavenly glory. I was no longer in this world. After the performance, I roamed the streets aimlessly. When I got home I didn't say anything and begged not to be questioned. My ecstasy kept singing within me through half the night, and when I awoke on the following morning I knew that my life was changed. A new epoch had begun: Wagner was my god, and I wanted to become his prophet.[13]

Walter's response to Wagner's sound-world mirrored that of Weingartner, who declared as a student: 'One of the goals I had set myself besides my own creative work was to stand up for Wagner wherever I could.'[14] Like that of Nikisch some twenty years earlier, Walter's thirst for Wagner could be satisfied only by studying his operas secretly. Unable to share his enthusiasm with either his family or his professors, Walter became a frequent visitor at the Royal Library, where he read and digested the composer's scores covertly. His passion for Wagner's music was fuelled further when he received a '*stipendium* entitling [him] to a free trip to Bayreuth and admission to three performances at the Festspielhaus'.[15] There, he visited Wagner's grave and attended performances of *Parsifal* and *Tristan und Isolde* conducted by Hermann Levi and *Der fliegende Holländer* conducted by Felix Mottl.

It was clear to Walter that if he wanted to pursue his passion for Wagner he would have to find a job at an opera house. But with his youth and his lack of experience counting against him, he was unable to secure a post. He decided, therefore, to continue working at the piano, to remain the accompanist of Jenny Meyer's students and to begin conducting lessons with Radecke. As Radecke's pupil, Walter progressed quickly and was soon invited to conduct his *Meerestille und glückliche Fahrt*[16] and to act as soloist in the first movement of Anton Rubinstein's Piano Concerto No. 1 at a student concert with the Berlin Philharmonic on 18 March 1893.[17] To all who attended that concert, it was obvious that Walter's talent was developing at speed and that a professional post needed to be found. Radecke's successor at the Stern Conservatory, Arno Kleffel, formerly a Kapellmeister at the Stadttheater in Cologne, was also impressed by Walter's abilities and soon became his mentor. Kleffel quickly set about championing Walter's cause and used his professional contacts with the Intendant of the Cologne Stadttheater, Julius Hofmann, to secure Walter a post there from September 1893.[18]

Walter travelled to Cologne with his parents at the end of August 1893. He was struck immediately by the architecture of the city and its famous cathedral but was less impressed by the Rhine, which he considered 'serious, efficient, and industrious'.[19] He was impressed, however, by Julius Hofmann, whom he considered a capable administrator and 'a born impresario . . . [with] the gift of discovering talented artists, of placing and bringing out the best in them'.[20] Engaged as a vocal coach, Walter found his duties at Cologne often routine and tedious. Although he had no experience of professional theatre life, he was soon conscious of the poor standard of the music staff and the pall of apathy that hung over the company.[21] Eager not to be drawn into the mire of indifference that surrounded him, Walter decided to attack his work with vigour and to use his post as a means by which to further his education. After completing his day-to-day tasks as a coach, therefore, he regularly took his place in one of the two staff boxes for the evening's performance, where he was able to further his knowledge of the repertoire and to observe his colleagues at work.

Walter's first chances to conduct came with Carl Reinecke's *Von der Wiege bis zum Grabe*, 'a cross between pantomime and ballet',[22] and the incidental music to Johann Nestroy's play *Lumpazivagabundus*, 'a fairy extravaganza'.[23] As neither work was from the front rank, Walter was allowed the chance to gain necessary experience in relative anonymity. The performances were a success and Hofmann then entrusted Walter with a revival of Lortzing's *Der Waffenschmied*. Having prepared meticulously for the performance by coaching the singers personally, Walter took the podium confidently and later recalled: 'My hand knew automatically what to do: it had the ability to hold the orchestra together and keep the soloists and the chorus in harmony with it.'[24] But the critics took a slightly different stance, and although they recognized his undoubted talent they questioned some of his tempi, felt that he gave some unnecessary cues to the singers and thought that he left many of the instrumentalists at the back of the orchestra to fend for themselves.[25] While such criticisms were hardly surprising in view of Walter's inexperience, he was a quick learner, and when he was presented with a change of cast at a subsequent performance at very short notice, he was able to meet the challenge and gain the admiration of all concerned.

In September 1894, Walter moved to the Hamburg Stadttheater. As a junior member of the music staff he was directly accountable to Gustav Mahler, the theatre's First Kapellmeister. Having been introduced to him shortly after arriving at the Stadttheater, Walter was struck immediately by Mahler's physical appearance, which he considered in keeping with the composer of the 'Titan' Symphony. At that first encounter, a short but decisive conversation took place between Mahler and Walter, which he later recounted with relish in his autobiography:

'So you are the new coach,' Mahler said. 'Do you play the piano well?' 'Excellently,' I replied, meaning simply to tell the truth, because a false modesty seemed inappropriate in front of a great man. 'Can you read well at sight?' Mahler asked. 'Oh yes, everything,' I said again truthfully. 'And do you know the regular repertoire operas?' 'I know them all quite well,' I replied with a great deal of assurance. Mahler gave a loud laugh, tapped me on the shoulder pleasantly, and concluded the conversation with 'Well, that sounds fine.'[26]

Keen to see if Walter was as good as his word, Mahler soon tested his abilities. At a piano rehearsal of Humperdinck's *Hänsel und Gretel* conducted by Mahler, the répétiteur failed to meet his standards and Walter was asked if he was prepared to take the pianist's place at short notice. The young coach agreed confidently and, after performing admirably, he became the conductor's preferred assistant. As Mahler's right-hand man, Walter was able to observe him closely. Mahler quickly superseded Bülow as Walter's model, and although the young conductor began to adopt some of hero's podium gestures, he withstood the urge to emulate Mahler's abusive and often aggressive manner, which only served to alienate all those who were subjected to it.

Promotion came quickly for Walter at the Stadttheater and, after being made chorus master, he took charge of works by Mascagni, Lortzing, Flotow and Verdi.[27] In the autumn of 1895, Walter was promoted to Kapellmeister and was allocated Marschner's *Hans Heiling*, Wagner's *Tannhäuser*, Auber's *Fra Diavolo*, Weber's *Der Freischütz* and Verdi's *Aida*. But at a performance of *Aida* on 21 November 1895, Walter was found wanting. His technique failed him in the 'Triumphal Scene', he took inappropriate tempi for some of the arias and he failed to accompany some of the singers satisfactorily. As the opera is a formidable spectacle that is taxing both musically and technically, it is unsurprising that a conductor of Walter's experience performed it badly. Mahler was responsible, at least in part, for Walter's predicament, because he had suggested to Pollini that Walter was ready to conduct the work. More worrying, having exposed his relatively inexperienced protégé unnecessarily, Mahler was also critical of him.[28]

The *Aida* incident did little to shake Mahler's fundamental admiration for Walter, and when Mahler decided to leave Hamburg for Vienna, he wanted Walter to accompany him. Walter was concerned, however, that if he were to do so, Mahler's dominant personality would have an adverse affect on his development as an individual. It was agreed mutually, therefore, that Walter would seek work elsewhere. Mahler considered the Breslau Stadttheater to be an appropriate move, and he wrote to its director, Theodor Löwe, on Walter's behalf. Löwe responded favourably to Mahler's request and offered Walter a contract for the 1896–7 season. Löwe stipulated, however, that Walter should change his name before taking up his post, 'because of its frequent occurrence in the capital of Silesia'.[29] Until that point, Walter continued to be known both personally and professionally as Bruno Schlesinger and was deeply unhappy about the change. But as he was keen to join the staff of the Stadttheater, he eventually acquiesced and explained in later life that he had adopted the name Walter because of its Wagnerian connections.[30]

Breslau was an unattractive town that did little to inspire Walter. The Stadttheater was unimpressive and, like many theatres of its size and status in Germany, had a repertoire that was unexceptional and that was given with little or no rehearsal. As in Cologne and Hamburg, Walter was a junior member of the music staff and his duties reflected that status. In early October 1896, however, the situation changed when Löwe allocated him a performance of Lortzing's *Der Waffenschmied*, the work with which he made his operatic début in Cologne. Again, his interpretation sparked a critical debate that centred on his manipulation of tempi. It was argued that his chosen speeds were erratic and inappropriate for the work,[31] a criticism that dogged Walter regularly during his years as an apprentice. But Löwe was unconcerned by those worries and asked Walter to prepare and to perform Donizetti's *Lucrezia Borgia* with the luxury of 'a sufficient number of rehearsals',[32] and a revival of Mozart's *Die Zauberflöte*,[33] which he later admitted probably reflected 'a twenty-year-old conductor's maturity'.[34] Despite his increasing success at Breslau, Walter was unhappy with the atmosphere of apathy that dominated the 'mediocre municipal theatre'[35] and was unwilling to compromise his musical standards by remaining there.

After resigning from Breslau at the end of the 1896–7 season, Walter was offered the post of First Kapellmeister at the Riga Stadttheater. But as his contract was not scheduled to begin there until the 1898–9 season, he was faced with an extended period of unemployment. Fortunately, however, the director of the Pressburg Stadttheater had heard of his ability and had offered him the post of First Kapellmeister for part of the 1897–8 season. Pressburg, now called Bratislava, 'a handsome little town'[36] close to Vienna, had three attractions for Walter: first, he would be employed fully until he was scheduled to begin in Riga; second, he could visit Vienna, a lifelong ambition, and, third, he was able to attend Mahler's rehearsals and performances at the Vienna Hofoper. The theatre in Pressburg was small but was staffed by enthusiastic young artists who were happy to work closely with Walter. The orchestra was tiny and he was often required to reorchestrate many of the larger operas for the forces available. As part of his contract, Walter also had to take the company to Temesvár in Hungary, where the orchestral situation was even worse than that at Pressburg. Although a resilient musician with a determination to succeed, Walter quickly became dispirited by the artistic privations of the Pressburg company, and when his six-month contract ended, he moved to Riga as planned.

Riga's population during the late nineteenth century was an uneasy mix of diverse cultures. Although part of the Russian empire, its inhabitants divided into three ethnic groups: Russians, who were the occupying power and therefore governors of Latvia; Germans, who pursued their commercial and cultural interests, among which was the financial control of the Stadttheater, and Letts, who were the subjugated native population. Russian imperial law also subjugated other racial minorities, and Jews were treated particularly harshly. Even though Walter was a German citizen, he was also an ethnic Jew and, as such, was unable to move freely within the Russian territories. He decided, therefore, to convert to Catholicism before beginning his duties at Riga. Some commentators have likened his conversion to that of Mahler, who became a Catholic shortly before being appointed Director of the Vienna Hofoper. Unlike Mahler's conversion, however, that of Walter was not an act of convenience but the gesture of a believer, who continued to practise his new faith for much of his life.[37]

As First Kapellmeister at Riga, Walter took charge of a theatre that was well managed and well maintained. Since Wagner's departure some sixty years earlier, the orchestra, singers and administration had improved considerably and had risen to a satisfactory standard. That transformation was due to the local German community, who were proud of their theatre, took an active interest in its administration[38] and saw it as a positive expression of their ethnicity and culture. Because of his status at Riga, Walter was able to explore repertoire that formed the core of his mature performance style.[39] The significance of performing Wagner's *Der fliegende Holländer*, *Lohengrin* and *Tannhäuser* at Riga would not have been lost on Walter, and the chance to perform Mozart's *Die Zauberflöte* and *Le nozze di Figaro* – works that Wagner had performed in the Latvian capital – would also have appealed to his heightened sense of hero worship. These parallels, however, would have been of only passing importance to Walter, whose principal concern was to programme repertoire that was relevant to the ethnicity and the expectations of his audience. As German-speakers dominated the Stadttheater audience, many of the works given were from the Austro-German canon that was taking shape and, of those, many drew heavily upon fairy tales, myths and the idea of triumph over adversity, all notions that would have appealed to dislocated, ethnic Germans. It should come as no surprise, therefore, that Walter made his début with Weber's *Der Freischütz*, an opera of special significance to German-speaking audiences. But Walter and the administration also broadened the company's repertoire to include French and Russian operas in an attempt to appeal to the Russian ruling class.[40] Although Germans ran the Stadttheater, it is inconceivable that Russians were excluded altogether, and by appealing to both ethnic groups, the management and Walter not only reduced the probability of serious financial loss, but also made the theatre less exclusive. But as the Stadttheater was part of the German theatre system, and 'was listed in the *German Stage Almanac*',[41] it can be assumed that the French and Russian operas were performed in German. If that was the case, it seems that the hand of friendship was extended only conditionally.

From the 1900–1 season, Walter was engaged by the Berlin Hofoper. The Berlin appointment was the culmination of a series of offers that Walter received during his stay in Riga which included invitations from Mahler in Vienna and the management of the Hofoper in Mannheim. But the chance to return triumphant to his home town, to perform in the theatre in which he had heard Wagner's *Tristan und Isolde* for the first time and to join a conducting staff that boasted Richard Strauss and Karl Muck appealed most. Nevertheless, Walter was concerned that he was once again a junior member of the music staff and that the operas he would be scheduled to perform would be those rejected by either Strauss or Muck. Walter was also worried about the theatre's management, which was controlled by Prussian court officials whose understanding of the arts was often limited, partisan and self-serving. Even so, he was impressed by the orchestra, the singers and the chance to work alongside some of the leading conductors of the day.[42]

Walter made his Hofoper début with Bizet's *Carmen*. Because of its popularity, the opera's technical difficulties have often been underestimated by audiences and musicians alike.[43] Walter, however, had performed the opera in Riga and was able to negotiate its problems successfully. His experiences in Latvia and Hamburg were also invaluable when tackling much of the other repertoire that he was given to perform in Berlin, which included operas by Weber, Mozart, Richard Wagner, Siegfried Wagner, Auber and Lortzing.[44] But not all the works that he performed at the Hofoper were familiar to him, and he was also asked to conduct Wagner's *Der Ring der Nibelungen* and the Berlin premières of Weber's *Abu Hassan* and Pfitzner's *Der arme Heinrich*.[45] Walter had encountered Pfitzner's music for the first time in Hamburg and had been impressed immediately by it. *Der arme Heinrich* was a popular success in Berlin and Walter was pleased that the audience shared his enthusiasm. The Hofoper première, however, was not Walter's first performance of a work by Pfitzner in Berlin, for he had already conducted the March from Pfitzner's *Die Rose vom*

Liebesgarten at the Berliner Tonkünstler-Orchester's third subscription concert the previous month.[46] At that concert, he also performed Berlioz's *Symphonie fantastique*, Wagner's overture to *Der fliegende Holländer* and Beethoven's Violin Concerto (Willy Burmester, violin). While the critics felt that the programme was too long, they did recognize Walter's spirited conducting and commended him for the positive effect he had on the orchestra's precision.[47]

Although his concert with the Tonkünstler Orchester was a success, Walter was becoming increasingly dissatisfied with Berlin and wanted to leave. He was in constant conflict with the management and, after it decided to stage productions simultaneously at the Hofoper and at the Kroll Theatre, matters came to a head. Walter was assigned Sullivan's *The Mikado* and Lecocq's *La Fille de Madame Angot* at the Kroll. Although the Sullivan work was a Berlin première, which Walter enjoyed conducting, both were operetta. As the operetta conductor was, and still is, the lowest rung on the conducting ladder, Walter probably felt sidelined. When a conflict of casting occurred between the Kroll and the Hofoper that directly affected an opera that Walter was performing, he used it as an excuse to leave Berlin. But his decision to leave was no surprise to the management, which probably knew of his secret negotiations with Mahler in Vienna. Happy to be rid of a troublesome young conductor whose ambitions were elsewhere, the management annulled Walter's five-year contract after only one year, freeing him to join Mahler in the Austrian capital from the beginning of the 1901–2 season.

Vienna had always fascinated Walter. Aware of its cultural history and its importance as a centre of musical excellence, he saw in his appointment at the Hofoper the culmination of a long-cherished ambition. Over the next thirty-seven years, Vienna would be central to his activities as a performer and, in later life, he averred, 'Countless memories of my lifelong affiliation with Vienna . . . left an echo in my soul.'[48] With a salary of 6000 florins and the security of a two-year contract, Walter began his tenure at the Hofoper in a spirit of optimism. Ironically, he made his début on 27 September 1901 with Verdi's *Aida*, the opera that had proved so problematic in Hamburg. But by performing *Aida* successfully in the presence of his mentor, Walter was able to lay the ghosts of the Hamburg performance to rest.[49] Moreover, with a cast of international renowned singers performing an opera that was central to their repertoire,[50] Walter was likely to attract the attention of both press and public. But press attention can be a double edged-sword: as Natalie Bauer-Lechner recalled, the 'gentlemen [of the press] were already furious with [Walter] because they had found out that Mahler had summoned him [to Vienna] and thought highly of him. They also tried to make out that he imitated Mahler's movements and copied his outward mannerisms.'[51]

The other operas that Walter conducted during his first season at the Vienna Hofoper were an amalgam of those that were new to him and those that he had given previously.[52] Curiously, none of the operas performed by Walter during that period was a house première. In Berlin, where Walter worked to superiors who were at best ambivalent to his career development, he gave at least three local premières in one season, a figure that is surpassed only marginally during his six seasons with Mahler in Vienna, where he conducted only four.[53] In contrast, Mahler, as Director, performed a series of historic new productions and premières that included many of the important operas of Mozart, Wagner and Beethoven. Moreover, Mahler entrusted important premières and new productions of opera to other members of the music staff, including Francesco Spetrino and Franz Schalk,[54] conductors no longer associated closely with Mahler. Given Mahler's interest in Walter, it is curious that he did not accord him preferential treatment.

During his first years at the Vienna Hofoper, Walter suffered from health problems, was attacked critically for some of his performances and was the subject of vilification by the anti-Semitic press. Throughout much of that period he was depressed, and at the end of 1905 he had problems with his right arm, a source of extreme concern for Walter, who continued to perform regularly as a chamber musician.[55] Although active as a pianist for much of his early career, conducting dominated his activities during his period at the Hofoper, and on 27 January 1907 he performed with the Vienna Philharmonic for the first time. For that concert, he programmed Schumann's Symphony No. 1 ('Spring'), a work by a composer whose abilities as an orchestrator he doubted.[56] In view of his concerns, it is strange that he performed the piece at such an important engagement. The symphony was of particular significance to him during his early career, however, and he programmed it often when introducing himself to a new orchestra or organization. If Walter considered the work a kind of symphonic talisman, it produced the desired result, for a year later, on 5 January 1908, he returned to the Musikverein to conduct the Vienna Philharmonic in concert that commemorated the twenty-fifth anniversary of Wagner's death. But by the time of that concert, Mahler had left Vienna and Walter was working under Felix Weingartner.

As Weingartner had been one of only a handful of contenders for the post and the most celebrated internationally, his appointment as

Director of the Vienna Hofoper came as no surprise to Walter. Having observed Weingartner at work in Berlin, Walter was acquainted with his approach and was impressed by his abilities as an orchestral conductor. But he had reservations about Weingartner's skills as an opera conductor and was particularly concerned by his lack of dramatic flair and his heavy reliance on the régisseur, Wilhelm von Wymetal.[57] Although Walter was on friendly terms with Weingartner, they were never close and, in later life, he described him as 'an exceedingly well-read and well-bred man, and the member of an old Austrian family'. While Weingartner's intellectual and musical abilities are not in question, he was certainly no better 'bred' than Walter. As both musicians came from similar socio-economic backgrounds, had attended conservatories of distinction, were products of the Central European opera-house system, were excellent pianists and had failed to impress as composers, their experiences and aspirations would have given them much in common. Because of those commonalities, it is likely that Weingartner felt a kind of affinity with Walter. If that was indeed the case, it might explain why Weingartner assigned him a series of important premières and new productions that eclipsed those given to him by Mahler.[58] Moreover, when Enrico Caruso sang in Verdi's *Rigoletto* and Bizet's *Carmen* at the Hofoper in 1911,[59] Walter was given the responsibility of conducting the performances. As Caruso's popularity was at its peak and as the performances were high-profile events, the involvement of the Hofoper's Director might have been expected. But Weingartner passed the responsibility for these operas to Walter, an act of delegation that was not common during Mahler's time.

Walter conducted outside Central Europe for the first time on 3 March 1909. Engaged by the Philharmonic Society of London to conduct its orchestra, Walter gave a programme that included Schumann's Symphony No. 1, Beethoven's Piano Concerto No. 5 ('Emperor') (Emil Sauer, piano) and overture *Leonore* No. 3 and Ethel Smyth's overture to *The Wreckers*.[60] Walter had met Smyth in Vienna during Mahler's tenure and had been impressed immediately by her abilities. From the correspondence between Walter and the Society, it seems that she had reciprocated his faith and was active on his behalf with the organization.[61] Walter appreciated Smyth's efforts and included works by her at his concerts with the Society in November and December 1909 and November 1926. The juxtaposition of British music with works from the Austro-German canon soon became a feature of Walter's concerts for the organization, and on 4 December 1924 he performed Elgar's Symphony No. 1 alongside works by Weber, Wagner and Mozart.[62]

Walter's success with the Philharmonic Society attracted the attention of Thomas Beecham, who invited him to make his Covent Garden début with Wagner's *Tristan und Isolde* on 21 February 1910. Two nights earlier, Beecham had opened the 1910 Beecham Opera Season with the London première of Strauss's *Elektra*. The British capital was alive with talk of the sensational new opera and expectation was high. Although *Elektra* overshadowed Walter's début, his interpretation of Wagner's score did not disappoint, with the critics responding favourably to his performance.[63] At Covent Garden, Walter was also able to pursue his interest in Smyth's music by sharing the conducting of a series of performances of *The Wreckers* with Beecham.[64] What is striking about Walter's repertoire at Covent Garden is its similarity to that of his Philharmonic Society concerts. At both, Walter juxtaposed a modern British work with one from the Austro-German tradition. By agreeing to perform Smyth's opera Walter was able to dismiss any notion of tokenism, and by performing *Tristan und Isolde* he was able to be compared directly with other leading Central European conductors of the period, such as Hans Richter, Arthur Nikisch and Franz Schalk, all of whom had conducted the opera at Covent Garden between 1905 and 1907.

Weingartner left the Vienna Hofoper at the end of 1911 and was replaced by Hans Gregor as Director. Unlike Weingartner, Gregor was not a conductor but a régisseur who did little to impress Walter. Increasingly dissatisfied with his situation in Vienna, Walter leapt at the opportunity of becoming the new Generalmusikdirektor of the Munich Hofoper after the death of Felix Mottl on 2 July 1911. Although he was unable to accept immediately, it was agreed that if he could free himself from Vienna the post at Munich would be his. But Walter's release was not achieved easily and was only reluctantly granted. After extended negotiations with Count Montenuovo, the court official responsible for the Hofoper, it was agreed that Walter's Vienna contract would be cancelled if he promised to return as Director when his Munich tenure expired. Confronted with a *quid pro quo* that suited all parties, Walter agreed willingly,[65] and with a salary of 36,000 marks,[66] the title of Generalmusikdirektor, the power to programme operas of his choice and the authority to engage and to dismiss singers and musicians, Walter began work at the Munich Hofoper on 1 January 1913 optimistically.

Having performed at Munich as a guest conductor in the period directly preceding his appointment as Generalmusikdirektor, Walter was no stranger to Bavarian audiences. As a guest in both the concert hall and the opera pit, he signalled his interest in new music from the outset by conducting the world première of Mahler's *Das Lied von der Erde* on 20 November 1911 and the local première of Bittner's *Der Bergsee* on 10 December 1911.[67] Walter continued to champion contemporary works during the first months of his tenure with the house premières of Strauss's *Ariadne auf Naxos* and Pfitzner's *Der arme Heinrich*, on 30 January and 17 April 1913 respectively. The production of Strauss's opera proved particularly problematic and was the cause of friction with the composer. At the time of the performance, only the first version of the work existed, a juxtaposition of the play *Der Bürger als Edelmann* with the chamber opera *Ariadne auf Naxos*. Because of the work's intimate nature, Strauss and Hofmannsthal were keen for it to be performed in small theatres. Walter was aware of this but still wanted to give it in the cavernous Nationaltheater. Knowing that he was acting against the spirit of the piece and the wishes of the composer, he asked the work's librettist to approach Strauss on his behalf. Clearly unhappy to be asked to act in that capacity and to learn that *Ariadne auf Naxos* was scheduled for performance in the Nationaltheater, Hofmannsthal wrote:

> My dear Dr. Strauss,
>   I write to you at the express request of Bruno Walter . . . to tell you of my violent distaste for any *Ariadne* and *Bourgeois* performances in the big Munich House (instead of the admirably suited Residenztheater), and to remind you of all the many reasons you yourself advanced to me in Stuttgart in favour of small theatres for this work
>   After a talk with me, Walter seems to realize that a letter he appears to have written to you is pretty absurd (this strange man seems to be constantly in a fever, pro or contra, and never able to weigh anything calmly). Now he apparently wants me to attenuate the effect his letter may have on you; hence this note.[68]

In spite of the concern of Strauss and Hofmannsthal, Walter performed the work in the Nationaltheater. Strauss was appalled and in a note to Hofmannsthal wrote, 'they are massacring *Ariadne*. . . . Performance in the big house means complete murder.'[69] Strauss was also shocked that a répétiteur was to conduct the final performance of the series. Determined to put the matter right the composer presented Walter with the ultimatum that unless the opera was moved to the smaller Residenztheater, permission to perform it would be withdrawn.[70] Strauss's demands were met but relations between Walter and

Strauss had soured and never recovered fully.[71] Nevertheless, Walter's interest in new music continued for much of the remainder of his Munich tenure and he led the world premières of Klenau's *Sulamith*, Korngold's *Der Ring des Polykrates* and *Violanta*, Pfitzner's *Palestrina*, Courvoisier's *Lanzelot und Elaine*, Schreker's *Das Spielwerk* and Braunfels's *Die Vögel* at the Hofoper between 16 November 1913 and 30 November 1920.[72]

At Munich, Walter balanced his interest in new music with performances of familiar works. Keen to ensure that familiar did not mean routine, he reinvigorated well-known works by establishing a series of reforms that included the coaching and rehearsal of singers with an emphasis on 'order in detail and a seemingly improvised freedom in the flow of a presentation',[73] a new repertoire built around the twin pillars of Wagner and Mozart, a balanced use of young, talented singers with more experienced colleagues and a guarantee that singers of the front rank were always available for premières and new productions. Two composers who benefited from this approach were Verdi and Wagner. Although most modern listeners associate Walter primarily with music from the Austro-German tradition, he was also a passionate advocate of Verdi's music and celebrated the centenary of the composer's birth by conducting new productions of *Un ballo in maschera* and *Falstaff* on 12 October and 30 October 1913 respectively.[74] That year also marked the centenary of Wagner's birth and his anniversary was celebrated by a new production of *Rienzi, der letzte der Tribunen* on 1 May 1913.[75]

Part of Walter's remit as Generalmusikdirektor was direction of the Hofkapelle's Academy Concerts. From the programme of his first concert, on 29 September 1912, which included his symphonic talisman, Schumann's Symphony No. 1, Mozart's Violin Concerto No. 4 and Beethoven's Symphony No. 7, the public might have been forgiven for thinking that Walter's passions lay solely in the music of the past. That was not the case, and during the course of his tenure he challenged many concert-goers by performing established masterpieces side by side with new works by Carl Ehrenberg, Hugo Wolf, Paul Graener, Karl Bleyle, Walter Braunfels, Paul von Klenau, Clemens von Frankenstein, Hans Pfitzner, Max Trapp and Arnold Schoenberg. To those familiar with Walter's antipathy to Schoenberg's music, his performance of *Gurrelieder* at Munich on 12 April 1920 might seem strange. But his objection to the composer's works was not absolute and in his autobiography he explained candidly, 'Much as I admired Schönberg's courage and unwavering attitude, profoundly though I was impressed by his exquisite musicianship, and attracted though I was by much of his later chamber music and vocal compositions, I felt increasingly unable to follow him on his way, because I considered it a devious way. The heroic romanticism, the lofty lyricism, and the bizarre boldness of his *Gurrelieder* have become dear to my heart. I performed the powerful work on a number of occasions.'[76]

By 1922, it was clear to Walter that his position at the Munich had become untenable. During his period as Generalmusikdirektor, both the Hofoper and Germany had changed enormously. The country was defeated in World War I, the imperial house of Hohenzollern had fallen, national and state politics were in turmoil and violence on the streets was common. Because of the political unrest that dominated the postwar years, working practices at the Hofoper had altered sharply. Walter was no longer answerable to court-appointed officials, but, instead, to the new republic's ministry of education and the complex array of workers' councils that flourished at the Nationaltheater. With the shifting political climate, Walter had begun to suffer personally and, having become increasingly distressed by the behaviour of the anti-Semitic press and the financial effects of hyperinflation, he decided to leave Munich in October 1922.[77]

No longer in full-time employment, Walter faced the daunting prospect of earning his living as a guest conductor. As Germany was in the grip of extreme political and financial turmoil, he attempted to raise cash by accepting engagements in the USA at the beginning of 1923. By leaving Germany at that time, he felt that he was abandoning 'a task to which [his] nature seemed to have predestined [him]: to be the guardian and keeper of a cultural institute and to make its blood circulate by the force of [his] heart'.[78] Nevertheless, American dollars were extremely attractive at a time of fiscal unrest and those that Walter earned proved valuable. For his American début at Carnegie Hall on 15 February 1923 with the New York Symphony Orchestra, he performed a programme that included Beethoven's overture *Leonore* No. 2, Mozart's Symphony No. 35 and Brahms's Symphony No. 1. Outwardly, the programme appears to have been an attempt to establish Walter's credentials in America as a worthy advocate of the Austro-German canon. But as neither the Beethoven overture nor the Mozart symphony was regular fare in New York, his juxtaposition of the familiar with the unfamiliar was more likely to have been an attempt at arousing the curiosity of both the press and the public. Whatever the case, the evening was a triumph and he went on to present a second programme of Austro-German music with the New York Symphony Orchestra at the Aeolian Hall on 18 February 1923.[79] Again, the concert was a success, with the critics commenting favourably on his controlled podium manner, his approach to tempo modification and the serious tone of his programmes.[80]

On his return to Europe, Walter performed with the Berlin Philharmonic on 23 April 1923[81] and made his débuts with the Leipzig Gewandhaus Orchestra and the Concertgebouw Orchestra of Amsterdam on 28 August and 11 October 1923 respectively.[82] Those concerts were followed by regular visits to London during the mid 1920s. His success at Covent Garden in 1910 had not been forgotten and the management was keen for him to conduct some of its German repertoire at its Grand Opera Season.[83] Although concerned that Londoners still harboured anti-German feelings following World War I, he was delighted to discover that his fears were without substance and that he was welcomed warmly by the public and praised widely by the critics. As the decade progressed, his Covent Garden appearances became increasingly important to him and he returned annually to the theatre between 1924 and 1931.[84] Although he performed operas and operettas by Richard Strauss, Johann Strauss and Mozart, the overwhelming majority of the works given were those by Wagner, and, of those, *Der Ring des Nibelungen* was heard most often. Walter's appetite for performing the tetralogy was insatiable and, with the exception of the 1925 season, he performed a complete cycle annually.[85] Today, few opera houses would be able to stage *Der Ring des Nibelungen* yearly. To do so would be a logistical, musical and financial nightmare. In the 1920s and early 1930s, however, casts were more stable, singers and conductors were often familiar with each other's work, and the public's interest in the music of Wagner was at its peak.[86] Curiously, Walter performed no early Wagner or any of the more recent works of Strauss at Covent Garden. It could be argued that the theatre did not benefit from the same financial conditions as opera houses in Munich and Vienna, and, therefore, was in no position to challenge popular taste. But that argument is only partially convincing, because it is also likely that the management wanted to market Walter as an leading exponent of the great Austro-German canon, an image that he was unlikely to challenge.

Walter's 'predestined [task, as] . . . the guardian and keeper of a cultural institute' was restored when he was appointed Generalmusikdirektor at the Städtische Oper, Berlin, on 1 August 1925. Working to the Intendant Heinz Tietjen, Walter's responsibilities were comparable to those of Erich Kleiber[87] at the Staatsoper and later those of Otto Klemperer at the Kroll Opera. Aware of the unease that dominated Germany's political life, Walter was wary about accepting the post but set aside his political concerns when Tietjen agreed to meet all his

musical demands. Although pleased to be back in tenure, he was dis-
missive of the theatre's architecture, which he considered 'uninspiring',
'unmagical' and 'prosaic'.[88] That said, the stage and lighting equipment
was of a high standard and the large wings meant that big productions
could be mounted with ease. With those advantages at his disposal and
with a cast that included Lotte Lehmann and Igor Kipnis, he began his
tenure with a production of Wagner's *Die Meistersinger von Nürnberg*
on 18 September 1925 that he hoped would set a standard against
which all future performances at the theatre would be judged. It was
immediately obvious, however, that the building had acoustic problems
and that it was difficult to balance the orchestra with the stage. He was
also worried about the repertoire, which was often standard fare. For a
musician who had spent the greater part of his career challenging public taste, the thought of performing established repertoire for an
extended period was unappealing. Nevertheless, he did have an opportunity to perform some less familiar operas, but such works as Pfitzner's
Der arme Heinrich, Debussy's *Pelléas et Mélisande*, Korngold's *Das
Wunder der Heliane* and Bittner's *Mondnacht*[89] were the exceptions
rather than the norm. Walter was also troubled by Tietjen's often duplic-
itous management style, and having become increasingly dissatisfied
with, and distrustful of, him, Walter was unwilling to continue at the
Städtische Oper and announced his resignation in 1929.[90]

Careful to balance his activities in the opera house with engagements
in the concert hall, Walter maintained his long-established relationship
with the Berlin Philharmonic throughout his tenure at the Städtische
Oper. Between 1924 and 1933, he conducted an annual series of six
concerts with the orchestra that ran parallel to its main subscription
series given by Wilhelm Furtwängler.[91] Heard between late autumn and
early spring, the repertoire for the two series had elements in common,
including a high percentage of works by Austro-German composers, an
interest in the music of Russia and regular performances of new compositions. Given Walter's relationship with Mahler, it was to be
expected that he would use the series as a vehicle for the composer's
music and, with the exception of his last season, he performed at least
one major work by him annually.[92] Walter also challenged the Berlin
public with twelve world or local premières and a series of performances of works from music's cutting edge.[93] He was also interested in
the music of Russia, a country he enjoyed visiting, and took particular
pleasure at presenting works by Tchaikovsky, Rachmaninov, Stravinsky, Mussorgsky, Borodin, Prokofiev, Shostakovich and Lopatnikoff to
his Philharmonic audiences. But to suggest that Walter placed undue

emphasis on the works of Mahler, foreign novelties and contemporary music would be to create a false impression, for he frequently performed compositions by Mozart, Beethoven, Schubert and Brahms.[94]

No longer contracted to the Städtische Oper, Walter was a free agent. That situation changed, however, when he was appointed Gewand-hauskapellmeister from the beginning of the 1929–30 season. Having conducted ten of the Gewandhaus Orchestra's twenty subscription con-certs the previous season, he was well acquainted with the players and 'felt a "selective affinity"'[95] with them. Mindful of his 'responsibility to keep alive a great past and to champion valuable contemporary cre-ations', he decided to dedicate himself to 'its continued mission and its enduring importance in the musical life of Europe' regarding this a 'a worthy task for the rest of [his] life'.[96] Although linked to Leipzig pro-fessionally, he was unwilling to be associated with it domestically and with the exception of the orchestra's famous home, the Gewandhaus, which he considered beautiful, he found the city's architecture wholly uninteresting. He decided, therefore, to continue to live in Berlin and to commute to Leipzig for rehearsals and concerts.

The notion of keeping 'alive a great past' while championing 'valu-able contemporary creations' was central to Walter's programme policy at Leipzig. He regularly performed established works alongside new music, with twenty of his forty-two subscription concerts containing a work by a living composer.[97] As in Berlin, the music of Mahler featured prominently with a work by him being heard each season.[98] Bruckner's music was also heard regularly at Leipzig with Walter performing at least one of his symphonies with the Gewandhaus Orchestra annually.[99] The conductor's sympathy with, and understanding of, Bruckner's music had begun to strengthen towards the end of the 1920s, and the interpretations that he gave in Leipzig were manifestations of that increased awareness. Walter would have known of Nikisch's passion for Bruckner's music and the special place that Leipzig occupied in the history of Bruckner performance. It was appropriate, therefore, that Walter's growing passion for Bruckner's compositions coincided with his Gewandhaus tenure. But no Leipzig season would have been com-plete without the music of Beethoven, and during his time there Walter performed all nine symphonies, with Symphony No. 9 ('Choral') occupying its traditional place at the end of each season.[100]

With the rise of the Nazis, Walter's career was affected adversely. Although he had long been the target of the anti-Semitic press, matters worsened severely in early 1933. After returning from a tour of the USA, he was contacted by the manager of the Gewandhaus Orchestra,

Max Brockhaus, who said that Manfred von Killinger, a Nazi supporter and head of the police in Leipzig, would stop the orchestra's eighteenth subscription concert unless the management abandoned it willingly. Brockhaus tried desperately to negotiate with the authorities, but to no avail. To help the orchestra, Walter offered to resign, a gesture that the management refused to accept. Although the situation was bleak, Walter still hoped that the matter could be resolved amicably. But his hopes were dashed when he arrived at the Gewandhaus for the general rehearsal to find that the police had already cancelled the concert in the name of the Saxon Ministry for the Interior. Walter's tenure as Gewandhauskapellmeister was effectively at an end. Unable to be of any use in Leipzig, he returned to Berlin for his next concert with the Philharmonic. There, he faced a similar situation. The management had been warned by the Nazis that Walter's safety could not be guaranteed and that, if he insisted on performing with orchestra on 20 March, there would be violent demonstrations in the hall. The Nazis made it clear, however, that they still wanted the concert to proceed, but without Walter as conductor. As it was a 'Bruno Walter Concert', the management dismissed the idea and continued to support him. But when it was obvious that the Nazis did not intend to allow the concert to proceed peacefully, that the danger to all concerned was too great and that he was considered suspicious politically, Walter withdrew from the performance and left the country immediately.[101]

Having fled Germany, Walter took refuge in Austria. From there, he began to reconstruct his career through guest conducting by accepting engagements from leading ensembles and festivals in Europe and North America. His performances at the Salzburg Festival were of particular importance to him during that period because he continued to be judged there by his musicianship and not his ethnicity. Although his career seemed little harmed by his period of exile, Walter always enjoyed tenure and when he was offered the post of Director of the Vienna Staatsoper in 1936, he accepted willingly. After opening the 1936–7 season with Wagner's *Tristan und Isolde*, an opera that had been of importance to him since boyhood, Walter proceeded to perform a series of new productions that reflected his catholic taste rather than his increasing stature as an interpreter of the Austro-German tradition.[102] Surprisingly, he failed to conduct any new productions of operas by Mozart, Wagner or Beethoven during his Vienna tenure. As he was no longer under the shadow of Mahler and as each of the composers mentioned was at the centre of his programming policy, it is strange that those operas were not produced afresh. But because of Austria's *Anschluss* with Germany in March 1938, Walter's tenure at the Staatsoper was short and he was unable to pursue his interests fully.

With the fall of Austria, Walter's career and personal life had been affected twice by the growing presence of Nazism.[103] As it was clear that he would be unable to return to Vienna, he reluctantly severed his connections with the Staatsoper and the Salzburg Festival and moved with his family to Lugano in Switzerland. From there he again pursued his career as a guest conductor, but for an ethnic Jew life in Central Europe remained precarious, so he sailed for America on 1 November 1939.[104] Despite his émigré status, transition from the Old World to the New was made relatively easy because of his contacts with fellow refugees such as Lotte Lehmann, Thomas Mann, Adolf Busch and Bronislaw Huberman. As he had made a number of tours to the USA after World War I, he was known professionally to American arts organizations and was able to develop strong links with not only the Metropolitan Opera, New York, but also the NBC Symphony, Los Angeles Philharmonic and New York Philharmonic Orchestras. In general, the repertoire that Walter performed with these bodies was less adventurous than with European institutions and centred largely on works from the Austro-German canon.[105] There were some exceptions, however, and with the Los Angeles Philharmonic, he was able to give West Coast or local premières of music by John Alden Carpenter, David Stanley Smith, Ralph Vaughan Williams, Sergei Rachmaninov and Gustav Mahler.[106] But Walter's performances of new music became increasingly rare in America, and orchestras and opera companies welcomed him there as a curator of a grand tradition rather than a musician of catholic taste.

Walter as curator was also attractive to record companies. Ever eager to benefit commercially from the public's insatiable thirst for established masterpieces from Central Europe, record companies used Walter's status as an interpreter of those works to exploit the market. While the strategy may have been beneficial financially in the short term, it has proved unsound historically in the long term. By emphasizing the conservative elements of his repertoire, the record industry has created a discography that gives a completely distorted picture of Walter's interests in general.[107] With the exception of Barber, Berlioz, Bizet, Cherubini, Dvořák, Smetana and Tchaikovsky,[108] all the other compositions documented by Walter were written by Austro-Germans between the late eighteenth century and the first decade of the twentieth. Moreover, of the exceptions listed, the only symphonies that he recorded by non Austro-German composers were those of Barber, Berlioz, Dvořák and Tchaikovsky and, of these, only Barber's was written after the first decade of the twentieth century. This stands in stark contrast to his activities in the concert hall, where his programming was broad and less influenced by commercial concerns. Of his recordings made before World War II, those of Wagner and Mahler are of particular interest. Walter rarely performed extracts from Wagner's operas at his concerts in Leipzig and Berlin but recorded a series of excerpts for Columbia and Victor between the mid 1920s and the mid 1930s. Some of these were made with British orchestras, and were obviously intended to capitalize on Walter's success at Covent Garden during the same period. No complete commercial recording of an opera was made by Walter, and his interpretation of Act 1 and Act 2, Scenes 3 and 5, of Wagner's *Die Walküre* for HMV in June 1935 is the most extended extract from an opera recorded by him.[109] The following year, on 24 May 1936, Columbia documented a concert performance of Mahler's *Das Lied von der Erde* with Walter and the Vienna Philharmonic,[110] and a little over eighteen months later the company's production crew returned to Vienna to record a concert performance of that his Symphony No. 9 with the same forces at the Musikvereinsaal on 16 January 1938. These discs are not only milestones in the history of recorded sound but are interesting insights into Walter's pre-war Mahler style. After World War II, Columbia recorded, or re-recorded, many of the works with which Walter had become associated, including symphonies by Beethoven, Brahms, Bruckner, Mahler, Mozart, Schubert and Schumann, but although these are valuable and interesting, they do little to dismiss the incorrect impression that Walter was a reactionary musician with a conservative repertoire.

In America, Walter had an opportunity to write extensively, and as well as his autobiography, *Theme and Variations*, he published his treatise, *Of Music and Music-making*, in which he documents his ideas on music and the function of the conductor. As a committed Wagnerian, he argues in support of the composer's treatise on conducting, stating: 'I remember gratefully how as a young musician I was helped and stimulated by Richard Wagner's essay *On Conducting*.'[111] Central to that monograph were the composer's ideas on melos, with which Walter agrees totally. Like Wagner, Walter argues that only through the melos of a work can the correct tempo be found and that the '*right tempo*' is necessary if the true character of the phrase is to be uncovered. For Walter, 'a well-constructed piece of music in organic form' has only one 'right' tempo. But because the 'mood and technical requirements' alter during the course of a work, the speed should be 'adapted' accordingly. It is clear, then, that the 'right' tempo is relative and that any modifications to the speed must be done 'imperceptibly'. Concerning alterations to the musical text, Walter also agrees with Wagner's approach, but has reservations about the extent of his modifications, stating: 'Whatever can be adduced against [retouching] on the grounds of *literary fidelity*, I must declare myself against the radical rejection of retouching . . . [but Wagner's] suggestions about the performing of Beethoven's Ninth . . . seem to go too far'.[112] Curiously, Walter makes no mention of Mahler's amendments to the symphonies of Beethoven or his extensive reorchestration of those by Schumann, where, according to Walter, 'instrumental retouching becomes an unavoidable duty . . . [because] the original orchestration is unable to do justice either to the spiritual content of the work or to its thematic clarity, either to the spirit or to the letter'.[113]

Walter also uses *Of Music and Music-making* as a didactic tool. He dispels the common misconception that the principal task of the conductor is to keep the musicians together. For him, this is only part of the conductor's function, which also includes shaping the performance through his or her 'inner sound-image, or rather, sound-ideal'.[114] Along with an exceptional ear for intonation and rhythm, Walter emphasizes the importance of the hand as a conduit between the conductor and the musicians and argues that 'the clumsiness of the hand will prevent the work from making the right impression'.[115] In obtaining the correct impression, he stresses the importance of the baton, which 'In the hands of the *born* conductor' becomes an extension of the artist; to conduct without the baton 'carries the seeds of decay'.[116] He underlines the usefulness of the pianoforte, an instrument that allows the conductor to realize an orchestral score in a domestic situation when studying. Walter also acknowledges the importance of attending concert and opera performances, the need to be well read and to understand religion, the knack of motivating colleagues, the capacity to balance an orchestra precisely and the humanity to use power correctly. Concerning the thorny subject of performing from memory, he takes a pragmatic stance. For conductors with good memories, performing without the score increases spontaneity, intensity and eye contact with the musicians, but if a conductor's memory is poor he should use the music, and in rehearsals the score is 'indispensable'.[117]

In the years following World War II, Walter toured extensively, performing with leading orchestras throughout Europe and North America. His work at the Edinburgh Festival from 1949 was of particular importance, and the concerts that he gave with the British contralto Kathleen Ferrier are a vivid memory for all those who attended. As one of the last conductors with direct links to the nineteenth century, he had acquired a status as an exponent of established masterpieces from Central Europe that continued to grow after the hostilities. His relationship with Mahler remained important to him in his late years and he was seen increasingly as an authoritative interpreter of the composer's works. He never lost touch with his European roots and, unlike some émigrés, he returned regularly to Germany and Austria after the war. Like other returning expatriates, he was shocked by the level of destruction that he witnessed, and although he believed fully in reconciliation and forgiveness, he continued to live in the USA until his death on 17 February 1961. But after his cremation,[118] his ashes were returned to Europe, where his 'changeful, active, music-blessed life . . . [came] to rest' and from where he was able to 'look into the past, look into the future – and look on high'.[119]

Peter Heyworth
zu guter Erinnerung.
Otto Klemperer
1957

CHAPTER 7

A Troubled Mind: Otto Klemperer

Otto Klemperer was an imposing figure. His immense height, his bipo-lar condition,[1] his conversion from Judaism to Roman Catholicism in maturity, his return to the Jewish faith in old age[2] and his refusal to compromise musically all helped to create a Faustian image that domi-nated the way in which he was perceived by musicians and audiences alike. Like Bruno Walter, Klemperer came under the influence of Gustav Mahler early in his career and was a devoted disciple of the composer for the rest of his life. Hans Pfitzner and Richard Strauss also influenced Klemperer during his formative years as a musician and he aspired to be their creative and interpretative equals. As a composer, Klemperer cre-ated a substantial oeuvre but failed to impress either the critics or the public with his music. Nevertheless, he continued to compose until the end of his career and used the insights gained through composition to understand better the music of his time. As a champion of the moderns in the immediate post-Weimar Republic period, he faced the wrath of Germany's new fascist government. He was not only vilified as both a Jew and a Bolshevik but also had to face the humiliation of exile. Today, he is remembered as one of the great Beethoven interpreters of his age whose recordings are benchmarks against which other performances are often judged.

The second of three children of Nathan and Ida Klemperer, Otto was born in Breslau on 14 May 1885.[3] During Otto's childhood, Nathan worked unsuccessfully in commerce and Ida supplemented the family income by working as a piano teacher. Although Nathan's business acu-men was poor, he never allowed his financial situation to hamper his interest in the arts, and when the family moved to Hamburg in 1889 both he and Ida attended theatre and opera productions regularly. Nathan was also a good amateur singer and, with Ida as accompanist, he performed Lieder by Schumann, Schubert and other composers at home. That environment influenced Otto heavily and his interest in vocal music stemmed from those early, domestic experiences.

Having heard his parents perform regularly in the parlour, Otto soon became interested in music and began to take piano lessons with his mother from the age of six.[4] With the advantage of perfect pitch, he progressed quickly and he was soon able to play four-hand arrangements of symphonies and chamber music from the Austro-German repertoire.[5] Although Ida was an accomplished pianist and teacher, it was decided that Otto should be taught by Hans Havekoss, a local piano teacher, with whom he studied until the age of fifteen.[6] Keen to ensure that Otto's music education was not restricted to instrumental lessons, Nathan and Ida regularly took him to Hamburg's theatres, opera house and concert hall. At those venues, he attended a performance of Schiller's *Wilhelm Tell*, heard operas by Mozart, Beethoven and Verdi and was present at the first Hamburg performance of Richard Strauss's *Tod und Verklärung*.[7] Having 'learnt a lot'[8] from Havekoss, Klemperer was tested in 1900 by Max Mayer, a pianist and friend of Ida, to determine the true extent of his abilities. For this assessment, Klemperer performed sonatas by C. P. E. Bach and Beethoven, had his ear tested for pitch recognition and played one of his early compositions. Mayer reported that Klemperer might not be another Hans Richter, but he was confident that he would be a good musician.[9] Encouraged by Mayer's report, Ida and Nathan decided to withdraw Otto from the Realgymnasium of the Johanneum at Hamburg[10] and to send him to the Hoch Conservatory at Frankfurt am Main in the autumn of 1901.

At the Hoch Conservatory, Klemperer studied piano, violin and composition. His piano teacher was a Dutchman, James Kwast, whom Klemperer had heard in Hamburg. Isolated from family and friends, Klemperer was able to concentrate fully on music and often practised the piano for eight hours a day. In the evenings, he regularly attended concerts and operas, and it was at the Frankfurt Opera that he heard Wagner's *Der Ring des Nibelungen* for the first time. Klemperer's progress as a pianist was rapid, and he was invited to perform Beethoven's Sonata in D Op. 10 No. 3 and Schumann's Piano Concerto in 1901 and 1902 respectively.[11] In 1902, Kwast was appointed to the staff of the Klindworth–Scharwenka Conservatory in Berlin and left the Hoch Conservatory. Klemperer followed his teacher to the capital, where he continued to study piano with Kwast, was accepted into the theory class of Philipp Scharwenka and joined the orchestration and score-reading classes of Wilhelm Berger. Kwast's tenure at the Klindworth–Scharwenka Conservatory was short, and when he moved to the Stern Conservatory in 1905 Klemperer again followed him. There, Klemperer joined the conducting and composition classes of Hans Pfitzner, whom he considered 'an excellent teacher'.[12] He particularly valued Pfitzner's conducting lessons, where '[o]ne pupil would play the piano while another conducted' and where Pfitzner would sing the vocal parts of operas. For Klemperer, those experiences were invaluable and were of help in 'acquir[ing] a thorough knowledge of the work in question'.[13]

But Klemperer did not restrict his education to the classroom, and he complemented his formal studies by attending performances at Berlin's opera houses and concert halls. During the first decade of the twentieth century, the Prussian capital was a lively cultural centre and Klemperer heard there Mozart operas conducted by Richard Strauss at the Hofoper and orchestral concerts conducted by Arthur Nikisch at the Philharmonie. Strauss's performance of Mozart's *Don Giovanni* on 7 April 1907 impressed him particularly, and the composer-conductor's new approach[14] influenced his mature Mozart style directly. Klemperer was also impressed by Strauss's restrained podium manner, which enabled him 'to let the orchestra breathe. . . . *He* didn't throw himself around like a madman, but [let] the orchestra [play] as though *it* was possessed.'[15] Klemperer, however, was less convinced by Nikisch, whom he considered 'a better conductor than he was a musician'.[16]

An encounter that proved seminal to Klemperer was his first professional meeting with Gustav Mahler. As a child in Hamburg, Klemperer had seen Mahler in the street and recognized him immediately from the Stadttheater programme booklets that his parents had kept. As a student in Berlin, Klemperer attended the Berlin première of the composer's Symphony No. 5 on 20 February 1905[17] and was asked to conduct the off-stage music for Symphony No. 2 ('Resurrection') under Oskar Fried later that year.[18] Mahler attended both the rehearsals and the concert of the latter and found Klemperer's treatment of the off-stage music too loud. Klemperer protested to the composer and pointed out that he had marked the passage fortissimo. The composer agreed that the passage should be played fortissimo but from a distance. As the spatial effect that Mahler required was impossible to fulfil physically, Klemperer instructed the players to perform the music more softly at the concert. Klemperer's ploy satisfied Mahler and the composer congratulated him after the performance.

In 1906, Oskar Fried invited Klemperer to act as chorus master for Max Reinhardt's new production of Offenbach's *Orphée aux enfers* at the Neues Theater, Berlin. Although the operetta opened on 13 May,[19] it nearly closed after the second performance when Fried withdrew from the production after an argument with one of the singers.[20] Unable to engage an experienced conductor at short notice, Reinhardt instructed Klemperer to act as Fried's replacement. Even though Klemperer had little professional experience, Reinhardt was confident that he was equal to the task and, on 16 May 1906,[21] Klemperer made his début as a conductor. The performance was a success and Reinhardt entrusted the remaining fifty performances to him.

On 14 January 1907, Mahler returned to Berlin to conduct his Symphony No. 3 with the Berlin Philharmonic for an indisposed Arthur Nikisch. Klemperer was engaged as Mahler's assistant conductor and was given the task of directing the off-stage side drum in the first movement. Although the symphony was not to Klemperer's taste, Mahler's conducting style was a revelation to the young musician, who was determined to work with him regularly. In an attempt to impress Mahler, Klemperer made an arrangement of the composer's Symphony No. 2 for solo piano, which he played to him at Vienna in April 1907. After performing the Scherzo to Mahler from memory, Klemperer broached the thorny issue of work at the Hofoper. Mahler told Klemperer that there were no vacancies at the theatre but suggested that he should apply to the Volksoper instead. As that theatre was also unable to engage him, Klemperer returned to Mahler, who attempted to help him by writing on a visiting card: 'Gustav Mahler recommends Herr Klemperer as an eminently good and, despite his youth, experienced musician who is predestined for a conductor's career. He vouches for the successful outcome of any trial with him as *Kapellmeister*, and will gladly supply further information about him in person.'[22] The card remained one of Klemperer's most treasured possessions and he carried a copy of it in his wallet for the rest of his life.

On his return to Berlin, Klemperer had Mahler's testimonial copied photographically. Although he sent it to all the major German opera houses, only a few responded with the offer of a post and, of those, none was salaried. As he was unable to support himself financially, accepting a voluntary position was out of the question. His luck changed, however, when he attended the Allgemeiner Deutscher Musikverein in Dresden during the summer of 1907. There, he overheard a conversation between two critics, one of whom, Richard Batka from Prague, mentioned that the Deutsches Landestheater in Prague needed a new conductor. For Klemperer, the opportunity was too good to overlook and he later presented Mahler's testimonial to the critic.

Impressed by the tone and content of Mahler's comments, Batka suggested that Klemperer visit the theatre's Director, Angelo Neumann, who was spending the summer at Marienbad. Neumann was also impressed by Mahler's recommendation and announced proudly, 'I herewith offer you the position that twenty years ago I offered to Nikisch.'[23] With that flamboyant gesture, Klemperer was engaged from August 1907 for a period of five years as chorus master and Kapellmeister at the Landestheater.[24] But Neumann's offer was unwritten, and Klemperer was unwilling to accept the post without a contract. Although amazed that Klemperer should doubt his word, Neumann agreed reluctantly to his request and confirmed the post in writing.[25]

Klemperer's caution soon proved justified. With Neumann absent and the other members of the management team unaware of his appointment, Klemperer was greeted blankly when he arrived for duty at the Landestheater. Fortunately, he was able to produce his written contract and the matter was resolved easily. As chorus master and Kapellmeister in Prague, Klemperer was responsible to Angelo Neumann as Director and Arthur Bodansky as First Kapellmeister.[26] Because the Deutsches Landestheater catered for the operatic needs of Prague's German-speaking minority, it had to present a repertoire that was viable financially, interesting musically and acceptable ethnically. Klemperer's performance of Weber's *Der Freischütz* for his début at Prague on 4 September 1907 met all those criteria. As the production that he conducted was already in the theatre's repertoire, he was allocated one rehearsal only. While Central European opera companies regularly revived productions with one rehearsal, Klemperer felt that the allocation was insufficient for his needs. He argued that at least two rehearsals – one with the orchestra alone followed by one with singers and orchestra – were necessary. To his surprise, his request was granted; he later argued sagaciously that young conductors should not agree automatically to the demands of management.[27] Although Klemperer's performance of *Der Freischütz* was a critical and popular success, his sense of euphoria was short-lived, because he was then allocated mainly operettas for the remainder of the season. Clearly, he would have liked to perform more substantial works, but, as junior conductor at a repertory house, the works that he was given were in keeping with his position.

A high point of Klemperer's first season at Prague was a concert conducted by Mahler, at which the overture to Smetana's *The Bartered Bride*, the Prelude to Wagner's *Tristan und Isolde* and Beethoven's Symphony No. 7 were performed. Although Klemperer was able to attend one rehearsal only, he was again overwhelmed by Mahler's approach and later recalled that his 'one reaction afterwards was . . . to abandon the profession unless one could conduct as Mahler did'.[28] But Klemperer did not abandon the profession and he continued to conduct the seemingly unending series of repertory operas that dominated his schedule during his second season at Prague.[29] The monotony of his position soon began to take its toll on Klemperer, and in December 1908 he wrote to Hans Pfitzner in Strasbourg about the possibility of a post there. Nothing came of the request and Klemperer sank deeper into the dark side of his ever present bipolar condition.[30]

Although weakened psychologically Klemperer continued to work assiduously, and when Bodansky moved to the Mannheim Hofoper at the end of the 1908–9 season he was entrusted with a revival of Wagner's *Lohengrin*. His performance was a success, and Neumann promoted him to the rank of Second Kapellmeister from the start of the 1909–10 season. As Second Kapellmeister, his first task was to conduct Rossini's *Guillaume Tell*, an opera of great length but of little public appeal. Although Klemperer's interpretation was successful critically, Neumann began to doubt Klemperer's loyalty to the theatre. Neumann felt increasingly threatened by the local press and accused Klemperer wrongly of campaigning against the theatre with his friend, the critic Felix Adler. As Neumann was sure that Klemperer was colluding with Adler, he presented him the ultimatum that unless he dissociated himself from the critic, he would have to leave the theatre. Never given to intimidation, Klemperer chose the latter.[31] But points of principle can be problematic financially and, with no income from the beginning of the 1910–11 season, he needed a new post urgently. Having contacted a string of theatres, Klemperer soon learned of vacancies at Hamburg and Mannheim. With little chance of a recommendation from Neumann, Klemperer turned to Mahler in New York, who responded quickly with cables to the managements of both theatres. As a result, Klemperer was offered both jobs.[32]

To choose between Mannheim and Hamburg must have been difficult for Klemperer. Mannheim boasted a fine court opera house that had a long and distinguished tradition, while Hamburg had a commercial theatre that was part of a wider, more vibrant cultural environment. But Hamburg was also Klemperer's home town, and the attraction of family and friends eventually proved greatest. Before beginning work in Hamburg, however, Klemperer attended some of the rehearsals for the première of Mahler's Symphony No. 8 at Munich in June and July 1910. He was particularly interested in the modifications that Mahler made to the text of the symphony and he later recalled that Mahler remarked: 'If, after my death, something doesn't sound right, then change it. You have not only the right but the duty to do so.'[33] Mahler also applied this principle when performing music by other composers, and when interpreting Beethoven's Symphony No. 6 ('Pastoral') he said to Klemperer: 'At first, of course, you will conduct as it is written, but later on you will see that some instrumental retouching has to be done.'[34] For Klemperer, Mahler's retouching was an essential part of the composer-conductor's performance aesthetic, but he lamented that 'a regrettable number of conductors [employed] it quite incorrectly [because as] Mahler once remarked . . . his retouchings were meant for him alone, and he bore full responsibility for them'.[35] While Klemperer acknowledged that Mahler 'retouched in the spirit of his age',[36] he felt that his adjustments to the text of Beethoven's Symphony No. 7 were 'wrong'.[37] Similarly, he considered that Wagner's alterations to Beethoven's Symphony No. 9 (Choral') 'sometimes [went] too far'.[38] Nevertheless, Klemperer, that 'All this talk that one shouldn't change a single note in a score is nonsense. *Werktreue*, that is, faithfulness to the work, is a very different matter from merely using the pure text.'[39]

At Hamburg, Klemperer's immediate superior was Gustav Brecher,[40] whom he considered 'an excellent *chef*'. Like the Deutsches Landestheater in Prague, the Hamburg Stadttheater was run privately and needed to balance its repertoire accordingly. The first opera that Klemperer conducted there was Wagner's *Lohengrin*, an opera that he had already performed at Prague. It is unlikely that, as a relatively junior member of the music staff, he would have been able to choose the opera for his first Hamburg appearance. But as the management allowed him to perform a familiar work for an important début, it seems that they were keen to assist him where possible. To the relief of both conductor and administration, Klemperer's interpretation of *Lohengrin* on 3 September 1910 was a success and he was subsequently allocated Gounod's *Faust*, Bizet's *Carmen* and Weber's *Der Freischütz*.[41] Although he was familiar with those operas, his schedule was both demanding and gruelling. As the Hamburg Stadttheater was a repertory house that was driven by commercial imperatives, the need to perform a wide and varied repertoire was central to its existence. Of course, for a young conductor, the repertory system provided an opportunity to become familiar with a large body of works quickly, but for a conductor of Klemperer's ability and vision, it was a depressing environment in which to work. His doubts about the system, however, were set aside temporarily in October 1910, when Enrico Caruso was engaged for a series of performances at the Stadttheater that included Verdi's

Rigoletto, Flotow's *Martha* and Bizet's *Carmen*. Klemperer was given the task of conducting these performances and was impressed immediately by the tenor, whom he considered musical, diligent and helpful.[42]

During the 1910–11 season Klemperer took eighteen months' leave from the Stadttheater because of depression[43] and when he returned to work two seasons later, Felix Weingartner had been engaged as permanent guest conductor and was effectively his immediate superior. Klemperer's initial perception of Weingartner must have been coloured by Mahler's scathing remarks about his performance style in general and his habit of cutting Wagner's operas in particular.[44] But if Weingartner was aware of Klemperer's admiration for Mahler, it was not apparent from the operas that he allocated his junior colleague, who was given responsibility for Beethoven's *Fidelio*, Mozart's *Le nozze di Figaro*, Strauss's *Der Rosenkavalier* and Wagner's *Tannhäuser*, *Lohengrin* and *Der Ring des Nibelungen* during the 1912–13 season.[45] Moreover, Weingartner appears not to have imposed his performance style on his subordinates at the Stadttheater, for when Klemperer came to interpret *Der Ring des Nibelungen*, he gave the cycle without cuts.[46] It seems, therefore, that Weingartner's policy of excising material from Wagner's stage works, like Mahler's retouching of scores by others, was meant for him alone.

After being involved in a spectacular affair with the singer Elisabeth Schumann,[47] Klemperer fled the Hamburg Stadttheater and was eventually appointed First Kapellmeister at Barmen from September 1913. Although the modest Barmen theatre was of a lower status than that of Hamburg, Klemperer gave a wide and varied repertoire there, including memorable performances of Wagner's *Parsifal* and Mozart's *Così fan tutte*.[48] As a devoted Wagnerian, Klemperer was keen to conduct *Parsifal*, which had been released from its Bayreuth copyright on 31 December 1913. With the enthusiasm of a zealot, Klemperer rehearsed the work meticulously and performed it from memory on 4 January 1914.[49] His performance – one of the first to be given after the work's official release to other theatres[50] – was such a success that it had to be repeated twenty-two times to sold-out houses after its local première.[51] When Klemperer performed *Così fan tutte* at Barmen on 14 March 1914, he acted as both conductor and producer. Although he was aware of Mahler's 'extremely accomplished interpretation'[52] of the work some seven years earlier at Vienna, it was Strauss's approach to the opera that affected his Barmen interpretation most. Like Strauss, Klemperer used the translation of Hermann Levi, acted as both conductor and continuo player, played a harpsichord in the secco recitatives, avoided altering the score's text and used a *Stilbühne* as a substitute for a revolving stage.[53]

When Hans Pfitzner applied for a sabbatical from his post as First Kapellmeister of the Strasbourg Stadttheater in 1914 to orchestrate his opera *Palestrina*, Klemperer was engaged as his temporary replacement. Keen to impress, he made his local début with an uncut performance of Beethoven's *Fidelio* on 10 January 1915. His decision to conduct the work whole upset Pfitzner, who regularly excised the first part of the last scene, which he considered 'too foursquare'.[54] Furious with Klemperer for abandoning the cut, Pfitzner demanded that it be restored. Klemperer, however, was unimpressed by Pfitzner's demand and replied simply that he preferred Beethoven's original to Pfitzner's 'version'.[55] Clearly influenced by Mahler's model, Klemperer continued to follow his hero's lead when he performed the overture *Leonore* No. 3 before the last scene. Although the production was a critical and musical success, Klemperer later had mixed feelings about using the overture as a kind of entr'acte and, in the late 1940s, refused to include it because of its lack of dramatic relevance. Nevertheless, by the 1960s he had reinstated the overture because it 'repeat[ed] the whole story . . . [and] added meaning to the performance as a whole'.[56] But ever the pragmatist, Klemperer refused to be bound by precedent and summarized his position in the 1960s by stating: 'that's my opinion today . . . [but] I can't tell you what it will be tomorrow'.[57]

After his début with *Fidelio*, Klemperer's Strasbourg repertoire included Bizet's *Carmen*, Pfitzner's *Der arme Heinrich* and Mozart's *Le nozze di Figaro*.[58] As Strasbourg was extremely close to Germany's border with hostile France and anti-French feeling was running high because of World War I, his decision to perform *Carmen* was particularly courageous. Perhaps less courageous was the inclusion of *Der arme Heinrich*, the work of an ardent nationalist with strong professional links with the Stadttheater. It could be argued that, by performing the opera, Klemperer was currying favour with Pfitzner. But Klemperer's musical principles would have precluded that possibility and it is more likely that he conducted the work because he held it in high regard. In contrast to his interpretation of Mozart's *Così fan tutte* at Barmen, Klemperer's approach to *Le nozze di Figaro* in Strasbourg had more in common with Mahler's Mozart style than that of Strauss. Klemperer was never constrained by musical dogma, and his inclusion of Mahler's setting of Beaumarchais's Judgement Scene[59] at Strasbourg is good example of his openness to various influences and his willingness to incorporate them into his performance style as a whole.

After a summer that involved much composition, a sign that he was experiencing a manic phase, Klemperer was invited to conduct at the prestigious Frankfurt Museum Concerts in December 1915. Having conducted only one concert previously,[60] he approached the engagement with little relevant experience. In the hope of establishing himself both as an interpreter of the Austro-German canon and as a credible concert conductor, he performed Mozart's overture to *Die Zauberflöte*, Strauss's *Don Juan* and Beethoven's Symphony No. 3 ('Eroica').[61] As the ability to perform Beethoven's music was the benchmark against which conductors were measured during the late nineteenth and early twentieth centuries, Klemperer's inclusion of a symphony by the composer was almost inevitable. But by programming a work that was central to the repertoire of most established conductors, he was in danger of being compared directly with senior colleagues. Aware that the risks were high, he also knew that the rewards could be great. Unfortunately, Klemperer's high-risk strategy proved disastrous, because he not only failed to impress critically but also failed to distinguish himself musically.

When Pfitzner left the Strasbourg Stadttheater at the beginning of 1916, Klemperer was appointed his permanent replacement. Unlike Pfitzner, Klemperer was a musician of diverse taste and enjoyed conducting works from a variety of national traditions. Nevertheless, works from the Austro-German canon continued to dominate his programme policy during the middle years of World War I and he reaffirmed his musical patriotism by conducting impressive performances of operas by Wagner, Mozart, Strauss, Pfitzner, Gluck and Korngold.[62] Although Klemperer was able both to consolidate and to expand his repertoire at Strasbourg, he was unenthusiastic about the theatre's adherence to the repertory system. He objected to performing operas with little or no rehearsal and he was not unduly distressed when his tenure ended at the close of the 1916–17 season.[63]

In January 1917, Klemperer conducted a guest performance of Beethoven's *Fidelio* at the Cologne Stadttheater. His interpretation made an immediate impact, and within days of the performance he was appointed First Kapellmeister from the beginning of the 1917–18 season. Although the Cologne Stadttheater's status was higher than that of the Strasbourg theatre, it also operated as a repertory house and presented operas with little or no rehearsal. As First Kapellmeister, Klemperer worked to the Intendant, Fritz Rémond, a producer and an administrator of conservative taste. Rémond had been active formerly as a tenor and insisted on producing many of the operas given at

Cologne. Klemperer considered Rémond's productions 'disagreeable' and it was for that reason that he 'eventually left [Cologne] seven years later'.[64] Klemperer's frustration with Rémond was evident from the start, and the Intendant's indifferent staging of Mozart's Le nozze di Figaro, with which Klemperer made his début as First Kapellmeister on 1 September 1917, left him completely unmoved. Although he acted as both conductor and continuo player, he was unable to pursue his approach to Mozart fully and as a consequence the production fell far short of his expectations.

In the seasons that followed, Klemperer either revisited works that were familiar to him or performed operas that formed the basis of the repertory system.[65] A highlight of his tenure was a production of Mozart's Don Giovanni for which Klemperer used the Prague version, the preferred choice of Richard Strauss, whose Mozart style he had begun to adopt. Although Klemperer's reputation as a Mozart conductor flourished after his appointment to the Cologne Stadttheater, he performed only five of the composer's operas during his career: Die Entführung aus dem Serail, Le nozze di Figaro, Don Giovanni, Così fan tutte and Die Zauberflöte. His disinclination to explore Mozart's operatic oeuvre further is a conundrum but as the majority of his work as an opera conductor took place in theatres that either subscribed to the repertory system or were private enterprises, marketplace economics may have influenced his programme policy. Moreover, as a child of his time, he would have also considered Mozart's early stage works the jottings of an apprentice composer and therefore unworthy of performance, an unfortunate view that is still held widely today.

While Rémond was hardly a standard bearer for the avant-garde, he did allow Klemperer to pursue his interest in new music. As a conductor who aspired to composition, Klemperer demonstrated a vested interest in modern works which soon proved unsettling for the conservative Cologne audience. It was apparent to public and colleagues alike that he was a musician of broad taste when, within weeks of beginning his tenure, he conducted Weingartner's one-act opera Cain und Abel in a double bill with Klenau's ballet Klein Idas Blumen. These performances were followed later in the season by Bittner's Das höllisch Gold and Chelius's Die vernarrte Prinzessin. As his tenure progressed, Klemperer became more innovative in his programming and included new and colourful works by Mussorgsky, Janáček, Busoni, Strauss, Pfitzner, Korngold, Schreker, Zemlinsky and Stravinsky,[66] thus ensuring that national and international attention was focused on Cologne. Of course, some of the new stage works were not to his taste but he considered it his duty to make certain that audiences should experience contemporary music regularly and without 'preconceived opinions'.[67] That did not mean, however, that he programmed indiscriminately: he could be particularly scathing of music that he disliked.[68]

Although Klemperer's career in the theatre had progressed quickly, he had directed very few concerts during his previous tenures and was keen to expand his profile as an orchestral conductor at Cologne. It might be assumed that Klemperer, as the Stadttheater's First Kapellmeister, would have been invited to perform at the Gürzenich Orchestra's subscription concerts. Because of the Orchestra's position as one of Germany's leading ensembles and its prominence in Cologne, the importance of such an invitation would have significantly enhanced Klemperer's prestige as a concert conductor. But the orchestra's permanent conductor, Hermann Abendroth,[69] was unwilling to allow other conductors frequent opportunities to work with it and Klemperer performed only twice with the orchestra during his Cologne tenure.[70] Unwilling to remain in a city that constricted his career in that direction, Klemperer announced that he would be leaving Cologne in 1919. The news of his departure soon provoked a public outcry and it was agreed that Klemperer could conduct an annual series of concerts with the Stadttheater Orchestra in the opera house.

With an orchestra that he later described as 'splendid',[71] Klemperer embarked on a series of performances that proved both influential and innovative. As an acolyte and a champion of Mahler, Klemperer conducted the composer's Symphony No. 2 ('Resurrection') at his first opera-house concert on 4 October 1919. Mahler's music then became a regular feature of Klemperer's Cologne series with *Lieder eines fahrenden Gesellen*, *Das Lied von der Erde*, *Kindertotenlieder* and Symphonies Nos. 7 and 9 being given between 1920 and 1923. Missing from that repertoire were Symphonies Nos. 1, 3, 5, 6 and 8, works with which Klemperer had little sympathy. Although a keen Mahlerian, he later explained that he was 'not a stupid, enthusiastic boy' and that he did not like everything the composer had written.[72] For Klemperer, the last movements of Symphonies Nos. 1 and 5 were too long, the slow movement of Symphony No. 5 reminded him of 'salon music' and the meaning of Symphony No. 6 eluded him.[73]

Of the other works that Klemperer conducted at the opera-house concerts, those of Mozart, Beethoven, Bruckner and Schoenberg were of particular interest. Although he had been presenting Mozart's operas regularly during his theatre career, his performance of Symphony No. 40 on 17 January 1920 was his first of an orchestral work by the composer. Significantly, he chose the Mozart symphony that was given most frequently during the late nineteenth and early twentieth centuries. Apart from the work's obvious box-office appeal, Klemperer's programming of it meant that he would be compared directly with other Mozart interpreters. Similarly, by performing the works of Beethoven on a regular basis, he was again attempting to establish himself as a major interpreter of the Austro-German canon. His all-Beethoven concert on 11 December 1920 was a means to that end and did much to enhance his reputation as conductor Beethoven's music.[74] Of course, his Mozart and Beethoven performances were sure to attract popular support, but his readings of Bruckner's Symphony No. 8 and Schoenberg's *Pelleas und Melisande* had little audience appeal. His programming of them at his opera-house series served only to alienate further the more conservative elements of Cologne's concert-going public and to reinforce his image as a musical iconoclast.

Having established a successful concert series in Cologne, Klemperer soon attracted the attention of major German orchestras.[75] His first important concert engagement outside the Rhine–Main area took place on 16 April 1921 when he conducted the Berlin Philharmonic for the first time. At that concert, he gave an all-Schoenberg programme that included *Verklärte Nacht* and *Pelleas und Melisande*. Although those works were not as challenging as the composer's later compositions, it was a bold gesture for a début. The concert was a success and Klemperer conducted the Berlin Philharmonic again on 18 May 1921. As this second concert marked the tenth anniversary of Mahler's death, it included the composer's Symphony No. 2.[76] While his concerts with the Berlin Philharmonic were important to Klemperer personally, their significance should not be stressed too heavily. They were only two of the 110 concerts that the Berlin Philharmonic gave in the German capital during the 1921–2 season and were not part of the orchestra's prestigious subscription series. Moreover, Klemperer's performance of Mahler's Symphony No. 2 was only one of nine concerts given by the Berlin Philharmonic during the 1920–1 season that contained a work by the composer.[77]

The Philharmonic was not the only Berlin organization interested in Klemperer in the early 1920s; the Deutsches Opernhaus, the Staatsoper and the Grosse Volksoper were all keen to engage him. As Klemperer had become dissatisfied with his position at Cologne, he welcomed these approaches increasingly. His dissatisfaction was fuelled by the financial crisis that Germany faced during the early 1920s and the problems that the Rhineland experienced when the French occupied it after World

War I. Like most other major opera houses in Germany during that period, the Cologne theatre fell victim to hyperinflation. The privations that the theatre's employees suffered following Germany's financial collapse were not restricted to food shortages but also affected artistic matters. Of course, Klemperer's experiences in the early 1920s were not all bad and his elevation to Generalmusikdirektor in 1922 by Cologne's Bürgermeister, Konrad Adenauer,[78] was particular pleasing. Nevertheless, by 1924 Klemperer was ready to leave Cologne, and when he was offered the job of Director of the Grosse Volksoper in Berlin he tendered his resignation. But the Berlin company had fallen on hard times and it disbanded before Klemperer was able to begin work. While he hoped to withdraw his resignation from Cologne, the authorities there decided that it should stand. The prospect of unemployment at a time of fiscal uncertainty was worrying for Klemperer, but he need not have concerned himself, because he was soon offered the post of First Kapellmeister at Wiesbaden from the 1924–5 season.

As the theatre at Wiesbaden was of a lower status than that of Cologne, Klemperer later recalled that his move to the spa town 'was a diminuendo in my career rather than a crescendo', but he affirmed nevertheless that in all his life he had 'never felt so happy as during those three years in Wiesbaden'.[79] His happiness was based on the wide-ranging powers and the enviable conditions of employment that he secured when negotiating his appointment. For a salary of 25,000 marks, he was required to work at Wiesbaden for only six months of the year, he was given the direction of six concerts with the orchestra[80] and he was awarded control over all artistic matters.[81] These conditions were secured for Klemperer by the Intendant at Wiesbaden, Carl Hagemann. Hagemann was born at Harburg bei Hamburg in 1871 and, after periods as Intendant at Mannheim, Hamburg and Wiesbaden, he held a teaching position at Berlin.[82] Hagemann was a distinguished theatre director and opera producer, whose comments about the musicians with whom he had worked were both objective and insightful. In later life, Hagemann recalled that Klemperer was one of the few musicians with whom he worked who could balance the needs of the stage with those of the pit. In achieving a satisfying synthesis of the musical, the theatrical and the decorative, Hagemann stated that Klemperer worked tirelessly with producers, lighting directors and set designers. Moreover, he claimed that Klemperer supported the singers fully and used his fine memory and ready wit to achieve a satisfactory whole. Hagemann maintained, therefore, that Klemperer was the ideal artist to lead 'a modern opera theatre'.[83] But Hagemann's encomium failed to mention

Klemperer's legendary temper. The conductor could be rude and off-hand to singers and musicians alike. For those he was conducting, his rages were often frightening and intimidating and could be linked directly to shifting phases of his manic-depressive condition. While his outbursts lessened in old age, they often created a distressing environment in which to work.

Klemperer's colleagues at Wiesbaden included the set designer Ewald Dülberg, whom he had met for the first time during his Hamburg period. Dülberg was born in the Rhineland in 1888, and after a period as a scene designer and teacher at Hamburg joined Klemperer at Wiesbaden for productions of Beethoven's *Fidelio* and Mozart's *Don Giovanni*. Because of the works on which they collaborated and the revolutionary nature of the designs used, Klemperer's relationship with Dülberg has often been likened to that of Gustav Mahler and Alfred Roller in Vienna. The influence of Mahler and Roller was apparent in the production of *Fidelio* that Dülberg designed and with which Klemperer made his Wiesbaden début on 3 September 1924. Dülberg's spectacular use of colour and block formations had direct links with Roller's designs at Vienna and the effect created was both innovative and controversial. The audience found the sets particularly unsettling and Klemperer later argued that Dülberg's designs for *Fidelio* were 'perhaps too severe'. Nevertheless, the production was the first of many at Wiesbaden that freed Klemperer from the repertory system.

Having introduced himself controversially, Klemperer then programmed a series of operas that juxtaposed new works with standard repertoire.[84] Although it is clear from the works performed that Klemperer relished the freedom to programme creatively at Wiesbaden and to be free of the repertory system, he still had to balance box-office imperatives with public taste and personal development. As the theatre catered to the needs of a predominant conservative, bourgeois audience, Klemperer's emerging interest in the cutting-edge works of Stravinsky, Busoni and Hindemith had to be tempered by works from the established repertoire. Even so, the productions of works by Wagner, Weber and Mozart that he gave in collaboration with Dülberg and Hagemann also challenged Wiesbaden audiences, and their innovative set designs and rejection of scenic naturalism soon became the basis for his mature operatic style.

After the Theater am Platz der Republik – commonly known as the Kroll Opera – reopened in 1924, it functioned for a period as a subsidiary of the Berlin Staatsoper. In 1926, however, it was decided that it should operate independently, and Klemperer was offered the job of

Director from the beginning of the 1927–8 season. But before signing a contract that would tie him to the theatre for a period of ten years, Klemperer made three demands: first, that he be given an annual concert series with the orchestra; second, that he be allowed to engage Ewald Dülberg as scene designer, and, third, that Hans Curjel be appointed as dramatic advisor.[85] All three demands were met and, along with Dülberg and Curjel, Klemperer engaged the conductors Alexander von Zemlinsky and Fritz Zweig.[86] Like Klemperer, Zemlinsky was a Mahler acolyte, a composer and a passionate advocate of new music. Klemperer had conducted the world première of Zemlinsky's opera *Der Zwerg* at Cologne and considered him to be 'an excellent musician . . . [and an] uncommonly sympathetic and attentive' colleague.[87] Zweig brought different qualities to the Kroll's music staff. He was not a composer of promise and, although he had been a pupil of Arnold Schoenberg, he was conservative musically. Nevertheless, he had risen through the ranks of the opera-house system and this meant that he had an outstanding knowledge of the standard operatic repertoire.

Klemperer's primary objective at the Kroll Opera was 'To make good theatre'.[88] He had no interest in the repertory system and was determined that his performances in Berlin should be given under the most favourable circumstances possible. To achieve that goal, it was decided that the theatre would mount only a few productions annually and that they would be repeated often. It was essential, therefore, that 'the Kroll was a good opera house that would be untouched by the bad practices of the repertory system and illuminated by the light of a new direction'.[89] The first opera to benefit from Klemperer's 'new direction' was Beethoven's *Fidelio* on 19 November 1927. For that performance, Klemperer acted as both producer and conductor and Dülberg created cubist sets. The public welcomed the new approach but the critics were less enthusiastic. Klemperer recalled that the press disliked the stylized scenery, the lack of naturalism and the weak voices.[90] The objections raised were a direct consequence of new management policies that resulted in the Kroll sharing singers, chorus and orchestra with the Linden Opera[91] until autumn 1928.

The next production that Klemperer gave at the Kroll was Mozart's *Don Giovanni* on 11 January 1928. Again, Klemperer acted as both conductor and producer and Dülberg designed the sets. Dülberg's concept was based on two fixed pillars around which the production functioned. Although this allowed for quick scene changes, it provided little visual variety and Klemperer later argued that '*Don Giovanni* is a very difficult opera. . . . [It] really needs a revolving stage and the Kroll didn't have one.'[92] On 25 February 1928, Klemperer conducted a daring all-Stravinsky triple bill, consisting of *Oedipus Rex*, *Mavra* and *Petrushka*. The conductor had met the composer first in May 1914 and again in 1927, when he attended a concert performance of *Oedipus Rex* under Stravinsky's baton in Paris. Klemperer was keen to mount a production of the opera in Berlin, and his interpretation of the work, with cubist sets by Dülberg, was given two days after the first staged performance at the Vienna Staatsoper under Franz Schalk.[93] Klemperer's enthusiasm for *Oedipus Rex* was typical of his response to Stravinsky's music as a whole, and he later confirmed that Stravinsky was the twentieth-century composer to whom he felt closest.[94] Another composer with whom Klemperer had an affinity at that time was Paul Hindemith, whose opera *Cardillac* he performed in Wiesbaden. Although Klemperer had mixed feelings about some of Hindemith's later music, he liked *Cardillac* and conducted the first Berlin performance on 30 June 1928. Unfortunately, the audience did not share Klemperer's enthusiasm for the work, and the severe sets that Dülberg created for the production did little to engender public sympathy.

When Klemperer returned for his second season at the Kroll, he was no longer Director. In the months before the production of *Cardillac*, he had become increasingly depressed and felt unable to fulfil the administrative demands of the post. It was agreed, therefore, that he would continue as Generalmusikdirektor at a reduced salary and that Ernst Legal would be appointed Director.[95] Klemperer's change of status affected his day-to-day activities little and he continued to control the Kroll's artistic programme. The extent of his influence was immediately evident from the challenging works that he scheduled for the 1928–9 season, which included a performance of Stravinsky's *Histoire du soldat* on 11 October 1928. Klemperer had a particular fondness for the piece and argued that it 'always manage[d] to find an audience . . . [because of] its variety and colour, . . . the strength of its melody and the refinement of its orchestration'.[96] But the same could not be said for the Krenek triple bill that Klemperer conducted on 2 December 1928. The introduction of *Der Diktator*, *Das geheime Königreich* and *Schwergewicht* into the Kroll's repertoire attracted little support from the public, and the topical nature of *Der Diktator*, with Mussolini as its subject, reinforced the impression that the Kroll's music staff harboured left-wing sympathies, an impression that would later contribute to the theatre's closure.

In January 1929, Klemperer conducted a controversial production of Wagner's *Der fliegende Holländer* that attempted to shed new light on an established masterpiece. Klemperer argued that the works of Wagner had been performed too frequently in Berlin and that the public's enthu-siasm had been sated. In response to a poll published in the Berlin peri-odical *Skizzen*, he said that the waning in public interest in Wagner's operas during the 1920s and the early 1930s was 'a natural reaction to the fact that Wagner [was] played too much'.[97] It seems that with the new production of *Der fliegende Holländer* he hoped to reverse that trend. To ignite public interest, Klemperer chose the 1843 Dresden ver-sion of the work and conducted from the score and orchestral parts that Wagner had used in Berlin in 1844.[98] Klemperer's choice of score and edition was only part of his approach to the composer's works as a whole. In 1933, he argued against excising music from Wagner's scores and in favour of complete observance of the composer's musical and theatrical instructions. That said, he was opposed to 'stiff, dry, anxious compliance with his directions. On the contrary: a free, imaginative, courageous treatment of these instructions will always . . . be the most Wagnerian.'[99] In realizing his vision of *Der fliegende Holländer*, Klemperer collaborated with Dülberg, whose cubist set and expression-ist production were criticized heavily, resulting in the Kroll's interpreta-tion being considered further evidence of Klemperer's left-wing tendencies.

Between 29 September 1927 and 24 April 1931, Klemperer con-ducted an annual concert series with the Berlin Staatskapelle at the Kroll Opera. He believed firmly that 'an opera orchestra plays far bet-ter if it can gain the extra experience of performing symphonic music from time to time'.[100] Of course, the Staatskapelle had given concerts throughout its history and the new series had to operate in tandem with the orchestra's regular subscription series under Erich Kleiber. By the time that Klemperer was appointed to the Kroll Opera, Kleiber had reached the peak of his career, having worked previously at Darm-stadt, Wuppertal and Mannheim. His abilities as an orchestral trainer were formidable and his programmes with the Staatskapelle between 1924 and 1933 were an interesting mix of the new and the unfamiliar. To make his programmes more distinctive, Klemperer placed a greater emphasis on new music and, of the twenty-six concerts that he con-ducted with the Staatskapelle between 1927 and 1931,[101] sixteen con-tained at least one work by a living composer. Of these, the most commonly heard was Paul Hindemith, whose music was performed every season. In later life, Klemperer recalled that he performed 'a lot of Hindemith's music' at Berlin,[102] and his championing of Hin-demith's works was a high point in the performance history of the composer's music.

Igor Stravinsky was another composer who benefited from Klemperer's adventurous programme policy with the Staatskapelle and, with the exception of the 1927–8 season, a work by him was performed annually.[103] Less often performed at the Kroll were the works of Arnold Schoenberg. Only his arrangement of Bach's Prelude and Fugue in E flat major and the world première of *Begleitmusik zu einer Lichtspielszene* were included in the series.[104] As Schoenberg was a leading figure in Berlin's musical life during the Weimar Republic, was Alexander von Zemlinsky's brother-in-law and was Fritz Zweig's former teacher, the absence of his more important works from Klemperer's programmes might seem strange. But Klemperer had reservations about some of Schoenberg's music and, while the *Begleitmusik zu einer Lichtspielszene* 'impressed [him] particularly',[105] he, like Bruno Walter, 'found no point of contact with [Schönberg's later] work'.[106] Other new or vibrant works that Klemperer conducted with the Staatskapelle fell into two groups: those that he had performed already either in Wiesbaden or as a guest conductor, and those that were new to him. Those that he revisited in Berlin were Janáček's *Sinfonietta* and Ravel's *Alborado del gracioso*, and among those that he prepared freshly were world premières of Krenek's *Kleine Sinfonie*, a 'delightfully parodistic piece',[107] Hauer's *Sinfonietta* and *Wandlungen* and Weill's *Der Lindberghflug*.[108]

With the exception of an all-Stravinsky concert on 17 June 1929,[109] Klemperer preferred to juxtapose new music with established masterpieces in his Staatskapelle series. In keeping with contemporary trends, the composer that he performed most frequently at the Kroll was Beethoven, with twelve works in four seasons.[110] With the exception of Symphony No. 2, Klemperer conducted all of the composer's symphonies with the orchestra and observed the traditional programming of Symphony No. 9, when he performed it as the last work of the 1930–1 season.[111] Along with Beethoven's music, Klemperer conducted at least one work by Bach each season,[112] a symphony by Mozart at two concerts,[113] music by Mahler at three seasons,[114] orchestral works by Brahms during his first and last seasons[115] and Symphonies Nos. 7 and 9 by Bruckner in 1927 and 1929 respectively.[116]

Klemperer's policy of juxtaposing new music with established repertoire in the concert hall extended to his work in the opera theatre. But his attempt at shedding new light on established operatic masterworks was often contentious, and his involvement in the controversial productions of Offenbach's *Les Contes d'Hoffmann*, Hindemith's *Neues vom Tage* and *Hin und züruck*, Mozart's *Die Zauberflöte* and *Le nozze di Figaro*, Krenek's *Leben des Orest* and Schoenberg's *Die glückliche*

Hand polarized the public and critics alike.[117] For some, the Kroll productions represented a worrying shift to the political left and, with the rise of the right and the parlous state of Germany's finances during the early 1930s, the future of the Kroll Opera was questioned increasingly. Some argued that its perceived leftist tendencies were unacceptable, while others considered it foolhardy for Berlin to support three opera houses at a time of financial crisis.[118] The debate concerning the Kroll Opera's future came to a head in November 1930, when its closure was announced. Klemperer tried desperately to defend its existence and to secure its future, but the government was not prepared to negotiate its decision. Although Klemperer was able to muster support from the public, critics and other artists, he was unable to prevent the inevitable and the Kroll Opera closed its doors on 3 July 1931.[119]

Although the Kroll Opera had shut, Klemperer was still under contract as Generalmusikdirektor, and it was announced that he would join Leo Blech[120] and Erich Kleiber at the Linden Opera. This meant that Klemperer would be involved in repertory performances of works that had not been prepared by him, a prospect that did little to raise his flagging spirits. The operas that he conducted during his time at the Linden Opera included Mozart's *Così fan tutte* and *Le nozze di Figaro*, Verdi's *Falstaff*, Strauss's *Der Rosenkavalier* and Wagner's *Lohengrin*. While the last two were new productions, the rest were revivals. Part of Klemperer's duties at the Linden Opera was the direction of some concerts with the Staatskapelle. Although he no longer had his own discrete series with the orchestra, he was still able to pursue his interest in new music and the four concerts that he conducted between 6 June 1932 and 12 January 1933 contained works by Hindemith, Busoni, Janáček and Krenek.[121]

In February 1929, the renowned conductor of the Philharmonischer Chor, Siegfried Ochs, died and Klemperer was engaged as his successor.[122] The first worked that he performed as the choir's new permanent conductor was Bach's *St John Passion* on 18 December 1929. For that interpretation, he juxtaposed new and period instruments,[123] avoided the use of appoggiaturas, terraced the dynamics, and reduced the string strength of the Berlin Philharmonic. Klemperer's Bach style was influenced heavily at that time by the organist of the Thomaskirche in Leipzig, Günther Ramin,[124] whom Klemperer consulted frequently before performing the composer's music. In later life, Klemperer remained faithful to Ramin's ideas and continued to juxtapose new and period instruments, to reduce the strength of the strings, to avoid unmarked ornaments, to consult the autograph scores and to terrace the dynamics.

In the years following his début with the Philharmonischer Chor, the works that Klemperer performed with it included Beethoven's Missa solemnis, Verdi's Requiem, Bach's St John and St Matthew Passions and Mass in B minor; and the world première of Hindemith's Das Unaufhörliche.[125] It could be argued from the repertoire listed that Klemperer's programming of choral music was overwhelmingly conservative. But it should be remembered that the Philharmonischer Chor was an amateur body that competed for members with other leading Berlin choirs, including the Chor der Sing-Akademie and the Bruno Kittel'scher Chor. Both the Chor der Sing-Akademie and the Bruno Kittel'scher Chor performed regularly with the Berlin Philharmonic and the former gave a series of between nine and ten concerts annually with the orchestra. As ticket sales and membership fees are the lifeblood of any choral group, the type and quality of the works given need to be judged carefully, and the performance of major works from the choral canon is essential if members are to be retained, standards are to be maintained and audiences are to be attracted. By meeting these criteria, Klemperer not only ensured the goodwill of the choir but also gained valuable insights into works that he had not conducted previously.

With the Nazis' victory at the elections of January 1933, Klemperer's position at the Staatsoper was in jeopardy. Although he had been accepted into the Roman Catholic faith in 1919, he was an ethnic Jew whose conversion to Christianity did little to protect him from the Nazis' anti-Semitic policies. Like many other German Jews of the period, he did not believe that Hitler and the Nazis were a long-term threat, but when it became clear that he had misunderstood the situation badly, he decided to leave Germany. Having made the decision to go, Klemperer fled to Switzerland on 4 April 1933.[126] But with exile came uncertainty, and because he no longer had a tenured post, he had to rely on guest conducting for income. While Switzerland was attractive geographically it provided few opportunities musically, so he decided to live in Vienna and to use the city as his professional base.

As a resident of Vienna, it was almost inevitable that Klemperer would conduct the Vienna Philharmonic. At his first concert with the orchestra on 23 April 1933, he performed Beethoven's Symphony No. 1 and Bruckner's Symphony No. 5.[127] For Klemperer, the Vienna Philharmonic represented the ideal Bruckner orchestra and he later recalled its April 1933 performance of Symphony No. 5 with great affection.[128] It seems that his affection was reciprocated, because Klemperer conducted the orchestra on ten further occasions between 20 August 1933 and 25 October 1936.[129] His pre-war repertoire in Vienna resembled that of his Berlin period, during which he juxtaposed new and colourful music with works from the Austro-German canon.[130] Of particular interest were his concerts in October 1936, when he conducted an all-Bruckner programme and the world première of Alban Berg's Violin Concerto.[131] For Klemperer, the relationship between place, creation and re-creation was an important consideration when performing a work of art. He felt that this was particularly true of Berg's Violin Concerto and wrote shortly after the première, 'the violin concerto belongs . . . to Vienna, to Austria, where it was created and where . . . it is intimately bound up'.[132]

As an exile, Klemperer was keen to explore the possibilities that America had to offer. At first he had hoped to secure a permanent appointment with one of the major East Coast orchestras, but when that proved impossible he reluctantly accepted the music directorship of the Los Angeles Philharmonic. After his first concert with the orchestra on 19 October 1933,[133] Klemperer conducted it on a further 289 occasions between 1933 and 1940, a schedule that was both demanding musically and taxing physically.[134] While he was relieved to find steady employment at a time of extreme international turmoil, he gained little pleasure from working and living in Los Angeles and considered the attitude of its citizens shallow and culturally naïve. Although many leading cultural émigrés resided in Los Angeles in the immediate pre-World War II period, their presence did little to improve the artistic apathy that shrouded the city like a pall. The local orchestra had been affected particularly badly by the cultural indifference of the local citizens, and by the time that Klemperer replaced Artur Rodzinski[135] as the orchestra's conductor, the organization was failing financially and disbandment was a real possibility. It was clear, therefore, to both the management and Klemperer that his programmes had to be attractive musically and viable economically.

To achieve a synthesis that would attract audiences and be interesting artistically, Klemperer needed to alter his approach to programming. Unlike the Berlin Staatskapelle, the Los Angeles Philharmonic Orchestra relied heavily on private subsidy and ticket sales to fund its concert season. Its programmes had to appeal to a broad audience, and the inclusion of extracts from opera was one way of achieving that goal. Because Los Angeles had no permanent opera company, Klemperer and the orchestra were able to fill a gap by frequently performing extracts from Wagner's stage works. Having argued in Germany that interest in Wagner's music was diminishing, Klemperer must have been pleasantly surprised by the demand for his music in Los Angeles. Of course, audiences in California only wanted to hear the most popular excerpts from Wagner's operas and it is debatable whether their interest would have extended to complete performances of the music dramas. Nevertheless, Wagner's music was heard at twenty-five per cent of all concerts given by Klemperer and the Los Angeles Philharmonic Orchestra and, of those, two were all-Wagner programmes.[136]

As audience approval was a critical criterion when programming in Los Angeles, it is hardly surprising that the composer heard most frequently was Beethoven. No less than a third of the concerts contained a work by him and, of those, twenty-four were devoted to his music. During his first season in California, Klemperer conducted all nine symphonies and, with the exception of Symphonies Nos. 2, 4 and 6, gave multiple performances of each work. In keeping with contemporary trends, the work by Beethoven that he conducted most was Symphony No. 5, with twenty-two performances in seven seasons.[137] Along with the music of Beethoven, the works of Mozart, Brahms, Bach and Haydn featured regular in Klemperer's Los Angeles programmes. As each of these composers represented a guaranteed box-office success for the management, their frequent appearance was to be expected. Less attractive to Californian audiences during the 1930s was the music of Bruckner and Mahler, and Klemperer was able to programme only the former's more popular Symphonies Nos. 4 ('Romantic') and 7 and the latter's *Das Lied von der Erde* and Symphony No. 2 with the Los Angeles Philharmonic.[138]

But Klemperer's programmes were not based solely on popular works from the Austro-German canon; he also conducted new and exciting music from Central Europe and elsewhere. Having championed the music of Hindemith at his Kroll concerts, Klemperer continued to support the composer by programming the symphony *Mathis der Maler*, *Trauermusik*, *Symphonic Dances*, *Der Schwanendreher* and *Nobilissima visione* at Los Angeles.[139] Another composer whose works Klemperer performed with both the Berlin Staatskapelle and the Los Angeles Philharmonic was Arnold Schoenberg, who had also fled to the USA after the rise of the Nazis.[140] Although Klemperer held Schoenberg's early works in high regard, he had little affinity with his later style, and the works that he programmed at Los Angeles reflected that reticence. With the exception of the Suite for Strings, *Verklärte Nacht* and the 'Lied der Waldtaube' from *Gurrelieder*,[141] the only works by Schoenberg that Klemperer conducted in California were the Cello Concerto, based on music by the eighteenth-century composer Georg Monn, and the arrangement of Brahms's Piano Quartet in G minor.[142]

Another living Central European composer whom Klemperer hoped to promote at Los Angeles was Kurt Weill.[143] Having conducted his *Kleine Dreigroschenmusik* in Berlin, Klemperer thought that the jazz-inspired work would be a suitable choice for his West Coast audience, but he was badly mistaken and the composition was greeted poorly.

Most modern listeners might not associate Klemperer with French, Russian, Scandinavian or American music but, during his tenure as Music Director in Los Angeles, his programmes contained a variety of works from those traditions. Of the French composers performed, the music of Franck, Debussy and Ravel was heard most frequently. Klemperer's biographer, Peter Heyworth, claimed that the conductor had a 'lack of enthusiasm' for Franck's Symphony in D minor,[144] but, if that was true, he seems to have set aside his doubts in Los Angeles, because he conducted the work on eighteen occasions in seven seasons. The Debussy repertoire that Klemperer performed in California included, amongst others, 'Fêtes' and 'Nuages' from *Nocturnes*, *La Mer* and *Prélude à l'après-midi d'un faune*, which he conducted at least sixteen times during his Los Angeles tenure. Ravel's *Alborado del gracioso* had been part of Klemperer's repertoire since the 1920s and it was natural that it should also be heard at his California concerts. The vibrancy of Ravel's music seems to have appealed to West Coast audiences: during his time with the Philharmonic Klemperer also conducted *La Valse*, *Rhapsodie espagnole*, *Boléro*, *Tzigane*, *Pavane pour une infante défunte*, *Le Tombeau de Couperin*, *Daphnis et Chloé* Suite No. 2 and Ravel's orchestration of Mussorgsky's *Pictures at an Exhibition*.

Of the works by living Russian composers, Stravinsky's music was heard most frequently with six of Klemperer's seven seasons in Los Angeles containing a work by him. But unlike the works he programmed with the Berlin Staatskapelle, the compositions performed were restricted to the suites from *Petrushka*, *The Firebird* and *Apollon Musagète*. Klemperer also conducted three performances of Shostakovich's Symphony No. 1 and two of his Piano Concerto No. 1.[145] The symphony must have had some popular support, because Klemperer conducted it on three further occasions during the 1938–9 season.[146] Similarly, the music of Sibelius must have appealed to Californian audiences, because he performed Symphonies Nos. 1, 2, 4, 5 and 7 and *The Swan of Tuonela* on no fewer than twenty-eight occasions in seven seasons. Less appealing to both the public and Klemperer was American music. Among the native composers that he performed in California were Barber, Carpenter, Gruenberg,[147] Harris, Hill, Mason, McDonald, MacDowell, Sessions, Still, Strang and Taylor.[148] As works by these composers were heard at only eleven per cent of the concerts given by Klemperer at Los Angeles between 1933 and 1940, it seems that his interest was nothing more than a token gesture to placate local vested interests.[149]

Klemperer's Los Angeles Philharmonic tenure came to an abrupt end when it was discovered that he was suffering from a brain tumour in the summer of 1939. Although it was removed successfully in the September of that year, the lengthy period of recuperation necessary meant that he was unable to fulfil his duties in California and that his contract had to be terminated in October 1940.[150] A side effect of removing the brain tumour was a partial loss of function on the right side of his body, resulting in him being unable to hold a baton to beat time with his right hand. But physical gestures were only of passing consequence to Klemperer, who later stated that when conducting he paid little attention to conducting technique because it distracted him from the music he was performing.[151] For him, the essence of conducting was the ability to exert influence over the performance by the 'power of suggestion'.[152] On the use of the baton he had mixed feelings, and when asked about it in later life he stated that, although he stopped using the baton after his operation in 1939, he took it up again because he felt that it aided precision. But Klemperer was never given to thinking in absolutes and he concluded enigmatically, 'Now I use a stick. But perhaps tomorrow I won't.'[153]

Over the next six years, Klemperer suffered increasingly from his manic-depressive condition. His often bizarre behaviour meant that he was overlooked by most of the important orchestras and that the majority of the work that he undertook was with second-rate organizations. His fortunes began to change, however, when he visited Europe in the spring of 1946. That year, he was engaged as a guest conductor by, among others, the Stockholm Philharmonic, the Paris Conservatoire, the Santa Cecilia and the Concertgebouw Orchestras. He was also one of the first German-Jewish conductors to perform in Germany after World War II, and his concert at Baden-Baden on 30 June 1946 was an attempt 'to heal the wounds' that had been 'inflicted' by the Nazi period. For him, reconciliation could be achieved through music and he hoped that his return to Germany would be viewed 'in [that] light'.[154]

Klemperer returned to Europe again in 1947 and began a particularly fruitful relationship with the Hungarian State Opera in the October of that year.[155] Although engaged only as a guest conductor, he gave 110 performances of fifteen operas by eight composers over three seasons.[156] In keeping with house policy, all the works were sung in Hungarian and most were repertory productions.[157] Operas from the Austro-German canon dominated Klemperer's Budapest schedule and, with the exception of Strauss's *Der Rosenkavalier*, all those performed were composed in the eighteenth and nineteenth centuries. If his activities in Budapest are compared with those of his tenures at Wiesbaden or the Kroll, the absence of cutting-edge works might seem strange. But Klemperer was not the music director of the Hungarian State Opera and was in no position to challenge that company's programme policy. Moreover, Klemperer's career had faltered by the 1940s and he needed the work. Although he was violently opposed to the repertory system, survival had to take precedence over principles.

Klemperer also worked as a concert conductor at Budapest, where he directed no fewer than sixty-four concerts with the Budapest Philharmonic, Capital and Hungarian Radio Orchestras. Although he was engaged as a guest conductor only, the repertoire that he performed in the Hungarian capital indicates an increasing shift from the adventurous to the conservative. The composer that dominated Klemperer's programmes during the late 1940s was Beethoven. Of the sixty-four concerts that he gave with the Budapest orchestras, thirty-seven contained a work by him, and, of those, eighteen were all-Beethoven programmes. The symphonies that he performed most frequently were Symphonies Nos. 1 and 9, which he gave on eight and nine occasions respectively. For Klemperer, Symphonies Nos. 1 and 9 were complementary and he programmed them together on five occasions.[158] Apart from Beethoven, the composers that Klemperer performed most frequently at Budapest were Mozart and Bach.[159] Of the concerts given, twenty-three contained a work by Mozart, ten contained a work by Bach, three were all-Mozart programmes and two were all-Bach programmes. Klemperer had little interest in the early or lesser-known works by Mozart and Bach and centred his repertoire on the late symphonies of the former and the Orchestral Suites and the Brandenburg Concertos of the latter.

Klemperer's reluctance to programme adventurously also extended to living composers. Apart from a few of his own compositions, he conducted only a handful of works by Bartók, Stravinsky, Strauss, Shostakovich and Kodály. For a conductor whose name had become linked increasingly with that of Stravinsky, the virtual absence of the composer's works is surprising.[160] Similarly, the paucity of new music by Hungarian composers is also strange. Apart from Bartók's Violin Concerto No. 2 (Endre Zathureczky, violin) and Kodály's *Summer Evening* with the Capital Orchestra on 12 December 1949 and 19 January 1950 respectively, Klemperer conducted no other recent Hungarian music. But he did revisit the music of Shostakovich with performances of Symphonies Nos. 1 and 9 with the Capital and Budapest Philharmonic Orchestras on 7 March and 21 November 1949 respectively. Of the newly composed works by German composers, only Strauss's *Metamorphosen* was heard.[161] Klemperer had reservations about the composer's late music and later described Strauss's most tragic composition as 'basically quite nice',[162] a curiously facile remark by a serious musician about a work of deep emotional intensity.

The small number of new or recent works that Klemperer conducted in Budapest was not indicative of his response to contemporary works in general during the post-war period. He remained passionate about composition throughout his long life and took a keen interest in new trends and developments. As a composer, he wrote, among others, six symphonies, nine string quartets, four major works for chorus and orchestra, three completed operas, twenty-eight works for voice and orchestra, 110 songs for voice and piano and numerous instrumental works. While Klemperer's compositions were generally received coolly, their genesis allowed him to identify more closely with the music of others. Younger colleagues appreciated his interest in all things new, and the conductor-composer Pierre Boulez recalled that Klemperer 'retained a surprising openness of spirit, a permanent desire to keep himself informed, to know, to listen, to follow'.[163] This, then, raises the question: why did Klemperer, a musician with a strong commitment to contemporary music, continue to reduce the number of new works in his programmes after his return to Europe in 1946? A primary reason was his physical condition. He had been affected adversely by his brain tumour and he no longer had the physical coordination that some newer works required. His inability to meet the technical demands of those works was noticed by musicians and critics alike, and his uneasy readings of newer music drew poor reviews. Another reason for the small number of twentieth-century works in his post-war programmes was the way in which he was perceived by audiences and impresarios. His readings of the Austro-German canon had gradually acquired an iconic status and concert promoters were keen to present him as a curator of that tradition, guaranteeing box-office success for managements and kudos for him.

Klemperer terminated his relationship with the Hungarian State Opera abruptly in 1950. In the years that followed, he was sought after increasingly as a guest conductor elsewhere and worked with most of the leading American, British and European orchestras. Of particular importance were his engagements with the Philharmonia Orchestra at the Royal Festival Hall, London, on 3 May and 29 June 1951.[164] The Philharmonia Orchestra had been founded as a recording orchestra by the record producer Walter Legge in 1946. Legge, who had risen through the ranks of the Gramophone Company, was an important power broker in the London music scene in the immediate post-war years. During the inter-war period, he worked as a music critic for the *Manchester Guardian* and assisted Sir Thomas Beecham at the Royal Opera House, Covent Garden. After the outbreak of war in 1939, he worked for the Entertainments National Services Association (ENSA) and later married the renowned soprano Elisabeth Schwarzkopf.[165] Legge was an opinionated and headstrong individual, who had the ability to alienate colleagues with ease. But he did have an instinct for spotting musicians of talent and he had the knack of marketing them successfully to audiences and record buyers alike. His flair in both areas led to the appointment of the Austrian musician Herbert von Karajan,[166] as conductor of the Philharmonia Orchestra in 1948. Karajan's period with the orchestra was particularly fruitful but, by 1959, his relationship with the orchestra had begun to wane and Legge needed to appoint a major musical figure to replace him. As Klemperer's concerts in May and June 1951 were a success and as his engagements with the orchestra had increased steadily thereafter, he was appointed by Legge as the orchestra's Principal Conductor for Life in 1959.

As one of the few remaining Central European conductors of stature with direct links to the nineteenth century, it was almost inevitable that the majority of Klemperer's repertoire with the Philharmonia was music from the past. With the exception of Bartók's Divertimento for Strings, Stravinsky's *Pulcinella* Suite and his own Symphony No. 1,[167] he performed no music composed after the death of Mahler publicly. As in Budapest, the majority of his concerts with the Philharmonia Orchestra contained a work by Beethoven.[168] Of the fifty-seven performances that he conducted at the Royal Festival Hall with the orchestra between 1959 and February 1964, twenty-seven contained a work by that composer and, of those, twenty-three were devoted to his music.[169] Klemperer also performed Mozart's works regularly at the Royal Festival Hall, with fifteen concerts containing a work by him and six being devoted to his music.[170] Other composers that he performed frequently with the orchestra at the hall were Bach, Brahms, Mahler and Bruckner. Brahms's music was heard at eight concerts, of which four were all-Brahms programmes,[171] Bach's compositions were restricted to the Brandenburg Concertos, Orchestral Suites Nos. 2 and 3 and the *St*

Matthew Passion,[172] Mahler's works were confined to *Das Lied von der Erde* and Symphonies Nos. 2 and 4[173] and Bruckner's symphonies were limited to Nos. 7, 8 and 9.[174]

As conductor of the Philharmonia Orchestra, Klemperer found that his profile as a recording artist increased sharply. Before World War II, he made records for Polydor, Parlophone and HMV. Unlike those of his colleagues Bruno Walter and Wilhelm Furtwängler, some of Klemperer's pre-war recordings documented his catholic approach to programming. With Polydor, for example, he recorded Ravel's *Alborado del gracioso* and two of Debussy's *Nocturnes* in 1926 and Weill's *Kleine Dreigroschenmusik* in 1931. The three recordings were made with the Berlin Staatskapelle and were part of a wider pre-war discography that included symphonies, or movements from symphonies, by Brahms, Beethoven, Bruckner and Schubert,[175] overtures by Beethoven, Mendelssohn, Weber, Brahms, Auber and Offenbach,[176] and stage and orchestral music by Strauss[177] and Wagner.[178] The works that he documented had clear links with his activities in the concert hall and it seems that the companies for whom he worked were willing to risk profits by recording repertoire that was not only appealing and challenging to the average record buyer but also to connoisseurs.

When Klemperer came to record for Vox between 1946 and 1951, the company was small and in no position to record adventurous repertoire. It was understandable, therefore, that they restricted their activities to music composed between the late eighteenth and the first decade of the twentieth centuries.[179] Although the repertoire recorded by Vox did little to indicate Klemperer's wide taste, the performances documented do give an insight into his shifting approach to tempo. For many modern listeners, the broad speeds that Klemperer adopted in some of his late recordings is an important issue. But to assume that those tempi were representative of his approach as a whole would be wrong. If, for example, his Vox recording of Bruckner's Symphony No. 4 is compared both with his later recording for EMI and with those of some of his contemporaries, it is immediately obvious that his speeds in the Vox recording are markedly faster. This is also true of his studio recording of Schubert's Symphony No. 4 ('Tragic') for Vox and of his live recording of Mahler's Symphony No. 2 with the Concertgebouw Orchestra at the Holland Festival on 12 July 1951 for Decca.[180] As Klemperer's manic-depressive condition meant that his behaviour swung wildly from extended periods of intense activity to bouts of near lethargy, it would not be unreasonable to assume that his mental state affected his chosen tempo. If this was so, it is clear that when he was manic his speeds would be quicker than when he was depressed. But little or no research has been undertaken concerning the impact of Klemperer's mental state on the works that he interpreted and, until that has been attempted, the exact nature of his performance style remains unclear.

Profit and marketing also dictated the works that Klemperer recorded with the Philharmonia Orchestra for EMI from 1954. The record producer Walter Legge was keen to capitalize on Klemperer's increasingly iconic status as an interpreter of the Austro-German canon and recorded accordingly. In general, Klemperer was uninterested in either recordings or the recording process but saw it as means of earning additional income. When conducting a score with the Philharmonia Orchestra that was also to be recorded, Klemperer preferred to document it in the studio before performing it in the concert hall. The relationship between concert hall and recording studio was important for Legge, whose marketing strategy linked both areas. As British and American audiences were impressed by Austro-German musicians and considered that their interpretations of works from the Central European repertoire had greater authority than those of conductors from other ethnic backgrounds, most of the works recorded by Klemperer for EMI were of composers from that canon. This meant that Klemperer and EMI were able to challenge the market share held by Bruno Walter and Columbia, whose marketing strategy was similar to that of their British rivals. With the exception of Klemperer's *Merry Waltz* and *One Step*, Weill's *Kleine Dreigroschenmusik*, Strauss's *Metamorphosen*, Stravinsky's Symphony in Three Movements and *Pulcinella* Suite, all the music that Klemperer recorded with the Philharmonia Orchestra between 1954 and February 1964 was by composers who were active before the end of the first decade of the twentieth century.

In March 1964, Legge announced the disbandment of the Philharmonia Orchestra. While this came as a shock to the orchestra, it was an inevitable result of the depressed market for recordings of art music in the early 1960s. For those involved with the orchestra, it was not simply the news of the disbandment that distressed them but the way in which it was handled. Legge gave little notice to the musicians and he made no attempt to address Klemperer's contract for life.[181] It was soon clear to all those affected by the disbandment that their only alternative was to re-form as the self-governing New Philharmonia. Legge, however, did not make this easy, because he objected to them using the name 'New Philharmonia' and refused to sell them the orchestra's existing music library.[182] But Legge was unable to prevent the inevitable and the orchestra began to perform as the New Philharmonia in October 1964.

As a new ensemble, the New Philharmonia needed a major artist as its conductor and Klemperer seemed the natural choice. By late 1964, however, old age and poor health meant that he was unwilling to accept the challenge of tenure. But he did agree to become the orchestra's President, and continued to perform and to record in that capacity until his last concert with it on 26 September 1971. Fittingly, his London swansong consisted of Beethoven's overture *König Stephan* and Piano Concerto No. 4 (Daniel Adni, piano) and Brahms's Symphony No. 3, works that reflected his increasingly narrow programming policy from 1964. Of course, during the last years of his career, he continued to perform works from other cultures and periods but, in general, his activities in the concert hall, opera house and recording studio were restricted to the Austro-German canon. It was inevitable, therefore, that after his death in Zürich on 6 July 1973, record companies marketed him as one of the last exponents of that tradition, but Klemperer was more than a curator of a musical museum; he was an artist of broad taste whose intellectual curiosity ensured that he remained receptive to new ideas to the end of his long life.

CHAPTER 8

The Transcendental Furtwängler

Wilhelm Furtwängler holds a unique place in the history of conducting. Unlike the conductors who preceded and succeeded him, he is perceived universally as a transcendental figure who was able to imbue established masterpieces with fresh insights at each successive performance. While it is true that his work always had a sense of the new, he was in fact a meticulous musician who planned his effects well in advance of execution.[1] Throughout his life Furtwängler aspired to composition but, like Klemperer, he never achieved the status that he desired. Although more successful than Klemperer as a composer, Furtwängler was unable to convince fully as a creative artist and his works are now performed more for their curiosity value than for their intrinsic worth. Nevertheless, his activities as a composer meant that he had an interest in new music and that he was passionate in putting modern works before the public. But his achievements in championing the compositions of his contemporaries have often been overshadowed by his activities during the Third Reich. Although clearly not in sympathy with the aims and the ideals of the regime, his decision to stay in Germany affected his career in the post-war period and the way that he is perceived to this day. For some he is a hero who remained behind the government and worked against it from within, but for others he was simply a collaborator who lacked the courage to leave. Whatever the case, he remains a central figure in the dissemination and reception of German music and an artist whose stature is as relevant today as it was in the middle of the twentieth century.

Born in Berlin on 25 January 1886 to the renowned archaeologist Adolf Furtwängler and his wife Adelheid, Wilhelm was the first of four children.[2] As he was raised in an educated, middle-class environment, it was almost inevitable that he would begin piano lessons at an early age. Studying first with his mother and then with his aunt, Minna, Wilhelm not only progressed quickly at the keyboard but also displayed a precocious interest in composition. He completed his first piece at the age of seven and although it is very rudimentary and clearly not the work of a composing prodigy, it was his first step on the road to composition, a journey that he would travel for much of his life.[3]

Having moved to Munich with the family at the age of eight, Wilhelm entered the city's Humanistisches Gymnasium in the mid 1890s. Unable to come to terms with its strict academic regime, he soon rebelled and it was decided that he would be removed from the school and would be tutored privately. Concerned that Wilhelm should have the best education possible, Adolf then engaged the services of Ludwig Curtius and Walter Riezler, fellow archaeologists, to supervise his son's academic studies.

Furtwängler's music education was equally unorthodox. As a youth, he never attended a school of music but had private lessons with a series of individual teachers instead. His first formal piano teacher was the pianist and composer Anton Beer-Walbrunn, who quickly recognized. Furtwängler's outstanding potential and recommended him to the renowned teacher and composer Joseph Rheinberger, the director of the Münchener Musikakademie. Although Rheinberger no longer accepted private students, Furtwängler made such a deep impression that he was prepared to make an exception. Rheinberger was a notoriously conservative musician who preferred the music of Beethoven to that of Wagner. That preference influenced the young Furtwängler, who later recalled that after hearing Der Ring des Nibelungen under 'the famous Wagner conductor Franz Fischer with the best singers of the Munich stage . . . my illusion and love of Wagner [was destroyed] for years afterwards'.[4] Inevitably, Rheinberger's conservatism failed to stimulate Furtwängler fully, so he turned to the progressive composer Max von Schillings, with whom he began to explore the works of Wagner in detail. Schillings's influence was significant, and in later years Furtwängler attempted to repay his debt to the composer by performing his works wherever possible. Furtwängler completed his formal music studies with Conrad Ansorge, with whom he studied the piano in Berlin between 1902 and 1903.

While Furtwängler's training was less than orthodox, his route to the podium followed the classic path through the ranks of the Central European opera-house system. His first post was at the Breslau Stadttheater, where his mother's cousin, Georg Dohrn, engaged him as a répétiteur for the 1905–6 season. Despite having been introduced to German theatre life through family connections, Furtwängler never conducted publicly at Breslau, but he did gain some valuable early experience there by conducting off-stage bands and by coaching singers. As an ambitious young musician, Furtwängler had little interest in such menial tasks and hoped to raise his profile at Breslau with the world première of his Symphony in D major. Although prepared and performed with care by Dohrn, the work failed to ignite the interest of either the critics or the public and disappeared from the repertoire. Furtwängler's father, however, refused to allow his son to be defeated by the audience's response, so he arranged for a performance of a work by Wilhelm at Munich. By drawing upon personal connections, Adolf not only persuaded the management of the Kaim Orchestra to allow his son to perform his Symphonic Poem in B minor but also to conduct the rest of the concert.

For his début as a conductor on 19 February 1906, Furtwängler chose a taxing programme that included his Symphonic Poem, Beethoven's overture *Die Weihe des Hauses* and Bruckner's Symphony No. 9. While neither the Beethoven nor the Bruckner is an easy work to perform, the critique in the *Münchner Neueste Nachrichten* indicates that Furtwängler acquitted himself adequately.[5] In a review that was more positive than negative, the critic argued that although Furtwängler's excessive daring and self-confidence was less than desirable, his musicianship was such that, with time, he could develop into a capable conductor.

With his 1906 performance of Bruckner's Symphony No. 9, Furtwängler began his lifelong association with the composer's works. In an article that he penned about the symphonies in 1939, his devotion to Bruckner's music is immediately apparent. While he openly acknowledges the composer's lack of popular appeal, he raises the thorny question of cuts, the crude tool used by some conductors when attempting to make the symphonies more accessible. For him, the excisions could not be justified because they affected the music's 'greater organic cohesion'.[6] In later years, Symphony No. 9 remained of particular importance to Furtwängler, and in 1952 he wrote, 'I think in all sincerity I could suggest to the Holy Father that this grandiose work should be officially acknowledged as a sacred work.'[7]

Furtwängler's début with the Kaim Orchestra, later known as the Munich Philharmonic, was the beginning of an extended relationship that continued until 10 January 1950.[8] With the exceptions of Berlioz's overture to *Benvenuto Cellini*[9] and Tchaikovsky's Symphony No. 6 ('Pathétique'),[10] his repertoire with the orchestra was entirely Austro-German. In contrast to his activities as a tenured conductor, his Munich concerts were dominated by the music of Beethoven, with eight of the thirteen programmes containing works by the composer.[11] The piece by Beethoven that Furtwängler gave most often at Munich was Symphony No. 5, with three performances. During the course of his career the work became a kind of talisman for Furtwängler, who conducted it often at important engagements, generally as the final work in the programme.

Passionate about composition, Furtwängler would have preferred to earn his living as a creative rather than a recreative artist. As this was not possible, he decided to pursue a career as a conductor and accepted the post of chorus master at the Zürich Stadttheater for the 1906–7 season. There he conducted Lehár's *Die lustige Witwe*, his first performance of a stage work. After its première at Vienna on 30 December 1905, at which it had been an instant success, the operetta was given widely. Although the thought of conducting a string of operetta performances would hardly have inspired Furtwängler, he took his task seriously and studied the score assiduously. But repetition is a major hazard for conductors of light opera and Furtwängler was its victim: he lost concentration during one of the performances, failed to hear a dialogue cue, brought the performance to a standstill and was dismissed from Zürich. With his career in disarray, Furtwängler returned to Munich, where he was appointed répétiteur at the Hofoper in 1907. While his duties there did not include conducting, he was involved in the preparation of the world première of Beer-Walbrunn's *Don Quijote, der sinnreiche Junker von Mancha* and the first Munich performance of Schillings's *Moloch*, works by two of his former teachers.[12]

After Munich, Furtwängler was engaged by Hans Pfitzner as Third Kapellmeister at the Strasbourg Stadttheater for the 1909–10 season. Like Walter at Cologne, Furtwängler used his position educationally by attending Pfitzner's performances and questioning him about his conducting style. Even though Furtwängler later had doubts about Pfitzner's methods,[13] he was particularly keen to study his approach to Wagner, Beethoven and Weber. More important, Pfitzner represented the young Furtwängler's ideal: a successful composer-conductor. In later life, however, his belief in the importance of the composer-conductor altered, and he argued: 'Great composers are seldom completely satisfactory performers . . . because they never wholly dedicate themselves, even to their own works. . . . Their coolness, or mistrust, towards their own passion, which has so ruined their concepts, so often betrayed them, gives them that suspicious coolness, that objectively stand-offish attitude that we can see in Strauss, Pfitzner, Reger, etc. Only Wagner, the epitome of the expressive person, seems to have been an exception here too.'[14] In 1909, however, Furtwängler was not plagued by these concerns and his admiration for Pfitzner was reciprocated. The composer-conductor was immediately impressed by the young musician's potential and allowed him to perform some light and Italian operas at the Stadttheater.[15] But Furtwängler's performances received mixed reviews and his abilities were judged particularly harshly by the eminent German critic Rudolf Louis, who considered him a hopeless case with no future as a conductor.[16]

At Strasbourg, Furtwängler was acutely aware of his technical short-comings as a conductor and tried to eradicate them by practising in front of a mirror and by experimenting with gestures while walking. In later years, his controversial conducting technique developed into something of a *bête noire* and was the source of lively discussions by performers and audiences alike. In his essay of 1937, *Vom Handwerkszeug eines Dirigenten (The Tools of the Conductor's Trade)*,[17] he confronts his critics, outlines his ideas on conducting and defends his approach. For him, the art of conducting is mysterious and cannot be defined easily. He acknowledges that conducting requires the transmission of thoughts and ideas through gesture, and that these vary little because of their relationship to tempo and rhythm. While he inveighs against prescribed methods of conducting, which he suggests can often fail to serve the music adequately, he emphasizes the importance of a correct use of gesture, which can convey more in a short time than extended periods of rehearsal. A primary function of the conductor is to set the tempo, and this, he maintains, can affect the ensemble and other fundamentals of performance. Of particular importance is the relationship of technique and line – specifically, the ability to achieve a true cantabile, which is vital rhythmically. To this end, visual preparation is important and the upbeat rather than the downbeat is crucial to the effect required. For Furtwängler, a strong downbeat can restrict the music's line and affect its expressive qualities adversely. Moreover, to conduct rhythmically, emphasizing individual beats, is to underestimate the importance of the melodic content. The result of such a practice is that, rhythm and tempo benefit at the expense of the music as a whole and this is unacceptable. He was aware that those trained in schools of music and some critics found his approach untenable, but he maintained that the results he achieved with the orchestras with which he performed stood as his defence.

Clearly, much of the above is a reaction to the methods of Arturo Toscanini and his followers. In the essay Furtwängler makes no overt reference to the Italian, but in his notebooks he was less circumspect. Of Toscanini's interpretation of Debussy's *La Mer*, for example, Furtwängler wrote in 1930 that his 'primitive and unintellectual manner so consistently, and with such a naïve lack of awareness, ignored Debussy's sensitive tonal language, that one could only wonder why he had performed the work at all'.[18] And of Toscanini's understanding of Beethoven's Symphony No. 3 ('Eroica'), he is even more damning, arguing that the Italian's 'lack of acquaintance with and his naïve ignorance of one of the main demands of properly symphonic music, the demand for organic development, . . . fail[ed] to exist for Toscanini. There are technical reasons for this too.'[19] Furtwängler was notoriously sensitive to criticism, and his harsh judgement of Toscanini was probably a result of his own insecurities. Those insecurities plagued Furtwängler for much of his life and his approach to conducting technique was an especially thorny subject.

Hermann Abendroth resigned as conductor of the Lübeck Orchestra in 1911. Although the vacancy had been advertised widely, Furtwängler was alerted to the opening only after the closing date for applications. As only four of the ninety-seven conductors who applied for the job would be admitted to the final audition stage,[20] Furtwängler held out little hope for his late application. But when it emerged that one of the candidates had already been earmarked for the job, another withdrew his application in protest and Furtwängler was accepted as the fourth contender. Having qualified by default, he now faced an audition process that consisted of two parts: a rehearsal with the local chorus and one with the orchestra. At the rehearsal with chorus, Furtwängler failed to impress and was certain that he was no longer in contention for the post. At the orchestral rehearsal, however, his fortunes were reversed and it was clear to all that he was the right man for the job. While his conducting style had little in common with that of Abendroth – Abendroth's technique was precise while Furtwängler's was twitchy and uneven – the orchestra had little trouble in responding to his intentions and he was appointed unanimously as Kapellmeister of Lübeck's Verein der Musikfreunde.

As conductor in Lübeck, Furtwängler was responsible for eight major subscription concerts and thirty popular concerts each winter.[21] This schedule must have been extremely taxing for him, for he had conducted only one major symphony concert and was plagued by technical difficulties. Although he lacked experience, he was undaunted by his task and began by tackling repertoire that was challenging both technically and musically. At the subscription concerts, he conducted

Bruckner's Symphony No. 8, Beethoven's Symphonies Nos. 3 and 9 ('Choral') and Tchaikovsky's Symphony No. 5, while at the popular concerts, where the patrons could sit, smoke and consume alcohol, he conducted programmes that resembled Gustav Kogel's popular concerts in Berlin and Henry J. Wood's Promenade Concerts in London. Initially, the Lübeck popular concerts were divided into three parts: the first usually contained a symphony, overture or concerto; the second was devoted to light music and instrumental solos, and the third was given over to familiar music and often ended with a march. As his tenure progressed, however, Furtwängler began to alter the shape and content of those programmes and, by the time of his last popular concert on 28 April 1915, the concert consisted of Bach's Orchestral Suite No. 2, Beethoven's Violin Concerto, Weber's overture to *Oberon*, Brahms's Hungarian Dances, Liszt's Hungarian Rhapsody No. 4 and Wagner's Prelude to *Die Meistersinger von Nürnberg*.[22]

Although Furtwängler's contractual duties in Lübeck were based firmly in the concert hall, he was aware that, if his career was to develop fully in Germany, he would have to raise his profile as an opera conductor. With a heavy schedule that left little time for accepting guest engagements elsewhere, his options were limited. But by the time of his last season at Lübeck, his popularity with both public and orchestra was such that he was invited to conduct Beethoven's *Fidelio*, Nicolai's *Die lustigen Weiber von Windsor* and Wagner's *Die Meistersinger von Nürnberg* at the local opera house. Although he gave three operas only, two of those performed – *Fidelio* and *Die Meistersinger von Nürnberg* – would occupy a special place in his mature performance aesthetic. Moreover, by performing the three operas, he was able to add a new dimension to a predominantly symphonic repertoire that had developed largely out of his thirty-two symphony concerts, seven oratorio performances and 120 popular concerts that he conducted at Lübeck.[23]

Arthur Bodansky resigned from the Mannheim Hofoper in 1914, leaving a vacancy for the position of Hofkapellmeister. Bruno Walter, who had formed a high opinion of Furtwängler after they had met in Strasbourg and was eager to promote his career, recommended Furtwängler for the post. Around the time of the Mannheim vacancy, Walter wrote to the Munich Intendant, Ernst von Possart, 'If I can [persuade] you to hear [Furtwängler], I'll be able to forgo any further recommendation of the young artist. I have the highest opinion of his talent and ability, his deep and true musicality, and his effectiveness before an audience.'[24] While Walter wrote a similar testimonial to the Mannheim management, they had little faith in paper recommendations and wanted to audition Furtwängler personally. As the theatre's previous conductors included Felix Weingartner, Emil von Rezniček and Arthur Bodansky, the directors naturally hoped that a candidate of similar calibre was among the applicants. Furtwängler was aware that the successful candidate would be required to conduct not only the six Academy Concerts given annually by the orchestra but also the majority of the operas. Clearly, he lacked the necessary operatic experience, but this did not prevent Bodansky and members of the Mannheim management team from travelling to Lübeck, where they heard him conduct Beethoven's *Fidelio*. Although Furtwängler was unhappy about his performance, the Mannheim visitors took a different stance and offered him the job immediately.[25]

As Mannheim's new Hofkapellmeister, Furtwängler introduce himself as an opera conductor with Weber's *Der Freischütz* and as a concert conductor with Brahms's Symphony No. 1. Having quickly established his authority as an interpreter of German music with his performance of *Der Freischütz*, he then undertook a taxing programme of operas that would have challenged even the most experienced theatre conductor. In his first season, he continued the early German Romantic theme with Marschner's *Hans Heiling* and then began to explore works from the mid and late nineteenth century with performances of Wagner's *Der fliegende Holländer*, *Tristan und Isolde*, *Parsifal* and *Der Ring des Nibelungen*. Furtwängler's interest in the music of Wagner deepened during his Mannheim period, and he later recalled in his notebook: 'only after I began to conduct the works [of Wagner] myself, did I understand the entire range of their greatness'.[26] Nevertheless, he continued to have mixed feelings about aspects of Wagner's iconic status and later proclaimed himself to be 'no Wagnerian, in so far as I see Wagner as a genius who provides us with norms and a sense of direction . . . [rather he] is and remains an exceptional case as musician'.[27]

Some commentators have expressed surprise at the overwhelming number of operas by Austro-German composers that Furtwängler conducted during his Mannheim period. Although it has been suggested that this was a consequence of German cultural policies during World War I, it had more to do with Furtwängler's approach to programming in general. As his interest in operas from cultures other than his own remained limited throughout his career, and as he rarely allowed political concerns to affect his programme policy in the pre-Nazi period, his approach at the Hofoper was an expression of personal taste rather than the result of external influences.

An important element of his programme policy at Mannheim was his interest in new music. After challenging audiences with Paul von Klenau's *Sulamith*, he repaid debts of gratitude to two of his mentors with performances of Max von Schillings's *Mona Lisa* and Pfitzner's *Der arme Heinrich*, *Christelflein* and *Palestrina*. While it is clear from the other works performed that he was more interested in laying the foundations of a professional working repertoire than acknowledging the help of his teachers, his penchant for works by Richard Strauss, Schillings, Pfitzner, Sekles and Klenau meant that he not only actively challenged the taste of the provincial Mannheim audience but also alienated some of his listeners.[28] The Intendant of the Mannheim Hoftheater, Carl Hagemann, was also less than impressed by Furtwängler's approach and was highly critical of his abilities as an opera conductor. Hagemann opined that Furtwängler was 'not a man of the theatre, neither in the broad sense as an organizer, nor in detail as an artist, or . . . as a musician. Furtwängler [had] a sense of the theatre, but he [did] not have the theatre in his blood.'[29]

While Hagemann might have questioned his abilities in the opera pit, Furtwängler's qualities as a concert conductor were not in doubt. Recognized quickly as a musician of potential, he was invited to make his début with the Berlin Philharmonic on 14 December 1917 with works by Wagner and Strauss.[30] As the orchestra had performed part of the programme the previous day,[31] it is likely that Furtwängler conducted with little or no rehearsal. Nevertheless, he obviously impressed both orchestra and management, because he was asked to conduct the Philharmonic again on 25 January and 8 March 1918.[32] A string of high-profile engagements then followed, including invitations to succeed Ferdinand Loewe as conductor of the Vienna Tonkünstler Orchestra,[33] Richard Strauss as conductor of the Berlin Staatskapelle's Abonnement Concerts and Willem Mengelberg as director of the Frankfurt Museum Concerts. Furtwängler was also appointed concert director of the Gesellschaft der Musikfreunde in Wien, a position he retained for life, and was invited to preside over the concerts of the Deutsche Brahms-Fest in Hamburg.

Furtwängler made his début as Richard Strauss's successor with the Berlin Staatskapelle on 2 April 1920.[34] That was the first of twenty-one concerts that he gave with the orchestra between that date and 28 April 1922.[35] Of those, seventeen were devoted to Austro-German composers, fourteen contained a work by Beethoven, thirteen were performed without a soloist, three were all-Beethoven concerts, two contained a symphony by Bruckner and one contained a symphony by

Mahler.[36] Although the number of works by Beethoven seems high, it was proportionately smaller than that given by Richard Strauss during his tenure. Under Strauss, eighty per cent of the concerts contained a work by Beethoven; under Furtwängler, the figure dropped to sixty-three per cent. Like Strauss, Furtwängler was passionate about new music, and along with established masterpieces he conducted recent compositions by Kaun, Schillings, Busoni, Koch and Reger and the Berlin premières of music by Schoenberg, Hausegger, Reznicek and Braunfels. [37]

After the death of Nikisch on 23 January 1922, Furtwängler was appointed Gewandhauskapellmeister in Leipzig and conductor of the Philharmonic Concerts in Berlin.[38] With the exception of his final years in Leipzig, Nikisch had presided over nearly all the concerts given by the Gewandhaus Orchestra. After the appointment of Furtwängler, however, the number of concerts conducted by the Gewandhauskapellmeister dropped sharply. This was due partly to the reduction in subscription concerts given each season from twenty-two to twenty but also to the other commitments undertaken by Nikisch's successors. Between the beginning of the 1922–3 and the end of the 1927–8 seasons, Furtwängler conducted on average fourteen of the twenty concerts given each year. Of those not conducted by him, Karl Straube gave annual or biannual performances of choral music and Edwin Fischer, Gustav Brecher, Gerhard von Keussler, Hans Pfitzner, Otto Klemperer, Ernst Wendel, Fritz Busch, Felix Weingartner, Erich Kleiber, Bruno Walter, Carl Schuricht, Georg Göhler and Georg Dohrn appeared as guest conductors.[39]

Modern music was prominent at Furtwängler's Leipzig concerts, with sixty-three per cent containing a piece by a living composer. Much of the new music was cutting-edge and included premières of works by Schoenberg, Graener, Kempff, Trapp, Braunfels, Georg Schumann, Raphael, Jarnach and Toch.[40] Of the other contemporary composers that Furtwängler performed at Leipzig, some of the more prominent included Strauss, Pfitzner, Respighi, Sibelius, Korngold, Stravinsky, Prokofiev, Hindemith, Busoni, Schoeck, Casella, Vaughan Williams, Ravel, Nielsen and Honegger.[41] It may come as a surprise that Furtwängler performed Stravinsky's *Le Sacre du printemps* with the Gewandhaus Orchestra.[42] For a conductor who was concerned about stick technique and who preferred to conduct in phrases rather than rhythmic points, the complex rhythms of the concluding 'Danse sacrale' must have challenged both conductor and orchestra. Also surprising is that although Furtwängler performed all nine Beethoven symphonies at

Leipzig, he never conducted a complete cycle of them in any one season.[43] Brahms's symphonies, too, were given regularly but never performed as part of a cycle. The works of Mahler and Bruckner were also a regular feature at Leipzig, with Furtwängler performing four works by the former during his tenure and continuing Nikisch's tradition of performing at least one work by the latter each season.[44]

In contrast to his activities in Leipzig, Furtwängler conducted nearly all of the Berlin Philharmonic's subscription concerts between the beginning of the 1922–3 season and 26 November 1934.[45] As he directed all but one of the 124 concerts given, it is obvious that he performed on average more concerts in Berlin than in Leipzig.[46] Aside from the differences in the quality of the two orchestras, the German capital was at the centre of the cultural whirlwind that swept through the country during the 1920s. For Furtwängler, the opportunity to be part of the new cultural environment would have been too good to miss, and the number of cutting-edge works that he performed with the Philharmonic reflects not only his interests but also the direction of the new artistic trends. At the concerts that he gave between 1922 and 1934, for example, sixty per cent contained a work by a living composer, including fifty local, Philharmonic or world premières.[47] Many of the new works were conducted by Furtwängler at both Leipzig and Berlin,[48] but of those that he conducted solely in the capital the most significant were the world premières of Schoenberg's Variations for Orchestra, Prokofiev's Piano Concerto No. 5 with the composer as soloist and Hindemith's symphony *Mathis der Maler*.[49] During the 1920s and 1930s the music of Hindemith and Schoenberg benefited greatly from the patronage of Furtwängler, whose interest in their music went beyond the superficial. This is apparent from an entry that he recorded in his notebook in 1932, which reads: 'who can fail to have the highest respect for Hindemith's simple and authentic attitude to work, or the consistency, bordering on self-mortification and despair, of Schönberg?'[50]

When performing works from the established repertoire, Furtwängler adopted a policy in Berlin that was similar to his approach in Leipzig. Again, he restricted his performances of Beethoven, with only forty-four per cent of the concerts given containing a work by him. No cycle of the symphonies was performed and no work was repeated during any one season. Even so, to suggest that Beethoven's music was not of critical importance to Furtwängler would be to misrepresent his approach to programming, because a work by the composer was performed at the final subscription concert of each season between 1922 and 1934.[51] Furtwängler was also circumspect when programming concerts devoted

to the music of one composer: he conducted only six all-Beethoven concerts in twelve seasons and two all-Brahms.[52] But the most striking
aspect of Furtwängler's approach to the performance of works by established composers was his lack of adventure. When performing symphonies by Mozart and Schubert, for example, he simply followed
contemporary trends and conducted only Nos. 38 ('Prague') to 41
('Jupiter') by the former and Nos. 7 ('Unfinished') in B minor and 8
('Great') in C major by the latter. Similarly, when performing symphonies by Bruckner, a composer with whom he had a special affinity,
he again lacked adventure and gave only Nos. 3 to 9.

On 24 January 1924, Furtwängler conducted in London for the first
time. For the Royal Philharmonic Society at the Queen's Hall, he gave a
programme that included Handel's Concerto grosso in D minor,
Strauss's Don Juan, Brahms's Symphony No. 1 and the first performance of the new version of Vaughan Williams's On Wenlock Edge.
Although Vaughan Williams is not a composer with whom Furtwängler
is usually associated, his introduction to the composer's music in 1924
must have been favourable, because he later performed Fantasia on a
Theme of Thomas Tallis at Leipzig and Norfolk Rhapsody at Vienna.[53]
As Furtwängler had originally hoped to include a symphony by Mahler
in the concert, the final shape of his first London programme is decep-
tive. But the Society did not share his enthusiasm for the composer's
music and rejected the suggestion for box-office reasons.[54] Nevertheless,
the programme given was well received and Furtwängler was invited to
open the following season with a concert that again included music by
Strauss and Brahms.[55] Curiously, Furtwängler's second Philharmonic
programme contained no new music and stood in sharp contrast to the
concerts conducted later in the season by Eugene Goossens, Ernest
Ansermet and Malcolm Sargent, all of which contained a London
première of a work by a living composer.[56]

New York had long attracted the attention of conductors from
Central Europe. Furtwängler was not immune to the benefits that the
USA had to offer, and on 3 January 1925 he made his début with the
New York Philharmonic Orchestra at Carnegie Hall.[57] For that concert,
he conducted a programme that was strongly reminiscent of his first
London appearance and that again included Strauss's Don Juan and
Brahms's Symphony No. 1.[58] Although he was keen to establish his
authority as a performer of the Austro-German canon, he was aware
that New York audiences had already experienced those works regu-
larly under Gustav Mahler, Richard Strauss, Felix Weingartner and
Bruno Walter. It was clear, therefore, that some of his programmes

needed to contain music from other traditions. As Furtwängler had begun to conduct Russian music regularly in Berlin and Leipzig, the inclusion of Tchaikovsky's Symphony No. 5 was a natural extension of his touring repertoire, but his decision to perform Stravinsky's *Le Sacre du printemps* was less obvious. Nevertheless, as a careerist Furtwängler was aware that by conducting Stravinsky's work he would be able to demonstrate his versatility as a performer. When it became clear, however, that part of his duties in New York included socializing with committee members and the press, he was unwilling to be flexible. For him, duties were unnecessary and unpalatable distractions, and his reluctance to participate in New York's social life quickly alienated him from both the all-important Ladies Committee and the critics. Although he returned in 1926 and 1927, he never regained the critical status that he had enjoyed during his first visit and was particularly distressed when the press compared him unfavourably with Willem Mengelberg and Arturo Toscanini. For a musician who was highly sensitive to criticism this was too much, and he departed at the end of his third visit feeling disillusioned and angry. He never returned to the USA.

Furtwängler's career as a recording artist began in 1926 with Beethoven's Symphony No. 5 and Weber's overture to *Der Freischütz*. In general, he was unimpressed by the dissemination of music by electronic, mechanical or broadcast means and argued that the new technology served only to distort and to mangle the music that it was trying to transmit. That said, he was encouraged by the progress that was being made in the USA in the 1930s and knew of Leopold Stokowski's enthusiasm for the pioneering work being undertaken there. Even so, he remained unconvinced by recording and considered gramophone records to be less than ideal sound documents. Sceptical of the gramophone's ability to represent his approach fully, he recorded only five major compositions between 1926 and 1939,[59] preferring instead to document short works, arrangements or extracts from operas and incidental music. Moreover, all the works recorded were composed in the eighteenth and nineteenth centuries. While this did much to strengthen Furtwängler's image as a curator of the great Austro-German canon, it also created a distorted picture of his activities as a whole. Of course, the works that were recorded in the years following World War II did little to change that image,[60] and although his enthusiasm for the gramophone had increased by the time of his post-World War II recordings for HMV, he remained unconvinced by the process to the end of his life.

Felix Weingartner resigned as conductor of the Vienna Philharmonic in 1927. He had held the post since 1908 and had developed a formidable reputation as a concert conductor. Furtwängler considered him to be 'a superior kind of musician . . . with classical training and experience'[61] and was honoured to be named his successor. As with his appointments in Berlin and Leipzig, Furtwängler was following in the footsteps of a major artist whose tenure had been both long and distinguished. But even Nikisch and Weingartner never had the honour of leading the German-speaking world's three finest orchestras – the Berlin Philharmonic, the Leipzig Gewandhaus and the Vienna Philharmonic Orchestras – concurrently. Having conducted the Vienna Philharmonic for the first time on 26 March 1922, Furtwängler was no stranger to its members. Over the following thirty-two years, he developed a strong bond with the orchestra and conducted it on no fewer than 460 occasions in Vienna, Salzburg and on tour.[62] Otto Strasser, a member of the Vienna Philharmonic between 1922 and 1967, recalled that Furtwängler 'influenced us so much that we became the true "Furtwängler orchestra"'. His 'link [with the Vienna Philharmonic] was so strong that we came into conflict with other conductors who attempted to change us according to their will'. Strasser argued that this was due in part to Furtwängler's methods. He felt that 'Furtwängler understood extraordinarily well how to rehearse, and for the most part made no further interruptions at the last rehearsal, so that we didn't just discern the cohesion of the phrases at the actual performance; the dress rehearsal almost became the performance'. Moreover, 'In general, each of [Furtwängler's] interpretations followed what Richard Wagner wrote in his article *On Conducting*, namely that the tempo of the "Melos", upon which melody depended, and "modification of tempo" (i.e. a sense of *rubato*) are the essential things in performing a musical art-work.'[63]

Having conducted eighty-four concerts with the Berlin, Leipzig and Vienna orchestras during the 1927–8 season,[64] Furtwängler found the workload too much and decided to withdraw from at least one of the organizations. As the Leipzig orchestra was the least distinguished of the three, he terminated his tenure as Gewandhauskapellmeister at the end of the 1927–8 season. In terms of the volume of work undertaken, Furtwängler's repertoire at the Vienna Philharmonic's Abonnement and Nicolai Concerts between 20 November 1927 and 23 March 1930 was similar to that which he performed in Berlin and Leipzig. His clear commitment to German art was obvious and each of the twenty-two concerts contained a work by an Austro-German composer. This statistic reflected his programme policy as a whole and matched his Berlin and Leipzig activities, where a work by an Austro-German composer was also heard at each concert. This unity of approach was obvious, too, in the performance of new music: in Vienna, fifty-four per cent of the concerts contained music by a living composer. Much of the new music performed was also heard in Berlin and Leipzig, but Furtwängler did present works by Prohaska and Weigl solely in Vienna.[65] Again, he was circumspect when programming Beethoven, with only forty-five per cent of the concerts containing a work by the composer. As with his concert series in Germany, the symphonies were not presented in cycles and only two concerts were devoted solely to Beethoven's music.[66] He continued to champion Bruckner's music at Vienna and, in keeping with his practice in Berlin and Leipzig, he conducted one symphony by that composer each season.[67]

Furtwängler's period as conductor of the Philharmonic concerts in Vienna was short. The Berlin Philharmonic had suffered a financial crisis at the end of the 1920s and new subsidy arrangements had to be established. Under the new plan the orchestra was to become a limited company, and the city of Berlin, the state of Prussia and the German government were to provide funds. A condition of this arrangement stipulated that Furtwängler was to remain as conductor of the orchestra for ten years, and although this affected his capacity to accept engagements in Vienna and elsewhere, he felt obliged to agree. He therefore relinquished his duties in Vienna at the end of the 1929–30 season and was appointed Städtischer Generalmusikdirektor of Berlin.

From the late 1920s, Furtwängler returned regularly to the opera pit. One of the first major engagements of that period was a new production of Wagner's Das Rheingold at the Vienna Staatsoper, which he conducted for the first time on 17 October 1928.[68] Two years later, Richard Wagner's son Siegfried died, leaving the Bayreuth Festival without a music director. To fill the void, Furtwängler and Toscanini were asked to share the direction of the 1931 festival. Although Toscanini had appeared there in 1930 with Tannhäuser and Tristan und Isolde,[69] Furtwängler was new to Bayreuth. It was decided, therefore, that Toscanini would conduct Tannhäuser and Parsifal in 1931 and that Furtwängler would make his début with Tristan und Isolde.[70] For the conductors, the opportunity to perform Wagner's music dramas at his theatre was something akin to a religious experience, but the devotion that they felt soon faded when Siegfried Wagner's English-born widow, Winifred, proved difficult. Both Furtwängler and Toscanini left at the end of the 1931 festival feeling angry and disillusioned, and although Furtwängler was determined never to return, his wrath dissipated quickly and he conducted there again between 1936 and 1954.[71] His

Bayreuth experience did little to damage his enthusiasm for opera conducting, and on 1 September 1933 he began his duties as Director of the
Berlin Staatsoper.[72] Having made his début there on 12 November 1931
with the world première of Pfitzner's *Das Herz*,[73] he was no stranger to
the theatre. Even so, those experiences did little to prepare him for the
difficulties ahead, because as principal conductor of both the Berlin
Staatsoper and the Berlin Philharmonic he soon came into daily contact
with Hitler and his new administration, a contact that quickly proved
explosive.

Furtwängler believed passionately that music and politics were
incompatible. During the first months of the Nazi regime,[74] he was
shocked and distressed by the behaviour of the new government and
took particular offence at the termination of Bruno Walter's activities in
Leipzig and Berlin and the attempt to dismiss Jewish members of the
Berlin Philharmonic. Consequently, he wrote an open letter to the
Minister for Propaganda, Joseph Goebbels, on 12 April 1933. In that
document, he states that race and religion should not be criteria for
artistic excellence, that he was prepared to acknowledge only the 'divid-
ing-line . . . which separates good art from bad art', and that Bruno
Walter, Otto Klemperer and Max Reinhardt should have the right to
practise their professions.[75] Although Goebbels published the letter, he
used it to further his own ends and responded with a reply that stressed
the link between art and politics and the need to eradicate 'foreign elements' in favour of 'German' artists. Nevertheless, Goebbels was aware
that Furtwängler was passionately opposed to the government's stance
and that he might leave Germany in protest. As that would have been a
major propaganda blow for the new administration, Goebbels ordered
that the conductor should be treated sensitively. This, however, did
nothing to placate Furtwängler who, in an attempt to counter the methods of the Nazi government, decided to discuss his concerns with Hitler
personally in August 1933. Unable to change the Chancellor's policy
concerning Jewish musicians, Furtwängler then decided to make a stand
by inviting leading Jewish soloists to perform with the Berlin
Philharmonic. He hoped that with their solidarity he could alter the
government's anti-Semitic line, but the soloists felt that this was a futile
gesture and were unwilling to participate in the exercise.

With a situation that deteriorated quickly, matters came to a head
when Furtwängler's open letter 'Der Fall Hindemith' ('The Case for
Hindemith') was published in the *Deutsche Allgemeine Zeitung* on 25
November 1934. Paul Hindemith was an excellent violist and composer
with whom Furtwängler had strong professional links. The conductor

had engaged him as the viola soloist for a performance of Berlioz's *Harold en Italie* with the Berlin Philharmonic on 31 October 1932 and had performed a string of his works with the Leipzig Gewandhaus, Berlin Philharmonic and Vienna Philharmonic Orchestras between 1923 and 1934.[76] By the time that Hitler came to power, the composer was already well known for his exotic and challenging stage works and had created sensations in 1921 with *Mörder, Hoffnung der Frauen* and *Das Nusch-Nuschi* and in 1929 with *Neues vom Tage*.[77] Unfortunately for Hindemith, Hitler attended a performance of the latter and considered it depraved. Consequently, when Furtwängler programmed the composer's next opera, *Mathis der Maler*, Hermann Göring, the minister directly responsible for the Berlin Staatsoper, told the conductor that he needed Hitler's approval to stage the work. Before permission could be given, however, Furtwängler performed the composer's symphony based on music from the opera at a concert with the Berlin Philharmonic Orchestra on 12 March 1934. The response to the work was overwhelming favourable and the government interpreted the audience's enthusiasm as a demonstration against Nazism. The opera was banned immediately and Furtwängler went to the defence of Hindemith in his open letter. The document prompted a storm of abuse from the Nazi press, which had been encouraged and sanctioned by the government. Furtwängler confronted Göring about the attacks and demanded that the minister put a stop to them. Enraged by the government's behaviour, he also made it clear that he would resign from all his official posts if the situation continued. Göring told Furtwängler that he was unable to help him personally and that he needed to consult Hitler about his demand. The Führer was in no mood for compromise, however, and the conductor's resignation was accepted.[78] Nevertheless, the government was keen for him to remain as conductor of the Berlin Philharmonic, a suggestion that was unacceptable to Furtwängler, who demanded that his ultimatum be accepted in its entirety or not all.

Having removed himself from all official duties, Furtwängler hoped to visit friends in Egypt. But the government, concerned that if he left Germany he might not return, confiscated his passport. Undaunted and unbowed, he then left for Bavaria where he used his time to compose. It was clear, however, that the situation needed to be resolved, so he contacted Goebbels's office in 1935. At the very least, Furtwängler wanted permission to perform abroad, but the minister delayed meeting the conductor in the hope that he could persuade him to acquiesce in the government's policies. This, however, was not an option for Furtwängler and he threatened to emigrate. As the government was reluctant to lose one of the country's cultural icons and as Furtwängler was loath to leave Germany, a compromise was reached whereby he would conduct in Germany but without any formal position. Although the deal was satisfactory to both Goebbels and Furtwängler, it needed to be ratified by Hitler. The Führer approved the agreement on 10 April 1935 and Furtwängler was free to conduct his first concert under the new deal two days later.[79]

During the period immediately before World War II period, Furtwängler continued to be associated closely with the Berlin and Vienna Philharmonics. With the former, he conducted some, but not all, of the Philharmonic Concerts and toured domestically and internationally. Of the international tours that he led, probably the most important were those to Britain. Having performed in the United Kingdom regularly before the rise of the Nazis,[80] conductor and orchestra returned in 1935, 1937 and 1938. While Furtwängler was concerned only with the dissemination of German art, the last three tours were also valuable propaganda tools for Hitler's government. With the Vienna Philharmonic, he conducted regularly at its Abonnement Concerts and performed in Budapest, Salzburg, Berlin, Nuremberg, Pressburg (Bratislava) and Munich.[81] Of Furtwängler's other guest conducting activities abroad in the mid 1930s, those in Britain were again of importance. Having performed regularly in London with the Berlin Philharmonic, Furtwängler made his Covent Garden début with Wagner's *Tristan und Isolde* on 20 May 1935. It was almost inevitable that his interpretation would be compared with that of Sir Thomas Beecham, who had conducted the opera twice earlier that season. Although the critics were divided over Furtwängler's approach, that did not prevent Beecham from inviting him to return to the theatre in 1937 and 1938 to conduct Wagner's *Der Ring des Nibelungen*.

Furtwängler made his Salzburg Festival début with Beethoven's Symphony No. 9 on 27 August 1937. Toscanini was also scheduled to appear at the Festival that year but withdrew when he learned of Furtwängler's engagement. Toscanini argued that Furtwängler had capitulated to the Nazis by continuing to perform at Bayreuth after 1933 and, therefore, should not be allowed to perform at Salzburg. As Toscanini had recommended Furtwängler to the New York Philharmonic as his successor the previous year, the German was astonished by the Italian's attitude. Although Furtwängler stressed that he was opposed to the policies of the Nazi government, Toscanini refused to be placated and remained adamant. Eventually, the Maestro agreed to perform at Salzburg but with two conditions: first, he was not to meet Furtwängler and, second, the German was not to be engaged by the Festival again.[82] Neither condition was observed and the conductors met. There are at least two reports of that famous encounter and they differ sharply. According to Toscanini, when Furtwängler entered his dressing room he accused the German of being a Nazi. Furtwängler then tried to defend his position but was unsuccessful and had to leave crestfallen. Furtwängler, on the other hand, recalled that they met in the street, where he argued that he was against the policies of the German government, stressed his belief that art and politics were incompatible and affirmed his willingness to forgo his activities at Salzburg if Toscanini would continue to perform at the Festival.[83] Whichever account is correct, it is obvious that Toscanini was not prepared to listen to reason. Furtwängler's tireless defence of racial and religious minorities throughout the duration of the Third Reich has been documented extensively and Toscanini's reaction was clearly unwarranted.

Having made his Salzburg début in stressful circumstances, Furtwängler continued to perform there until 30 August 1954. Although he was one of the leading conductors of his generation, his commitment to the music of Mozart was not wholehearted and it could be argued that he was not an ideal choice for a festival that paid homage to the composer. It was reported in 1937 that Furtwängler found Mozart's Symphony No. 41 'too cool for his temperament',[84] an admission that is in keeping with his programme policy at Berlin, Leipzig and Vienna during the 1920s and 1930s. Surprisingly, this policy was continued in Salzburg and none of the sixteen concerts that he gave there contained a work by Mozart. Instead, he performed music by Bach, Beethoven, Brahms, Bruckner, Hindemith, Mahler, Mendelssohn, Pfitzner, Schubert, Strauss, Stravinsky, Uhl, Wagner, Weber and Wolf.[85] While Furtwängler did conduct a total of thirty-three performances of Mozart's Die Zauberflöte, Don Giovanni and Le nozze di Figaro between 1949 and 1954 at Salzburg,[86] they too were only part of a wider repertoire that included Beethoven's Fidelio, Wagner's Die Meistersinger von Nürnberg, Weber's Der Freischütz and Verdi's Otello.[87] It seems, then, that Furtwängler considered the Salzburg Festival a vehicle for promoting his own performance preferences rather than an opportunity to celebrate the music of the city's most famous son.[88]

During World War II, Furtwängler's activities were centred mainly on the Berlin and Vienna Philharmonics. Although he performed with them regularly, he generally refused to conduct them in Nazi-occupied territories.[89] He also resisted the regime in other ways throughout the course of the war and showed his disobedience publicly by refusing to give the

German salute. Of course, the cultural policies of the Third Reich affected his music-making profoundly, and the programmes that he conducted during the hostilities reflect the constraints within which he worked. From the concerts that he conducted in Berlin and Vienna during the 1940–1 season,[90] for example, it is clear that the repertoire available to him had been reduced sharply. Although Furtwängler still performed music by living composers at twelve of the fifteen Berlin performances,[91] the music of Stravinsky, Hindemith and modern Jewish composers was noticeably absent. Nevertheless, Furtwängler's personal commitment to new music did not diminish during the war years and he peppered his concerts with contemporary pieces when and where possible. Similarly, at six of his eight concerts with the Vienna Philharmonic during the 1940–1 season a work by a living composer was also included.[92] In keeping with his pre-war practice, the concerts that he gave in Berlin and Vienna had works in common, with all the Vienna concerts containing at least one piece that Furtwängler had performed in Berlin. Moreover, he continued to perform the works of Beethoven as an integral rather than the dominant element of his programme policy and abstained from devoting whole concerts to the music of one composer.[93]

Towards the end of World War II, Furtwängler fled from Vienna to Switzerland. Having entered neutral territory in February 1945, he then performed the two concerts with L'Orchestre de la Suisse Romande at Geneva and Lausanne that had provided the pretext for his entry visa.[94] Following those engagements, he was scheduled to perform with the Tonhalle Orchestra in Zürich on 20 and 25 February but was prevented from doing so by the local authorities. He did conduct Bruckner's Symphony No. 8 at Winterthur on 23 February, however, but his presence provoked civil disobedience outside the hall. The unrest was met with a sharp response by the emergency services,[95] and this was the last concert that Furtwängler conducted until 1947.

Although Furtwängler was never a member of the Nazi Party, he did hold official posts during the early years of the Third Reich. This meant that he would have to undergo the denazification process, and until that was completed he was unable to perform in territories occupied by the Allies. Never given to atrophy, he returned to composition and not only completed his Symphony No. 2 but also began his Symphony No. 3 during his enforced sabbatical. At his denazification tribunal in December 1946, he was acquitted unanimously and was officially approved for work by the Allied Kommandatura on 27 April 1947.[96]

Having been cleared by the authorities, Furtwängler performed with the Berlin Philharmonic on 25 May 1947. As this was his first concert with the orchestra since the end of the war, he celebrated his return with an all-Beethoven programme that was repeated three times over the following days.[97] With his honour restored, Furtwängler also began to perform regularly elsewhere. Because of the financial problems that he faced at the end of the war, he was keen to accept many of the engagements offered and performed widely throughout Western Europe. In 1948, he was invited to become Music Director of the Chicago Symphony Orchestra but rejected the offer in favour of an extended visit as a guest conductor during the 1949–50 season. But when the news of his engagement became common knowledge, protests by other musicians and the public ensued and he was eventually forced to forgo the concerts.

The hostility that Furtwängler faced in the USA was not repeated in Great Britain. Courted by HMV in the immediate post-war period, he made a series of recordings for the company between 1947 and 1954. During the course of those recordings, he developed an uneasy relationship with the influential record producer Walter Legge, who was also interested in Herbert von Karajan. Legge's enthusiasm for Karajan contributed to Furtwängler's well-documented antipathy towards the younger conductor. Furtwängler had not forgiven Karajan for his meteoric rise to fame in the years preceding the war and he actively set out to prevent the Austrian from profiting at his expense after the hostilities. While Karajan had begun to rebuild his career after the war with a string of highly successful performances with the Vienna Symphony Orchestra, the orchestra of La Scala, Milan, and the Philharmonia, he conducted the Berlin Philharmonic twice only between 1945 and 1954.[98] Similarly, the number of concerts that Karajan gave with the Vienna Philharmonic was dwarfed by the 152 performances that Furtwängler conducted with the orchestra in Vienna, Salzburg and on tour after the war.[99] As the managements of those organizations were concerned that Furtwängler would withdraw his services if they employed Karajan, they opted to engage the iconic Furtwängler rather than the highly talented but less influential Karajan.

With the final session of his HMV recording of Wagner's *Die Walküre* at Vienna on 6 October 1954,[100] Furtwängler conducted for the last time. He felt unwell on the journey home,[101] and his condition worsened considerably over the next few weeks; on 2 November he was moved to a clinic at Baden-Baden in Germany,[102] where he died on 30 November. His sudden and unexpected death shocked the music world. Even though his hearing had been failing for some time, he was only in his mid sixties. He was considered to be at the peak of his interpretative powers and to be the leading conductor of his generation. His transcendental performances were admired by musicians and audiences alike and his conducting style continued to be a source of lively debate. Although his podium manner and his performance style were inimitable, they were influential. The South American-born Israeli conductor Daniel Barenboim certainly thought this to be true, and he summed up the enduring influence of Furtwängler when he wrote: 'When you hear the Berlin Philharmonic today, after so many generations . . . many of the things you associate with Furtwängler are still there. . . . [Their relationship] was so fruitful and positive because, ultimately, you cannot tell what he gave to them and what they gave to him. . . . He could achieve only with them the interpretation he wanted, but at the same time, he gave them something which continues to be transmitted from one generation to the next.'[103]

CHAPTER 9

'Das Wunder Karajan'

Herbert von Karajan was the quintessential virtuoso conductor. Unlike many of the conductors who came before him in Central Europe, his aspirations were solely interpretative and he made no attempt at composition. As a young musician, he was determined to become a conductor from the beginning of his professional career and pursued that goal relentlessly. The image of him as an imperator was a direct result of his single-minded approach and his sometimes stormy relationships with the organizations and individuals he encountered during the course of his career. He was a charismatic figure whose leadership qualities stemmed from a combination of his musical and extra-musical activities. With an adventurous spirit that drew him to sport, fast cars, mountaineering, flying and sailing, he soon captured the imagination of musicians and non-musicians alike and was admired for being both a style icon and an artist of distinction.

Born Heribert Ritter von Karajan at Salzburg on 5 April 1908,[1] Karajan was the second son of Dr Ernst von Karajan, a physician, and his wife Martha. As both a great-great-grandson of the ennobled Greco-Macedonian cloth manufacturer Georg Johann Karajoannes[2] and a son of a well-respected and successful doctor, Herbert looked back on his antecedents with pride. As a youth, he was encouraged by his father, a fine amateur clarinettist and occasional member of the Mozarteum Orchestra, and by his mother, a housewife who doted on him, to pursue his musical studies. The Karajans often held soirées at their home by the Makartsteg in Salzburg, and the young Herbert and his older brother Wolfgang spent their formative years surrounded by high-quality domestic music-making. As a natural extension to that environment, Wolfgang and Herbert were introduced to the piano at an early age, with the latter starting lessons at the age of three.

Having shown an early talent for the piano, Karajan gave his first public performance at the age of four.[3] With a talent that was precocious, he was admitted to the Mozarteum during his school years and studied harmony with the organist Franz Sauer, piano with Franz Ledwinka, and composition and chamber music with Bernhard Paumgartner.[4] At the Mozarteum, Karajan progressed quickly and played at the institution's annual 'Mozart-Feier' between 1917 and 1919. Those celebratory concerts marked the anniversary of the composer's birth and Karajan played the Rondo K. 485, the Fantasy in D minor K. 397 and the Rondo for piano and orchestra K. 382.[5] But his performances at the Mozarteum were not restricted to the music of Mozart, and he also gave virtuoso and chamber works by Beethoven, Brahms, Corelli, Franck, Liszt and Vladigerov during his years there.[6]

The impact of Karajan's teachers at Salzburg on his early musical development was profound. Of particular importance was the influence of Bernhard Paumgartner, who was the first to encourage Karajan to consider conducting as a career. Although dismissed by some commentators as a musician who spread his talents too thinly, Paumgartner was instrumental in establishing the modern Salzburg Festival in 1920. Along with Hugo von Hofmannsthal, Max Reinhardt and Richard Strauss, Paumgartner realized Salzburg's potential as a festival venue and conducted the incidental music for Hofmannsthal's play *Jedermann* at the first Festival in 1920. Paumgartner was associated particularly with the Festival's serenade and matinée concerts until his death and was a member of the management committee for most of that period. As one of the principal instigators and supporters of the Festival, Paumgartner also ensured that Karajan benefited educationally from it and encouraged him to attend rehearsals and performances during his summers at Salzburg. Although the Festival was unable to provide a full programme of events because of the financial chaos that gripped the German-speaking countries during the early 1920s,[7] it did provide Karajan with the opportunity to perform as a member of a boys' choir, to work as a stage extra and to act as a conducting assistant, cueing offstage singers and musicians, during his student years in Vienna.[8]

Having successfully completed his *Matura* at Salzburg during the spring of 1926, Karajan had to make a critical decision about his tertiary studies. Although he had shown remarkable skill as a pianist during his youth and was determined to make music his life's work, his parents were concerned that a career in the arts was risky and that he should pursue a more stable profession. As Karajan had an interest in engineering and technology, it was suggested that he should attend the Technische

Hochschule in Vienna while continuing to take music lessons privately. While Karajan agreed reluctantly to follow his parents' wishes, the compromise that they had reached soon foundered and, after only a short period, he abandoned his studies at the Technische Hochschule and enrolled at the Akademie für Musik. There he was soon advised by his piano teacher, Josef Hofmann,[9] with whom he studied from the beginning of his time in Vienna, to abandon the piano in favour of conducting.[10] Having been urged by both Hofmann and Paumgartner to consider a career on the podium, Karajan duly joined the conducting class at the Akademie. Understandably, he hoped to begin his studies with an expert practitioner but was disappointed to learn that his teacher, far from being a professional conductor, was Alexander Wunderer, the principal oboe of the Vienna Philharmonic. Although Karajan later recalled that Wunderer was a very popular figure in Vienna and was part of the management teams of various organizations in the Austrian capital,[11] he considered him no substitute for a conductor of experience. To supplement his education, therefore, Karajan attended performances at the Staatsoper, before which he prepared himself by playing through the operas at the piano in duet with some of his classmates and by singing solo and chorus parts to their accompaniment.

In later life, Karajan claimed that he heard 'everything at the Opera and Musikverein'[12] during his student years and was particularly impressed by Richard Strauss's interpretations of his own operas and those of Mozart.[13] While Strauss did conduct Elektra, Ariadne auf Naxos, Die Frau ohne Schatten, Der Rosenkavalier, Salome, Intermezzo and Die ägyptische Helena and the ballets Josephslegende and Schlagobers at the Staatsoper between 1926 and the end of 1928,[14] he performed no operas by Mozart there during that period. It is difficult to see, therefore, how Karajan could have heard Strauss interpret the composer's music in Vienna. But he did hear Franz Schalk perform regularly at the Staatsoper, and among the new productions and premières that Schalk conducted during Karajan's student years were Puccini's Turandot, Verdi's Il forza del destino, Beethoven's Fidelio, Saint-Saëns's Samson et Dalila, Korngold's Das Wunder der Heliane and Stravinsky's Oedipus Rex.[15] Karajan recalled in later life that he had learned much from Schalk and that, unlike some of the conductor's critics, he found him 'a most sensitive and competent man'.[16]

Along with attending rehearsals and performances at the Staatsoper and the Musikverein, Karajan spent much time listening to gramophone records during his student years and was often found practising for his future career as a conductor by beating time to those recordings.[17] But his fantasies quickly turned into reality when he was allowed to direct an orchestra at the Akademie for the first time and, after making an immediate impact with his reading of Weber's overture to *Euryanthe*, he was soon considered one of the conducting class's leading lights. Nevertheless, his prospects of graduating were in doubt because of his refusal to submit a work for the composition class as his course required. He argued that he was unable to compose anything worthwhile and that an alternative means of assessment would be more appropriate. At first his composition teacher, the cellist and composer Franz Schmidt, was insistent that Karajan should fulfil the conditions of the course but eventually he relented and allowed Karajan to submit an example of orchestration instead.[18] Having brokered a suitable compromise, Karajan then joined his fellow conducting students for their final conducting examination. The tasks to be undertaken included accompanying a series of vocal items and to perform Rossini's overture to *Guillaume Tell*. Although expected simply to conduct the overture without a break, Karajan began to rehearse the work instead. His improvised rehearsal seems to have impressed his examiners, because within ten minutes, they were satisfied with his ability and he was allowed to graduate from the Akademie in December 1928.

As a successful alumnus of one of Europe's leading conservatories, Karajan returned triumphant to Salzburg. During his period in Vienna, he continued to be involved with the Salzburg Festival and acted as répétiteur for Max Reinhardt's production in German of Shakespeare's *A Midsummer Night's Dream* in 1927.[19] It was, however, Karajan's sensational public début as a conductor in his home town on 22 January 1929 that proved decisive to his future career. For that performance, he directed the Mozarteum Orchestra in a programme that consisted of Tchaikovsky's Symphony No. 5, Mozart's Piano Concerto No. 23 (with Yella Pessl as soloist) and Strauss's *Don Juan*. Underwritten financially by his father, who also played clarinet in the orchestra, the concert was an overwhelming success. With a programme that was challenging both technically and musically, Karajan managed to impress the local critics, who commented favourably on his discipline, his restrained manner and his assured baton technique.

Karajan also impressed the Intendant of the Ulm Stadttheater, Erwin Dieterich, who attended the concert. Dieterich needed a new Second Kapellmeister for his theatre and Karajan's obvious potential encouraged him to invite the young musician for a trial performance. With a degree of self-assurance that verged on arrogance, Karajan dismissed the notion of a single test performance and insisted that he be allowed to show his worth by taking charge of a new production. Intrigued by Karajan's attitude, Dieterich agreed to his demand and allowed him to conduct a new production of Mozart's *Le nozze di Figaro*. Performing in a theatre with a tiny stage barely six metres wide,[20] Karajan led a successful performance of Mozart's opera on 2 March 1929 and, within days of that reading, it was announced that he was the Ulm Stadttheater's new Second Kapellmeister.

Working under the Stadttheater's First Kapellmeister, Otto Schulmann, and the Intendant, Dieterich, for a token salary of 80 marks a month,[21] Karajan was able to explore a wide and varied repertoire at Ulm with an orchestra of thirty-two musicians and chorus of between twelve and twenty singers.[22] From 2 March 1929 to 31 March 1934, he conducted no fewer than 134 operatic performances of twenty-four operas by sixteen composers. Of the operas performed, eighty-seven were by Austro-German composers, forty-three were by Italian composers and four were by a French composer.[23] The works that Karajan performed mainly from memory ranged from Handel's *Giulio Cesare* to Richard Strauss's *Arabella*.[24] Many of the operas that Karajan led at Ulm would become closely associated with him, and the juxtaposition of works from the Austro-German canon with important operas by Italian and French composers would be a hallmark of his operatic style in later life. For a young musician with little experience of the operatic repertoire, the task undertaken by Karajan at Ulm was formidable. Few, if any, of the works that he tackled were easy and the inclusion of *Arabella*,[25] a recent work of some difficulty, in his allocated operas underlines the faith that both Schulmann and Dieterich had in his ability. But Karajan was helped in part by the Ulm Stadttheater's use of the *stagione* system when formulating its programme policy. Unlike the repertory system, the *stagione* system ensured that a limited number of operas were performed in short, freshly rehearsed runs.[26] That method was ideal for a fledgling conductor with little experience and, in the case of Karajan, it allowed him to concentrate on performing one opera while preparing the next in detail.

As Second Kapellmeister at Ulm, Karajan also took part in at least ten concert performances. Aptly for a musician from Salzburg, the first concert in which he participated with the Stadttheater Orchestra was an all-Mozart programme on 17 March 1929. For that performance, he was the pianist in the Trio for piano, clarinet and viola ('Kegelstatt'), the soloist in a four-hand arrangement of Piano Concerto No. 20 in D minor[27] and the conductor of *Eine kleine Nachtmusik*. He then shared the conducting of two concerts on 31 December 1930 and 1 March

1931 with his senior colleague, Otto Schulmann, before conducting a programme that included Beethoven's Symphony No. 3 ('Eroica'), Weber's overture to *Euryanthe* and Strauss's *Tod und Verklärung* on 11 and 23 November 1931. The only piece that Karajan had conducted previously was the Weber overture, with the other two works being new to his fast developing repertoire. After two further concerts in which he appeared as a pianist, he returned to the podium on 22 February 1933 to perform Mozart's Piano Concerto No. 20, which he conducted from the keyboard, Debussy's *Prélude à l'après-midi d'un faune* and Tchaikovsky's Symphony No. 6 ('Pathétique'). Following his participation as a piano accompanist in a *Lustiger Abend* (Light Evening) on 28 February 1933, he gave his last concert with the Stadttheater Orchestra on 26 November 1933. On that occasion, he programmed an all-Strauss concert, which included *Don Juan*, *Allerseelen* and *Die heiligen drei Königen aus dem Morgenland* (with Thea Halbeck as soprano soloist) as well as *Ein Heldenleben*. With the exception of *Don Juan*, which he gave at his Salzburg début, all the works were new to his repertoire. *Ein Heldenleben* must have proved particularly taxing because of the demands that it would have placed on the small provincial Ulm orchestra, but it is a testament to his courage as an artist that he tackled such a difficult work during his formative years as a conductor.

During his Ulm period, Karajan maintained his professional contacts in Salzburg. Although confronted with a schedule at the Stadttheater that would have occupied a lesser musician fully, Karajan seems to have been able to meet the demands of his job while exploring new repertoire and building important contacts in his home town. His first engagement at Salzburg after accepting his post in Ulm was a performance of Strauss's *Salome* with the Mozarteum Orchestra at the Festspielhaus on 19 April 1929. This was followed by Lortzing's *Der Waffenschmied* for the opera class of Professor Gross at the Mozarteum on 27 June 1929, Mascagni's *Cavalleria rusticana* at the Festspielhaus on 6 June 1930 and Puccini's *Tosca* at the Stadttheater on 23 July 1930. While only *Cavalleria rusticana* was familiar to him professionally through performances at Ulm, his potentially foolhardy decision to perform the notoriously difficult *Salome* soon paid dividends, with the critics commenting favourably on his knowledge of the score. During the summers of 1930, 1931 and 1934, Karajan was also active as a concert conductor at Salzburg, where he performed at an open-air concert with the Vienna Symphony Orchestra on 22 July 1930, a garden concert with the Mozarteum Orchestra at Max Reinhardt's impressive Salzburg residence, Schloss Leopoldskron, on 19 August 1930, a concert with the

Mozarteum Orchestra at the Mozarteum on 22 July 1931,[28] and a private open-air concert with the Vienna Philharmonic at the Mirabell Garden on 21 August 1934.[29] But it was Karajan's involvement with Reinhardt's production of Goethe's *Faust* at the 1933 Salzburg Festival that was of greatest importance. For this production, Karajan's former teacher Bernhard Paumgartner composed incidental music that Karajan was engaged to conduct. The first of the four performances, on 17 August 1933,[30] marked Karajan's début as a conductor at the Salzburg Festival and was the beginning of a relationship with the Festival that lasted until his death.

Karajan's continuing involvement with Salzburg and its festival during the late 1920s and the early 1930s was also important to him educationally. During that period, the Festival flourished and some of the leading conductors of the day performed there regularly. Richard Strauss, Franz Schalk, Clemens Krauss, Hans Knappertsbusch, Bruno Walter and Sir Thomas Beecham all conducted at the Salzburg Festival between 1929 and 1933 and must have been of interest to the young Karajan. Of particular importance were the concerts that Arturo Toscanini conducted with the Vienna Philharmonic at the Festival on 23, 26 and 30 August 1934.[31] Karajan had already heard Toscanini conduct on a number of occasions[32] and was overwhelmed by the Italian conductor's meticulously rehearsed performances of Verdi's *Falstaff* with the La Scala company when it visited Vienna in 1929. Karajan likened the effect of hearing Toscanini for the first time to being 'struck by a blow'[33] and, when he visited Salzburg on a regular basis between 1934 and 1937, it was almost inevitable that Karajan took every opportunity to attend his rehearsals and to absorb his approach to both the Austro-German and Italian repertoires.[34]

Karajan not only continued to develop musically at Salzburg during the late 1920s and early 1930s but also contributed to the musical education of others. A born educator who remained passionate about teaching for much of his life, he was engaged as a conducting tutor at the Salzburg Festival from 1929. One of the young conductors who attended some of his classes was the future Music Director of the Boston Symphony Orchestra, Erich Leinsdorf.[35] Leinsdorf was particularly impressed by Karajan's meticulous and serious approach and recalled in later life:

In 1930 I attended summer courses at the Mozarteum in Salzburg. . . . One of the instructors of the conducting class was the twenty-two-year-old Karajan. It seems to me now, looking back, that even in those

very early days his basic interpretive approach gave priority to sound.
. . . He was . . . a thoroughly prepared and serious musician even
then. This may seem a superfluous statement considering Karajan's
remarkable career, but I make it nonetheless because over the years
his detractors often tried to dismiss him as a mere showman. . . . A
musician friend of mine once observed Karajan giving a master class
to a student orchestra. Karajan, my friend told me, got straight down
to business and rehearsed the students in exemplary fashion. I gained
a very similar impression during the classes at the Mozarteum – that
of a perfectly well-prepared and enthusiastic young conductor whose
personality and tastes were already formed. I recall in particular his
spirited discussion of Richard Strauss's *Tod und Verklärung*. . . . Of
course, this will sound like wisdom of hindsight, but it seems to me
now that even in those days a gambler would happily have staked
much money on the young Karajan.[36]

Although Karajan's fortunes seemed to be going from strength to
strength between 1929 and 1934, his fledgling career was threatened
when he was dismissed from his post in Ulm at the end of March 1934.
His position at the Stadttheater had been fragile from 1933, but he was
able to persuade Dieterich to re-engage him for the 1933–4 season. In
later life, Karajan always argued that Dieterich had dismissed him for
his own good and quoted the Intendant as saying: 'I don't want you
back here at the end of this summer [1934]. . . . Next season we'll probably be giving the same operas that you have already conducted here.
You've learned all you could learn in Ulm. It's time for you to move on.
You'll either go to the dogs or else you'll make a career for yourself – as
I firmly believe. But you can't come back here.'[37]

'Thrown out' of Ulm by Dieterich after a performance of *Le nozze di
Figaro* on 31 March 1934, Karajan travelled to Berlin to find work.[38]
Although relatively experienced by the time of his unemployment, he
found it difficult to gain work as a conductor in the German capital.
After he spent the summer of 1934 accompanying singers for various
agencies and visiting provincial theatres in the hope of finding a job,
Karajan's luck changed when the Intendant of the Aachen Stadttheater,
Edgar Gross, visited Berlin in search of a new conductor for his theatre.
Keen to ensure that he was not overlooked by Gross, Karajan secured
an interview with him during which he told the Intendant that he would
not leave until he gained something from the meeting.[39] Seemingly
impressed by Karajan's insistence, Gross offered him a trial rehearsal at
Aachen on 8 June 1934.[40] Performing in front of a panel that consisted

of orchestral representatives, management and local music critics, Karajan conducted Weber's overture to *Oberon*, the first movement of Mozart's Symphony No. 35 ('Haffner') and Wagner's Prelude to *Die Meistersinger von Nürnberg*. At first, the orchestra were hostile towards Karajan because of his demanding manner, but they were soon impressed by his light and flexible beat, a characteristic of his conducting technique that he practised throughout much of his career. Nevertheless, most of those gathered were of the opinion that he was too young for the post of First Kapellmeister. An exception, however, was the critic Wilhelm Kemp who disagreed, arguing that the orchestra played better under Karajan than they had for a long time.[41] Kemp's opinion eventually prevailed and Karajan was appointed conductor of the Aachen Stadttheater from the beginning of the 1934–5 season.

As the principal operatic conductor at the Aachen Stadttheater, Karajan was able to consolidate and to expand his repertoire during his tenure there and, after introducing himself musically with a critically acclaimed performance of Beethoven's *Fidelio*, which he conducted from memory on 18 September 1934, he performed no fewer than twenty-nine operas by ten composers.[42] While ten of the works had been conducted previously by Karajan at either Salzburg or Ulm,[43] the majority were new to his repertoire. As Nazi cultural policy had already begun to shape the programming of German theatres, it is hardly surprising that the overwhelming majority of the works performed were by Austro-German composers. Of the performances given, a great many were composed by a member of that group. It is probably unsurprising, therefore, that Richard Wagner was the composer whose operas and music dramas were performed most frequently, with Karajan conducting all his stage works from *Der fliegende Holländer* onwards at Aachen. Of particular significance were his performances of the music dramas from *Der Ring des Nibelungen*. Having never conducted the tetralogy either in part or whole previously, he performed for the first time *Das Rheingold* on 9 November 1936, *Die Walküre* on 23 October 1934, *Siegfried* on 26 May 1935 and *Götterdämmerung* on 2 December 1936, and a complete cycle of the works between 21 and 28 November 1937 at the Stadttheater.[44] It was also with a work by Wagner at Aachen that Karajan combined the functions of conductor and producer for the first time. With his 1940 reading of *Die Meistersinger von Nürnberg*,[45] he joined both roles as 'an entirely natural reaction ... to a situation which arises time and again in every opera house in the world, when a conductor notices during the rehearsals that the producer he's working with does not know the work that he's producing'.[46] As Karajan found working with producers a largely unhappy experience, he 'had to become [one] . . . in order to solve the problems involved'.[47]

Of the other operatic composers whose works Karajan performed at Aachen, those of Richard Strauss were the most frequently heard. Included in Karajan's repertoire was the recently composed *Friedenstag*, Strauss's twelfth opera.[48] This differs from the composer's other stage works in that the principal voices are those of two males, the Kommandant and the Holsteiner. The setting is the last day of the Thirty Years War and the opera's overriding message is that of peace. As a pacifist work, it was largely unwelcome on the German stage after 1939 and Karajan's programming of it in the immediate pre-war period was a reflection of his interest in Strauss's music rather than an expression of his political views. Other operas that Karajan added to his Strauss repertoire at Aachen were *Die Frau ohne Schatten* and *Elektra*, which he conducted for the first time on 1 November 1935 and 15 June 1938 respectively. Unlike *Friedenstag*, which Karajan never performed again after leaving Aachen, *Die Frau ohne Schatten* and *Elektra* remained in his operatic repertoire until the mid 1960s. While Karajan conducted the former on only two further occasions after he left the Stadttheater, the latter was given at least nineteen performances by him during the course of his career.

Having been headhunted by theatres in Berlin and Karlsruhe,[49] Karajan was secured for the Aachen Stadttheater when the management promoted him to Generalmusikdirektor. With a three-year contract that gave him sweeping powers and financial security,[50] Karajan took charge of the town's principal operatic and concert organizations. Previously, the roles of opera conductor and concert conductor at Aachen had been separated. Under his new contract, which was announced on 12 April 1935,[51] Karajan was to continue working in the theatre while also taking direction of the orchestra's subscription series. As Generalmusik-direktor, he was also required to join the Nazi Party. Having joined the NSDAP first in Salzburg in April 1933 for 5 schillings, he rejoined the organization again in May 1934.[52] In later life, he was often challenged about his membership of the Party and responded by stating: 'It is sometimes said, unthinkingly, that I would have sold my own grandmother to get [the Aachen] position. Yet this sentence sums up fairly accurately what I was capable of doing at that time, young, hungry conductor that I was. Entry into the party was a condition of my becoming general music director in Aachen. For me it was the price you sometimes have to pay to get exactly what you want if there is a particular goal you must achieve at all costs.'[53]

As the youngest Generalmusikdirektor in Germany,[54] Karajan was responsible for the Städtisches Orchester's Abonnement, Popular (Volks) and Chamber Concerts from October 1935.[55] At his disposal was a well-appointed concert hall, an orchestra of some seventy musicians and two skilled choirs. From the overall shape and content of his concerts, it seems that he was keen to balance new music with works from the Austro-German canon. Like Furtwängler, Klemperer and Walter, Karajan used his positions as conductor to introduce new and unusual music to his audiences. No fewer than forty-five per cent of his concerts at Aachen included a work by a living or recently deceased composer. During his first season as Generalmusikdirektor, he challenged local audiences with two all-contemporary programme that included works by Wunsch, Frommel, Waertisch, Atterberg, Pepping, Georg Schumann, Palmgren and Ravel.[56] Although they were the only concerts devoted to new music that Karajan conducted at Aachen, he continued to pepper his programmes with works by living composers throughout his tenure. In general, the new works that he performed were placed at or near the beginning of a concert, thereby ensuring the audience's attention. His commitment to modern music during his Aachen period was profound but, like many of his colleagues, he became cautious with age and never conducted such a high percentage of new works when tenured.

Karajan's interest in the new at Aachen was a reflection of his catholic programming in general. While keen to explore the masterpieces of the Austro-German canon, he never conducted a cycle of symphonies by a composer from that tradition. When performing symphonies by Beethoven, for example, he conducted only Nos. 3, 5, 6 ('Pastoral'), 7, 8 and 9 ('Choral'). Although he gave an all-Beethoven programme at his début concert as Generalmusikdirektor on 10 October 1935,[57] he never conducted more than three of the composer's symphonies in any one season, and he gave multiple performances of only Symphonies Nos. 7 and 9 during the 1940–1 and 1939–40 seasons respectively.[58] When conducting the latter, he programmed no other work in the same concert, underlining the monumental character of the music and the iconic place that the symphony holds within the public consciousness as a whole. Karajan did not restrict this selectivity to Beethoven but was also careful in the programming of the orchestral works by other Austro-German composers. When performing music by some Classical and early Romantic composers, for example, he restricted himself to Mozart's Symphonies Nos. 33 and 40, Schubert's Symphonies Nos. 7 ('Unfinished') and 8 ('Great') and Schumann's Symphonies Nos. 3 and 4. He was less cautious, however, when programming the music of

Bruckner, and although he did not perform any of the composer's less familiar early works, he did conduct Symphonies Nos. 4 ('Romantic'), 5, 7, 8 and 9.

When Karajan performed Bruckner's Symphony No. 9 on 8 December 1938, he coupled it with the composer's Te Deum. Although the juxtaposition of these works in a single programme was not particularly unusual for the period, it was an example of Karajan's emerging interest in choral music during his Aachen tenure. The city's two main choral groups, the Städtischer Gesangsverein and the chorus of the Stadttheater, were trained by the highly gifted chorus master Wilhelm Pitz. Having worked formerly as a violinist in the Städtisches Orchester, Pitz would later achieve international recognition through his work with the chorus of the Bayreuth Festival and the Philharmonia Chorus, London. Of the concerts that Karajan conducted as Generalmusikdirektor, twenty-eight per cent contained a choral item and, of those, eighty-three per cent were programmes devoted solely to a major work for chorus.[59] Along with Bruckner's Te Deum, the choral works performed included Bach's Cantata BWV 50, the Mass in B minor and the St Matthew-Passion, Mozart's Mass in C minor, Haydn's *Die Jahreszeiten* (*The Seasons*) and *Die Schöpfung* (*The Creation*), Beethoven's Missa solemnis, Brahms's *Ein deutsches Requiem*, Verdi's Requiem and Te Deum, Kodály's *Psalmus hungaricus*, Nuffel's Three Psalms for organ, chorus and orchestra, Pfitzner's *Von deutscher Seele*, Philipp's *Sinfonische Friedenmesse* and Orff's *Carmina burana*. Some of those works had multiple performances and a number of them were taken on tour by Karajan.[60] It is obvious, then, that choral music was an important part of his Aachen repertoire and it was appropriate that his last performance as Generalmusikdirektor was a reading of Bach's St *Matthew-Passion* on 22 April 1942.

Karajan's star was in the ascendant throughout his Aachen tenure. Although he was a conductor of a provincial opera house, his talents were soon recognized by managers in some of Europe's leading musical centres. With his piercing blue eyes, his striking good looks and a talent that was prodigious, his success outside Aachen was swift and impressive. Having begun to tour with the orchestra and singers of the Stadttheater from 1936, Karajan was invited to make his Vienna début on 1 June 1937. For his first professional performance in the Austrian capital, he conducted Wagner's *Tristan und Isolde* at the Staatsoper without an orchestral rehearsal. Originally promised three rehearsals, Karajan was informed by letter two weeks before the performance that he would have to make do with two rehearsals. As the date of the performance grew closer, he received another letter stating that only one rehearsal would be available to him. When he arrived in Vienna, the leader of the orchestra said that one rehearsal was pointless and, if he were to forgo it, the musicians would play their best for him.[61] Karajan learned subsequently that the leader's suggestion was a standard ploy to avoid work and it was used regularly on unsuspecting young conductors.[62] Nevertheless, the performance was a success and press and public alike were impressed by both his technique and his musicianship.

The year after making his first appearance at the Vienna Staatsoper, Karajan made his Berlin début at a concert with the Berlin Philharmonic on 8 April 1938.[63] Like his Vienna performance, the concert was a popular and critical success, and six months later he conducted at the Berlin Staatsoper for the first time. Having been asked by the Intendant, Heinz Tietjen, to present the world première of Wagner-Régeny's *Die Bürger von Calais*, Karajan replied that he would rather make his début at the Staatsoper either *Fidelio*, *Tristan und Isolde* or *Die Meistersinger von Nürnberg*. At first Tietjen dismissed Karajan's demands, but after a period of haggling it was agreed that he could make his début with *Fidelio* on 30 September 1938. While this performance was a critical success, it was his reading of *Tristan und Isolde* on 21 October 1938 that secured his place as Central Europe's brightest young conducting star. Describing him as 'Das Wunder Karajan' in the Berlin newspaper *B.Z. am Mittag* the day after the concert, the critic Edwin van der Nüll argued that Karajan's outstanding performance of *Tristan und Isolde* meant that he must be considered, along with Wilhelm Furtwängler and the Italian Victor de Sabata,[64] one of the leading opera conductors in Germany. For the hypersensitive Furtwängler, such a comparison was unthinkable. He objected strongly to van der Nüll's comments and thereafter considered Karajan a rival. It was obvious to Karajan from the beginning, however, that Tietjen and van der Nüll 'were playing [him] off against . . . Furtwängler' and that he was being used 'to make life difficult for him'.[65] But Karajan 'wanted to seize all the opportunities offered [him] . . . [and that] meant that Furtwängler suffered as a result'.[66]

Some of the 'opportunities offered' to Karajan in Berlin included the title of Staatskapellmeister, multiple performances of *Tristan und Isolde*, *Fidelio*, *Die Meistersinger von Nürnberg*, *Die Bürger von Calais*,[67] *Die Zauberflöte* and *Elektra* as well as the direction of the Berlin Staatskapelle's subscription concerts. Of the operatic performances that he gave at the Staatsoper, those of *Die Zauberflöte* and *Elektra* were of particular importance to him. *Die Zauberflöte* was a new production by the Régisseur, Gustaf Gründgens, whom Karajan admired greatly. In contrast to the rehearsals of some other producers, those of Gründgens 'were a sheer delight',[68] because he had the ability to 'achieve thrilling effects . . . without any grand gestures'.[69] The impact of Gründgens's technique on Karajan was profound and he later recalled that what he 'learned [from him] as a producer . . . [could] be used in any opera'.[70] Karajan's encounter with Richard Strauss in February 1940 also made a deep impression.[71] Having gone backstage to congratulate Karajan after one of his performances of *Elektra* at the Berlin Staatsoper, Strauss arranged to meet him for lunch the next day. During their initial meeting and over the meal that followed, Karajan had an opportunity to discuss his interpretation with Strauss. The composer was impressed by Karajan's ability to conduct the score from memory and to clarify key aspects of the music in performance. For Karajan, that was high praise, as he had always admired Strauss, both as a composer and as a conductor.[72]

It would have been with some pride, therefore, that Karajan took responsibility for the Berlin Staatskapelle's subscription concerts from the beginning of the 1940–1 season. With Strauss's former orchestra, Karajan conducted no fewer than forty-four concerts of twenty-seven programmes between 20 October 1940 and 18 February 1945. As he was commuting regularly between Aachen and Berlin during the years 1938–1942, it is understandable that many of the symphonic works that he conducted in one city were repeated in the other. A common thread between the two centres was his interest in the music of Bruckner. In Berlin, he continued to perform Symphonies Nos. 5, 7, 8 and 9, with No. 8 being heard most frequently with readings on 3 and 4 May 1941 and 4 and 5 October 1944.[73] As in Aachen, Karajan's Beethoven repertoire was restricted, consisting of only Symphonies Nos. 3, 5, 6 and 7 in Berlin. He did give, however, a performance of the Missa solemnis with the Aachen Städtischer Gesangverein and the Berlin Staatskapelle on 19 January 1941, but because he did not have a first-rate chorus with which to perform masterpieces of the choral repertoire in the German capital, he presented no further choral concerts during his period with the Staatskapelle.

Karajan's interest in contemporary composers also continued in Berlin. During his time with the Staatskapelle, no less than forty per cent of the concerts given contained music by one of those artists. While the works of Strauss are included in that statistic – Karajan conducted at least one major work by Strauss in each of his seasons with the Staatskapelle, including an all-Strauss programme on 14 and 15 May

1944[74] – he also promoted the music of lesser-known composers. Included in that repertoire were Rasch's Toccata for large orchestra, Berger's *Legende vom Prinzen Eugen* and the world première of von Einem's Concerto for orchestra.[75] Unsurprising for a busy commuting musician, and in keeping with his practice of maximizing his repertoire as a whole, some of the unfamiliar music that Karajan performed at Berlin was also given in Aachen, including Borck's *Sinfonisches Vorspiel*, Knaak's *Sinfonisches Vorspiel* and Viski's *Enigma*.[76] Sensibly, he performed those works first at provincial Aachen before presenting them to the more cosmopolitan audience in Berlin. As in Aachen, Karajan generally placed less familiar works at or near the beginning of the concert, ensuring maximum attention and attendance. In contrast to his practice in Aachen, however, he did not present an all-contemporary programme but preferred instead to perform modern works side by side with established masterpieces.

While each of Karajan's Berlin programmes contained at least one work by an Austro-German composer, as would be expected for a concert series given under the nationalist cultural policies of the Third Reich, he did attempt to achieve variety by including works by composers from other cultures. Of particular importance was his programming of the orchestral music of Sibelius, a composer whom he would perform widely and record comprehensively throughout his career. Having already conducted Symphony No. 6 in Stockholm and Berlin and *En Saga* in Aachen,[77] Karajan began to consolidate his interest in Sibelius's music by programming Symphonies Nos. 1 and 4 with the Berlin Staatskapelle on 9 February 1942 and 19 April 1943 respectively. The Italian repertoire also attracted Karajan, and he gave performances at both Berlin and Aachen of orchestral works by Respighi and concerti grossi by Locatelli and Geminiani.[78] Karajan's inclusion of Baroque works was not restricted to the music of Italian composers: he added variety and scope to his programming at Berlin and Aachen with performances of Bach's Concerto for Four Keyboard Instruments, Brandenburg Concerto No. 2, Concerto for Two Violins and Orchestral Suites Nos. 2 and 3, and Handel's Concerti grossi Op. 6 Nos. 5 and 12.[79]

Although a relative newcomer to major concert series, Karajan soon attracted leading soloists to perform with him at both Aachen and Berlin. With the Städtisches Orchester, the major international artists with whom he worked included the pianists Walter Gieseking, Edwin Fischer, Wilhelm Backhaus and Ely Ney, the violinist Georg Kulenkampff and the cellists Gaspar Cassadó and Enrico Mainardi.[80] As leading stars in Europe's firmament of soloists, these artists added lustre to Karajan's career and at the same time increased the profile of the Aachen Abonnement series, both nationally and internationally. Even though some of the soloists mentioned also performed with Karajan at the Berlin Staatskapelle's subscription series, the number of high-profile artists with whom he worked did begin to wane as World War II progressed. Of the twenty-seven programmes that he gave with the Staatskapelle, only five involved an internationally renowned soloist and, of those, all had performed earlier with him at Aachen.[81] More worrying was the sharp decrease in major artists appearing with him at Berlin after the 1941–2 season, with only Walter Gieseking from the front rank of soloists collaborating with him during his final seasons with the Staatskapelle. The question that must be asked, therefore, is why Karajan failed to attract high-profile artists to his Berlin series during the last years of the war. It is possible that many were aware of Furtwängler's increasing hostility towards Karajan and were not prepared to be associated publicly with the younger, less well-established musician, or perhaps they were aware that Karajan no longer enjoyed the support of senior government officials and arts managers in the German capital after marrying his partly Jewish second wife, Anita Gütermann, on 22 October 1942. Whatever the reason, the absence of prominent soloists from his Berlin concerts was only part of a general malaise that affected Karajan's career during the last three years of the war.

Karajan's tenure at Aachen was terminated by the Stadttheater's Intendant, Otto Kirchner, from the end of the 1941–2 season. Although he 'continued to take [his] work [there] seriously',[82] Karajan's frequent absences caused problems for the Stadttheater's management, which needed a musician who would devote himself more fully to the job.[83] In later life, Karajan maintained that he was sacked without warning, that he learned of his dismissal only after reading about it in a newspaper while on tour in Italy,[84] that he was 'enormously offended' by the action, and that he never received an adequate explanation from Kirchner.[85] What is certain is that he no longer had the security of his Aachen tenure and his standing in the capital was increasingly shaky. His last performance for the Berlin Staatsoper was a reading of Orff's *Carmina burana* at the Kroll Theatre on 19 February 1942 and his only engagements in the city from 1943 were as a concert conductor. While he continued to act as sole conductor of the Staatskapelle's Abonnement- and Sonderkonzerte for the 1943–4 season, conducting ten concerts of five programmes, his situation changed dramatically during the following season, when he gave only seven of the orchestra's sixteen symphonic concerts.[86]

Like most Berlin residents, Karajan suffered privations and hardships during the closing months of the war. After his apartment was destroyed by bombs, he stayed in hotel accommodation and was seen at one point sheltering from the bombing in the basement of the Hotel Adlon without shoes and dressed in a trench-coat.[87] Fearing that the invading Russians would seize him because of his high profile, he escaped to northern Italy shortly after his last concert with the Berlin Staatskapelle in February 1945.[88] He travelled first to Milan and later moved to a boathouse on Lake Como, where he was soon discovered by the German authorities and ordered back to Berlin. Having already lost Wilhelm Furtwängler to Switzerland, the members of the Nazi government were keen to ensure that at least one of their star conductors was available to them. Aware of the consequences that the loss of both artists meant for morale and propaganda, the authorities quickly arranged for Karajan to fly back to Germany. Events were moving fast, however, and when he returned to Milan to collect some of his belongings before returning to Berlin, he was confronted with the German retreat and the subsequent American occupation. No longer in danger of being repatriated to Berlin by the German authorities, Karajan remained in Italy for much of 1945 before returning to his parents' house in Salzburg towards the end of the year.[89]

Karajan faced a bleak future at the end of the war. When he left Berlin, his finances and career were at a nadir. Having conducted only three concerts since fleeing Germany,[90] Karajan was keen to resume work but had to undergo the denazification process first. After he was interviewed by an American tribunal towards the end of 1945, his case was processed quickly and he was issued with a permit to perform that December.[91] It seemed, therefore, that he would return to normal concert life at the beginning of 1946. Encouraged by an invitation from the Vienna Philharmonic to conduct three concerts with the orchestra at the Musikverein on 12, 13 and 19 January 1946, Karajan's career appeared to be rising phoenix-like from the ashes of Vienna. The invitation soon foundered, however, when the Russians objected to the concerts because they might inspire pro-Nazi demonstrations outside the hall. After some frantic negotiations, the Russians did agree to allow the first two concerts to proceed but reserved the right to review the situation before the third. Although the first two concerts were a resounding success, the Russians were still unconvinced by Karajan's defence at the American tribunal and banned the third. Matters then seemed to deteriorate when Karajan was summoned to appear before another denazification tribunal at Vienna in February 1946. For that hearing, Karajan had to testify in front of the Austrian authorities. Quizzed about his membership of the Nazi Party during the period 1933–8, he claimed that he had no interest in politics and that his sole reason for joining the Party was to secure the post of Generalmusikdirektor in Aachen. The Austrian tribunal accepted his argument and responded by finding him not guilty of acting illegally during the period in question.[92]

Cleared by both the American and the Austrian tribunals, Karajan began to resurrect his career in earnest from October 1947. Using the Vienna Philharmonic and Vienna Symphony Orchestras as the basis for his return to the podium, he then began an extended association with the latter that resulted in no fewer than 236 concerts in Vienna and on tour. Although he was never tenured with the Vienna Symphony Orchestra, his meticulous rehearsal methods and comprehensive programme policy did much to heighten the orchestra's profile. Karajan also used guest conducting to raise his own profile outside Vienna in the first decades after World War II and performed in that capacity throughout much of Europe, Britain, the Americas and Japan. Of the opera houses where he worked as a guest conductor, La Scala, Milan, was of particular importance and, with the exception of 1962, he performed annually with its company in Milan and on tour, conducting at least sixteen operas by nine composers.[93] Apart from Bizet's *Carmen*, the repertoire that he directed at La Scala was either Austro-German or Italian and, apart from Donizetti's *Lucia di Lammermoor*, the operas that he conducted had all been performed previously by him. Although the ratio of composers whose works Karajan conducted at La Scala was 4 Austro-German : 4 Italian : 1 French, the majority of the operas performed were by the first-named group and, of those, Wagner was dominant. It seems, therefore, that while Karajan was perceived increasingly outside Italy as a major interpreter of Puccini, Donizetti and Verdi, inside the country his services as a conductor of Mozart, Beethoven, Wagner and Strauss were still in greatest demand.

Another organization with which Karajan performed regularly in the years following World War II was the Philharmonia Orchestra of London. His first concert with the orchestra, on 11 April 1948, was also his London début, and he conducted a programme that included Strauss's *Don Juan*, Schumann's Piano Concerto (Dinu Lipatti, piano) and Beethoven's Symphony No. 5. The inclusion of *Don Juan* in the programme underlines the importance that Karajan placed on the engagement, because that work was included not only at his official début at Salzburg in 1929 but also at his first major concert in Vienna after the cessation of hostilities in 1945.[94] With the Philharmonia Orchestra,

Karajan led no fewer than ninety-two performances in London and on tour. While some of the players found his habit of conducting with his eyes closed unnerving, they admired his flexible but clear stick technique, his insistence on dynamic accuracy, his use of humour to defuse tense situations, his masculine athleticism, his ability to overlook small mistakes in favour of the wider musical picture, his ability to achieve a sense of line, his capacity to balance the orchestra superbly, his fine sense of ensemble and his controlled use of the upper body as the basis for his podium manner.

Karajan's involvement with the Philharmonia Orchestra began as a direct result of an encounter with the EMI record producer, Walter Legge, at Vienna in January 1946. Legge was talent-spotting in the Austrian capital for conductors to record for EMI and to perform with the recently established Philharmonia Orchestra. Having arrived two days after Karajan's concert with the Vienna Philharmonic, he was only able to attend a subsequent rehearsal. Legge recalled later that he was 'absolutely astonished at what the fellow could do' and thought that the 'enormous energy and vitality he had was hair-raising'.[95] He contacted Karajan immediately and the two arranged to meet at the conductor's dilapidated flat on the eight floor of an apartment block in Vienna. They had an instant rapport and, after an extended period of negotiation, Legge engaged Karajan to record for EMI from September 1946.[96]

Karajan's recordings for Legge were not his first, for he had made his début as a recording artist with the Berlin Staatskapelle in 1938 with Mozart's overture to *Die Zauberflöte*. As a passionate technophile from childhood, Karajan inevitably had an interest in recordings and the recording process. Like the English-born conductor Leopold Stokowski, Karajan saw recordings as a didactic tool, a means by which to promote his own career and a complement to his activities in both the concert hall and the opera house. Having recorded first on shellac, he quickly saw the advantages of magnetic tape and, later, the digital process. His interest in technology continued throughout his life and he agreed willingly to take part in the launch of Sony's new CD format in 1981. Karajan was also the first conductor since Stokowski to use the medium of film as a major vehicle for the dissemination of music. When making films of orchestral and operatic works, Karajan was often involved as producer, director and/or editor and was keen to superintend the process as a whole. Aware of the advantages of skilful marketing, Karajan ensured that his image dominated his record sleeves and insisted that leading photographers like Siegfried Lauterwasser be engaged to capture the right pose and mood. Karajan was also an astute businessman, who used his commercial acumen to determine with which company he would record and the best means of marketing the final product.

Given the breadth of Karajan's repertoire, it is unsurprising that his discography was extensive. With EMI, DGG, Decca and others, he made over 950 commercial sound recordings by 116 composers and appeared in films of 108 works, some of which were unpublished, by thirty-one composers.[97] Like the discographies of Walter, Klemperer and Furtwängler, that of Karajan does little to reflect his early interest in new music and, while he did record commercially music by at least thirty-one composers who were still writing after his 1929 Salzburg début, many of those were hardly cutting-edge.[98] But he did document some music by composers with little public appeal, and was particularly proud of his recordings of works by Schoenberg, Webern and Berg that he made with the Berlin Philharmonic between 1972 and 1974.[99] These recordings were probably his most important contribution to the discography of twentieth-century music in general and did much to dispel the notion that recordings of music by the Second Viennese School were always problematic financially for record companies. His preference, however, was for music from the Austro-German canon and he recorded four cycles of symphonies by Beethoven, three of symphonies by Brahms, one each of symphonies by Bruckner, Mendelssohn, Schubert and Schumann and two sets of Bach's Brandenburg Concertos. When recording the orchestral music of Haydn and Mozart, Karajan was less comprehensive, documenting Symphonies Nos. 82 ('L'Ours') to 87 and Symphonies Nos. 93 to 104 ('London') by the former and Symphonies Nos. 29, 32, 33 and 35 to 41 ('Jupiter') by the latter.[100] Apart from Austro-German composers, Tchaikovsky was the most fully documented, with his symphonies being recorded complete by Karajan between 1939 and 1984.[101]

As a conductor of opera, operetta and music theatre, Karajan recorded commercially at least thirty-six complete works by fifteen composers.[102] Having developed a reputation as an outstanding opera conductor from near the beginning of his career, he took the opportunity to record, more than once and with different companies and ensembles, stage works with which he had an extended association. As in the opera house, his preference was for works from the Austro-German canon and operas composed in the late nineteenth and early twentieth centuries by a handful of Italian, French and Russian composers. In general, he recorded works that had already secured their place in the standard operatic repertoire and largely ignored new and early operas.

Similarly, when recording operas by established composers, he did not explore any of their earlier or less familiar works, tending instead to document financially viable operas that were well known to the average music consumer. Although he was a committed interpreter of Richard Strauss's music, his interest in the operas was largely restricted to works composed in the first two decades of the twentieth century and, of those, he recorded only *Salome, Der Rosenkavalier* and *Ariadne auf Naxos* commercially. A serious omission from Karajan's commercial discography was Strauss's *Elektra*, an opera for which he had a special affinity.[103] Similarly, Karajan was also a committed interpreter of Mozart's operas but did little to explore the composer's early or less familiar works in the theatre or in the recording studio. His complete recordings of *Le nozze di Figaro, Don Giovanni, Così fan tutte* and *Die Zauberflöte* therefore reflect his selective commitment to Mozart in particular and his approach to performing operatic music from the late eighteenth century in general.

Karajan's recordings did much to shape his professional profile for many listeners. His various cycles of Beethoven's symphonies were enormously popular with many consumers who often preferred his lush, highly polished sound to that of his rivals. Marketed heavily by DGG during the last decades of his career, his recordings were often awaited eagerly by record buyers. The quality of the pressings, the impressive photos of him on the record sleeves and his use mainly of the Berlin and Vienna Philharmonics gave Karajan an authority and cachet that many consumers valued. But, with the increasing artistic and commercial power of the 'authentic' movement, his readings were often considered overblown and outmoded. Although Karajan adhered more strictly to the text than any of his predecessors, many educated listeners rejected his interpretations of late eighteenth- and early nineteenth-century works in favour of more historically aware performances. For a period after his death, it seemed that Karajan's performance style would affect his place in the history of recordings and that he might lose some of his iconic status. While that was certainly true of the Hungarian-born British conductor Sir Georg Solti, whose career as a recording artist was helped greatly by his exclusive contract with Decca, it has not been the case for Karajan, whose recordings continue to sell in their millions.

In the decade following World War II, Karajan was virtually excluded from Berlin's musical life because of Wilhelm Furtwängler's continuing hostility. During that period, the bulk of the Berlin Philharmonic's concerts were conducted by the outstanding young Romanian musician Sergiu Celibidache.[104] Although Celibidache was a gifted artist, his acerbic manner alienated many of the musicians he conducted. His long-winded and pernickety approach to rehearsal often angered the players, and he was regularly at loggerheads with them both personally and musically. With Furtwängler's return to musical life in 1947, the Berlin Philharmonic was able to call upon his services until his death in November 1954 and, although he took no part in the orchestra's Abonnement Series after the war, he did conduct it regularly at Berlin and on tour. One of the tours that he was scheduled to lead with the orchestra was to North America in 1955, his first post-war engagement outside Europe. His death in November 1954, however, put the tour in doubt and, to salvage the situation, Karajan was asked to act as his replacement. Although keen to accept the engagement, Karajan insisted that he would perform only if he were named the orchestra's conductor for life. With pressure coming from the tour's American organizers, Columbia Artists, to secure the services of Karajan for the Philharmonic's visit,[105] it was announced on 13 December 1954 that the orchestra had asked its Intendant, Gerhard von Westermann, to invite Karajan 'to conduct the major Philharmonic concerts and tours for a period of time as yet unspecified'.[106] Although the 'resolution was taken unanimously',[107] it did not meet Karajan's demands for a lifetime contract, but, with time running short before the orchestra's departure for North America, he eventually relented and toured with the Berlin Philharmonic as conductor designate.

Karajan and the Berlin Philharmonic visited twenty-two cities in North America between 27 February and 1 April 1955.[108] With memories of Nazi atrocities still fresh in the minds of the American public, his visit was a catalyst for demonstrations by war veterans, trade unionists and members of the Jewish community. Although Karajan had been cleared of any wrongdoing by the denazification process, he was still considered representative of Nazi social and cultural policies by some elements of American society. The most vociferous of the demonstrations occurred during his visits to New York, where pickets paraded outside Carnegie Hall before his first concert with banners that read 'Tonight at Carnegie Hall The Musical Dictators of the Nazi Regime'.[109] Understandably, security was at a premium during the tour and it was thought advisable that Karajan should register at his hotel under an assumed name.[110] At the press conference that he gave at New York on 3 March 1955, he was quizzed heavily about his activities during the Third Reich and justified his behaviour by declaring: 'I automatically became a member of the NSDAP when I took over the Aachen town orchestra in 1934, which was a state appointment'; he went on to say that he had 'never been interested in politics – not in the slightest' and that nothing apart from his music had 'any significance, nothing that is, except for science, art and sport'.[111] Although Karajan continued to chant this mantra of justification for the rest of his life, young members of the New York Jewish community were unimpressed, and when he returned to the city at the end of the tour, he was again confronted with a protest that linked his tour with the atrocities of the Holocaust.[112]

Karajan signed his contract with the Berlin Philharmonic on 25 April 1956[113] and took over direction of the orchestra's Philharmonic Concerts from the 1956–7 season. As conductor of the series, he followed in the footsteps of Bülow, Strauss, Nikisch and Furtwängler. Like those artists, he was concerned that the series should offer an interesting and exciting mix of music from various eras and cultures. Unlike them, however, Karajan restricted the number of performances that he gave at the Philharmonic and Abonnement Concerts[114] to a minimum and conducted the majority of his performances with the Berlin Philharmonic outside the subscriptions series and on tour. At the Philharmonic and Abonnement Concerts, Karajan gave no fewer than 312 concerts. Outside those series, he gave at least 206 concerts at Berlin, 694 on tour and 237 at the Berlin Philharmonic's residencies at the Salzburg Easter and Whitsun Festivals.[115] Those who experienced Karajan only on gramophone, video or on tour might be forgiven for thinking that his preferred repertoire with the Berlin Philharmonic was centred firmly on nineteenth-century composers from the Austro-German canon. While it is true that ninety-three per cent of all Karajan's Philharmonic and Abonnement Concerts contained a work by an Austro-German, and forty-two per cent of all the subscription concerts that he conducted were devoted to music from that tradition, he did offer a wide and varied repertoire that drew heavily upon music from the twentieth century and other cultures.[116]

Unlike Bruno Walter, who lacked sympathy with the late music of Arnold Schoenberg, Karajan was a passionate advocate not only of his music but also that of Berg and Webern. The pride with which he recorded their music with the Berlin Philharmonic in the early 1970s was not simply a fleeting gesture but, rather, an expression of his interest in the music of the Second Viennese School in general. Karajan conducted no fewer than fifty-seven performances of music by those composers at the subscription concerts between the 1958–9 and 1984–5 seasons.[117] For him, the most moving work by any Second Viennese School composer was Berg's Three Orchestral Pieces Op. 6, the impact of which often affected him for days after its performance.[118] But

Schoenberg, Berg and Webern were not the only twentieth-century composers who interested Karajan, and he also gave multiple readings of works by Honegger, Stravinsky, Bartók, Martin, Martinů, Blacher, Vaughan Williams, Prokofiev, Shostakovich, Britten, Henze, Messiaen, Nono, Penderecki, Ligeti, Fortner, Voss, Thärichen and Wimberger. At least four of the works that Karajan conducted were given their world premières by him, including Voss's Variations for wind and timpani on 9 November 1960, Henze's *Antifone*, which was dedicated to Karajan, on 20 January 1962 and Thärichen's Piano Concerto Op. 39 (Alfred Brendel, piano) on 29 December 1961 and *Der Paukenkrieg* on 25 September 1977. In all, twenty-three per cent of the Philharmonic and Abonnement Concerts that Karajan directed at Berlin contained music by a living composer. Inevitably, his interest was greatest during the early years of his tenure, with the number of new works performed diminishing sharply towards the end of his time with the orchestra. But the sheer volume of twentieth-century works performed underlines their importance within Karajan's repertoire as a whole.

Because he recorded four cycles of symphonies by Beethoven, modern listeners would be forgiven for thinking that Karajan's Berlin subscription concerts would be dominated by the composer's music. This, however, was not the case, and at the Philharmonic and Abonnement Concerts he ensured that Beethoven's music was an integral, rather than dominant, element of his programme policy as a whole. In those series, he never gave more than three symphonies in any one season or conducted a complete cycle of them. He did perform the symphonies regularly outside the subscription series, however, and between 29 December 1973 and 2 January 1974 he conducted a cycle of them in Berlin. At the Philharmonic and Abonnement Series, Symphony No. 9 was heard only during the 1967–8 season,[119] but was given more frequently outside the subscription concerts. In keeping with tradition, Karajan programmed it as a festive piece and used it when marking special occasions. His performances at the subscription series, for example, were given as part of the New Year celebrations at the end of 1967 and, when the new Philharmonie was opened in Berlin in 1963, he gave performances of the work to mark the occasion on 15 and 16 October. Although circumspect when performing Beethoven's symphonies at the subscription concerts, Karajan regularly included them when touring with the Berlin Philharmonic. Having been marketed heavily by EMI and DGG as one of the world's leading Beethoven conductors, he did little to dispel that image when performing in France, Great Britain, the USA and Japan, countries in which his profile as a conductor of Beethoven's music was particularly high, and presented cycles of the symphonies in Paris, London, New York, Tokyo and Osaka between 1960 and 1970.[120]

The works of Brahms, Bruckner, Strauss and later Mahler were the other threads that ran through Karajan's tapestry of performances with the Berlin Philharmonic. Having taken over the Philharmonic Concerts from the 1956–7 season, Karajan set about performing all four symphonies by Brahms over the next four years. These works became increasingly associated with Karajan during his years with the orchestra and, at the subscription concerts, he conducted no fewer than twelve all-Brahms concerts.[121] He also regularly performed the symphonies outside the Philharmonic and Abonnement Series and on tour, and he directed cycles of the works at London in 1964 and 1974 and at the Berlin Festwochen in 1968.[122] As a Bruckner advocate, Karajan regularly included the composer's symphonies in his Berlin subscription series but, although passionate about those works, he limited his performances to Symphonies Nos. 4 to 9. In contrast, when performing the orchestral music of Strauss, Karajan had a more wide-ranging approach, conducting works from *Don Juan* to the Oboe Concerto at his Philharmonic and Abonnement Concerts. Unlike the music of Strauss, which Karajan had conducted from the beginning of his career, the symphonies of Mahler were a late addition to his repertoire. Although he had decided against performing Mahler's works in the immediate post-war years because of insufficient rehearsal time,[123] Karajan tackled this repertoire in earnest from the 1970s. Having conducted three performances of *Lieder eines fahrenden Gesellen* on his 1955 tour of North America with the Berlin Philharmonic,[124] he went on to give multiple performances of *Das Lied von der Erde* from 1960 and Symphonies 4, 5, 6 and 9 with the orchestra from 1960.[125]

From the beginning of the 1980s Karajan's relations with the Berlin Philharmonic were strained. In January 1981 the young clarinettist Sabine Meyer auditioned for one of the orchestra's vacant posts. Karajan was impressed immediately by her sound and wanted to engage her. Some members of the orchestra, however, were less keen and suggested that she be employed occasionally as a freelance. The question of her appointment then gave rise to a power struggle between the orchestra and Karajan, who ultimately wanted to impose his will. Karajan took the orchestra's rejection of Meyer as a professional slight and announced that he would be reducing his commitments with the orchestra to his contractual minimum. The affair soon became public and was reported widely in the press. With emotions running high, matters went from bad to worse in 1984, when Karajan engaged the Vienna

Philharmonic at his own expense to perform at that year's Salzburg Whitsun Festival. Karajan did try to mend fences that September, however, by suggesting in a letter to the Berlin Philharmonic that they should attempt to resolve some of their disagreements during the annual Berlin Festwochen concerts.[126] At meetings held during the Festwochen, Karajan and the orchestra reached a series of compromises that allowed them to continue, albeit in a relationship that was often strained. But his health had been failing badly for some time and, with his relations with the orchestra still far from perfect, he resigned as conductor of the Berlin Philharmonic after the Salzburg Easter Festival in April 1989. In his autobiography, Karajan maintained that, his bad relations with the orchestra stemmed from the contract that he signed in 1956 and that when it came to key issues of orchestral and artistic management, his contract provided only for his consultation and not his agreement. For Karajan, that distinction was tantamount to deception, reducing his contract with the Berlin Philharmonic to 'no more than a scrap of paper'.[127]

During his tenure with the Berlin Philharmonic, Karajan also held, or continued to hold, a series of other high-profile posts with the Singverein der Gesellschaft der Musikfreunde (Wien), the Vienna Staatsoper, the Salzburg Festival and the Orchestre de Paris. The Singverein had a long and distinguished history dating back to the nineteenth century, and it could boast collaborations with artists that included Brahms and Mahler. In 1947, Karajan was appointed Konzertdirektor der Gesellschaft der Musikfreunde for life and began an extended and fruitful relationship with the organization that continued until 1989. Together, they performed and recorded regularly and made a particularly deep impact with their reading of Bach's Mass in B minor. The recording was made in London and Vienna with the Philharmonia Orchestra for EMI in 1952–3 and was praised in the 1950s for its scholarly approach and its lively and vibrant tempi. When performing with the choir, Karajan regularly abandoned the baton, preferring instead to conduct with his bare hands, made greater eye contact with the performers and had the choristers sing from memory.[128] Even though his professional activities were dominated by his concerts with the Berlin Philharmonic from the mid 1960s, he continued to take his responsibilities with the choir seriously and used it regularly when recording works by Bach, Beethoven, Brahms, Haydn, Mozart and Verdi.[129]

As Artistic Adviser of the Orchestre de Paris between 1969 and 1971, Karajan worked with the ensemble in both the concert hall and the recording studio. The orchestra was founded in 1967 under the baton of the Alsatian conductor Charles Münch, and when he died in November 1968, the orchestra's management turned to Karajan as his successor. Although he was a great admirer of Paris as a city and his third wife, Eliette,[130] was French, he initially rejected their approach. Having reflected on his decision, Karajan changed his mind and accepted the somewhat nebulously named post of Artistic Adviser from 1969. Because of his commitments in Berlin and Salzburg, the time that he could offer the Orchestre de Paris was very limited. Although he was contracted to work with the orchestra for a minimum of ten weeks annually, it soon became clear that he was having difficulty meeting that commitment. Moreover, by the time of his appointment, his diary was dominated by his engagements with the Berlin and Vienna Philharmonics. These orchestras were of a considerably higher standard than that of the fledgling Orchestre de Paris and Karajan quickly realized that to raise its standard to that of the Berlin or Vienna ensembles he would have to devote a considerable amount of time and effort to its development. With little appetite for such a venture, he began to spend less time with the French orchestra, and when it became apparent that it ranked a very poor third in his hierarchy of commitments, the management asked him to resign.[131]

On 5 March 1956, Karl Böhm resigned as Director of the Vienna Staatsoper. As a native Austrian,[132] Böhm had seemed the ideal choice to lead the company after its reconstruction following World War II, but his tenure was far from successful and he quickly fell foul of the local press and opera-going public. Keen to replace the dour Böhm with a more charismatic figure, the Vienna authorities looked to Karajan as his logical successor. Like Böhm, Karajan was an Austrian who had risen through the ranks of the Central European opera-house system. By the time of his appointment he had had considerable success as a guest conductor with La Scala, Milan, after World War II and had made a sensational guest appearance with the company in Vienna in June 1956 with Donizetti's *Lucia di Lammermoor*. Aware that the post of Director of the Staatsoper was a problematic appointment and subject to intense press and public scrutiny, Karajan was nevertheless both ready to accept the job and willing to make the sweeping changes needed to improve the theatre's fortunes. After extensive talks with senior Austrian civil servants and politicians, during which he outlined some of the reforms that he intended to implement, Karajan signed a contract on 14 June 1956 that appointed him Director from 1 January 1957.[133] Sure of his ability to improve standards at the Staatsoper, he quickly set about changing the theatre's working practices and replaced the old repertory system with a modified version of the *stagione* system, insisted on original-language productions, took charge of important first nights, engaged singers of world renown, established production links with other major theatres, and acted as both producer and conductor for some of his productions. The appointment also allowed Karajan to develop both musically and theatrically, and he later affirmed that he had 'really learned ... the tools of the trade' at the Staatsoper through having become 'deeply involved in stage technology' from the outset, and having 'learned all that [he] still had to learn as a producer'.[134]

During his tenure at Vienna, Karajan conducted a broad and interesting repertoire. After making his début as Director with his own new production of Wagner's *Die Walküre* on 2 April 1957, he conducted a further 234 performances of twenty-nine operas by thirteen composers.[135] As in Berlin with the Philharmonic, variety was the key to Karajan's programme policy at the Staatsoper. Along with works by composers with whom he had become associated closely over the years, he also took charge of operas by Claudio Monteverdi and Ildebrando Pizzetti. By conducting the former's *L'incoronazione di Poppea* and the latter's *Assassinio nella cattedrale*[136] he not only continued to signal his interest in all things Italian but also provided Vienna audiences with an overview of shifting trends in opera composition from the mid seventeenth to the mid twentieth centuries. As a producer-conductor, he presented new productions of *Falstaff*, *Otello*, *Die Walküre* and *Siegfried* in 1957, *Das Rheingold* in 1958, *Tristan und Isolde* in 1959, *Götterdämmerung* in 1960, *Parsifal* in 1961, *Fidelio* and *Pelléas et Mélisande* in 1962, *Tannhäuser* and *Il trovatore* in 1963 and *Die Frau ohne Schatten* in 1964. With the exception of Debussy's *Pelléas et Mélisande*, which was praised for its beauty and delicacy, all the operas that Karajan produced and conducted at the Staatsoper were by Beethoven, Strauss, Verdi or Wagner. Given his championing of their works, it is hardly surprising that he should attempt to mould their musical and theatrical elements into a cohesive whole by acting as producer-conductor, but what is surprising is the absence of Mozart's operas from the list. Even more surprising was the absence or virtual absence of Mozart's mature operas from Karajan's Vienna repertoire. With the exception of *Le nozze di Figaro*, which he performed relatively frequently, he conducted *Don Giovanni* only twice and *Die Zauberflöte* on just one occasion during his tenure at the Staatsoper.[137] And, in keeping with nineteenth- and early twentieth-century trends, he showed either little or no professional interest in Mozart's early operas and considered *Così fan tutte* unsuitable for the stage.[138]

Concurrently with his duties at the Staatsoper, Karajan was appointed Artistic Director of the Salzburg Festival in 1956 with effect from 1957.[139] Having been largely excluded from the Festival after World War II because of Furtwängler's continuing jealousy,[140] Karajan was keen to make his mark as Artistic Director by attempting a number of reforms. As a native Salzburger and the most famous son of the city since Mozart, he felt that he was in a strong bargaining position to influence the conservative Festival committee. Keen to remove the near monopoly that the Vienna Philharmonic had enjoyed at the Festival's Orchestral Concerts series since its inception,[141] he suggested that the series should be opened on a regular basis to other orchestras. He also argued that it was necessary to increase fees to attract front-rank singers, soloists and conductors. He felt that if these changes were implemented, wealthy patrons would continue to attend the Festival and the revenue needed to help finance the new Festspielhaus would be assured.[142] While not all the reforms were popular universally, they were introduced eventually and the Festival's image as a major musical and social event was again secure.

Of the reforms implemented, the ending of the Vienna Philharmonic's dominance of the Orchestral Concerts was of greatest importance artistically. Karajan's modification to the existing arrangement began in 1957, and between that year and 1964, six orchestras directed by twenty-two conductors supplemented the work of the Vienna Philharmonic.[143] Karajan's reform of the Orchestral Series was less a means of raising his conducting profile at the Festival than a way of providing variety for audiences. Of the thirty-nine performances given by orchestras other than the Vienna Philharmonic at that series during this period, Karajan directed only four. Similarly, at the forty concerts given by the Vienna Philharmonic during his time as Artistic Director, thirty-two were taken by conductors other than Karajan and, when performing opera at Salzburg during his tenure, Karajan conducted only fifty-eight of the 236 performances given.[144] It seems, therefore, that the basis for his programme policy at Salzburg was artistic balance rather than professional advantage.

In 1964, Karajan resigned as Artistic Director of the Salzburg Festival and Director of the Vienna Staatsoper. Although his decision to leave the Staatsoper caused shock waves that rocked Austrian cultural life to its foundations, it was hardly a rash action, but rather the culmination of a series of events that dated back several years. From 1961, Karajan's tenure at the Staatsoper had begun to suffer a series of crises that led to his departure. That year, a serious dispute with the unions threatened to

disrupt the day-to-day running of the theatre. The stagehands felt over-
worked and underpaid, and although Karajan was sympathetic to their
cause, he was constrained by government financial controls. The situation reached crisis point when the workers' actions threatened the
famous Opera Ball, a highlight of Vienna's social season. To avoid the
embarrassment of cancelling the Ball, a deal was reached between
the unions and the government during one of Karajan's frequent
absences from the Staatsoper. Feeling that his position as Director had
been undermined, Karajan resigned immediately. Supported by the
press and the opera-going public, he soon rescinded that decision and
resumed his position as head of the theatre. A second, more serious
crisis occurred after the appointment of Egon Hilbert as Karajan's co-
director in 1963. Although Karajan retained artistic control of the
theatre, he soon began to resent Hilbert's interference in matters
beyond his remit. The professional relationship between the two deteriorated quickly and Karajan left the Staatsoper at the end of the
1963–4 season. Feeling angry and betrayed, he distanced himself from
the theatre for many years and returned only as guest conductor in
1977 for performances of Verdi's *Il trovatore*, Mozart's *Le nozze di
Figaro* and Puccini's *La Bohème*.

Despite his resignation as Artistic Director of the Salzburg Festival in
1964, Karajan continued to play an active role in its day-to-day running
by accepting a place on the committee of management.[145] In the years
following his resignation, he continued to conduct operas and concerts
annually at Salzburg and remained firmly at the centre of the Festival's
musical life until 1989. By freeing himself from his duties at the
Salzburg Festival and the Vienna Staatsoper, Karajan was able to focus
his attention firmly on the establishment of the Salzburg Easter Festival.
Prompted by a remark by the conductor Christoph von Dohnányi,
Karajan soon became interested in establishing a venue at which he
could conduct and produce operas to his own standards. Working without subsidy and accepting no fee, Karajan conducted the first Easter
Festival in 1967. Unlike the Salzburg Festival, the Easter Festival was
largely a personal vehicle for him to explore works that were central to
his repertoire. He established the format, tone and quality of the Festival from the outset by juxtaposing operatic performances with choral
and orchestral concerts and by engaging the Berlin Philharmonic as its
resident orchestra.[146] Karajan then extended his influence over
Salzburg's artistic life with his involvement in the city's Whitsun Festival
from 1973. This Festival usually involved a short series of orchestral
concerts with the Berlin Philharmonic as the resident orchestra and, like

the Easter Festival, was used by Karajan to explore music for which he had a particular affinity.[147]

By the summer of 1989, Karajan's health had been failing for some time,[148] and although his physical decline had been public knowledge throughout the late 1980s, his sudden death on 16 July 1989 struck the musical world as if by lightning.[149] The summer Festival was about to begin and Karajan was scheduled to conduct a production of Verdi's *Un ballo in maschera*.[150] Within hours of his passing, Salzburg was swathed in black and many of its citizens began a period of unofficial mourning. By the time of the Requiem for him at Salzburg Cathedral on 23 July,[151] it was apparent to all present that they had witnessed the passing of the last great icon of the Central European tradition. It was almost inevitable that the death of one of the most discussed musicians of the late twentieth century should spark a debate that would polarize musicians and non-musicians alike. On the one hand, there were his detractors who criticized his dominance as pernicious and, on the other, there were his supporters who argued his importance as a musical and a historic figure. His emphasis on orchestral sonority and his links with the traditions of the past meant that some doubted his aesthetic judgement. But those who performed with him at the height of his career were often prepared to overlook those doubts, preferring instead to revel in the image of Karajan as 'a real man, a real general man, [a man who] drove fast cars and flew an aeroplane, as well as being a fine musician'.[152]

Conclusion

The subjects of group biographies inevitably share similar hopes, expectations and experiences. The decision to become a musician, the need to specialize as a conductor and the responsibilities that come with that profession meant that the subjects of this book had more in common than most. Central to that commonality was their sense of responsibility. They saw themselves as curators of a tradition that had its roots firmly planted in the soil of German culture. For them, Austro-German music was 'die heilige deutsche Kunst' ('the holy German art')[1] and it was their destiny to act as its high priests. In fulfilling that destiny, they ensured that the content of the masterworks they performed took on a near mystical status. They believed fully that there was a natural artistic progression from J. S. Bach to Richard Strauss and that the integrated nature of that progression could have been achieved only within the context of Central Europe. For them, the music that they performed was not only an expression of their culture but also a means by which to promote that culture elsewhere. Because of their high profiles, they became the public face of German art and they were soon exploited by politicians for propaganda purposes. Even though their interest in politics was generally minimal, the stigma of their involvements often continues to detract from their achievements as musicians to this day.

Without exception, the conductors examined in this book were all products of the middle class. Although their place in that demographic altered slightly from individual to individual, they benefited greatly from the security that that social group provided. As the cost of scores, books and instruments meant that the working class were often excluded from art music in general, it became the responsibility of the middle class to become the standard-bearers for high culture in Central Europe. As the ownership of a pianoforte was a symbol of bourgeois respectability during the late nineteenth and early twentieth centuries, it was common for middle-class homes to have a keyboard instrument in their parlour or drawing room. For aspiring conductors of the period, the pianoforte was an essential tool with which they could familiarize themselves with the music that they would later perform professionally. The ability to experience practically, in a domestic situation, the major works from what was becoming the Austro-German canon not only extended their understanding of the works in general but also prepared them for life in the opera house in particular. As the ability to sight-read difficult scores with ease was a prerequisite for all répétiteurs, the techniques that they first learned in the parlour were often the basis for their early experiences as professional musicians.

Although Richard Wagner approved of conductors who had gained their experiences through working in either an opera house or an orchestra, he was damning of those who came from the conservatory system. It is slightly ironic, therefore, that with the exceptions of Hans von Bülow, Richard Strauss and Wilhelm Furtwängler each of the conductors discussed in this book was an alumnus of a school of music. Unlike modern conservatories, those that aspiring conductors attended during the late nineteenth and early twentieth centuries did little to prepare them for a career in either the concert hall or the opera house. Very few of the schools of music offered courses in conducting and, in those that did, only basic instruction in stick technique was available. The lessons offered to Felix Weingartner by the Leipzig Conservatory were rudimentary, with one student beating time while another played a piano arrangement of the score being studied, while, at the Akademie für Musik in Vienna, Herbert von Karajan was taught by an oboist rather than a professional conductor. It is unsurprising, therefore, that aspiring conductors turned to their local concert halls and opera houses to supplement their educations. At those venues, young musicians were able to watch experienced conductors at work and to hear much of the repertoire that they would later interpret. As gramophone recordings were either non-existent or were in their infancy, the only chance for students to hear both masterworks from the past and new compositions was at the performances of their local orchestra or opera company. It is little wonder, then, that the practices of the conductors performing with those organizations were passed from one generation to the next.

Having graduated from their schools of music, young conductors were keen to begin their careers as conductors. The most obvious route to the podium in Hohenzollern Germany and Habsburg Austria was by the opera-house system. All of the conductors discussed in this book began their careers in the theatre and all gained early experience by working as répétiteurs or as chorus masters. By starting at the bottom of the operatic ladder, they were able to work closely with conductors who had also risen through the same system. Although the repertoire performed would vary from theatre to theatre, its basis was established firmly in works from the emerging Austro-German canon and the Italian nineteenth-century tradition. The works that conductors were allocated depended largely on rank and seniority. The Third Kapellmeister would conduct mostly operettas and light opera, the Second Kapellmeister would generally take charge of revivals of more important works, and the First Kapellmeister, Hofkapellmeister, Generalmusikdirektor or Direktor would undertake many of the premières and new productions. Of course, there were many exceptions to those rules but, in general, that hierarchic structure dominated the working practices of the Central European opera-house system and the conductors discussed were comfortable with it.

In the concert hall, the repertoire that each conductor performed had much in common. At the heart of their activities were the works of Beethoven. For the conductors of Central Europe, he was the foundation upon which they built their programme policies. Although they admired the works of Bach, Mozart and Schubert, those composers were represented usually by only a handful of popular works. In contrast, Beethoven's compositions were common fare, with all nine symphonies being performed repeatedly at the major subscription series. Although all the conductors recognized the importance of Beethoven as a barometer for their skills as interpreters, the number of performances given varied from conductor to conductor. Arthur Nikisch, for example, considered Beethoven's music to be an integral rather than a dominant part of his programme policy, while Richard Strauss performed a work by the composer at no less than ninety per cent of his concerts with the Berlin Staatskapelle.

New music also featured at the subscription concerts of Central European conductors. As most were composers, they had a passionate interest in works from music's cutting edge. They considered it their duty to promote recent compositions and to perform them in the most favourable circumstances possible. In achieving those goals, they regularly performed new works side by side with established masterpieces. Rarely did they devote whole concerts to modern compositions, because concert promoters would have suffered at the box office and new works would have been exposed only to niche audiences. Established composers like Richard Strauss were particularly active on the part of their less successful colleagues, while some less popular composers, such as

Gustav Mahler, used their status as conductors to promote their own music at their guest engagements. With the exception of Herbert von Karajan, none of the Central European conductors had a strong affinity with the music of the Second Viennese School. They were largely baffled by Schoenberg's move from tonality to atonality and could not come to terms with the rigours of the twelve-tone system. In contrast, many respected the music of Stravinsky and took particular pleasure in championing the composer's music in the years directly preceding World War II. Even though the conductors began to perform new works less frequently in old age, they continued to have an interest in the music of their time and made a point of attending performances of modern compositions when and where possible.

Although the conductors were passionate advocates of new music, little evidence of their enthusiasm is evident in their discographies. While Richard Strauss did record many of his tone poems, much of the music that he documented was composed by him in the years preceding the first decade of the twentieth century. Record companies in both North America and Europe preferred to promote the conductors as curators of the Austro-German canon rather than as enthusiasts for the new. Even though recordings were more affordable and more widely available after the introduction of vinyl long-play discs, companies continued to record the conductors' interpretations of established works rather than their readings of twentieth-century music. Keen to profit from the conductors' reputations as Beethoven interpreters, the companies recorded his symphonies regularly. Although only Karajan made more than one complete set of the Beethoven symphonies, other conductors such as Felix Weingartner, Bruno Walter, Otto Klemperer and Wilhelm Furtwängler recorded individual symphonies more than once. Many of those recordings have since become important historically and are benchmarks against which other recordings are often judged. While each of the conductors' interpretations reflected the thoughts and practices of Wagner, those of Walter and Klemperer were also influenced by the approach of Gustav Mahler. In an attempt to repay their debt to him, they not only included his music in their concerts but also documented some of his works on disc. Although neither conductor recorded all nine symphonies by Mahler, they did record works with which they felt a particular affinity. Those discs have since become important sound artefacts and are distinguished by the performers' links with the composer.

Having gained notoriety at home and abroad through public performance and recorded sound, Central European conductors soon became iconic figures. The level of respect that they were accorded and the awe with which they were greeted had few parallels in the performing arts. They became celebrities in their own right and were in constant demand for interviews and personal appearances. Even though some of them were uncomfortable with that lifestyle, they soon learned to adapt to it and to make use of it. Their fame as artist-celebrities probably reached its peak with Herbert von Karajan. With his flair for mixing financial acumen with artistic excellence, he was able to secure a place in the public consciousness that has yet to be surpassed. Of today's artists from Central Europe, Wolfgang Sawallisch, Christoph von Dohnányi and Kurt Masur are arguably the most distinguished. Their career paths have much in common with those of previous generations and they have all held important posts in Europe and North America. Although they have benefited from expert marketing, improved global communication and speedy international travel, they have failed to achieve the iconic status of their antecedents. Their failure has often been seen as evidence of the decline and fall of the Central European conducting tradition. If that is the case then, Western art music will have lost one of its greatest treasures. Only time will tell.

Notes

Introduction: Richard Wagner, *Zukunftsdirigent*

1 Richard Wagner was born at Leipzig on 22 May 1813 and died at Venice on 13 February 1883.

2 This overview of Wagner's conducting career will be restricted to the years 1833–55, the period in which he worked primarily as a professional conductor.

3 Wagner's début performance with the Magdeburg company, on 2 August 1834, was not given at Magdeburg but in the spa town of Lauchstädt as part of the company's summer season there.

4 Stage works that Wagner conducted with the Magdeburg company included Bellini's *I Capuleti e i Montecchi* and *Norma*, Rossini's *Il barbiere di Siviglia*, *Tancredi* and *Otello*, Weber's *Preciosa*, *Oberon* and *Der Freischütz*, Boieldieu's *La Dame blanche*, Spohr's *Jessonda*, Marschner's *Der Templer und die Jüdin* and Cherubini's *Les Deux Journées*. C. von Westernhagen, 'Wagner', *The New Grove Dictionary of Music and Musicians* (London, 1980), p. 105.

5 R. Wagner, trans. M. Whittall, ed. A. Gray, *My Life* (Cambridge, 1983), pp. 112–13.

6 Ibid.

7 F. Praeger, *Wagner as I Knew Him* (New York, 1893), p. 61.

8 Wagner, *My Life*, p. 148.

9 J. Köhler, trans. S. Spencer, *Richard Wagner: The Last of the Titans* (New Haven and London, 2004), p. 105.

10 Wagner, *My Life*, p. 247.

11 'Über eine Aufführung des Don Juan auf dem Dresdener [*sic*] Hoftheater', *Zeitschrift für die elegante Welt* – 43:19, 10 May 1843, pp. 463–4. As found in E. W. Galkin, *A History of Orchestral Conducting in Theory and Practice* (New York, 1988), p. 578.

12 See Chapter 1.

13 The practice of doubling the woodwind and the brass in loud passages is still popular today.

14 In the second movement of Beethoven's Symphony No. 9 ('Choral'), for example, Wagner strengthened the woodwind with 'at least . . . four horns' at the 'second theme' (bars 93 to 109), because the melody and the accompaniment lacked balance when performed with the original orchestration. Similarly, at the beginning of the last movement, what he called the 'Schreckenfanfare', he doubled the woodwinds with the trumpets, because 'the limitations of the natural trumpets had here again prevented Beethoven from thoroughly fulfilling his intention'. R. Wagner,

'Zum Vortrage der neunten Symphonie Beethoven's' ('Performing Beethoven's Ninth Symphony'), trans. W. Ashton Ellis, *Actors and Singers* (Lincoln, Nebr., and London, 1995), pp. 236–41.

15 Wagner, *My Life*, pp. 329–32.

16 The orchestra of the Allgemeine Musikgesellschaft was drawn from Zürich's pool of professional and amateur musicians and its permanent conductor was the German conductor and composer Franz Abt (1819–85). Wagner conducted only Beethoven's Symphony No. 7 at his first Zürich concert; the remainder of the programme was conducted by Abt. C. Walton, 'Richard Wagner als Dirigent in Zürich', *Tribschener Blätter*, No. 55/56, September 1998, pp. 2–45.

17 Wagner, *My Life*, p. 429.

18 Ibid., p. 458.

19 In Zürich, Wagner conducted at one public concert in 1850, three each in 1851 and 1852, eight in 1853, seven in 1854 and five in 1855. Along with these, he gave two private performances for his friends the Wesendoncks: one each in 1857 and 1858. Information concerning Wagner's activities in Zürich was kindly provided by Professor Chris Walton.

At the Aktientheater, Wagner conducted Bellini's *Norma*, Boieldieu's *La Dame blanche*, Mozart's *Don Giovanni* and *Die Zauberflöte* and Weber's *Der Freischütz* in 1850, Beethoven's *Fidelio* in 1851 and his own *Der fliegende Holländer* in 1852 and *Tannhäuser* in 1855. The Aktientheater was built in 1833 and was destroyed by fire in 1890. Opera performances were then given in the Stadttheater, which opened in 1891; this theatre was renamed 'Opernhaus' in 1964.

20 While Wagner did not perform the whole of Beethoven's Symphony No. 9 at Zürich, he did give the Scherzo and Adagio from the work at a private concert for the Wesendoncks on 31 March 1858. At the same concert, he also performed the Finale from Symphony No. 3 ('Eroica'), the Adagio and Scherzo from Symphony No. 4, the Andante from Symphony No. 5, the Andante and Scherzo from Symphony No. 7 and the Menuetto and Scherzando from Symphony No. 8.

At the public concerts, Wagner conducted Beethoven's Symphony No. 3 three times, Symphony No. 4 once, Symphony No. 5 four times, Symphony No. 6 ('Pastoral') twice, Symphony No. 7 five times and Symphony No. 8 three times.

21 For detailed descriptions of Wagner's period with the Philharmonic Society, see: M. B. Foster, *The History of the Philharmonic Society of London 1813–1912* (London, 1912), pp. 239–45; R. Elkin, *Royal Philharmonic: The Annals of the Royal Philharmonic Society* (London, 1946), pp. 49–57, and C. Ehrlich, *First Philharmonic: A History of The Royal Philharmonic Society* (Oxford, 1995), pp. 87–92.

22 Michael Costa (1808–84): Italian-born British composer and conductor, appointed conductor of the Philharmonic Society in 1846.

23 C. Ehrlich, *First Philharmonic*, p. 88.

24 On 30 May 1853, Berlioz shared the podium with Costa. Berlioz conducted the first half of the concert, which consisted solely of his own works; these were: *Harold en Italie*, 'Le Repos de la Sainte Famille' from part 2 of *L'Enfance du Christ* and the overture *Le Carnaval romain*.

25 According to Wagner's autobiography (pp. 514–15), Prosper Sainton, a violinist and director of the Society, had been encouraged by a German musician named Lüders, who had read Wagner's article 'Opera and Drama', to engage the composer-conductor; neither Sainton nor Lüders had seen Wagner conduct. Without further evidence, however, this story should be treated with caution.

26 Franz Paul Lachner (1803–90): German conductor. Hofkapellmeister and later Generalmusikdirektor at the Munich Hofoper from 1836 to 1868. A composer as well as a conductor, he was personally acquainted with Schubert and

Beethoven. His activities in Munich were curtailed with the arrival of Wagner and Bülow.

27 Wagner's letter of agreement, dated 27 January 1855, is held in Royal Philharmonic Society Letters Vol. 35 (Vi–Wh), British Library, RPS MS 367.

28 Although Wagner accepted the Philharmonic's offer, his stipulations concerning an assistant conductor and sufficient rehearsal time were not met.

29 With the exception of the concert on 26 March 1855, at which Beethoven's Symphony No. 9 was performed and for which Wagner was allowed two rehearsals, the Philharmonic policy of allowing one rehearsal for each concert was applied strictly.

30 At the Philharmonic Concerts, Wagner performed fourteen symphonies (seven by Beethoven, two each by Mendelssohn and Mozart, and one each by Cipriani Potter, Spohr and Haydn), twenty-three vocal works (six by Mozart, three by Spohr, two each by Cherubini, Meyerbeer, Weber and Paër, and one each by Beethoven, Marschner, Pergolesi, Handel, Haydn and an unnamed composer), six concertos (two by Beethoven and one each by Mendelssohn, Spohr, Chopin and Hummel) and seventeen overtures (five by Weber, three by Wagner, two each by Mendelssohn and Cherubini, and one each by Mozart, Onslow, Beethoven, Spohr and Macfarren).

31 Wagner conducted Beethoven's Symphonies Nos. 3 to 9 inclusive.

32 *Sunday Times*, 17 June 1855.

33 *Über das Dirigiren* (*On Conducting*) was first published in the *Neue Zeitschrift für Musik* and the *New Yorker Musik-Zeitung* in 1869. It was later incorporated into the *Gesammelte Schriften und Dichtungen von Richard Wagner* (Leipzig, 1871–83). 'Translator's Note' (E. Dannreuther), in R. Wagner, *On Conducting*.

34 Wagner, *On Conducting*, pp. 3–5.

35 Ibid., p. 1.

36 Ibid., p. 19.

37 Ibid.

38 Pierre Boulez (b. 1925): French composer and conductor. J. Vermeil, trans. C. Naish, *Conversations with Boulez: Thoughts on Conducting* (Portland, OR, 1996), p. 70.

39 Sir John Barbirolli (1899–1970): British cellist and conductor. J. Barbirolli, 'The Art of Conducting', as found in C. Bamberger, ed., *The Conductor's Art* (New York, 1965), p. 243.

40 Wagner, *On Conducting*, pp. 42–3.

41 Ibid.

42 Ibid, pp. 52–3.

43 Ibid., pp. 60–2.

Chapter 1. 'The master-conductor Hans von Bülow'

1 F. Weingartner, *Über das Dirigieren* (1895), trans. E. Newman as *On Conducting* (London, 1906), p. 12.

2 Bülow composed forty-seven works, the best known of which is *Nirwana*. Although his works are numbered Op. 1 to Op. 30, Op. 17 is subdivided into Op. 17a (*Souvenir de l'Opéra, Un Ballo in maschera de Giuseppe Verdi. Morceau de cour pour le Piano*) and Op. 17b (*Capriccio à la Polacca sur des motifs de la musique de 'Struensee' de Giacomo Meyerbeer*) and Opus 9 and Opus 25 are not listed. There also exist at least eighteen works without opus number. For a complete list of Bülow's compositions, see H.-J. Hinrichsen, *Musikalische Interpretation: Hans von Bülow* (Stuttgart, 1999), pp. 371–81.

3 Hans's sister Isidora was born on 15 June 1833.

4 Bülow's father was a businessman, literary translator and writer, and his mother was a good amateur musician.

5 The German pianist Friedrich Wieck (1785–1873) was the father of Clara Schumann, née Wieck. Louis Plaidy (1810–74): German pianist.

6 Bernhard Molique (1802–69): German conductor and composer. Joachim Raff (1822–82): Swiss-born German composer and administrator.

7 H. von Bülow, ed. M. von Bülow, *Briefe 1841–1853* (Leipzig, 1899), pp. 81–2.

8 14 March 1848.

9 F. Haas, *Hans von Bülow: Leben und Wirken* (Wilhelmshaven, 2002), p. 15.

10 R. du Moulin-Eckart, *Hans von Bülow* (Munich, 1921), p. 46.

11 Moritz Hauptmann (1792–1868): German teacher and editor.

12 Bülow, *Briefe*, Vol. 1, p. 195.

13 In Berlin, Bülow continued to pursue his musical and tertiary studies.

14 Haas, *Hans von Bülow*, p. 15.

15 See note 3.

16 Bülow, *Briefe*, Vol. 1, pp. 262–3.

17 Ibid.

18 R. Wagner, trans. M. Whittall, ed. A. Gray, *My Life* (Cambridge, 1983), p. 457.

19 Bülow made his local début at St Gallen with Lortzing's *Der Waffenschmied von Worms*. Bülow, *Briefe*, Vol. 1, p. 279.

20 Ibid., p. 289.

21 While Bülow had already conducted some operas that were popular nationally and internationally, the folkloric nature of *Der Freischütz* meant that it had a particular significance for German-speaking audiences.

22 Bülow, *Briefe*, Vol. 1, p. 295.

23 Bülow once remarked famously to the young Richard Strauss, 'You should have the score in your head and not your head in the score . . . even if you have composed the thing yourself.' R. Strauss, ed. W. Schuh and trans. L. J. Lawrence, *Recollections and Reflections* (London, 1953), p. 121. (Bülow's remark to Strauss was made after a performance of the young composer's tone poem *Macbeth* in Berlin on 29 February 1892. The other works on the programme were Berlioz' s overture to *Béatrice et Bénédict*, Hubay's Violin Concerto in A minor (Jenö Hubay, violin), violin solos by Svendsen and Hubay (Jenö Hubay, violin), Brahms's Symphony No. 2 and Beethoven's overture *Leonore* No. 3. Only *Macbeth* was conducted by Strauss; the rest of the programme was conducted by Bülow. The orchestra was the Berlin Philharmonic.)

24 Bülow performed the Choral Fantasy at Ballenstedt on 22 June 1852. The reading was conducted by Liszt and was the first of ten performances that Bülow gave of the work during his career. Bülow then performed Op. 47 with the Hungarian violinist, Joseph Joachim (1831–1907) at Erfurt on 3 September 1852 and Op. 57 at Jena on 13 December 1852.

25 Hinrichsen, *Musikalische Interpretation*, p. 478. The statistics concerning the total number of performances given by Bülow in this section are an extension of the figures found in Hinrichsen.

26 Of that statistic, 136 performances were of compositions for piano and orchestra with Bülow as soloist.

27 The Liebig'sche Kapelle was founded and managed by the German conductor and clarinettist Carl Liebig (1808–72).

28 The singers were the German soprano Rosa von Milde (1825–1906) and her husband, the German baritone Hans Feodor von Milde (1821–1899). By the time of that concert, Bülow had conducted Wagner's overture to *Tannhäuser* on 19 October 1855 and *Faust Overture* on 1 February 1856.

29 The soloist was the Polish pianist Carl Tausig (1841–71).

30 Later in his life, Bülow's interest in Liszt's works waned and, unlike the music of Berlioz and Wagner, whose overtures were heard regularly at Bülow's concerts throughout his career – he never performed Berlioz's *Symphonie fantastique* or Wagner's *Siegfried Idyll* – the symphonic poems of Liszt were performed seldom by him after the late 1870s. With the exception of *Les Préludes*, which Bülow performed six times between June 1860 and January 1892, his readings of *Tasso: Lamento e Trionfo, Orpheus, Prometheus, Mazeppa, Festklänge, Hungaria, Die Ideale* and *Eine Faust-Symphonie* were restricted to the period 1858–79, and *Mazeppa* and *Hungaria* were performed once only by him, on 12 March 1859 and 18 April 1866 respectively.

31 Bülow gave 98 performances of his works during his career. That figure does not include the performance of his four-hand piano transcription of Wagner's overture to *Tannhäuser* that he gave with Carl Tausig in Berlin on 29 January 1858.

32 The concert included Beethoven's Piano Concerto No. 4 (Hans von Bülow, piano), Berlioz's Overtures *Les Francs-juges and Le Corsaire* and an aria from *Benvenuto Cellini* (Rosa von Milde, soprano), Wagner's 'Prayer' from *Tannhäuser* (Rosa von Milde, soprano) and the Prelude to Act 1 of *Lohengrin*, Liszt's *Die Ideale* and Raff's Violin Concerto ('Die Liebesfee') (Ludwig Straus, violin).

33 Bülow first performed Beethoven's Piano Concerto No. 4 at Danzig on 15 December 1858 and later gave a further forty-seven performances of the piece during his career. While he gave Piano Concerto No. 4 regularly from 1858, his preference was for its successor, Piano Concerto No. 5 ('Emperor'), of which he gave seventy-eight performances between 1854 and 1892. Those statistics pertain only to those concerts at which Bülow acted as soloist. He also gave a further nine and five performances respectively of Piano Concertos Nos. 4 and 5 as conductor. Hinrichsen, *Musikalische Interpretation*, pp. 478, 490.

34 27 February 1859.

35 Liszt conducted *Die Ideale*, the 'Wanderer' Fantasy and the *Fantasie über Motive aus Beethovens 'Ruinen von Athen'*; Bülow was the soloist for the two last named. Liszt's *The Erl-King* and *Mignon* were also heard at the concert, sung by the soprano Emilie Genast.

36 Letter from Hans von Bülow to Richard Wagner, dated 4 March 1859. *Letters of Hans von Bülow to Richard Wagner and Others* ed. Richard Count du Moulin Eckart and S. Goddard, trans. H. Walter (New York, 1979), pp. 202–3.

37 For that reading of Wagner's Prelude to *Tristan und Isolde*, Bülow used his own concert ending.

38 R. Wuerst, *Allgemeine musikalische Zeitung*, 29 April 1863, as found in Haas, *Hans von Bülow*, pp. 153–4.

39 The choir that sang in Beethoven's Symphony No. 9 and *Meeresstille und glückliche Fahrt* was the Stern'scher Gesangverein. Bülow was soloist in Liszt's Piano Concerto No. 2 and Julius Stern was the conductor.

40 The soloist in Beethoven's Violin Concerto was August Kömpel, the concertmaster at Weimar.

41 Bülow performed Beethoven's Violin Concerto for the first time at Berlin on 17 March 1858 with Ferdinand Laub as soloist.

42 At St Petersburg, Bülow conducted Beethoven's Symphony No. 6 on 22 March 1864, and Meyerbeer's *Fest-Ouvertüre* and Mozart's Symphony No. 41 on 23 March 1864.

43 Cosima (1837–1930) was the daughter of Liszt. She married Bülow on 18 August 1857.

44 Haas, *Hans von Bülow*, p. 160.

45 Ibid., p. 161.
46 The first night was scheduled for 15 May 1865, but because of the indisposition of the Danish soprano Malvina Schnorr von Carolsfeld (1825–1904), the first Isolde, the première was delayed until 10 June 1865. H. Zehetmair and J. Schläder, eds., *Nationaltheater: Die Bayerische Staatsoper* (Munich, 1992), p. 65.
47 Letter from Hans von Bülow to Eduard Lassen, dated 31 July 1865. As found in K. Birkin, 'Une organisation musicale des plus rares', *Richard Strauss-Blätter* (June 2002), p. 17.
48 Bülow conducted four performances of *Tristan und Isolde* at Munich between 10 June and 1 July 1865.
49 The world première of Liszt's *Die Legende von der heiligen Elisabeth* was given at Budapest on 15 August 1865.
50 Karl Bechstein (1826–1900): German piano manufacturer.
51 Letter from Hans von Bülow to Karl Bechstein, dated 6 March 1866. *Letters of Hans von Bülow to Richard Wagner and Others*, p. 49.
52 The operas that Bülow conducted only once were Gluck's *Orfeo ed Euridice*, *Iphigenie in Aulis* (ed. Wagner) and *Armida*, Halévy's *La Juive*, Lachner's *Catharina Cornaro*, Nicolai's *Die lustigen Weiber von Windsor*, Rossini's *Guillaume Tell*, Verdi's *Il trovatore* and Weber's *Abu Hassan*.
53 *Sitzproben* are rehearsals where singers and orchestra rehearse the music seated and without stage action.
54 C. Fifield, 'Conducting Wagner: the Search for Melos', *Wagner in Performance*, ed. B. Millington and S. Spencer (New Haven and London, 1992), p. 4.
55 Hans Richter (1843–1916): Hungarian conductor.
56 C. Fifield, *True Artist and True Friend: A Biography of Hans Richter* (Oxford, 1993), p. 25.
57 Richter was appointed conductor of the Vienna Philharmonic's Abonnement series and First Kapellmeister at the Hofoper in 1875. From 1876, he conducted regularly at the Bayreuth Festival; from 1879, he gave an annual series of 'Richter Concerts' at the Queen's Hall, London; in 1899, he was appointed Music Director of the Hallé Orchestra, Manchester; from 1903, he was engaged regularly at Covent Garden, and, in 1904, he conducted the first concert of the newly formed London Symphony Orchestra.
58 The other new productions that Bülow conducted in the first months of 1868 at Munich were Cherubini's *Les Deux Journées* and Weber's *Abu Hassan*, given on 22 March and 14 April 1868 respectively.
59 Hinrichsen, *Musikalische Interpretation*, p. 515.
60 Information concerning Bülow's activities as a concert conductor in Munich kindly provided by Dr Kenneth Birkin of Vienna.
61 Works that Bülow added to his repertoire at Munich included Bach's Orchestral Suite No. 3 (16 December 1868), Beethoven's Symphonies Nos. 2 (12 April 1868), 4 (5 April 1868) and 7 (1 November 1868), ballet music to *Die Geschöpfe des Prometheus* (12 April 1868), Romance for violin and orchestra in F major (Joseph Venzl, violin) (1 November 1868) and overtures *Die Weihe des Hauses* (5 April 1868) and *Leonore* No. 1 (1 November 1868), Gade's Symphony No. 3 (18 November 1868), Haydn's Symphonies Nos. 85 (16 December 1868) and 101 (18 March 1868), Mendelssohn's Symphony No. 3 ('Scottish') (25 December 1868), overture *Meeresstille und glückliche Fahrt* (28 March 1869) and Violin Concerto (Ludwig Abel, violin) (5 April 1868), Meyerbeer's overture to *Struensee* (25 December 1868), Mozart's Symphony No. 39 (16 December 1868), Raff's overture *Ein' feste Burg* (21 March 1869), Rubinstein's Cello Concerto (Andante only) (2 December 1868) and Piano Concerto No. 4

(Anton Rubinstein, piano) (7 December 1867), Schubert's Symphony No. 8 in C major ('Great') (4 March 1869), Schumann's Symphonies Nos. 1 ('Spring') (18 November 1868) and 3 ('Rhenish') (26 March 1868), overtures to *Genoveva* (28 March 1869) and *Die Braut von Messina* (25 January 1869) and the Closing Scene from *Faust* (21 April 1869), Spontini's overture to *La Vestale* (26 March 1868) and Weber's overture *Der Beherrscher der Geister* (12 April 1868) and overture to *Euryanthe* (18 March 1868).

62 See note 61.

63 Karl Klindworth (1830–1916): German pianist, conductor and administrator.

64 Hans von Bülow's letter to Karl Klindworth, dated 29 July 1869. *Letters of Hans von Bülow to Richard Wagner and Others*, p. 10.

65 Hans von Bülow's letter to Karl Bechstein, dated 31 July 1869.

66 Haas, *Hans von Bülow*, p. 112.

67 From 1877, Bülow's profile as a guest conductor increased sharply. His engagements that year in Scotland, along with his performances in the USA, were of particular importance.

68 Haas, *Hans von Bülow*, p. 112.

69 The figure of 488 performances includes those that Bülow gave both as a pianist and as a conductor.

70 Bülow conducted Beethoven's Symphony No. 5 for the first time at Wiesbaden on 7 August 1873.

71 This statistic relates only to Bülow's activities at Hanover and does not include any compositions that he added to his repertoire while performing as a guest conductor.

72 The forty-five works that Bülow added to his repertoire at Hanover were Bach's Violin Concerto in A minor (Joseph Joachim, violin) (24 April 1878), Orchestral Suite No. 1 (1 December 1878) and excerpts from the *St Matthew Passion* (15 March 1879), Beethoven's Symphony No. 1 (11 October 1879), Berlioz's *Harold en Italie* (15 February 1879), Brahms's 'Haydn' Variations (16 February 1878) and Symphonies Nos. 1 (20 October 1877) and 2 (26 April 1879), Cherubini's overture to *Faniska* (2 February 1878), Chopin's Piano Concerto No. 2 (Vera Timanoff, piano) (2 March 1878), Glinka's overture to *Ruslan and Lyudmila* (1 March 1879), Gluck's ballet music to *Paride ed Elena* (arr. Reinecke) (20 October 1877), Goltermann's Cello Concerto (Andante and Finale only) (Georg Goltermann, cello) (11 January 1879), Handel's March from *Herakles* and excerpts from *Israel in Egypt* (28 September 1878), Haydn's Symphony No. 102 (2 February 1878), Joachim's overture *Dem Andenken des Dichters Heinrich von Kleist* (24 April 1878) and Violin Concerto No. 1 (Joseph Joachim, violin) (26 April 1879), Lalo's *Symphonie espagnole* (Pablo de Sarasate, violin) (29 September 1877), Liszt's *Die Loreley* (19 January 1878), Marschner's overture to *Der Vampyr* (13 February 1879), Méhul's overture to *Horatius Coclès* (2 February 1878), Mendelssohn's overture to *Ruy Blas* (2 March 1878), incidental music to *Athalie* (21 April 1878), overture *The Hebrides* (25 October 1878) and incidental music to *Ein Sommernachtstraum* (30 September 1879), Meyerbeer's *Fackeltanz* No. 1 (13 February 1879), Mozart's Violin Concerto No. 4 (movement 2 only) (Hugo Heermann, violin) (9 November 1878), Raff's Symphony No. 4 (19 January 1877) and Violin Concerto No. 2 (Hugo Heermann, violin) (9 November 1878), Rietz's *Festival Overture* (30 September 1878), Rubinstein's Fantasy for piano and orchestra in C major (Anton Rubinstein, piano) and Symphony No. 4 ('Dramatic') (1 March 1879), Saint-Saëns's *Phaéton* (13 October 1877), Cello Concerto No. 1 (Bernhard Cossmann, cello) (19 January 1878) and Piano Concerto No. 4 (Camille Saint-Saëns, piano) (15 February 1879), Scholz's aria from *Golo* (Gus-

tav Gunz, bass) (29 September 1877) and overture to *Iphigenie* (28 August 1879), Schubert's 'Wanderer' Fantasy (arr. Liszt) (Heinrich Lutter, piano) (16 February 1878) and *Gott in der Natur* (arr. Bülow) (26 October 1878), Schumann's Fantasie for violin and orchestra in C major (Joseph Joachim, violin) (24 April 1878) and *Der Rose Pilgerfahrt* (29 January 1879), Tchaikovsky's ballet music from *Voyevoda* (1 March 1879), Wagner's *Kaisermarsch* (26 October 1878) and Weber's *Jubel Overture* (25 August 1878). Hinrichsen, *Musikalische Interpretation*, pp. 488–510.

73 B. Weber, '"Hannover ist mir unersetzlich in der Welt . . . "': Hans von Bülows Kapellmeisterjahre in Hannover', in H. Müller and V. Gerasch, eds., *'Beiträge zum Kolloquium Hans von Bülow: Leben, Wirken und Vermächtnis [. . .] zum 100. Todestag Hans von Bülows*, Südthüringer Forschungen 28 (Meiningen, 1995), p. 73.

74 Haas, *Hans von Bülow*, p. 184.

75 During his Hanover period Bülow also conducted incidental music to plays and two performances of Delibes's ballet *Coppélia*, on 9 and 19 May 1879.

76 Bülow gave eight and nine performances of operas by Marschner and Meyerbeer respectively at Hanover.

77 Operas that Bülow conducted for the first time at Hanover included Beethoven's *Fidelio*, Berlioz's *Benvenuto Cellini*, Boieldieu's *Jean de Paris*, Donizetti's *Lucrezia Borgia*, Glinka's *A Life for the Tsar*, Marschner's *Der Holzdieb* and *Der Vampyr*, Meyerbeer's *Robert le diable*, *Le Prophète* and *Le Pardon de Ploërmel*, Mozart's *Le nozze di Figaro*, *Don Giovanni* and *La clemenza di Tito*, Reinthaler's *Edda*, Spontini's *Fernand Cortez* and Wagner's *Rienzi*. With the exception of *Der Holzdieb*, *Der Vampyr*, *Edda* and *La clemenza di Tito*, each was given multiple performances at Hanover.

78 Haas, *Hans von Bülow*, p. 184.

79 Weber, 'Hannover ist mir unersetzlich in der Welt', p. 73.

80 Previously, Bülow had conducted one performance only of an opera by Mozart: *Die Entführung aus dem Serail* at the Munich Hofoper on 30 April 1868.

81 Hinrichsen, *Musikalische Interpretation*, p. 514.

82 *Neue Hannoversche Zeitung*, 9 October 1877.

83 Anton Schott (1846–1913): German tenor.

84 Hans Bronsart von Schellendorf (1830–1915): German pianist, conductor, composer and administrator. Bronsart gave the première of Liszt's Piano Concerto No. 2, of which he is the dedicatee. After leaving Hanover, Bronsart was Intendant at Weimar between 1888 and 1895.

85 Herzog Georg II von Sachsen-Meiningen (1826–1914).

86 Helene (Ellen) Franz (1839–1923). German actress.

87 H. Müller and V. Kern, eds., *Die Meininger kommen!* (Meiningen, 1999), p. 89.

88 Bülow's contract at Meiningen began on 1 March 1880. Haas, *Hans von Bülow*, p. 202.

89 For his arrangement of Op. 133, Bülow added double basses to the scoring.

90 Bülow never performed Op. 49 No. 1, Op. 49 No. 2 or Op. 79 publicly.

91 Information concerning Bülow's programme policy at Meiningen is based on the information held at the Staatliche Museen Meiningen and was kindly made available to the present author by Herta Müller.

92 Bülow also shared an all-Beethoven concert with Emil Büchner on 25 December 1880. On that occasion, Bülow conducted Symphony No. 3 only.

93 At the Abonnement Concerts, Bülow conducted Symphonies Nos. 1 to 8, Piano Concerto No. 4 (Max Schwarz, piano), the Violin Concerto (Friedhold Fleischhauer, violin), the Triple Concerto (G. F. Hatton, piano; Friedhold Fleischhauer, violin; Friedrich Hilpert, cello), the Choral Fantasy (G. F. Hatton, piano;

Hilpert'scher Chorgesangverein, chorus), the overtures to *Coriolan*, *Egmont*, *Die Geschöpfe des Prometheus* and *Fidelio*, the overtures *Zur Namensfeier*, *Die Weihe des Hauses*, *König Stephan*, *Leonore* Nos. 1 and 3, the Romances for violin and orchestra in G (Friedhold Fleischhauer, violin) and F major (Max Grünberg, violin), the Rondino for wind instruments ('Herren Kirchhoff und Tamme (Hoboe), Mühlfeld und Schwarz (Clarinette), Hochstein und Truckenbrodt (Fagott), Leinhos und Müllich (Horn)'), *Meeresstille und glückliche Fahrt* (Hilpert'scher Chorgesangverein, chorus), *Elegischer Gesang*, the Scene and Aria Op. 65, *Adelaide* ('Herren [Max] Alvary [und Max] Schwarz [piano]'), extracts from *Die Ruinen von Athen* (Hilpert'scher Chorgesangverein, chorus), Leonore's Recitative and Aria from Act 1 of *Fidelio* ('Fräulein Oberbeck', soprano) and extracts from Act 2 of *Fidelio* (Max Avery, tenor).

94 2 April was Georg II's birthday.

95 Emil Büchner, Bülow's predecessor at Meiningen, assisted him between 1880 and 1882, and Franz Mannstädt assisted him between 1882 and 1885.

96 Strauss, *Recollections and Reflections*, p. 50.

97 The performance of Beethoven's Symphony No. 3 to which Strauss was referring was given at the end of January 1886 after Bülow had resigned his tenure at Meiningen.

98 Strauss's letter to his father, translated by the present author, dated 31 January 1886. R. Strauss, ed. W. Schuh, *Briefe an die Eltern 1882–1906* (Zürich, 1954), pp. 84–6.

99 The all-Mozart concerts were heard on 30 October 1881 (Symphonies Nos. 33 and 39, overtures to *Idomeneo*, *La clemenza di Tito* and *Le nozze di Figaro*, 'Ach nur einmal noch' from *La clemenza di Tito* (Louise Schärnack, mezzo-soprano), 'Neue Freuden, neue Schmerzen' ('Non so più') and 'Ihr, die ihr Triebe' ('Voi che sapete') from *Le nozze di Figaro* (Louise Schärnack, mezzo-soprano)) and 13 November 1881 (Symphonies Nos. 38 and 40, Sinfonia concertante for violin and viola (Friedhold Fleischhauer, violin; Hermann Ritter, viola), overtures to *Don Giovanni* and *Die Zauberflöte*); the all-Mendelssohn concert was heard on 6 November 1881 (Symphony No. 3, Violin Concerto (Friedhold Fleischhauer, violin), *Meeresstille und glückliche Fahrt*, *The Hebrides* and *Die schöne Melusine*, *Capriccio brillant* for piano and orchestra Op. 22 (G. F. Hatton, piano)); the all-Brahms concert was heard on 27 November 1881 (*Tragic* and *Academic Festival* Overtures, Piano Concerto No. 2 (Johannes Brahms, piano; Hans von Bülow, conductor), 'Haydn' Variations, Symphony No. 1 (Johannes Brahms, conductor)); the all-Haydn concert was heard on 4 December 1881 (Symphonies Nos. 88, 95 and 102, aria from *Die Schöpfung* (*The Creation*), recitative and aria from *Die Jahreszeiten* (*The Seasons*) (Fräulein Breidenstein, soprano)), and the all-Schumann concert was heard on 11 December 1881 (Symphony No. 1, Fantasy for violin and orchestra (Max Grünberg, violin), Cello Concerto (Friedrich Hilpert, cello), overtures to *Hermann und Dorothea* and *Die Braut von Messina*).

100 The all-Raff concert was heard on 23 January 1883 (overture *Ein' feste Burg*, Violin Concerto ('Die Liebesfee') (Friedhold Fleischhauer, violin), Piano Concerto in C minor (Hans von Bülow, piano; Franz Mannstädt, conductor) and Symphony No. 3 ('Im Walde')).

101 The all-Brahms concert was heard on 7 December 1884 (Symphonies Nos. 2 and 3, Piano Concerto No. 1 (Eugenie Menter, piano)); the all-French programme was heard on 14 December 1884 (Berlioz's *Rêverie et Caprice* for violin and orchestra (Friedhold Fleischhauer, violin) and overture and Sicilienne from *Béatrice et Bénédict*, Saint-Saëns's Tarantella for flute and clarinet ('Hofmusiker' Genennichen, flute, and Richard Mühlfeld, clarinet) and Symphony

No. 2, Lalo's *Symphonie espagnole* (Friedhold Fleischhauer, violin), Bizet's *Danse bohémienne* and Auber's overture to *Fra Diavolo*), and the all-Russian programme was heard on 21 December 1884 (Glinka's overture and ballet music from *A Life for the Tsar*, overtures to *Ruslan and Lyudmila and Kamarinskaya*, Tchaikovsky's Piano Concerto No. 1 (Hans von Bülow, piano; Franz Mannstädt, conductor), Borodin's *In the Steppes of Central Asia*, Rubinstein's Two Dances from *The Demon* and *Grande Ouverture triomphale*).

102 The figure of seventeen performances includes not only those of Bülow but also those of Brahms.

103 Brahms was the soloist in Piano Concerto No. 2 on 27 November 1881. He conducted Symphony No. 1 on 27 November 1881, a double performance of Symphony No. 3 on 3 February 1884 and the Violin Concerto (Adolf Brodsky, violin) and the world première of Symphony No. 4 on 25 October 1885.

104 Theodore Thomas (1835–1905): German-born American conductor.

105 E. Schabas, *Theodore Thomas, America's Conductor and Builder of Orchestras, 1835–1905* (Urbana and Chicago, 1989), p. 41.

106 Hermann Wolff (1845–1902): German music journalist, impresario and agent.

107 B. Walter, trans. J. A. Galston, *Theme and Variations: An Autobiography* (London, 1947), p. 39.

108 Bülow did not perform Beethoven's Symphony No. 2 on tour and he shortened Symphony No. 9, performing either the third movement only, movements 2 and 3, or movements 1 to 3. These truncated versions of Symphony No. 9 were necessary because a choir was not part of Bülow's touring ensemble.

109 During Bülow's tenure as Intendant of the Meininger Hofkapelle, six touring concerts were devoted to Brahms's music.

110 The figure of sixteen concerts does not include the all-Brahms concert that the composer conducted with the Meininger Hofkapelle at Wiesbaden on 25 November 1885.

111 Brahms conducted the world première of Symphony 4 at Meiningen on 25 October 1885.

112 Brahms conducted Symphony No. 4 in Frankfurt am Main (3 November 1885), Essen (6 November 1885), Elberfeld (8 November 1885), Utrecht (11 November 1885), Amsterdam (13 November 1885), The Hague (14 November 1885), Krefeld (21 November 1885) and Cologne (23 November 1885). Bülow conducted the work at Rotterdam (19 November 1885).

113 Richard Strauss was Bülow's immediate successor at Meiningen, but he stayed for only a very short period and never toured independently with the orchestra. Fritz Steinbach (1855–1916) conducted the Meininger Hofkapelle between 1886 and 1903, Wilhelm Berger (1861–1911) conducted it between 1903 and 1911 and Max Reger (1873–1916) conducted it between 1911 and 1914. Steinbach conducted the Hofkapelle 224 times on tour, Berger conducted it 123 times on tour and Reger conducted it 138 times on tour. See Müller and Kern, eds., *Die Meininger kommen!*, pp. 91–103.

114 The Philharmonische Gesellschaft performed under the direction of the German conductor Julius von Bernuth (1830–1902).

115 Bernhard Pollini (born Bernhard Pohl) (1838–97): German singer and impresario. Chéri Maurice (born Charles Maurice Schwartzenberger) (1805–96): French-born impresario.

116 The Stadttheater's orchestra was available to Bülow and Wolff only until the beginning of the 1888–9 season, at which point they had to establish a new ensemble.

117 *Hamburgischer Correspondent*, 3 October 1886, p. 7.

118 This statistic does not included the works performed at the three festival con-

certs that Bülow gave with the orchestra at the Hamburgische Gewerbe und Industrie Ausstellung in 1889.

119 Bülow conducted the first performance of Strauss's Horn Concerto No. 1 on 4 March 1885. The soloist was the principal horn of the Meininger Hofkapelle, Gustav Leinhos (1836–1906).

120 On 24 February 1887, Bülow conducted the overture *Die Weihe des Hauses*, the Choral Fantasy (Max Schwarz, piano; Bach-Gesellschaft, chorus) and Symphony No. 9 and, on 20 March 1893, he performed the overtures *Die Weihe des Hauses*, and *Egmont* and Symphonies Nos. 3 and 8.

121 See note 124.

122 24 November 1892.

123 *Hamburgischer Correspondent*, 26 November 1892, p. 1.

124 Bülow performed as a guest conductor at the Hamburg Stadttheater.

125 The other operas that Bülow conducted as part of the cycle were *Le nozze di Figaro* (5 November 1887) and *Don Giovanni* (4 November 1887). Bülow did, however, give three further performances of *Don Giovanni* and two further performances of *Le nozze di Figaro* during the 1887–8 season at the Hamburg Stadttheater that were not part of the advertised cycle.

126 See Chapter 4.

127 F. Weingartner, trans. M. Wolff *Buffets and Rewards*, (London, 1937), p. 162.

128 Gustav Mahler and Richard Strauss were also candidates to replace Franz Mannstädt; Strauss was appointed in 1885.

129 Bülow was displeased with Weingartner's tempi, which he considered more appropriate for operetta. Haas, *Hans von Bülow*, p. 234.

130 Bülow's repertoire at Bremen resembled that of Hamburg and Berlin. There were, however, a number of works that he added at Bremen, including Saint-Saëns's Introduction and Rondo capriccioso for violin and orchestra (Stanislas Barcewicz, violin) (15 March 1887) and the prelude to *Le Déluge* (20 December 1888), Brahms's Violin Concerto (Adolph Brodsky, violin) (11 October 1887), Reinecke's Harp Concerto (Wilhelm Posse, harp) (17 April 1888), Mendelssohn's *Rondo brillant* Op. 29 (Emil Sauer, piano) (9 October 1888), Reinthaler's overture to *Edda* (29 December 1888), Mozart's overture to *Der Schauspieldirektor* (15 January 1889) and Molique's Cello Concerto (Robert Hausmann, cello) (26 February 1889). Information concerning Bülow's activities in Bremen kindly provided by Dr Kenneth Birkin, Vienna.

131 This statistic pertains solely to the Philharmonic Concerts that Bülow conducted between 21 October 1887 and the end of the 1891–2 season, and not to those that he conducted with the Berlin Philharmonic outside the Abonnement series. The Philharmonic Concerts were the subscription series of the Berlin Philharmonic and constituted only a small part of its activities annually. Gustav Kogel conducted the overwhelming majority of the orchestra's other concerts during Bülow's Berlin period.

132 Bülow did perform Beethoven's Symphony No. 9 outside the Abonnement series with the Berlin Philharmonic, including a double performance of the work on 6 March 1889. He also conducted it on 16 December 1889, at a charity performance on 18 December 1889 and for the orchestra's pension fund on 4 April 1892.

133 At the Philharmonic Concerts, Bülow afforded composers the opportunity to conduct their works, including Eugen d'Albert (overture to *Esther* on 14 November 1887), Richard Strauss (*Aus Italien* on 23 January 1888, *Tod und Verklärung* on 23 February 1891 and *Macbeth* on 29 February 1892), Friedrich Gernsheim (Symphony No. 3 on 5 March 1888), Edward Grieg overture (*Im Herbst* and *Peer Gynt* Suite on 21 January 1889), Johannes Brahms (Piano

Concerto No. 1, with Bülow as soloist, and the *Academic Festival Overture* on 4 March 1889), Karl Goldmark (overture *Der gefesselte Prometheus* on 25 November 1889) and Waldemar von Baussnern (*Gesang der Sappho* on 13 January 1890). These performances are not included in the statistic relating to new music conducted by Bülow at the Philharmonic Concerts.

134 Although the German violinist and conductor Leopold Damrosch (1832–85) had died some five years before, his Violin Concerto No. 2 was new to Berlin audiences; it was performed by Bülow from the manuscript.

135 Leopold Damrosch's Violin Concerto No. 2 (Charles Gregorowitsch, violin), Robert Kahn's Serenade, Anton Rubinstein's overture *Antony and Cleopatra*, Ernst Rudorff's Symphony No. 2, Richard Strauss's *Burleske* (Eugen d'Albert, piano) and Robert Radecke's Capriccio for large orchestra were heard on 24 February 1890, 27 October 1890, 24 November 1890, 12 January 1891, 12 January 1891 and 9 November 1891 respectively.

136 The fifth Abonnement Concert of the 1892–3 season was conducted by Gustav Mahler, the sixth and seventh by Max Erdmannsdoerfer, the eighth by Anton Rubinstein and the ninth by Karl Muck.

137 At Berlin on 13 March 1893, Bülow conducted Haydn's Symphony No. 95, Brahms's Symphony No. 3 and Beethoven's Symphony No. 4; at Hamburg on 20 March 1893, he performed an all-Beethoven programme that included the overtures *Die Weihe des Hauses* and *Egmont* and Symphonies Nos. 3 and 8, and at Berlin on 10 April 1893, he gave Beethoven's overture to *Fidelio*, overture *Leonore* No. 3 and Symphonies Nos. 5 and 7.

138 Strauss, *Recollections and Reflections*, p. 118.

Chapter 2. The Magician of the Podium: Arthur Nikisch

1 August Nikisch was born in 1821.

2 F. Pfohl, in *Arthur Nikisch: Leben und Wirken*, ed. H. Chevalley (Berlin, 1922), p. 4.

3 Ibid.

4 Joseph Hellmesberger (1828–93): Austrian violinist and conductor.

5 [Felix] Otto Dessof (1835–91): German conductor and composer.

6 The chorus for Wagner's performance of Beethoven's Symphony No. 9 ('Choral') at Bayreuth was an amalgam of the Riedel-Verein from Leipzig and the Sternscher Gesangverein from Berlin. The soloists were Marie Lehmann, Johanna Jachmann-Wagner, Albert Niemann and Franz Betz.

7 Pfohl, *Arthur Nikisch*, pp. 10–14.

8 Ibid.

9 In Vienna, Verdi conducted his Requiem and *Aida* on 11 and 19 June 1875 respectively.

10 Josef Sucher (1843–1908): Austrian conductor.

11 Hans von Bülow's letter to his daughter Daniela, dated 17 August 1887. *Letters of Hans von Bülow to Richard Wagner and Others*, ed. S. Goddard, trans. H. Walter (New York, 1979).

12 C. Flesch, trans. H. Keller, *The Memoirs of Carl Flesch* (London, 1957), pp. 149–50.

13 J. Warrack and E. West, *The Oxford Dictionary of Opera* (Oxford, 1992), p. 502.

14 In 1882, Neumann founded a touring company specializing in the performance of Wagner's operas with which he toured Europe.

15 Max Staegemann (1834–1905): German impresario and administrator.

16 Karl Reinecke (1824–1910): German composer, pianist and conductor.
17 On 12 February 1880, Nikisch conducted Hauptmann's *Und Gottes Will' ist dennoch gut* for chorus and orchestra, Volkmann's Symphony in D minor, Mendelssohn's Psalm 114 for eight-part chorus and orchestra, Gade's *Frühlingsbotschaft* for chorus and orchestra and Schumann's Overture, Scherzo and Finale.
18 On 3 February 1881, Nikisch's programme included Haydn's Symphony in C ('L'Ours'), Mozart's Piano Concerto No. 20 (Clara Schumann, piano), Beethoven's overture to *Coriolan*, Mendelssohn's *Variations sérieuses* (Clara Schumann, piano) and Schumann's Symphony No. 4.
19 It was during that concert that Nikisch applied Wagner's thoughts on the performance of Beethoven's Symphony No. 9 for the first time.
20 When the Allgemeiner deutscher Musikverein met in Magdeburg in 1881, Nikisch also performed for the organization.
21 The other works that Nikisch performed on 30 December 1884 were Liszt's *Les Préludes* and extracts from Wagner's *Götterdämmerung*.
22 Nikisch continued to champion modern music at Leipzig during the mid 1880s, when he founded the Leipzig Lisztverein with the pianist Martin Krause in 1885.
23 Georg [Sir George] Henschel (1850–1934): German-born British baritone, composer and conductor. Nikisch conducted a performance of Henschel's Missa pro defunctis with the Gewandhaus Orchestra on 3 December 1903.
   Wilhelm Gericke (1845–1925): Austrian composer and conductor.
24 Henry Lee Higginson's letter to a German correspondent, dated 8 October 1888. As found in M. A. De Wolfe Howe, *The Boston Symphony Orchestra: An Historical Sketch* (Boston, 1914), p. 155.
25 Julius Epstein (1832–1926): Austrian pianist. Otto Dresel (1826–90): German-born American pianist.
26 De Wolfe Howe, *The Boston Symphony Orchestra*, p. 155.
27 Ibid., p. 156.
28 Ibid., p. 158.
29 Ibid.
30 The statistical information relating to Nikisch's tenure with the Boston Symphony Orchestra is based on material kindly provided by the orchestra's archivist, Bridget P. Carr. The subscription concerts were performed on Friday and Saturday evenings, with the Friday programme being repeated on the Saturday.
31 At the Subscription Concerts, Nikisch conducted works by Austro-German, American, Franco-Belgian, Polish, Russian, Italian, British, Scandinavian and Czech composers.
32 On 24 and 25 April 1891, Nikisch conducted Beethoven's overture *Leonore* No. 2, Act 1 of *Fidelio* and Symphony No. 5 and, on 16 and 17 December 1892, he conducted Symphonies 8 and 9.
33 On 18 and 19 December 1891, Nikisch conducted Mozart's overture to *Die Zauberflöte*, 'Non mi dir' from *Don Giovanni* (Mme Fursch-Madi, soprano), the *Maurerische Trauermusik*, 'Dove sono' from *Le nozze di Figaro* (Mme Fursch-Madi, soprano) and Symphony No. 39.
34 On 10 and 11 April 1891, Nikisch conducted the overture to *Der fliegende Holländer*, 'Legend and Farewell' from *Lohengrin* (Andreas Dippel, tenor), 'In neuen Thaten' from *Götterdämmerung* (Antonia Mielke, soprano; Andreas Dippel, tenor) and orchestral excerpts from *Die Meistersinger von Nürnberg*, *Siegfried* and *Götterdämmerung*. On 21 and 22 April 1893, he conducted the overture to *Rienzi*, the Prelude and Scene 1 from *Das Rheingold* (Felicia Kaschoska, soprano; 'Mrs Arthur Nikisch', soprano; Louise Leimer, contralto; Heinrich Meyn, baritone) and orchestral excerpts from *Die Meistersinger von Nürnberg*, *Siegfried* and *Götterdämmerung*.

35 The world premières that Nikisch conducted at his Boston Subscription Concerts were MacDowell's *Lancelot and Elaine* on 10 January 1890, Loeffler's *Nights in the Ukraine* on 20 November 1891, Chadwick's *A Pastoral Prelude* on 29 January 1892 and Margaret Lang's Dramatic Overture on 7 April 1893. Each work was repeated the day after the première.

36 Emil Paur (1855–1932), the Austrian violinist, composer and conductor was Nikisch's successor at the Boston Symphony Orchestra. Paur, like Nikisch, had been a conductor at the Leipzig Stadttheater. Nikisch was originally offered the post of Director in Budapest in 1888 but had declined the invitation. Mahler was appointed in his stead: see Chapter 3.

37 The new productions that Nikisch conducted at Budapest included Smetana's *The Bartered Bride* on 21 September 1893, Bizet's *Carmen* on 4 November 1893, Mozart's *Le nozze di Figaro* on 25 November 1893, Lortzing's *Der Wildschütz* on 10 February 1894, Puccini's *Manon Lescaut* on 17 March 1894, Massenet's *La Navarraise* on 4 October 1894, Wagner's *Die Meistersinger von Nürnberg* on 5 January 1895 and Humperdinck's *Hänsel und Gretel* on 2 February 1895. Dates and programme information for Nikisch's period in Budapest were kindly provided by Nóra Wellman, archivist at the Hungarian State Opera.

38 Puccini's *Manon Lescaut*, Humperdinck's *Hänsel und Gretel* and Massenet's *La Navarraise* were given their premières at Turin, Weimar and London on 1 February 1893, 22 December 1893 and 20 June 1894 respectively.

39 Nikisch conducted Beethoven's Symphony No. 7 on 8 November 1893, Piano Concerto No. 5 ('Emperor') on 6 December 1893, and overture *Leonore* No. 2 on 20 December 1893.

40 Nikisch conducted the Budapest Philharmonic on 8 November 1893, 22 November 1893, 6 December 1893, 20 December 1893, 10 January 1894, 26 January 1894, 14 February 1894, 23 February 1894 and 16 January 1895.

41 Nikisch conducted Erkel's *Magyar ünnepi nyitány* on 8 November 1893, Liszt's *Les Préludes*, 'Rakoczy' March and Hungarian Fantasy on 8 November 1893, 26 January 1894 and 14 February 1894 respectively, Moszkowski's Suite No. 1 on 22 November 1893, Berlioz's *Roméo et Juliette* and overture *Le Carnaval romain* on 10 January 1894 and 23 February 1894 respectively, Goldmark's overture *Sakuntala* on 26 January 1894, d'Albert's Symphony No. 1 and Piano Concerto (Teresa Carreño, piano) on 23 February 1894, Scharwenka's Piano Concerto in B minor (M. Pauer, piano) on 16 January 1895 and Volkmann's Symphony No. 2 on 16 January 1895.

42 At his London début, Nikisch conducted Beethoven's Symphony No. 5, Wagner's overture to *Tannhäuser*, Dvořák's overture *Carnival* and Grieg's *Peer Gynt* Suite No. 1.

43 For his concert at the Queen's Hall on 22 June 1895, Nikisch programmed Schubert's Symphony No. 7 ('Unfinished'), Smetana's *Lustspiel Overture*, Wagner's 'Waldweben' from *Siegfried* and 'Siegfried's Rheinfahrt' from *Götterdämmerung* and Mendelssohn's Violin Concerto.

44 *Musical Times*, 1 July 1895, pp. 455–6.

45 Ibid.

46 Ibid.

47 The statistic pertaining to Nikisch's duties with the Gewandhaus Orchestra excludes the seven Sonderkonzerte that he performed with the orchestra. Nikisch was rarely indisposed at Leipzig and was absent for only ten of the orchestra's 579 Abonnement Concerts between 10 October 1895 and 1 January 1922, his first and last concerts with the orchestra.

48 On 24 October 1895, Nikisch performed Tchaikovsky's Symphony No. 6 ('Pathétique'), Goldmark's overture *Sakuntala*, Schumann's Overture, Scherzo

and Finale, Mozart's 'Und Susanna kommt nicht' ('Dove sono') from *Le nozze di Figaro*, Schubert's *Die Liebe hat gelogen*, Grieg's *Solvejgs Lied*, Brahms's *Die Mainacht* and Strauss's *Ständchen* (Milka Ternina, soprano).

49 Sir Adrian Boult was less than impressed by Nikisch's interpretations of Beethoven. He said: 'if I had to make a list of the music I would prefer to hear conducted by Nikisch rather than any other conductor, that list would be small. It would include all the Schumann and Liszt symphonies; the three Weber overtures; a good deal of Wagner ... and the Verdi *Requiem*. ... But if it was Beethoven, well, Richter, Weingartner, and Steinbach all seemed to do greater justice to the music.' A. Boult, *Boult on Music* (London, 1983), p. 94.

50 At the subscription concerts that Richard Strauss gave with the Berlin Hof/Staatskapelle between 1908 and 1935, for example, a period that incorporates his work both as a staff and as a guest conductor, eighty per cent contained a work by Beethoven. This figure stands in sharp contrast to Nikisch's activities in Leipzig, where only thirty-eight per cent of the concerts contained a work by that composer.

51 Nikisch conducted cycles of Beethoven's symphonies in the 1912–13 and 1916–17 seasons.

52 During Nikisch's tenure with the Gewandhaus Orchestra, Beethoven's Symphonies Nos. 3, 5, 7 and 9 received twenty-three, twenty-five, twenty-six and twenty-seven performances respectively. During the 1914–15 season, Nikisch did not perform Beethoven's Symphony No. 9; during the 1920–1 season, it was performed earlier in the season as part of the 'Beethoven Feier'.

53 During his tenure with the Gewandhaus Orchestra, Nikisch gave the overtures *Leonore* Nos. 2 and 3, *Coriolan* and *Egmont* on ten, thirteen, nineteen and nineteen occasions respectively and the Violin Concerto and Piano Concertos Nos. 3, 4 and 5 on seventeen, six, thirteen and eleven occasions respectively.

54 Bruno Walter argued: 'There are scores which, as it were, resist live realization by the orchestra since they are written by an unskilled hand or have not sprung from the spirit of the orchestra; this is the case with Schumann's symphonic work.' B. Walter, *Of Music and Music-making*, trans. P. Hamburger (London, 1961), p. 140.

55 Nikisch gave eleven performances of Symphony No. 1, twelve of Symphony No. 2, eleven of Symphony No. 3, ten of Symphony No. 4 and five of the Overture, Scherzo and Finale.

56 During his tenure with the Gewandhaus Orchestra, Nikisch gave five performances of the moribund choral work, *Das Paradies und die Peri*, three of the music from *Manfred* and two of the music from *Faust*. He also performed Schumann's overtures on twenty-five occasions.

57 As conductor of the Abonnement Series at Leipzig, Nikisch gave twenty-one performances of Brahms's Symphony No. 1, twenty-three of Symphony No. 2, twenty-one of Symphony No. 3 and twenty-two of Symphony No. 4. He also gave fourteen performances of the Violin Concerto, four of Piano Concerto No. 1, seven of Piano Concerto No. 2, four of the Double Concerto, three of the *Academic Festival Overture*, nine of the *Tragic Overture*, eight of the 'Haydn' Variations, one of Serenade Nos. 1, two of Serenade No. 2, four of *Ein deutsches Requiem* and multiple performances of *Alto Rhapsody*, *Triumphlied* and *Schicksalslied*.

58 Nikisch also conducted a performance of the Adagio from Bruckner's Symphony No. 7 on 22 October 1896 in memory of the composer, who had died on 11 October 1896.

59 At the Leipzig subscription concerts, Nikisch gave two performances of Tchaikovsky's Symphony No. 4, six of Symphony No. 5, twelve of Symphony

No. 6 and two complete readings of the symphony *Manfred*; he also conducted two performances of excerpts from the latter. Nikisch also gave nine performances of Piano Concerto No.1, two of Piano Concerto No. 2, seven of the Violin Concerto and two of the 'Rococo' Variations. He also conducted, amongst others, performances of Suites Nos. 1 and 3, *Romeo and Juliet*, *Hamlet* and *Francesca da Rimini*.

60 In later life, Nikisch expressed doubts about Schoenberg's music and is reported to have said: 'If I had to conduct music of that character, I should change my profession.' M. Pearton, *The LSO at 70* (London, 1974), p. 37.

61 At the Abonnement Concerts at Leipzig, Gerhardt performed with Nikisch on twelve occasions. After her début with him, she sang with him regularly at most of the major musical centres in Europe. Their performances in London were important events in that city's concert calendar and they also made a number of gramophone recordings together. See note 96.

62 A. Schnabel, *My Life and Music* (New York, 1988), pp. 154–5.

63 Conductors who performed at the Philharmonic Concerts during the 1892–3 and 1893–4 seasons included Hans Richter, Raphael Maszkowski, Felix Mottl, Hermann Levi, Ernst von Schuch, Richard Strauss, Franz Mannstädt and Anton Rubinstein.

64 See Chapter 3 note 81.

65 En route to France, Nikisch and the Berlin Philharmonic gave concerts in Magdeburg (5 May 1897), Bonn (6 May 1897) and Liège (7 May 1897).

66 Nikisch and the Berlin Philharmonic's Paris concerts were given on 9, 11, 13, 15 and 16 May 1897.

67 L. Wolff, 'Arthur Nikisch und Berlin aus meinen Erinnerungen', *Arthur Nikisch*, ed. Chevalley, pp. 165–6.

68 After the Paris concerts, Nikisch and the orchestra continued the tour with five concerts in Switzerland and five in Germany.

69 The schedule for Nikisch's and the Berlin Philharmonic's 1899 tour of Russia was Königsberg on 29 April, St Petersburg on 1, 2, 9 and 10 May, Riga on 4 and 5 May, Dorpat on 6 and 7 May, Reval on 8 May, Moscow on 12, 13 and 14 May, Kiev on 17 and 18 May and Odessa on 20, 21 and 22 May.

70 On the 1901 tour, Nikisch and the Berlin Philharmonic performed forty concerts in six countries in forty-seven days. Between 15 April and 30 May 1901, they visited Austro-Hungary (Prague, Brno, Vienna, Graz and Trieste), Italy (Venice, Bologna, Florence, Rome and Genoa), France (Nice, Marseilles, Bordeaux, Toulouse, Lyon, Paris and Lille), Spain (Barcelona, Bilbao, San Sebastian and Madrid), Portugal (Lisbon) and Belgium (Brussels and Liège).

71 During the 1904 tour, Nikisch and the Berlin Philharmonic again performed in Königsberg on the outward journey and Warsaw on their return trip. The other cities they visited included St Petersburg, Moscow, Charkow (Kharkiv), Odessa, Kiev and Łódź.

72 Nikisch and the Berlin Philharmonic visited Copenhagen on 9 and 11 May 1917, Malmö on 14 and 15 May, Stockholm on 16 May and Göteborg on 18 May.

73 Nikisch and the Berlin Philharmonic visited Breslau (Wrocław on 22 May 1918, Kattowitz (Katowice) on 23 May 1918 and Vienna on 25, 26 (matinée and evening performances) and 27 May 1918.

74 Nikisch and the Berlin Philharmonic visited Copenhagen on 14, 15 and 17 May 1920 and Malmö on 16 May 1920.

75 Nikisch conducted fifty-nine performances of Beethoven between the 1895–6 and 1905–6 seasons.

76 Of the twenty-seven seasons that Nikisch led in Berlin, sixteen contained a work by Beethoven in the first concert of the season and twenty in the last. While

Symphony No. 5 was the work by Beethoven that was most often heard at the final concert of the Philharmonic Concert series, with six performances, Symphony No. 3 was also heard regularly, with five. Other works by Beethoven given in the final concerts of that series were Symphonies 2, 4, 6 ('Pastoral') and 7 and the overtures *Egmont* and *Leonore* Nos. 2 and 3.

77 Nikisch conducted Beethoven's Symphony No. 9 on 14 December 1896, 12 December 1898 and 15 December 1902. Although he does not seem to have placed any great emphasis on composer's anniversaries, nine of the twelve all-Beethoven concerts that Nikisch gave at the Philharmonic Concerts were heard during the middle of December and within a few days of Beethoven's birthday on the sixteenth of that month. Of the all-Beethoven concerts given, five were heard in the last decade of his tenure.

78 Nikisch also conducted Strauss's Festival Prelude, Violin Concerto, some of the songs with orchestra and extracts from *Feuersnot* and *Guntram*.

79 Nikisch also conducted the following works of Mahler in Berlin: the first performance of 'Was mir die Blumen auf der Wiese erzählen' from Symphony No. 3; *Kindertotenlieder*; *Lieder eines fahrenden Gesellen*, and various other songs with orchestra.

80 Letter from Richard Strauss to Gustav Mahler, dated 5 March 1905. *Gustav Mahler/Richard Strauss: Correspondence 1888–1911*, ed. H. Blaukopf, trans. E. Jephcott (London, 1984), p. 75.

81 Nikisch performed the 'Enigma' Variations, Symphony No. 1, the Violin Concerto and overture *Cockaigne* on 3 February 1908, 11 October 1909, 8 January 1912 and 27 October 1913 respectively. Those performances were all Berlin Philharmonic premières.

82 Nikisch also performed at Covent Garden in 1907 (*Der fliegende Holländer*, *Der Freischütz*), 1913 (*Der Ring des Nibelungen*) and 1914 (*Der Ring des Nibelungen*, *Lohengrin* and *Die Meistersinger von Nürnberg*).

83 Letter from Arthur Nikisch to the Philharmonic Society, date illegible. Royal Philharmonic Society Letters Vol. 25 (Mou–Nov), British Library, RPS MS 351.

84 Accounts for the year 1908. Directors' Minute Book (1898–1908), ibid., British Library RPS MS 000.

85 Letter from Francesco Berger to Arthur Nikisch, as found in R. Elkin, *Royal Philharmonic: The Annals of the Royal Philharmonic Society* (London, 1946), pp. 100–1.

86 Ibid., p. 102.

87 Nikisch's concert with the Philharmonic Society on 13 May 1909 included Wagner's Prelude to *Die Meistersinger von Nürnberg*, Elgar's Symphony No. 1 (first performance under Nikisch in England), Wagner's 'Forge Songs' from *Siegfried* and Tchaikovsky's *Francesca da Rimini*.

Nikisch's concert with the Philharmonic Society on 19 May 1910 included Handel's March from *Saul* (in memory of Edward VII), Rachmaninoff's Symphony in E minor (first English performance), Wagner's 'Elizabeth's Prayer' from *Tannhäuser* (Elena Gerhardt, soprano), Schelling's Fantastic Suite for Piano and Orchestra (Ernest Schelling, piano), Strauss's *Wiegenlied* and *Heimliche Aufforderung* (Elena Gerhardt, soprano; Arthur Nikisch, piano), piano music by Chopin and Liszt (Ernest Schelling, piano) and Liszt's Hungarian Rhapsody No. 1.

Nikisch's concert with the Philharmonic Society on 18 May 1911 included Schubert's Symphony No. 8 in C major ('Great'), Arthur Hinton's Piano Concerto in D minor (Katherine Goodson, piano), B. J. Dale's Romance and Finale from Suite for Viola and Orchestra (Lionel Tertis, viola) and Wagner's overture to *Tannhäuser*.

Nikisch's concert with the Philharmonic Society on 23 May 1912 included Elgar's *Dirge* (in memory of the King of Denmark) and Beethoven's overture *Leonore* No. 3, Violin Concerto (Efrem Zimbalist) and Symphony No. 9.

88 In a letter to the Philharmonic Society, dated 28 June 1906, from the Villa Magali in Ostende, Nikisch acknowledges the importance of the Society and thanks them for electing him an Honorary Member. Royal Philharmonic Society Letters Vol. 25 (Mou–Nov), British Library, RPS MS 357.

89 Pearton, *The LSO at 70*, p. 31.

90 The first concert, 27 October 1904, was conducted by Sir Frederic Cowen.

91 The statistics for Nikisch's activities with the London Symphony Orchestra are derived from data kindly provided by Libby Rice of the London Symphony Orchestra. The orchestra's programme information is incomplete and it has no record of the works performed at its concerts at the Queen's Hall on 8, 20 and 25 May 1908, 1 June 1908 and 11 June 1910.

92 Nikisch conducted Beethoven's Symphonies Nos. 3, 5, 7 and 9 with the London Symphony Orchestra on one, five, two and two occasions respectively.

93 The following works by Tchaikovsky were performed by Nikisch and the London Symphony Orchestra: Symphony No. 4 (one performance); Symphony No. 5 (four performances); Symphony No. 6 (one performance); the Violin Concerto (one performance); *Marche slave* (one performance); *Francesca da Rimini* (three performances); *Romeo and Juliet* (one performance), and the symphony *Manfred* (one performance). There was one all-Tchaikovsky concert, on 25 May 1908.

94 While Nikisch was unable to programme Schumann's symphonies with the London Symphony Orchestra, he did conduct the Piano Concerto on 7 March 1909 with Olga Samaroff as soloist. Of Brahms's symphonies, Nikisch gave three performances of Symphony No. 1, two of Symphony No. 3 and one of Symphony No. 4. Symphony No. 2 was not performed, but the Violin Concerto was performed once and the 'Haydn' Variations twice.

95 The conductors at the memorial concert were Sir Edward Elgar, Sir Henry Wood, Sir Thomas Beecham, Sir Landon Ronald and Willem Mengelberg.

96 Nikisch also recorded as a pianist. In 1907 and 1911, he accompanied Elena Gerhardt in the following: Strauss's *Wiegenlied, Ständchen* and *Wie sollten wir*; Wagner's *Schmerzen*; Wolf's *Der Freund, Und willst du deinen Liebsten sterben sehen, Heimweh* and *Verborgenheit*; Schumann's *Ich grolle nicht* and *Mondnacht*; Schubert's *An die Musik, Du bist die Ruh'* and *Wohin?*; Rubinstein's *Neue Liebe*; Bungert's *Ich hab' ein kleines Lied erdacht*, and Brahms's *Sapphische Ode, Der Schmied, O liebliche Wangen, Vergebliches Ständchen* and *Wiegenlied*. Nikisch also recorded piano rolls on a reproducing piano for Welte in 1905, documenting Brahms's Hungarian Dances Nos. 1, 4 and 6.

97 F. W. Gaisberg, *Music on Record* (London, 1946), pp. 137–9.

98 Although intended to be heard as a single unit, Nikisch's recording of Beethoven's Symphony No. 5 was released in Germany in 1914 by Deutsche Grammophon on four separate, double-sided 78-rpm discs: Record 1 (movement 1), catalogue number 040784–5; Record 2 (movement 2), catalogue number 040786–7; Record 3 (movement 3), catalogue number 040788–9, and Record 4 (movement 4), catalogue number 040790–1.

99 The footage of Nikisch conducting was released recently on Teldec Video 4509-95038-3.

100 Ibid.

101 As found in Boult, *Boult on Music*, pp. 103–4.

102 Nikisch was cremated at Leipzig on 26 January 1922.

103 Flesch, *Memoirs*, pp. 148–50.

Chapter 3. The Distiller's Son: Gustav Mahler

1 K. Blaukopf, trans. I. Goodwin, *Mahler* (London, 1973), p. 18.
2 While it would be wrong to belittle the level of personal devastation that the Mahlers felt at the loss of their children, the child mortality rate that the family suffered was in keeping with the statistic for that age group within the Austro-Hungarian Empire as a whole.
3 Iglau's citizens were predominantly German-speaking Roman Catholics. With the expansion of the Jewish community in the early 1860s, Bernhard became increasingly active as member of that group.
4 Before Mahler's seminal encounter with his grandparents' piano, he was able to pick out tunes on an accordion from the age of three.
5 K. and H. Blaukopf, trans. P. Baker and others, *Mahler: His Life, Work and World* (London, 2000), p. 18.
6 Franz Victorin taught Mahler piano and Heinrich Fischer taught him harmony. Ibid., pp. 18–19.
7 Ibid., p. 20.
8 Sigismund Thalberg (1812–71): Swiss-born Austrian pianist and composer.
9 Julius Epstein (1832–1926): Austrian pianist, teacher and editor. Mahler actually played to Julius Epstein at Baden, a spa town a short distance from Vienna. See chapter 2, note 25.
10 Interview with Gustav Schwarz, *Neues Wiener Journal*, 6 August 1905, as found in K. and H. Blaukopf, *Mahler: His Life, Work and World*, p. 22.
11 Epstein's published recollection of his first meeting with the young Mahler differs sharply from that of Schwarz. In an article in the *Neues Wiener Journal* on 19 May 1911, Epstein states that Gustav was accompanied by his father. The elderly teacher makes no mention of Schwarz. Some commentators believe that Epstein confuses that meeting with a subsequent one and that Mahler's first encounter with his future teacher was in the presence of Schwarz.
    Robert Fuchs (1847–1927): Austrian composer, teacher and organist. Franz Krenn (1816–97): Austrian composer, teacher and organist.
12 Letter from Gustav Mahler to Gustav Schwarz, dated 6 September 1877, as found in H.-L. de la Grange, *Mahler*, Vol. 1 (London, 1974), p. 29.
13 Ibid.
14 Mahler's first prize for piano followed a performance of a first movement of one of Schubert's sonatas in A minor, and his first prize for composition was for a first movement of a quintet. K. and H. Blaukopf, *Mahler: His Life, Work and World*, p. 24.
15 Ibid., pp. 25–6.
16 That year, he won first prize for piano with a performance of Schumann's *Humoreske*.
17 During the summer of 1877, Mahler returned to Iglau, where he completed his *Matura* (school leaving certificate) after two attempts. He also enrolled at the University of Vienna for the first time in 1877, but never completed his studies there.
18 Mahler was awarded the first prize for his Scherzo for piano quintet.
19 Guido Adler (1855–1941): Austrian musicologist and professor at the Universities of Prague and Vienna.
20 E. R. Reilly, *Gustav Mahler and Guido Adler: Records of a Friendship* (Cambridge, 1982), p. 20.
21 Hans Richter was appointed First Kapellmeister at the Hofoper in April 1875.
22 The new productions of *Tannhäuser* and *Lohengrin* were given first on 22 November 1875 and 15 December 1875.
23 The statistic pertains only to operatic premières and new productions at the

Hofoper between the date of Mahler's enrolment at the Vienna Conservatory and the end of the theatre's 1877–8 season.

24 The Vienna Conservatory offered no formal conducting lessons in the 1870s.

25 Gustav Löwy (d. 1901): Austrian singer, flautist and impresario.

26 Löwy deducted a commission of five per cent from Mahler's total income over the next five years. K. Blaukopf, *Mahler*, p. 45.

27 Ibid.

28 La Grange, *Mahler*, Vol. 1, pp. 76–7.

29 A. Mahler, trans. B. Creighton, ed. D. Mitchell and K. Martner, *Gustav Mahler: Memories and Letters* (London, 1990), p. 108.

30 Ibid., p. 109.

31 The exact dates of Mahler's engagement at Hall remain uncertain. La Grange states: 'The information so far provided by his biographers is vague, but some unpublished documents show that he was there as early as May 20 and as late as July 1 [1880]'. *Mahler*, Vol. 1, p. 76.

32 Ibid., p. 83.

33 *Laibacher Zeitung*, 26 September 1881, as found in K and H. Blaukopf, *Mahler: His Life, Work and World*, p. 38.

34 The *Laibacher Zeitung* reported on 4 October 1881 that 'the evening was a success[,] . . . Verdi's *Il Trovatore* went without any significant mishaps . . . [and the] orchestra . . . played strongly'. As found ibid., p. 39.

35 The stage works that Mahler conducted at Laibach included Weber's *Der Freischütz* (four performances) and *Preciosa* (one performance), Flotow's *Martha* (four performances) and *Alessandro Stradella* (two performances), Rossini's *Il barbiere di Siviglia* (five performances), Verdi's *Il trovatore* (seven performances) and *Ernani* (three performances), Nicolai's *Die lustigen Weiber von Windsor* (two performances), Gounod's *Faust* (three performances), Mozart's *Die Zauberflöte* (five performances), Donizetti's *Lucrezia Borgia* (four performances), Lecocq's *Giroflé-Girofla* (two performances) and *La Fille de Madame Angot* (one performance), Johann Strauss's *Der lustige Krieg* (11 performances), *Die Fledermaus* (two performances) and *Cagliostro* (two performances), Suppé's *Fatinitza* (two performances), *Boccaccio* (five performances), *Flotte Bursche* (one performance) and *Donna Juanita* (seven performances), Offenbach's *Pariser Leben* (*La Vie parisienne*) (two performances), *La Belle Hélène* (one performance) and *Barbe-bleue* (one performance), Genée's *Der Seekadett* (two performances), Planquette's *Les Cloches de Corneville* (three performances), Mendelssohn's *Ein Sommernachtstraum* (one performance) and Beethoven's *Egmont* (one performance complete). P. Kuret, *Mahler in Laibach: Ljubljana 1881–2* (Vienna, Cologne and Weimar, 2001), pp. 96–9.

Mahler also participated in an opera evening on 3 February 1882, where he acted as a piano accompanist.

At Laibach, Mahler also performed as a pianist and gave readings of Schumann's *Waldszenen*, Chopin's Polonaise in A flat major and Mendelssohn's *Rondo brillant* in B minor on 5 March 1882 and Vieuxtemps's Ballade and Polonaise for Violin and Piano (Hans Gerstner, violin) on 2 April 1882. K. Martner, *Gustav Mahler im Konzertsaal: Eine Dokumentation seiner Konzerttätigkeit 1870–1911* (Copenhagen, 1985), p. 11.

36 Hans Gerstner, 'Lebenserinnerungen', as found in K. and H. Blaukopf, *Mahler: His Life, Work and World*, p. 40.

37 Gustav Mahler's letter to Gustav Löwy, dated 4 April 1882, as found in *Selected Letters of Gustav Mahler*, trans. E. Wilkins, E. Kaiser and B. Hopkins, ed. K. Martner (London, 1979), p. 66.

38 *Iglauer Grenzbote*, 21 September 1882, as found in La Grange, *Mahler*, Vol. 1, p. 87.

39 Some sources give the conductor's name as Georg Kaiser.

40 Jacques Manheit's letter to Ludwig Karpath, as found in N. Lebrecht, *Mahler Remembered* (London, 1987), p. 30.

41 At the time of his Olmütz appointment, Mahler was still influenced by Wagner's *Religion and Art* and abstained from eating meat and drinking alcohol. In later life, he returned to both.

42 Lebrecht, *Mahler Remembered*, p. 31.

43 Mahler conducted *Robert le diable* on 18 January 1883, *La Muette de Portici* on 23 January 1883, *Un ballo in maschera* on 3 February 1883, *Rigoletto* on 14 March 1883, *Il trovatore* on 15 March 1883, *Joseph* on 13 February 1883 and *Carmen* on 10 and 17 March 1883. Mahler also accompanied singers from the theatre at the Olmütz Casino on 14 February 1883. D. Kučerová, 'Gustav Mahler v Olomouci', *Hudební věda* 4 (1968), English and German résumés, pp. 649–51, pp. 653–5. (La Grange mentions a third performance of *Carmen* on 11 March 1883. La Grange, *Mahler*, Vol. 1, p. 852 note 19).

44 Gustav Mahler's letter to Friedrich Löhr, dated 12 February 1883, as found in Mahler, *Selected Letters*, p. 68.

45 Lebrecht, *Mahler Remembered*, p. 30.

46 B. Walter, trans. L. W. Lindt, *Gustav Mahler* (London 1990), p. 81.

47 N. Bauer-Lechner, trans. D. Newlin, ed. P. Franklin, *Recollections of Gustav Mahler* (London, 1980), p. 109.

48 Ibid.

49 H.-J. Schaefer, 'Gustav Mahlers Wirken in Kassel', *Musica* 14:6 (1960), p. 350.

50 Ibid.

51 Lebrecht, *Mahler Remembered*, pp. 31–2.

52 Schaefer, 'Gustav Mahlers Wirken in Kassel', p. 350.

53 La Grange, *Mahler*, Vol. 1, p. 108.

54 In June 1884, Mahler composed music for the *tableau vivant*, *Der Trompeter von Säkkingen*.

55 For excerpts of Mahler's Kassel contract see Schaefer, 'Gustav Mahlers Wirken in Kassel', pp. 351–2.

56 Gustav Mahler's letter to Friedrich Löhr, dated 19 September 1883, as found in Mahler, *Selected Letters*, pp. 74–5.

57 The opera and operettas that Mahler conducted in Kassel included Adam's *Le Brasseur de Preston* and *La Poupée de Nuremberg*, Auber's *Fra Diavolo*, Bizet's *Carmen*, Boieldieu's *La Dame blanche*, Delibes's *Le Roi l'a dit*, Donizetti's *Lucia di Lammermoor* and *La Fille du régiment*, Flotow's *Alessandro Stradella* and *Wintermärchen*, Gounod's *Faust*, Kreutzer's *Das Nachtlager von Granada*, Lortzing's *Zar und Zimmermann*, *Der Waffenschmied* and *Die beiden Schützen*, Maillart's *Les Dragons de Villars*, Marschner's *Der Templer und die Jüdin* and *Hans Heiling*, Meyerbeer's *Robert le diable* and *Les Huguenots*, Nessler's *Der Rattenfänger von Hameln*, Nicolai's *Die lustigen Weiber von Windsor*, Offenbach's *Le Mariage aux lanternes*, Pillwitz's *Rataplan ou Le Petit Tambour*, Rossini's *Il barbiere di Siviglia*, Schubert's *Der häusliche Krieg* and Verdi's *Un ballo in maschera*.

58 On 24 January 1884, Bülow conducted Beethoven's *Egmont*, *Leonore* No. 1 and *König Stephan* overtures, Symphonies Nos. 1 and 8, Rondino for wind instruments in E flat major and the *Grosse Fuge*. On 25 January, he conducted Spohr's overture to *Faust*, Symphony No. 3 and Adagio from Clarinet Concerto No. 2 (Richard Mühlfeld, clarinet), Brahms's 'Haydn' Variations, Beethoven's Symphony No. 4 and Weber's overture to *Der Freischütz*.

59 Gustav Mahler's letter to Hans von Bülow, as found in K. and H. Blaukopf, *Mahler: His Life, Work and World*, p. 57.

60 Ibid., p. 59.

61 La Grange gives the place and date of Mahler's first concert with the Münden Choral Society as the Nickel Hall, Münden, on 14 February 1885, while Martner recorded the place and date as the 'Saal des Hotelgasthofes "Krone"' on 13 February 1885. La Grange, *Mahler*, Vol. 1, p. 123, and Martner, *Gustav Mahler im Konzertsaal*, p. 13.

62 The festival organizers eventually employed an orchestra drawn from the Hofkapellen of Brunswick, Meiningen and Weimar. The choirs that sang in the performance were the Casseler Oratorien-Verein, the Akademischer Gesang-Verein zu Marburg, the Mündener Chorverein and the Früh'scher Gesangverein zu Nordhausen. Ibid.

63 Gustav Mahler's letter to Friedrich Löhr, April 1885, as found in Mahler, *Selected Letters*, p. 85.

64 Ibid., p. 82.

65 The breaches of contract that Mahler was accused of committing in Kassel included the engagement of extra musicians for performances without the prior consent of his superiors, the restoration of the original ending of Nicolai's *Die lustigen Weiber von Windsor* without the prior permission of the management and being absent from rehearsals.

66 La Grange, *Mahler*, Vol. 1, p. 126.

67 Ibid.

68 Schaefer, 'Gustav Mahlers Wirken in Kassel', p. 355.

69 Blaukopf, *Mahler*, p. 68.

70 The Czech-speaking community outnumbered the German-speaking community in Prague by a ratio of three to two. P. Franklin, *The Life of Mahler* (Cambridge, 2001), p. 64.

71 Gustav Mahler's letter to Friedrich Löhr, undated, as found in Mahler, *Selected Letters*, p. 88.

72 The Hungarian-born conductor Anton Seidl (1850–98), was a leading Wagnerian and had worked with Neumann from the late 1870s. Having worked as the principal conductor of the impresario's touring Wagner company in the early 1880s, he later joined Neumann at the Bremen Opera. When Neumann moved to Prague in the spring of 1885, Seidl moved with him, but his period there was short and within weeks of arriving in the Czech city he left Europe to become Music Director of the Metropolitan Opera House, New York.

73 A. Neumann, 'Mahler in Prag', as found in K. and H. Blaukopf, *Mahler: His Life, Work and World*, p. 63.

74 Ibid.

75 Ibid.

76 Ibid.

77 String realizations of *Don Giovanni's* secco recitatives were common during the nineteenth century.

78 A. Neumann, 'Mahler in Prag', as found in Lebrecht, *Mahler Remembered*, p. 39.

79 *Prager Tagblatt*, 12 September 1885.

80 Ibid., 20 December 1885. Immediately after *Das Rheingold*, Mahler triumphed with *Die Walküre*. During his tenure, he also impressed local critics with performances of Mozart's *Die Entführung aus dem Serail* and *Così fan tutte*, Bellini's *Norma*, Marschner's *Hans Heiling*, Lortzing's *Undine*, Meyerbeer's *Le Prophète*, Gluck's *Iphigénie en Aulide* (ed. Wagner) and Beethoven's *Fidelio*.

81 Karl Muck (1859–1940): German conductor. After engagements in Zürich, Salzburg and Graz, Muck joined the staff of the Deutsches Landestheater in 1886. He later worked for Neumann as conductor of his touring Wagner company, with which he gave the first performances of *Der Ring des Nibelungen* in

Moscow and St Petersburg in 1889. He moved to Berlin in 1892 and he was later appointed Generalmusikdirektor there.

82 Karl Halir (1859–1909): Bohemian violinist, editor and conductor. After a period as Konzertmeister in Weimar, he was appointed Hofkonzertmeister in Berlin. As an editor, his edition of Beethoven's Sonatas for Piano and Violin, for Henry Litolff's Verlag, Brunswick, was influential. He was also a member of the Joachim Quartet and conducted the Hofkapelle Berlin.

83 Mahler accompanied the Lieder, songs and arias at the piano. The vocal works performed included three of his Lieder, the Romance from Meyerbeer's *Le Prophète*, Grieg's *Ich liebe dich*, Heinefetter's *Im wunderschönen Monat Mai*, Schumann's *Frühlingsnacht*, Rubinstein's *Gelb rollt mir zu Füssen*, an aria from Winter's *Das unterbrochene Opferfest*, Haydn's 'Und Gott sprach' from *Die Schöpfung* (*The Creation*), Schubert's *An Schwager Kronos* and national songs from Sweden. The singers were Marie Renard, Betty Frank and Johannes Elmblad. Martner, *Gustav Mahler im Konzertsaal*, p. 19.

84 Mahler conducted Mozart's Symphony No. 40 from memory.

85 Gustav Mahler's letter to Max Staegemann, dated 3 June 1886, as found in Mahler, *Selected Letters*, p. 95.

86 Ibid.

87 See Chapter 2.

88 Gustav Mahler's letter to Friedrich Löhr, undated, as found in Mahler, *Selected Letters*, p. 108.

89 Mahler conducted *Siegfried*.

90 The Leipzig Stadttheater Orchestra's letter to the Town Council, Leipzig, date unspecified, as found in K. and H. Blaukopf, *Mahler: His Life, Work and World*, p. 69.

91 Max Staegemann's letter to the Town Council, Leipzig, date unspecified, as found in ibid., p. 70.

92 Bauer-Lechner, *Recollections of Gustav Mahler*, pp. 35–6.

93 The works that Mahler performed during that period included Bruch's *Der Loreley*, Weber's *Der Freischütz* and *Preciosa*, Nessler's *Der Trompeter von Säkkingen*, Wagner's *Siegfried*, *Tannhäuser* and *Lohengrin*, Gounod's *Faust*, Donizetti's *La fille du régiment*, Rossini's *Il barbiere di Siviglia*, Gluck's *Armide*, Verdi's *Il trovatore* and *Aida* and Mozart's *Don Giovanni*. He also took part in an all-Wagner concert at the Leipzig Stadttheater on 30 November 1887 at which he conducted the closing scenes from Acts 1 and 3 of Wagner's *Parsifal*. The remainder of the programme – the Symphony, some Lieder and *Faust Overture* – was conducted by Nikisch.

94 K. Blaukopf, *Mahler*, p. 73.

95 David Popper (1843–1913): Czech cellist and teacher.

96 La Grange, *Mahler*, Vol. 1, p. 187

97 Sándor Erkel (1846–1900): Hungarian conductor and administrator. Ferenc Erkel (1810–93): Hungarian composer.

98 L. Lehmann, *My Path through Life* (New York, 1914), pp. 379–80.

99 Interview with Gustav Mahler published on 7 October 1888 in *Budapesti Hirlap*. As found in K. and H. Blaukopf, *Mahler: His Life, Work and World*, p. 78.

100 For the first months of his tenure, Mahler devoted himself to the preparation of *Das Rheingold* and *Die Walküre*, delegating all other public conducting duties to other members of the music staff.

101 Ferenc von Beniczky's open letter to Gustav Mahler, published in *Pester Lloyd* on 29 January 1889, as found in K. and H. Blaukopf, *Mahler: His Life, Work and World*, pp. 79–80.

102 Traditionally, *Don Giovanni* was performed at the Opernhaus with spoken dialogue instead of sung recitatives. Mahler restored the recitatives for his 1890
production and accompanied them using a pianino.

103 The first night of the new productions of Maillart's *Les Dragons de Villars*,
Wagner's *Lohengrin*, Nicolai's *Die lustigen Weiber von Windsor*, Marschner's
Der Templer und die Jüdin, Mozart's *Don Giovanni*, Franchetti's *Asraël*,
Mascagni's *Cavalleria rusticana*, Lortzing's *Der Waffenschmied* and
Mendelssohn's *Die Loreley* were given on 31 March 1889, 15 September 1889,
24 October 1889, 8 March 1890, 16 September 1890, 20 November 1890, 26
December 1890, 17 January 1891 and 1 March 1891 respectively. Information
kindly provided by Nóra Wellman, archivist at the Hungarian State Opera.

104 Other operas and operettas heard at the Königliches Opernhaus during his
tenure included *Merlin*, Bizet's *Les Pêcheurs de perles*, Kreutzer's *Das Nachtlager in Granada*, Donizetti's *La Fille du régiment*, Ferenc Erkel's *György
Brankovics* and *Bánk bán*, Auber's *La Part du Diable*, Offenbach's *Le Mariage
aux lanternes*, Mozart's *Le nozze di Figaro*, Thomas's *Mignon*, Verdi's *Aida* and
Un ballo in maschera, Goldmark's *Die Königin von Saba*, Adam's *La Poupée
de Nuremberg*, Beethoven's *Fidelio*, Massé's *Les Noces de Jeannette*, and
Huber's *A vig cimborák*. The ballets performed at Budapest during Mahler's
tenure were *Der neue Romeo*, *Csárdás*, Bayer's *Die Puppenfee* and *Sonne und
Erde* and Szabados's *Viora*. K. and H. Blaukopf, *Mahler: His Life, Work and
World*, pp. 89–90.

105 Mahler had already performed three of his songs, *Frühlingsmorgen*, *Erinnerung* and *Scheiden und Meiden*, at Budapest on 13 November 1889. At that
concert, he accompanied the soprano Bianca Bianchi at the piano.

106 The tone poem, later known as Symphony No. 1, which was performed in its
original five-movement version, was the central work in a programme conducted jointly by Mahler and Sándor Erkel. Mahler conducted his symphony
while Erkel conducted Cherubini's overture to *Les Abencérages*, two arias from
Mozart's *Le nozze di Figaro* and Bach's Prelude, Chorale and Fugue arranged
by Abert.

107 Of those seven performances, six were either benefit or gala performances.

108 Mahler performed Beethoven's overture *Leonore* No. 3 on 3 January 1890,
Beethoven's Symphony No. 5 on 24 February 1890, Liszt's *Festklänge* and
Mihalovich's overture to *Toldis Liebe* and *Königshymnus* on 29 October 1890, and
Weber's overture to *Oberon*, Mozart's Symphony No. 40, extracts from Thomas's
Mignon and Wagner's Prelude to *Die Meistersinger von Nürnberg* on 6 December
1890. Mahler also performed as a conductor at benefit concerts on 11 December
1889 and 16 April 1890 and as a piano accompanist on 12 March 1890.

109 The resignation demand appeared in *Pesti Hirlap* on 5 November 1890. As
found in K. and H. Blaukopf, *Mahler: His Life, Work and World*, p. 86.

110 Géza von Zichy (1849–1924): Hungarian pianist, composer and administrator.

111 With his loss of prestige, Mahler also had to settle for a lower salary: 12,000
marks annually.

112 Josef Sittard's review in the *Hamburgischer Correspondent* on 1 April 1891 as
found in K. and H. Blaukopf, *Mahler: His Life, Work and World*, p. 93.

113 B. Walter, trans. J. A. Galston, *Theme and Variations: An Autobiography* (London, 1947), p. 49.

114 Hans von Bülow's letter to his daughter, Daniela, dated 24 April 1891, as found
in *Letters of Hans von Bülow to Richard Wagner and Others*, p. 426.

115 Walter, *Theme and Variations*, pp. 85–6.

116 For Bruno Walter, see Chapter 6. Wilhelm Kienzl (1857–1941): Austrian
conductor and composer.

117 The premières and new productions that Mahler conducted at Hamburg
included Tchaikovsky's *Eugene Onegin* (19 January 1892) and *Yolanta* (3 January 1893), Bruneau's *La Rêve* (28 March 1892) and *L'Attaque du Moulin* (30
November 1895), Bizet's *Djamileh* (21 October 1892), Mascagni's *L'amico
Fritz* (16 January 1893) and *I Rantzau* (19 April 1893) Kaskel's *Hochzeitsmorgen* (23 March 1893), Tasca's *A Santa Lucia* (31 May 1893), Franchetti's
Cristoforo Colombo (5 October 1893), Verdi's *Falstaff* (2 January 1894),
Smetana's *The Bartered Bride* (17 January 1894), *The Kiss* (20 February 1895)
and *Dalibor* (11 February 1896), Humperdinck's *Hänsel und Gretel* (25 September 1894), Blodek's *Im Brunnen* (25 September 1894), Hochberg's *Der
Wärwolf* (28 March 1895), Massenet's *Werther* (10 October 1895), Haydn's
Der Apotheker (5 November 1895), Kienzl's *Der Evangelimann* (6 January
1896), Brüll's *Gloria* (15 October 1896), Goldmark's *Das Heimchen am Herd*
(26 October 1896) and Giordano's *Andrea Chénier* (5 February 1897). Information kindly provided by Christel Benner of the Hamburg Theatersammlung
and Barbara Neumann, archivist at the Hamburgische Staatsoper.
118 The figure of 144 performances is the total for both theatres. Information
kindly provided by Barbara Neumann, archivist at the Hamburgische Staatsoper. (La Grange gives a figure of 134 performances during the 1894–5 season. *Mahler*, Vol. 1, p. 318.)
119 Mahler performed the following works by Wagner during the 1894–5 season:
Tristan und Isolde (five performances), *Tannhäuser* (11 performances), *Die
Meistersinger von Nürnberg* (six performances), *Das Rheingold* (one performance), *Die Walküre* (four performances), *Siegfried* (five performances) and *Götterdämmerung* (three performances). Information kindly provided by Barbara
Neumann, archivist at the Hamburgische Staatsoper.
120 The Day of Penance (der Buss- und Bettag) occurs eleven days before Advent in
the German Evangelical Church's calendar. The Good Friday (Karfreitag) Concerts were held at the Stadttheater and the Day of Penance Concerts were held
normally at the Altona Theatre.
121 The policy of performing liturgical choral music on the Day of Penance was
waived, however, when the orchestra of the Stadttheater performed under
Mahler at the Lübeck Colosseum on 27 November 1891. At that concert,
Mahler conducted a programme that included Haydn's Symphony No. 101
('Clock'), vocal excerpts from Mozart's *Le nozze di Figaro*, Beethoven's *Fidelio*
and Wagner's *Die Walküre*, Beethoven's overture *Leonore* No. 3 and Wagner's
overture to *Tannhäuser*.
  The six Good Friday concerts were given on 15 April 1892 (Mozart's Requiem
and Bruckner's Te Deum), 31 March 1893 (Bruckner's Mass No. 1 in D minor
and Te Deum), 23 March 1894 (Haydn's *Die Schöpfung* and arias from
Mendelssohn's *Elijah* and *St Paul*), 12 April 1895 (Haydn's *Die Schöpfung* and
Mozart's Requiem), 3 April 1896 (Mozart's Requiem, arias by Krebs, Handel
and Mendelssohn, and the closing chorus from Bach's *St Matthew Passion*) and
16 April 1897 (Mozart's Requiem, Bruckner's Te Deum, Krebs's *Unser Vater* and
Handel's Largo for Strings and Organ (arr. Hellmesberger)). Mahler also conducted Haydn's *Die Schöpfung* for the annual Buss- und Bettags-Konzert at the
Altona Theatre on 22 November 1893 (with arias from Mendelssohn's *Elijah*
and *St Paul*), 21 November 1894 (with arias from Mendelssohn's *Elijah* and *St
Paul*), 20 November 1895 and 18 November 1896.
122 Gustav Mahler's letter to Anton Bruckner dated 16 April 1892, as found in
K. and H. Blaukopf, *Mahler: His Life, Work and World*, p. 95.
123 At the Hamburg Stadttheater, Mahler conducted Symphony No. 3 on 14
March 1892 and 24 April 1897, Symphony No. 5 on 15 April 1893, Symphony

No. 6 on 1 March 1895, 17 March 1895 and 26 March 1895, and Symphony No. 7 on 1 March 1894.

124 In all, Mahler conducted thirty-one concert performances of choral, vocal and symphonic works at the Lübeck Colosseum, the Hamburg Stadttheater and the Altona Theatre for Pollini. As for his performances of Beethoven's symphonies, many were heard in advance of an operatic performance on the same evening.

125 Mahler conducted the Fifth Abonnement Concert on 12 December 1892 in Bülow's stead. The programme was Mendelssohn's overture to *Ein Sommernachtstraum*, Lalo's *Symphonie espagnole*, Wagner's *Siegfried Idyll*, the first movement of Paganini's Violin Concerto in D major (Karl Halir, violin) and Beethoven's Symphony No. 5.

126 The performance on 26 February 1894 was both the Ninth Abonnement Concert of the 1893–4 season and Bülow's memorial concert. Originally, Richard Strauss was scheduled to conduct the performance but he withdrew after falling out with the concert's organizers over programming.

127 Instrumental and vocal solos were performed at five of the eight concerts. At three of those concerts – 22 October 1894, 19 November 1894 and 3 December 1894 – Mahler acted as piano accompanist.

128 Bruckner's Symphony No. 4 was heard on 18 February 1895. The rest of the programme comprised unaccompanied vocal trios by Mendelssohn, Fabricius and Rennes (Jeannette de Jong, Anna Corver and Marie Synders, voice), Brahms's Piano Concerto No. 1 (Robert Freund, piano) and the Prelude to *Die Meistersinger von Nürnberg*.

129 Beethoven's Symphonies Nos. 6, 7 and 9 and Schubert's Symphony No. 8 in C major were heard on 3 December 1894, 22 October 1894, 11 March 1895 and 5 November 1894 respectively.

130 The works performed on 27 October 1893 were Beethoven's overture to *Egmont*, 'Einst war so tiefe Friede' from Marschner's *Hans Heiling* (Clementine Schuch-Proska, soprano), an aria from Adam's *La Poupée Nuremberg* (Paul Bulss, baritone), Mendelssohn's overture *The Hebrides*, Mahler's *Das himmlische Leben*, *Verlor'ne Müh'* and *Wer hat dies Liedlein erdacht* (Clementine Schuch-Proska, soprano), *Der Schildwache Nachtlied*, *Trost im Unglück* and *Rheinlegendchen* (Paul Bulss, baritone) and *Titan, a Tone Poem in Symphonic Form* (later revised and renamed Symphony No. 1).

131 The Lieder performed were *Der Schildwache Nachtlied*, *Trost im Unglück* and *Rheinlegendchen* (Paul Bulss, baritone).

132 See Chapter 5.

133 The rest of the programme was conducted by Strauss and included Mendelssohn's overture *The Hebrides*, Saint-Saëns's Piano Concerto No. 4 (Josef Hofmann, piano), piano solos by Chopin and Liszt (Josef Hofmann, piano) and Weber's overture to *Oberon*.

   Mahler also conducted the first and second movements from Symphony No. 2 with the Orchestra of the Liszt-Verein at Leipzig on 14 December 1896. The other works on the programme included Schumann's Piano Concerto (Wassili Sapellnikow, piano) and Beethoven's overture to *Coriolan*. Martner, *Gustav Mahler im Konzertsaal*, p. 49.

134 Hermann Wolff, the manager of the Berlin Philharmonic, refused to take financial responsibility for the performance of Symphony No. 2 and the concert was sponsored privately by two friends of Mahler, Dr Hermann Behn and Wilhelm Berkhan. K. and H. Blaukopf, *Mahler: His Life, Work and World*, p. 112.

   The programme on 16 March 1896 included *Todtenfeier* (the first movement of Symphony No. 2), *Lieder eines fahrenden Gesellen* (Anton Sistermans, baritone) and Symphony No. 1 in the revised four-movement version. According to

Natalie Bauer-Lechner, the 'sale of tickets for the concert was very poor indeed
. . . [and the] takings at the box-office amounted [apparently] to only 48 marks,
whereas the performance cost Mahler thousands'. Bauer-Lechner, *Recollections
of Gustav Mahler*, p. 50.

135 Some orchestral musicians also travelled to London with Mahler to strengthen
Harris's existing orchestra.

136 H. Rosenthal, *Two Centuries of Opera at Covent Garden* (London, 1958),
pp. 723–4.

137 It seems that Felix Weingartner was among the first to move the position of the
conductor's podium from the middle of the pit to the pit wall during his first
period as Director of the Vienna Opera. M. Prawy, *Die Wiener Oper* (Vienna,
1969), p. 63.

138 Mahler conducted eighteen performances in London between 8 June and
23 July. La Grange, *Mahler*, Vol. 1, p. 255.

139 Mahler conducted: Beethoven's Symphony No. 5, Wagner's *Siegfried Idyll* and
the overture to *Rienzi*, Gounod's 'Ich will leben wie im Traum' ('Je veux vivre
dans ce rêve') from *Roméo et Juliette* (M. Antonova, soprano) and Simon's
Piano Concerto (V. Staub, piano) with the Philharmonic Orchestra at Moscow;
Wagner's Prelude to *Die Meistersinger von Nürnberg*, Berlioz's *Symphonie fan-
tastique* and Beethoven's Symphony No. 5 with the Kaim Orchestra at Munich,
and Wagner's overtures to *Rienzi* and *Tannhäuser* and 'Dich teure Halle' from
Tannhäuser (Sophie Sedlmair, soprano), the second movement from his own
Symphony No. 3, Weber's *Aufforderung zum Tanz* (arr. Weingartner) and
Beethoven's 'Abscheulicher!' from *Fidelio* (Sophie Sedlmair, soprano) and Sym-
phony No. 5 with the Philharmonic Orchestra at Budapest. Martner, *Gustav
Mahler im Konzertsaal*, p. 49.

140 Wilhelm Jahn (1834–1900): Austrian conductor.

141 The works that Mahler conducted as Jahn's subordinate at the Hofoper were
Wagner's *Der Ring des Nibelungen*, *Lohengrin*, *Der fliegende Holländer* and
Tannhäuser, Mozart's *Die Zauberflöte*, *Don Giovanni* and *Le nozze di Figaro*,
Gounod's *Margarethe (Faust)*, Meyerbeer's *L'Africaine* and *Le Prophète*,
Smetana's *The Bartered Bride*, Weber's *Der Freischütz* and Lortzing's *Zar und
Zimmermann*.

142 Hans Richter left the Hofoper in 1900 to become conductor of the Hallé
Orchestra, Manchester.

143 Wagner's works constituted 145 of the 648 performances of sixty-three operas
by thirty-eight composers that Mahler gave at the Hofoper between 11 May
1897 and 15 October 1907.

144 The figure of forty-two new productions includes the three world premières
(Goldmark's *Die Kriegsgefangene* on 17 January 1899, Zemlinsky's *Es war
einmal* on 22 January 1900 and Josef Forster's *Der Dot Mon* on 28 February
1902) and the twenty local premières that Mahler conducted at the Hofoper.

145 Before Mahler's twenty-one performances of the 1903 production of Wagner's
Tristan und Isolde, he conducted sixteen of an existing production at the
Hofoper.

146 Alfred Roller (1864–1935): Austrian artist and designer. The Secession, or the
Vereinigung bildender Künstler Österreichs, was established at Vienna in 1897,
by a number of leading artists, including Gustav Klimt, Carl Moll and Kolo-
man Moser as a reaction to traditional artistic trends.

147 G. Adler, 'Gustav Mahler', as found in Reilly, *Gustav Mahler and Guido Adler:
Records of a Friendship*, p. 26.

148 Mahler and Roller also collaborated on Wolf's *Der Corregidor*, Wolf-Ferrari's
Le donne curiose, Weber's *Euryanthe*, Verdi's *Falstaff*, Gluck's *Iphigénie en*

Aulide, Wagner's *Das Rheingold* and *Die Walküre*, Pfitzner's *Die Rose vom Liebesgarten* and Götz's *Der Widerspenstigen Zähmung*. The production of *Così fan tutte* on which Mahler and Roller collaborated in 1905 was not entirely new. Because of financial restraints, they had to refurbish some existing material.

149 B. Zuckerkandl, *Österreich intim*, p. 40, as quoted in H.-L. de La Grange, *Gustav Mahler*, Vol. 3: *Vienna: Triumph and Disillusion (1904–1907)* (Oxford, 1999), p. 6.

150 For Otto Klemperer, see Chapter 7. Lorin Maazel (b. 1930): American conductor. Like Mahler, Maazel was Director of the Vienna Opera (1982–4).

151 While the operas were produced to mark Mozart's anniversary year, the cycle was begun in 1905 with new productions of *Così fan tutte* (24 November 1905) (see note 148) and *Don Giovanni* (21 December 1905) and continued in 1906 with new productions of *Die Entführung aus dem Serail* (29 January 1906), *Le nozze di Figaro* (30 March 1906) and *Die Zauberflöte* (1 June 1906).

152 Adler, 'Gustav Mahler', p. 27.

153 Walter, *Theme and Variations*, pp. 157–9.

154 Ibid.

155 For a detailed description of Mahler's approach to *Così fan tutte* at Vienna, see B. Paumgartner, *Gustav Mahlers Bearbeitung von Mozarts 'Così fan tutte' für seine Aufführungen an der Wiener Hofoper* (Kassel, 1968).

156 For Strauss, see Chapter 5. Like Strauss, Mahler acted as both continuo player and conductor, but, whereas Strauss used a fortepiano in Munich, Mahler used a harpsichord in Vienna.

157 The Vienna Philharmonic's annual Nicolai Concert was named after the conductor Otto Nicolai (1810–49) and was held during Mahler's tenure to raise money for the Hofoper orchestra's medical fund.

158 The Abonnement Concerts that included soloists were 26 February 1899 ('Die Trommel gerühret' and 'Freudvoll und leidvoll' from *Egmont* with Marcella Pregi, soprano), 19 March 1899 (Beethoven's Piano Concerto No. 5 ('Emperor') with Ferrucio Busoni, piano), 17 December 1899 (Brahms's Violin Concerto with Marie Soldat-Roeger, violin), 14 January 1900 (Mahler's *Ging heut' morgen übers Feld*, *Die zwei blauen Augen*, *Das irdische Leben* and *Wo die schönen Trompeten blasen* with Selma Kurz, soprano), 18 March 1900 (Weber's Konzertstück for Piano and Orchestra (arr. Liszt) with Ferrucio Busoni, piano) and 2 December 1900 (Franck's *Symphonic Variations* with Carl Friedberg, piano). Information from the records of the Vienna Philharmonic kindly provided by Dr Clemens Hellsberg.

159 At the Nicolai Concerts, Mahler performed his Symphony No. 2 (L. von Barenfeld, soprano; Marcella Pregi, contralto; Singverein der Gesellschaft der Musikfreunde, chorus) on 9 April 1899, Beethoven's overture *Die Weihe des Hauses* and Symphony No. 9 (M. Katzmayr, soprano; Leonore Rellé, contralto; Franz Pacal, tenor; Wilhelm Hesch, bass; Singverein der Gesellschaft der Musikfreunde, chorus) on 18 and 22 February 1900 and Beethoven's Symphony No. 9 (Elise Elizza, soprano; Karoline Kusmitsch, contralto; Franz Naval, tenor; Moritz Frauscher, bass; Sing-Akademie der Gesellschaft der Musikfreunde and Schubertbund, chorus) on 27 January 1901. Information from the records of the Vienna Philharmonic kindly provided by Dr Clemens Hellsberg.

160 The works by living composers that Mahler conducted at the Vienna Philharmonic's Abonnement Concerts were his *Ging heut' morgen übers Feld*, *Die zwei blauen Augen*, *Das irdische Leben* and *Wo die schönen Trompeten blasen* (Selma Kurz, soprano) on 14 January 1900, his Symphony No. 1 on 18 November 1900, Dvořák's *Heldenlied*, *Die Waldtaube* and Serenade for winds, cello and double bass on 4 December 1898, 3 December 1899 and 24 February 1901,

Goldmark's overture *Im Frühling* on 18 March 1900 and Strauss's *Aus Italien* on 19 November 1899.

161 Mahler's Abonnement and Nicolai Concerts with the Vienna Philharmonic constitute only part of his activities with the orchestra between 6 November 1898 and 24 February 1901. During that period, he conducted thirty-six concerts with the orchestra in Vienna and on tour, including five concerts in Paris for the 1900 International Exhibition. The total number of concerts that he gave with the Vienna Philharmonic between 6 November 1898 and 24 November 1907, his first and last performances with the orchestra, was forty-four. Information from the records of the Vienna Philharmonic kindly provided by Dr Clemens Hellsberg.

162 Mahler conducted all-Beethoven concerts on 19 March 1899 (overture to *Fidelio*, Piano Concerto No. 5, Symphony No. 7), 18 February 1900 (overture *Die Weihe des Hause*, Symphony No. 9), 22 February 1900 (overture *Die Weihe des Hauses*, Symphony No. 9), 16 December 1900 (Symphony No. 1, overture to *Coriolan*, Symphony No. 4) and 27 January 1901 (Symphony No. 9). For soloists, see notes 158 and 159.

163 For a detailed description and analysis of Mahler's amendments to the scores of Beethoven and other composers, see D. A. Pickett, *Gustav Mahler as an Interpreter: A Study of his Textural Alterations and Performance Practice in the Symphonic Repertoire*, Ph.D. dissertation (1988), University of Surrey.

164 Review by Richard Heuberger in the *Neue Freie Presse*, 19 February 1900, as found in K. and H. Blaukopf, *Mahler: His Life, Work and World*, pp. 143–4.

165 Although the Vienna Philharmonic was known by that name on tour, it often operated in Vienna as Mitglieder des k. k. Hof-Opernorchesters (Members of the Royal Imperial Court Opera Orchestra).

166 This figure also excludes performances that Mahler gave with the Vienna Philharmonic on tour.

167 *Ich bin der Welt abhanden gekommen* was performed both independently and as part of one of the two groups of songs that he conducted as a guest conductor.

168 During the period 25 November 1901 to 9 November 1907, Mahler conducted the Concertgebouw Orchestra on 22 and 23 October 1903 (Symphony No. 3), 25 October 1903 (Symphony No. 1), 23 October 1904 (Symphony No. 4), 26 and 27 October 1904 (Symphony No. 2), 8 March 1906 (Symphony No. 5, *Kindertotenlieder* and *Ich bin der Welt abhanden gekommen* with Gerard Zalsman, baritone) and 10 March 1906 (*Das klagende Lied*). Mahler later returned to the Concertgebouw Orchestra on 2, 3 and 7 October 1909 (Symphony No. 7). At the concert on 7 October 1909 he also conducted Wagner's Prelude to *Die Meistersinger von Nürnberg*.

169 Willem Mengelberg (1871–1951) was one of Mahler's first and most enduring advocates. As Music Director of the Concertgebouw Orchestra between 1895 and 1945, Mengelberg was a passionate champion of new music and worked closely with not only Mahler but also Richard Strauss. Mengelberg quickly recognized the importance of their symphonies and tone poems and promoted them actively when and where possible. His festivals of music by Strauss and Mahler with the Concertgebouw Orchestra in London and Amsterdam in 1903 and 1920 respectively were of particular significance and attracted attention internationally. But Mengelberg is probably remembered best for his ability to train orchestras and his characteristic performance style. Although he was criticized by some musicians for his verbose and often histrionic rehearsal method, he was admired by string players for his understanding of bowing and string technique and by orchestras as a whole for his flexible and expressive conducting style. Like Mahler, he was notorious for his adjustments to the orchestrations of

established masterpieces and was later attacked for his continuing commitment to excessive string portamenti and tempo fluctuations. While many modern record collectors and musicians regard him as an interpreter of importance, some of his younger contemporaries were less convinced and would no doubt have agreed with Otto Klemperer's remark that Mengelberg was merely 'an excellent trainer rather than a great conductor'.

170 Heinrich Conried (1848–1909): German-born opera administrator.

171 Z. Roman, *Gustav Mahler's American Years 1907–1911: A Documentary History* (Stuyvesant, NY, 1989), p. 10.

172 Gustav Mahler's letter to Arnold Berliner, postmarked 17 June 1907, as found ibid.

173 With the Metropolitan Opera in New York and on tour, Mahler conducted six performances of Mozart's *Don Giovanni*, eight of Mozart's *Le nozze di Figaro*, four of Beethoven's *Fidelio*, four of Tchaikovsky's *The Queen of Spades*, seven of Smetana's *The Bartered Bride*, eleven of Wagner's *Tristan und Isolde*, five of Wagner's *Siegfried* and five of Wagner's *Die Walküre*. Information kindly provided by the Metropolitan Opera, New York.

174 Mahler performed *Tristan und Isolde*, *Don Giovanni*, *Die Walküre*, *Siegfried* and *Fidelio* for the first time in New York on 1 January, 23 January, 7 February, 19 February and 20 March 1908 respectively. Information kindly provided by the Metropolitan Opera, New York.

175 Unlike his performances of Wagner's operas and music dramas in Vienna, Mahler made cuts to that composer's works in New York.

176 For his performances of *Fidelio* in New York, Mahler used Roller's sets from Vienna. Mahler also conducted Beethoven's overture *Leonore* No. 3 at a benefit concert for Heinrich Conried on 24 March 1908.

177 *New York Times*, 5 April 1908.

178 Mahler conducted a programme of works by Beethoven, Smetana and Wagner on 23 May 1908 and the first performance of his Symphony No. 7 on 19 September 1908.

179 Giulio Gatti-Casazza (1869–1940): Italian impresario and administrator. Andreas Dippel (1866–1932): German tenor and administrator.

180 Arturo Toscanini (1867–1957): Italian 'cellist and conductor.

181 Toscanini made his début at the Metropolitan Opera with Verdi's *Aida* on 16 November 1908 and conducted Wagner's *Götterdämmerung* on 10 December 1908. Although the relationship between Mahler and Toscanini was never warm, each admired the other's abilities as a performing musician.

182 Under his contract with Conried, Mahler was prohibited from conducting concerts with other organizations. See Roman, *Gustav Mahler's American Years*, pp. 26–33.

183 At the second of those concerts (8 December 1908), Mahler conducted the first American performance of his Symphony No. 2.

184 Mahler continued to perform as guest conductor in Europe after October 1909, with concerts in The Hague (2 October 1909), Amsterdam (3 and 7 October 1910), Paris (17 April 1910), Rome (28 April and 1 May 1910) and Munich (12 and 13 September 1910). With the exception of the Rome performances, all the concerts contained a symphony by Mahler – Symphony No. 7 in The Hague and Amsterdam and Symphony No. 2 in Paris – and at the Munich concerts he gave the first and second performances of his Symphony No. 8.

185 As the orchestra was placed on a more permanent footing from the 1909–10 season, the concerts increased threefold during Mahler's first season and fourfold during his second. H. Shanet, *Philharmonic: A History of New York's Orchestra* (New York, 1975), p. 218.

186 Nearly half of the musicians who played under his predecessor, the Russian conductor Wasili Safonoff, were replaced by Mahler.

187 For the purpose of this statistical analysis, the concerts that Mahler conducted the Academy of Music in Brooklyn and Carnegie Hall in New York have been counted separately.

188 Beethoven's Symphony No. 9 was heard on 1 and 2 April 1910. The other work on the programme was the Choral Fantasy (Ernst Hutcheson, piano). As in Hamburg and Vienna, Mahler retouched Symphony No. 9 extensively at New York and, again, his alterations were a source of critical concern.

189 Mahler's all-Wagner concert was heard on 13 February 1910. The programme included the *Kaisermarsch*, *A Faust Overture*, Wotan's 'Abschied' and 'Feuerzauber' from *Die Walküre*, *Siegfried Idyll*, the Prelude to *Die Meistersinger von Nürnberg*, 'Wahn! Wahn!' from *Die Meistersinger von Nürnberg* and the overture to *Tannhäuser*.

190 Mahler also conducted an all-Wagner concert at Academy of Music in Brooklyn on the 18 March 1910. The programme included the overture to *Der fliegende Holländer*, *A Faust Overture*, *Siegfried Idyll*, 'Dich teure Halle' from *Tannhäuser*, the Prelude to *Lohengrin*, *Im Treibhaus*, *Schmerzen* and the *Kaisermarsch*.

191 Two of the five concerts that contained a work by Beethoven were all-Beethoven concerts. On 13 December 1910, Mahler conducted overture *Leonore* No. 3, Symphony No. 6 and Piano Concerto No. 5 (Xaver Scharwenka, piano) and he repeated the programme on 16 December 1910.

192 At Carnegie Hall, Mahler conducted Symphony No. 1 on 16 and 17 December 1909, *Kindertotenlieder* on 26 January 1910, *Ging heut' morgen übers Feld* and *Rheinlegendchen* (Alma Gluck, soprano) on 22 and 25 November 1910 and Symphony No. 4 on 17 and 20 January 1911. Mahler also conducted *Kindertotenlieder* at the Academy of Music in Brooklyn on 28 January 1910 and *Ging heut' morgen übers Feld* and *Rheinlegendchen* (Alma Gluck, soprano) at the same venue on 20 November 1910. Along with the above-mentioned works, Mahler also gave six performances of his arrangement of a Bach Orchestral Suite at Carnegie Hall during his tenure with the New York Philharmonic. For those readings, Mahler played the continuo on a modified modern piano.

193 At Carnegie Hall, Mahler conducted four performances of *Till Eulenspiegel*, two each of *Don Juan*, *Tod und Verklärung*, *Also sprach Zarathustra*, *Ein Heldenleben*, *Hymnus*, *Pilgers Morgenlied* and one only of the Preludes to Acts 1 and 2 of *Guntram*.

   Mahler performed Strauss's second opera, *Feuersnot*, at the Vienna Hofoper in 1902. He also hoped to stage the first Vienna performance of *Salome* at that theatre during his tenure but he was thwarted by the local censor.

194 On 5 February 1911, Mahler conducted MacDowell's Piano Concerto No. 2 (Ernest Hutcheson). On 14 and 17 February 1911, he conducted Chadwick's overture *Melpomene*, Stanford's 'Irish' Symphony, Elgar's *Sea Pictures* Nos. 1–4 (Louise Kirkby-Lunn, contralto), Loeffler's *La Villanelle du Diable*, Mac-Dowell's *Die Sarazenen* and *Lovely Alda* (Louise Kirkby-Lunn, contralto) and Hadley's *The Culprit Fay*.

   Mahler conducted his Symphony No. 4, Pfitzner's overture to *Das Käthchen von Heilbronn* and Strauss's *Ein Heldenleben* on 17 and 20 January 1911.

195 The programme included Sinigaglia's overture *Le baruffe chiozotte*, Mendelssohn's Symphony No. 4 ('Italian'), Martucci's Piano Concerto in B minor (Ernesto Consolo, piano), Busoni's *Berceuse élégiaque* and Bossi's *Intermezzi goldoniani*.

196 According to his wife, Mahler's last words were 'Mozartl! Mozartl!' ('little Mozart! little Mozart!). A. Mahler, *Gustav Mahler: Memories and Letters*, p. 200.

197 Julius Korngold, *Neue Freie Presse*, as found in Lebrecht, *Mahler Remembered*, p. 314.

Chapter 4. 'An unrecognised genius'? Felix Weingartner

1 The phrase 'an unrecognised genius' appears in C. Flesch, trans H. Keller, *The Memoirs of Carl Flesch* (London, 1957), p. 151.
2 Ibid., p. 150.
3 Although born Felix von Weingartner, he preferred to be known as Felix Weingartner.
4 In his autobiography, Carl Flesch wrote: 'The great tragedy of his life consisted in the unsatisfied need to be creative, a great composer. In this respect Weingartner regarded himself all his life as an unrecognized genius, whereas in reality he was no more than a clever eclectic, composing what was, fundamentally, the better kind of *Kapellmeistermusik* (lit. "conductor's music")'. Flesch, *Memoirs*, p. 151.
5 At the time of Weingartner's birth, Zara (now Zadar) was part of the Austro-Hungarian Empire.
6 Guido Weingartner died at Zara on 24 April 1868.
7 Weingartner's interest in Schubert's songs continued throughout his life. Among his possessions, some of which are housed at the Öffentliche Bibliothek der Universität Basel, a large number of that composer's songs can be found.
8 F. Weingartner, trans. M. Wolff, *Buffets and Rewards: A Musician's Reminiscences* (London, 1937), pp. 33–43.
9 In the summer of 1879, Weingartner also attend performances at the Vienna Hofoper, where he heard Weber's *Der Freischütz* and Wagner's *Der Ring des Nibelungen* under Hans Richter. The performances left an indelible impression on Weingartner. Ibid., pp. 46–7. (Weingartner probably attended performances on 8 September (*Der Freischütz*), 15 September (*Das Rheingold*), 16 September (*Die Walküre*), 17 September (*Siegfried*) and 19 September (*Götterdämmerung*)).
10 Ibid., p. 38.
11 Ibid., pp. 38–9.
12 Salomon Jadassohn (1831–1902): German music theorist.
13 Weingartner, *Buffets amd Rewards*, pp. 83–4.
14 Hermann Levi (1839–1900): German conductor.
15 On 14 March 1882, Bülow and the Meininger Hofkapelle performed an all-Brahms programme at Leipzig that included Piano Concerto No. 1 (Hans von Bülow, piano, and Franz Mannstädt, conductor), 'Haydn' Variations and Symphony No. 1.
16 Weingartner, *Buffets and Rewards*, pp. 89–90.
17 Eduard Lassen (1830–1904): Danish-born German composer and conductor. Lassen was Hofkapellmeister at Weimar between 1858 and 1895.
18 See Chapter 1 note 83.
19 Weingartner's description of his colleague's methods is a valuable insight into his thoughts on conducting technique in general: 'Kriebel belonged to a type of conductor that has now practically died out, the kind that beats exact time. Not a crotchet was out of place and each was exactly like the next. On the other hand there was no nervous subtlety about him and that was in some ways an advantage. If I had to choose to-day between one of those out-of-date automata and a modern super-conductor, who "individualizes" every crotchet by speeding it up or slowing it down, I think I should prefer the automaton.' Weingartner, *Buffets and Rewards*, pp. 112–13.
20 Ibid., p. 113.

21 Ibid., p. 114.
22 Weingartner's conditions of engagement at the Bayreuth Festival included a fee of 600 marks, free lodgings and free breakfasts. Ibid., p. 138.
23 Ibid., p. 171.
24 Ibid.
25 Graf Bolko von Hochberg (1843–1926): German theatre administrator and composer.
26 Weingartner, *Buffets and Rewards*, p. 189.
27 In 1888, Sucher was appointed Hofkapellmeister at the Berlin Hofoper. He remained in post until 1899.
28 Weingartner, *Buffets and Rewards*, p. 191.
29 Ibid.
30 Ibid.
31 Weingartner shared the direction of the Berlin Hofkapelle's Abonnement series with Josef Sucher and, later, Karl Muck. Sucher's last concert with the Hofkapelle was on 6 December 1892. That performance marked the 150th anniversary of the Berlin Hofoper. Sucher shared the podium with Muck, who was making his début with the orchestra.
32 G. Quander, *Klangbilder: Portrait der Staatskapelle Berlin* (Frankfurt and Berlin, 1995), p. 21.
33 Weingartner had a particular affinity with Berlioz's *Symphonie fantastique* and he later recorded it with the London Symphony Orchestra in 1925 for Columbia. Columbia, L 1708–1713.
34 Weingartner's first performance of Beethoven's Symphony No. 9 with the Hofkapelle, on 9 March 1892, was also the first of his career.
35 F. Weingartner, *Ratschläge für Aufführungen Klassischer Symphonien*, Vol. 3: *Mozart* (Leipzig, 1923).
36 Columbia L 1563–1565 (London Symphony Orchestra, 1923–5); Columbia 9450–9452 (Orchestra of the Royal Philharmonic Society, 1928); Columbia unpublished (Paris Conservatoire Orchestra, 1939); Columbia LX 881–883/LX 8483–8485 auto (London Philharmonic Orchestra, 1940). J. Hunt, *More 20th Century Conductors* (London, 1993), p. 139.
37 Weingartner had access to the autographs of Symphonies Nos. 95 and 96. In formulating their new edition, Breitkopf & Härtel arranged for the Philharmonic Society of London to lend these autographs to Weingartner in 1906. A. H. King, *Musical Pursuits* (London, 1987), p. 171.
38 On 31 January 1896, Weingartner performed his arrangement of Weber's *Aufforderung zum Tanz*.
39 Weingartner conducted his Symphony No. 2 with the Berlin Hofkapelle on 6 January 1905.
40 Weingartner conducted Smetana's *Vyšehrad* on 18 October 1892 and Borodin's Symphony No. 2 on 20 January 1893.
   Amongst the novelties conducted by Weingartner at the Berlin Hofkapelle's Abonnement Concerts was Schubert's Symphony No. 5, of which he gave the first Berlin performance on 23 January 1894. Today, this symphony has secured its place in the repertoire, but in 1894 it continued to be overshadowed by Symphonies Nos. 7 in B minor and 8 in C major ('Great'). Although Weingartner gave a second performance of Symphony No. 5 on 29 January 1897, and later, during the 1903–4 season, a performance of the little-performed Symphony No. 2, the majority of his Schubert performances centred on Symphonies Nos. 7 and 8 with seven and nine performances respectively.
41 Some of the works that Weingartner introduced to Berlin were Debussy's *Prélude à l'après-midi d'un faune* on 7 May 1906, Sibelius's *The Swan of Tuonela and*

The Return of Lemminkinen on 6 December 1901 and Symphony No. 1 on 10 January 1907, Pfitzner's Two Preludes from *Das Fest auf Solhaug* on 6 November 1903, 'Blütenwunder' and 'Siegnots Trauermarsch' from *Die Rose von Liebesgarten* and the overture to *Das Käthchen von Heilbronn* on 2 November 1905, Elgar's 'Enigma' Variations on 8 November 1901 and *In the South* on 2 December 1904 and Bruckner's Symphonies Nos. 4 ('Romantic'), 5, 6 and 8 on 9 March 1895, 3 January 1900, 5 December 1902 and 3 January 1902 respectively.

Along with the Berlin premières of Bruckner's Symphonies Nos. 4, 5, 6 and 8, Weingartner also conducted Symphony No. 7 on 4 November 1904; Karl Muck had already given the first Berlin performance of the work with the Hofkapelle Berlin on 6 January 1894. Weingartner also conducted a second performance of Bruckner's Symphony No. 4 with the Hofkapelle on 12 February 1897.

42 Franz Kaim (1856–1935): German literary historian and impresario.

43 A. Ott, ed., *Die Münchner Philharmoniker 1893–1968: Ein Kapitel Kulturgeschichte* (Munich, 1968), p. 23, and reprinted as A. Ott, 'Chronik des Orchesters bis zum Jahre 1938', *Die Münchener Philharmoniker von der Gründung bis heute*, ed. R. Schmoll gen. Eisenwerth (Munich, 1985).

44 Works that were given local premières in both Berlin and Munich by Weingartner included Elgar's Variations on an Original Theme (Berlin, 8 November 1901; Munich, 4 January 1904) and *In the South* (Berlin, 2 December 1904; Munich, 3 March 1905), Sibelius's *The Swan of Tuonela* amd *The Return of Lemminkäinen* (Berlin, 6 December 1901; Munich, 9 December 1901) and Hugo Wolf's *Penthesilea* (Berlin, 9 March 1904; Munich, 18 January 1904) and *Italian Serenade* (Berlin, 29 November 1905; Munich, 24 October 1904).

The figure of thirty-two local premières includes the world première of Adolf Sandberger's *Riccio*, the Symphonic Prelude to Björnson's *Marie von Schottland* (27 November 1899).

45 Weingartner conducted *Das Gefilde der Seligen* on 8 January 1900, Symphony No. 2 on 4 March 1901, *Des Kindes Scheiden* and *Der Traumgott* on 18 January 1904, Two Songs with Orchestra on 10 March 1904 and Three Songs with Orchestra on 13 March 1905.

46 Franz Kaim's letter to Weingartner was dated 27 March 1905.

47 Ott, *Die Münchner Philharmoniker*, p. 25.

48 Frederic Lamond (1868–1948): Scottish pianist and pupil of Liszt and Bülow.

49 Of the relationship between Weingartner and Mahler, Otto Klemperer remarked that the latter stated: 'My successor in Vienna, Mr Weingartner, naturally hates me. But he also hates Wagner, because now he makes cuts in *Die Walküre* and Siegfried [*sic*]'. P. Heyworth ed., *Conversations with Klemperer* (London, 1985), p. 36. This, however, is at odds with Weingartner's letter to Mahler dated 22 August 1907: 'What so lately appeared incredible has now come true: I am really to be your successor in Vienna. There is much I might say, but may I confine myself to the expression of one brief wish? . . . that the friendly relations which have existed between us, but seem to have lapsed for several years, may revive, and thereafter continue without interruption.' As found in A. Mahler, trans. B. Creighton, ed. D. Mitchell and K. Martner, *Gustav Mahler: Memories and Letters* (London, 1990), p. 302.

50 In a letter from Alfred Roller to Gustav and Alma Mahler, dated 22 January 1908, the designer states that Weingartner was pleased with the existing productions of *Il barbiere di Siviglia*, *Tristan und Isolde* and *Lohengrin* but was unhappy with *Le nozze di Figaro*, which he considered 'too heavy'. Roller also mentions Weingartner's habit as a conductor of 'rising on his toes' at fortissimo passages. Ibid., pp. 310–11.

51 Weingartner, *Buffets and Rewards*, p. 258.
52 The concert, given on 26 January 1908, contained the following works: Reger's Variations Op. 100 and Schubert's Symphony No. 8 in C major. Before his period as Director, Weingartner conducted two concerts with the Vienna Philharmonic: 29 March 1908 at the K.K. Hof-Operntheater and 19 May 1908 at the Palais Lobkowitz. Information from the records of the Vienna Philharmonic kindly provided by Dr Clemens Hellsberg.
53 New productions conducted by Weingartner during his tenure at the Vienna Hofoper included: Gounod's *Faust* (6 September 1909), Cornelius's *Der Barbier von Bagdad* and Blech's *Versiegelt* (4 October 1909), Verdi's *Otello* (22 October 1909), Wagner's *Die Meistersinger von Nürnberg* (17 December 1909), Puccini's *Tosca* (26 January 1910), Donizetti's *L'elisir d'amore* (26 February 1910), Goldmark's *Götz von Berlichingen* (18 May 1910), Wagner's *Götterdämmerung* (21 November 1910), J. Strauss's *Der Zigeunerbaron* (26 December 1910) and Berlioz's *Benvenuto Cellini* (25 February 1911).
54 The figure of 247 concerts includes the concerts, repeat concerts and open rehearsals at the subscription series. It also includes the Nicolai Concerts.
55 Franz Schalk conducted three concerts during the 1909–10 season for Weingartner who was ill, two concerts during the 1919–20 season, seven concerts during the 1920–1 season, and eight concerts during the 1924–5 season; Richard Strauss conducted one concert during the 1915–16 season and three concerts during the 1920–1 season, while Fritz Busch conducted two concerts during the 1924–5 season.
56 Unlike H. Kraus's and K. Schreinzer's statistics in *Wiener Philharmoniker 1842–1942* (Vienna, 1942) (p. 107), the above statistic also includes Weingartner's operatic performances with the Vienna Philharmonic in Buenos Aires in 1922 and Salzburg in 1935 and 1936.
57 Weingartner and the Vienna Philharmonic gave twelve concerts at Rio de Janeiro between 19 and 30 July, three concerts at Montevideo between 5 and 7 August and twenty-three performances of concerts and operas at Buenos Aires between 9 and 31 August 1922.
58 R. Turnbull, *The Opera Gazetteer* (New York, 1988), p. 217.
59 Of the 161 performances of works by Beethoven given by Weingartner with the Philharmonic at its Vienna series, 116 were of that composer's symphonies. These statistics take into account open rehearsals, concerts and repeat concerts.
60 These performances were part of a series of anniversary concerts that commemorated the composer's death in 1827.
61 Of Weingartner's performances of Beethoven's Symphony No. 9, Otto Strasser, a violinist in, and later a chairman of, the Vienna Philharmonic, wrote: 'Felix von Weingartner ... impressed me deeply with his performances of the Ninth.' O. Strasser, 'Beethoven's Ninth and the Vienna Philharmonic', notes accompanying Deutsche Grammophon CD, 435 325–2.
62 The other works on the programme were the overture to *Egmont* and Symphony No. 5. The programme was also heard at an open rehearsal on 18 December 1926.
63 In Vienna, Weingartner conducted his Symphony No. 1 on 9 January 1916, Symphony No. 2 on 18 March 1917, Symphony No. 3 on 27 November 1910 and on 21, 22 and 29 January 1922, Symphony No. 4 on 15 and 16 December 1917, the Violin Concerto (Carl Flesch, violin) on 19 and 20 January 1918, the Cello Concerto (Friedrich Buxbaum, cello) on 18 and 19 January 1919, the tone poem, *Das Gefilde der Seligen* on 28 January 1912, the 'Reisenauer' Variations on 6, 7 and 13 January 1923, *Der Sturm* Suite on 31 January and 1 February 1920, the *Lustige Ouvertüre* on 5 January 1913, overture *Aus ernster Zeit* on 8 November

1914 and three movements from the opera *Dame Kobold* on 16, 17 and 20 April 1921, Gluck's overture to *Alceste* (concert ending, Weingartner) on 8 November 1908, Bach's Orchestral Suite No. 1 (ed. Weingartner) on 6 November 1910, Beethoven's *Grosse Fuge* (arr. Weingartner) on 9 March 1913 and 29 and 30 December 1923 and Beethoven's Sonata Op. 106 ('Hammerklavier') (arr. Weingartner) on 18 and 19 December 1926.

64 At Vienna, Weingartner conducted Mahler's Symphony No. 1 ('Titan') on 2 and 3 March 1918 and on 16 and 17 January 1926, Symphony No. 3 on 22 and 23 March 1919, Symphony No. 4 on 14 March 1915, Symphony No. 5 on 5 November 1911 and Symphony No. 7 on 12 March 1916.

   Weingartner conducted a work by Strauss at ten of his nineteen seasons with the Vienna Philharmonic.

65 From the works performed at the Volksoper, the dialectic surrounding Weingartner's programme policy seems biased. The operas given included: *Maria von Magdala* (22 December 1919), *Fra Diavolo* (6 February 1920), *Der Goldschmied von Toledo* (20 February 1920), *Tosca* (3 June 1920), *Die lustigen Weiber von Windsor* (2 April 1921, 27 November 1922), *Oberon* (16 April 1921), *Le Prophète* (11 May 1921), *Karneval in Rom* (20 June 1921), *Die Zauberflöte* (7 September 1921), *Madama Butterfly* (17 September 1921), *Genesius* (8 October 1921), *Robert le diable* (5 November 1921), *Tristan und Isolde* (14 January 1922), *Otello* (20 January 1922), *Il piccolo Marat* (12 April 1922), *Die Fledermaus* (1 December 1922), *Der Wildschütz* (11 January 1923), *Les Contes d'Hoffmann* (12 February 1923), *The Children of Don* (29 March 1923), *Königskinder* (9 November 1923) and *La Muette de Portici* (29 December 1923).

66 With the end of World War I and the fall of the monarchies, Germany and Austria were in political and financial turmoil. Their opera companies suffered greatly during that period and were often a hotbed of political intrigue.

67 C. Höslinger, 'Zwei Jahrzehnte der Krise 1918–1938', *100 Jahre Wiener Volksoper* ed. U. Simek (Vienna, Cologne,Weimar, 1998), p. 49.

68 Characteristically, Weingartner's tenure at the Volksoper ended with rancour. In his autobiography, he recalled 'The Volksoper still owes me 2500 schillings, which I notified to the courts, but never collected.' Weingartner, *Buffets and Rewards*, p. 341.

69 In 1926, Weingartner visited Budapest, where he performed Verdi's *Aida*, Rossini's *Il barbiere di Siviglia*, Bizet's *Carmen* and Wagner's *Tannhäuser* at the City Theatre and was embroiled in a serious dispute with the management of the company.

70 Weingartner continued to conduct concerts as a guest with Vienna Philharmonic until 1937. His final concert with the orchestra was at the Musikvereinsaal on 26 February 1937.

71 Weingartner, *Buffets and Rewards*, p. 368.

72 Ibid.

73 The festivals followed a loose theme: in 1930 and 1931 the works of Mozart dominated; in 1932 Italian music; in 1933 the music of Beethoven, and in 1934 the compositions of Weber and Schubert.

74 New productions conducted by Weingartner at the Vienna Staatsoper between the beginning of 1935 and the end of 1936 included Ravel's *L'Heure espagnole* and Mussorgsky's *Sorochintsy Fair* (13 February 1935), Mozart's *Così fan tutte* (28 April 1935), Lortzing's *Zar und Zimmermann* (14 September 1935), Nicolai's *Die lustigen Weiber von Windsor* (29 September 1935), Offenbach's *Les Contes d'Hoffmann* (23 January 1936), Hubay's *Anna Karenina* (9 February 1936), Saint-Saëns's *Samson et Dalila* (28 March 1936), Millöcker's *Der Bettelstudent* (17 June 1936) and Kienzl's *Don Quixote* (22 November 1936).

75 Weingartner returned to the Vienna Staatsoper to conduct Kienzl's *Der Kuhreigen* on 12 January 1938.

76 Along with Welte, the American firms Duo-Art and Ampico also made reproducing pianos. Many of the leading artists of the day recorded their music for these companies, including Mahler, Grieg and Rachmaninoff.

77 For Welte, Weingartner recorded his *Vier Tonbilder zu Stifters 'Studien', Lose Blätter* and *Aus vergangener Zeit*, Bach's Prelude and Fugue in C major from Book 2 of *Das wohltemperierte Clavier*, Beethoven's Sonata in B flat major, Op. 106 ('Hammerklavier') (movements 1, 3 only), Chopin's Nocturne Op. 62 No. 2, Schubert's Sonata No. 21 (movements 2, 4 only) and Schumann's 'Eintritt' and 'Vogel als Prophet' from *Waldszenen*.

78 For detailed catalogue information, consult the following discographies: C. Dyment, 'Felix Weingartner', *Musica* 17 (Milan, April 1980), pp. 142–52, and J. Hunt, *More 20th Century Conductors* (London, 1993).

79 Weingartner was married five times.

80 Along with his *Frühlingsgespenster* and *Schäfers Sonntagslied*, Weingartner also recorded *Obstination* by Fontanaille with Marcel.

81 With the Columbia Symphony Orchestra, Weingartner recorded three of his songs with orchestra (Lucille Marcel, soprano), Bizet's Prelude and Adagietto from *L'Arlésienne* and Preludes to Acts 1 and 4 from *Carmen*, Schumann's *Frisches Grün* and *Die Lotosblume* (Lucille Marcel, soprano), an excerpt from the first movement of Tchaikovsky's Symphony No. 6 ('Pathétique'), Verdi's 'Ave Maria' from *Otello* (Lucille Marcel, soprano), Wagner's 'Liebestod' from *Tristan und Isolde* (Lucille Marcel, soprano) and 'Feuerzauber' from *Die Walküre* and Weber's *Aufforderung zum Tanz* (orch. Weingartner).

82 Weingartner also recorded with the British Symphony Orchestra, an ensemble of freelance musicians drawn from other London orchestras.

83 While willing to record Weingartner as an interpreter of the music of others, Columbia was reluctant to record music of his own creation. After 1913, Columbia restricted the recordings of his music to the following: Entr'acte from the incidental music to *Der Sturm* (London Symphony Orchestra, 1923); Scherzettino from the incidental music to *Der Sturm* (London Symphony Orchestra, 1923), and Scherzettino from the incidental music to *Der Sturm* (Basler Orchester-Gesellschaft, 1928).

84 Weingartner recorded Symphonies Nos. 2 and 3 and the 'Haydn' Variations with the London Philharmonic Orchestra, and Symphonies Nos. 1 and 4 and the *Academic Festival Overture* with the London Symphony Orchestra, between 1938 and 1940. For his 1928 recording of Brahms's Symphony No. 1, Weingartner used the orchestra of the Royal Philharmonic Society.

85 Weingartner recorded Beethoven's Symphony No. 5 with the London Symphony Orchestra in 1924, the orchestra of the Royal Philharmonic Society in 1927, the British Symphony Orchestra in 1932 and the London Philharmonic in 1933.

86 Weingartner later revised his treatise on Beethoven twice.

87 F. Weingartner, trans. E. Newman, *On Conducting* (London, 1906), p. 5.

88 Ibid., p. 9.

89 Ibid., p. 10.

90 Ibid., p. 39.

91 Ibid., pp. 28–9.

92 Ibid., p. 10.

93 Ibid., pp. 42–3.

94 The collection of Weingartner's possessions in Basel contains a number of batons, one of which is marked 'Weingartner, measuring 47.5 cm with a 9.5 cm grip. Both batons and handles are made of a light wood, possibly boxwood.

95 Weingartner, *On Conducting*, p. 44.
96 Weber, overture to *Der Freischütz*, Paris Symphony Orchestra (1932). Teldec Video 4509–95038–3.
97 *Musical Times*, June 1942, p. 192.

Chapter 5. Richard III: Richard Strauss

1 Richard III was Hans von Bülow's appellation for Strauss. Bülow argued that while there could be no Richard II after Wagner, Strauss was certainly Richard III.
2 Franz Strauss was born in Parkstein in 1822 and died in Munich in 1905.
3 F. Weingartner, *Über das Dirigieren* (1895), trans. E. Newman as *On Conducting* (London, 1906), p. 12.
4 Strauss's sister Berta Johanna was born on 9 June 1867.
5 August Tombo (1842–78). From 1861, Tombo was the harpist of the Munich Hofkapelle and was a teacher at the Royal School of Music in Munich. He taught Strauss piano from 1868.
6 R. Strauss, 'Reminiscences of Hans von Bülow', *Recollections and Reflections*, trans. L. J. Lawrence, ed. W. Schuh (London, 1953), p. 134.
7 The first opera that Strauss attended was Weber's *Der Freischütz*; he began violin lessons in 1872.
8 Friedrich Wilhelm Meyer (1818–93): German conductor and composer. In 1854, Meyer joined Lachner at the Munich Hofoper, becoming Hofmusikdirektor in 1858 and Hofkapellmeister in 1869. He taught Strauss between 1875 and 1880. The following works are dedicated to Meyer: Serenade in G major; WoO 32 Ouvertüre in A minor WoO 62 and Serenade in E flat major Op. 7. In 1875, Strauss became a piano student of Carl Niest.
9 Strauss's letter to Ludwig Thuille, dated 4 April 1878. As found in 'Selections from the Strauss–Thuille Correspondence', trans. S. Gillespie, ed. B. Gilliam, *Richard Strauss and His World* (Princeton, 1992), pp. 207–9.
10 Levi conducted Strauss's Symphony in D minor and Concert Overture in C minor at the Munich Odeonssaal on 30 March 1881 and 28 November 1883 respectively.
11 Strauss, *Recollections and Reflections*, p. 119.
12 The Odeonssaal was opened in 1828 and was one of Munich's principal concert halls. It was destroyed during World War II.
13 Strauss, *Recollections and Reflections*, p. 119.
14 Ibid., p. 120.
15 Strauss wrote his own cadenzas for the Mozart concerto at Munich in 1885 but they are now lost.
16 Strauss, *Recollections and Reflections*, p. 123.
17 Bülow's letter to Strauss's first publisher, Eugen Spitzweg, dated 20 October 1885. As found in W. Schuh, trans. M. Whittall, *Richard Strauss: A Chronicle of the Early Years, 1864–1898* (Cambridge, 1982), p. 94. On the day before Strauss's Meiningen début, Bülow wrote to Hermann Wolff: '[Strauss] is developing into an excellent musician in every way . . . [and] he's going to make a success of the Mozart Concerto as of everything else the first time he tries.' Ibid.
18 See Chapter 1 notes 101, 102, 103.
19 Strauss, *Recollections and Reflections*, p. 123.
20 Ibid., p. 124.
21 Ibid., p. 123.
22 Ibid., p. 118.

23 Ibid., p. 136.
24 Strauss removed the trombones from both the Lacrimosa and Quam olim Abrahae in the Requiem. Strauss's letter to his father, dated 7 November 1885. R. Strauss, ed. W. Schuh *Briefe an die Eltern 1882–1906* (Zürich, 1954), p. 69.
25 Letter from Strauss to his father, dated 31 January 1886. Ibid., p. 85.
26 During the 1886–7 season, Strauss conducted one performance each of Rheinberger's *Türmers Töchterlein* (26 January 1887) and Verdi's *Il trovatore* (23 June 1887), two each of Mozart's *Così fan tutte* (12 and 17 November 1886), Auber's *Le Domino noir* (1 February, 29 March 1887) and *Fra Diavolo* (8 February, 17 March 1887) and Lortzing's *Die beiden Schützen* (17 and 21 June 1887), three each of Goldmark's *Die Königin von Saba* (20 and 25 March, 15 April 1887) and Cherubini's *Les Deux Journées* (13, 20 and 24 May 1887) and four of Boieldieu's *Jean de Paris* (1 and 12 October, 16 November 1886, 7 May 1887).
27 See note 26.
28 During the 1887–8 season, Strauss conducted one performance each of Mozart's *Così fan tutte* (3 November 1887), Verdi's *Il trovatore* (18 November 1887), Cherubini's *Les Deux Journées* (22 March 1888), Flotow's *Alessandro Stradella* (30 April 1888) and Cornelius's *Der Barbier von Bagdad* (24 July 1888), two of Lortzing's *Zar und Zimmermann* (29 November, 22 December 1887) and three each of Lortzing's *Die beiden Schützen* (8 and 22 November 1887, 1 March 1888) and Weber's *Der Freischütz* (17 April, 21 June, 31 July 1888).
29 During the 1888–9 season, Strauss conducted one performance of Verdi's *Un ballo in maschera* (18 February 1889) and two each of Cornelius's *Der Barbier von Bagdad* (29 August 1888, 31 January 1889), Weber's *Der Freischütz* (6 September, 13 November 1888), Lortzing's *Die beiden Schützen* (18 December 1888, 21 February 1889) and Donizetti's *La Favorite* (2 and 7 February 1889).
30 Alexander Ritter (1833–1896): Estonian-born violinist and composer.
31 *Die Feen* was composed by Wagner during 1833–4.
32 Franz Fischer (1849–1918): German conductor. After a brief period as Hofkapellmeister at Mannheim (1877–9), Fischer joined the staff of the Munich Hofoper, where he worked until his retirement in 1912.
33 Strauss, *Recollections and Reflections*, p. 130.
34 Ibid., p. 131.
35 Information concerning Strauss's Weimar period was kindly provided by Dr Kenneth Birkin. For a detailed study of Strauss's activities in Weimar see K. Birkin, 'Richard Strauss in Weimar', *Richard Strauss-Blätter* 33 (June 1995), pp. 3–36; 34 (December 1995), pp. 3–56.
36 See Chapter 1 note 84.
37 The figure of sixteen Abonnement concerts does not include the concerts that Strauss directed for the Liszt Stiftung or those that he performed on behalf of the Hofkapelle's fund for widows and orphans.
38 At the Abonnement Concerts, Strauss conducted Beethoven's Symphony No. 3 on 13 October 1890 and 15 December 1893, Symphony No. 5 on 23 November 1891, Symphony No. 6 on 11 November 1889, Symphony No. 7 on 6 November 1893 and Symphony No. 8 on 26 January 1891. Strauss also conducted Symphonies Nos. 7 and 8 outside the Abonnement Concerts on 17 January 1880 and 5 January 1894 respectively.
39 Strauss conducted Beethoven's Piano Concertos Nos. 3 (Bernhard Stavenhagen, piano) and 4 (Margarethe Stern, piano) on 25 November 1889 and 30 January 1892 respectively, the Violin Concerto and the Romance in F major (Karl Halir, violin) on 17 November 1890 and 23 November 1891 respectively, Clärchen's 'Die Trommel gerühret' and 'Freudvoll und leidvoll' from the music to *Egmont* (Pauline de Ahna, soprano) on 26 January 1891 and the overtures *König*

Stephan, Leonore No. 1, *Egmont, Die Weihe des Hauses* and *Coriolan* on 28 October 1889, 25 November 1889, 26 January 1891, 30 January 1892 and 4 December 1893 respectively.

40 The other works by Mozart that Strauss conducted at the Abonnement Concerts were 'Der Stern meiner Liebe strahlt tröstend hernieder' from *Così fan tutte* and Piano Concerto No. 20 (Muriel Elliot, piano) on 19 October 1891 and Piano Concerto No. 26 (Bernhard Stavenhagen, piano) on 20 October 1893. At the pension fund concerts, Strauss and Lassen were soloists for a performance of the Concerto for Two Pianos on 11 January 1892 and Strauss conducted Violin Concerto No. 5 (Joseph Joachim, violin) and an aria with obbligato violin (Pauline de Ahna, soprano; Joseph Joachim, violin) on 5 January 1894.

41 In the first half of the Abonnement Concert on 26 January 1891, Strauss conducted Beethoven's Symphony No. 8, Clärchen's 'Die Trommel gerühret' and 'Freudvoll und leidvoll' from the incidental music to *Egmont* (Pauline de Ahna, soprano) and the overture to *Egmont*.

42 The other works by Wagner that Strauss conducted at the Abonnement Concerts were *A Faust Overture* on 9 December 1889 and 23 November 1891, *Huldigungsmarsch* on 9 December 1889 and the *Kaisermarsch* on 7 December 1891. Strauss also accompanied a performance of *Der Engel* (Pauline de Ahna, soprano) on 7 December 1891.

43 Strauss conducted *Die Ideale* on 28 October 1889, *Totentanz* (Bernhard Stavenhagen, piano) on 25 November 1889, *A Faust Symphony* on 17 November 1890, *Ce qu'on entend sur la montagne* on 12 January 1891, *Les Préludes* on 19 October 1891, *Mazeppa* on 7 December 1891 and *Festklänge* on 20 November 1893.

44 The three all-Liszt programmes in which Strauss took part were held on 28 April 1890, 13 April 1891 and 24 October 1892. At the 1890 concert, Strauss conducted *Hunnenschlacht*, Piano Concerto No. 2 (Bernhard Stavenhagen, piano) and an unspecified *Mephisto Waltz* (the remainder of the programme was given over to Lieder and solo works); at the 1891 concert, he conducted *Orpheus*, *Totentanz* (Bernhard Stavenhagen, piano), Liszt's arrangement of Schubert's *Die junge Nonne* (Agnes Stavenhagen, soprano), *Die Loreley* (Agnes Stavenhagen, soprano), Piano Concerto No. 2 (Bernhard Stavenhagen, piano) and 'Dante' Symphony, and, at the 1892 concert, he conducted *Orpheus, Totentanz* (Bernhard Stavenhagen, piano), *Freudvoll und leidvoll, Die Loreley* and *Lasst mich ruhen* (Hermine Fink, soprano) and *Tasso* (the programme also included solo works for piano played by Stavenhagen).

45 The remainder of the programme on 28 October 1889 was Beethoven's overture *König Stephan*, Lalo's *Symphonie espagnole* (Karl Halir, violin), Bülow's *Nirwana*, Lassen's *Frühling, Frühlingsgruss* and *Ich fühle deinen Odem* (Heinrich Zeller, tenor), Ritter's *Sternen ewig* (Heinrich Zeller, tenor) and Liszt's *Die Ideale*.

46 See R. Holden, 'Recording, *Don Juan*: The Composer's Perspective', *Richard Strauss-Blätter* 40 (December 1998), pp. 52–70.

47 Strauss, *Briefe an die Eltern*, p. 119 [trans. present author].

48 Ibid., p. 120.

49 Ibid., p. 120–1.

50 See R. Strauss, 'Is There an Avant-garde in Music?', *Recollections and Reflections*, pp. 12–17.

51 The Lieder that Strauss performed at Weimar included *Ständchen* (Heinrich Zeller, tenor) on 28 October 1889, *Seitdem dein Aug' in meines schaute* and *Nichts* (Heinrich Zeller, tenor) on 13 October 1890 and four Lieder from *Lotosblätter* Op. 19 (Heinrich Giessen, tenor) on 6 November 1893.

52 Strauss conducted Bülow's *Nirwana* on 28 October 1889, Saint-Saëns's Cello Concerto (Leonhard Halir, cello) on 11 November 1889, Lassen's Violin Con-

certo (Karl Halir, violin) on 17 January 1890, Weiss's Piano Concerto Op. 13 (Josef Weiss, piano) on 12 January 1891, Ritter's *Seraphische Fantasie* on 23 November 1891, Bruch's Violin Concerto No. 3 (Karl Halir, violin) on 23 November 1891, Humperdinck's *Die Wallfahrt nach Kevlaar* for soloists, chorus and orchestra (Louise Tibelti, mezzo-soprano; Heinrich Zeller, tenor Hoftheater Chor) on 30 January 1892, Brahms's Violin Concerto (Karl Halir, violin) on 6 November 1893, Halir's Violin Concerto (Karl Halir, violin) on 6 November 1893, Stavenhagen's Piano Concerto (Bernhard Stavenhagen, piano) on 20 November 1893 and Draeseke's Sinfonisches Vorspiel to *Das Leben ein Traum* on 15 December 1893.

Strauss included the following Lieder with piano accompaniment by contemporary composers at his subscription and non-subscription concerts: Lassen's *Frühling, Frühlingsgruss* and *Ich fühle deinen Odem* (Heinrich Zeller, tenor) on 28 October 1889, *Die Musikantin* (Fräulein Alt, soprano) on 11 November 1889 and *Dornröschen* (Frau Moran-Olden, soprano) on 17 January 1890; Brahms's *Ständchen* (Frau Moran-Olden) on 17 January 1890; Ritter's *Sternen ewig* (Heinrich Zeller, tenor) on 28 October 1889 and *Erklärung, Ich möchte ein Lied dir weihn* and *In Lust und Schmerzen* (Heinrich Zeller, tenor) on 13 October 1890; Thuille's *Botschaft* and *Waldesgang* on 13 October 1890, and Sommer's *Abschied, Froh im Gesang* and *Ganz leise* (Heinrich Giessen, tenor) on 19 October 1891 and *Der Mönch: O du seliges Wandern am Rhein* (Franz Schwarz, baritone) on 15 December 1893.

53 Operas that were conducted by Strauss as part of a double bill have been counted separately.

54 Strauss conducted the world première of Humperdinck's *Hänsel und Gretel* on 23 December 1893.

55 During his first season at Weimar, Strauss conducted Mozart's *Die Zauberflöte* (four performances), *Le nozze di Figaro* (three performances) and *Don Giovanni* (one performance), Wagner's *Lohengrin* (five performances) and *Tannhäuser* (four performances), Weber's *Der Freischütz* (five performances) and *Preciosa* (two performances), Méhul's *Joseph* (four performances), Lortzing's *Zar und Zimmermann* (four performances), *Der Waffenschmied* (three performances) and *Der Wildschütz* (five performances), Marschner's *Hans Heiling* (two performances), Flotow's *Alessandro Stradella* (two performances), Ritter's *Wem die Kron?* (three performances) and *Der faule Hans* (three performances) and Auber's *Le Cheval de bronze* (four performances).

56 Strauss conducted *Wem die Kron?* and *Der faule Hans* on 8, 10 and 17 June 1890.

57 The other performances of *Wem die Kron?* and *Der faule Hans* that Strauss conducted at Weimar were on 28 September and 7 October 1890, 17 November and 9 December 1891 and 16 February 1892.

58 As Strauss was absent from Weimar for much of the 1892–3 season, he did not perform *Tannhäuser* or *Lohengrin* during that period.

59 In the 1890–1 season, Strauss conducted Mozart's *Le nozze di Figaro* (three performances), *Die Zauberflöte* (three performances) and *Don Giovanni* (three performances), Ritter's *Wem die Kron?* (two performances) and *Der faule Hans* (two performances), Lortzing's *Der Wildschütz* (three performances) and *Der Waffenschmied* (three performances), Wagner's *Rienzi* (four performances), *Tannhäuser* (five performances) and *Lohengrin* (five performances), Marschner's *Hans Heiling* (two performances), Weber's *Der Freischütz* (four performances), Gluck's *Iphigénie en Aulide* (two performances), Kreutzer's *Das Nachtlager in Granada* (two performances) and Auber's *La Muette de Portici* (one performance).

In the 1891–2 season, Strauss conducted Mozart's *Die Entführung aus dem Serail* (two performances), *Die Zauberflöte* (three performances) and *Don Giovanni* (two performances), Wagner's *Tristan und Isolde* (six performances), *Lohengrin* (five performances, one of which was at Eisenach), *Rienzi* (one performance) and *Tannhäuser* (four performances), Gluck's *Iphigénie en Aulide* (three performances), Lortzing's *Der Waffenschmied* (two performances), *Der Wildschütz* (three performances) and *Zar und Zimmermann* (one performance), Ritter's *Wem die Kron?* (three performances) and *Der faule Hans* (three performances), Weber's *Der Freischütz* (three performances) and *Preciosa* (one performance), Kreutzer's *Das Nachtlager in Granada* (two performances), Beethoven's *Fidelio* (one performance), Cherubini's *Les Deux Journées* (three performances) and Sommer's *Loreley* (two performances).

60 During his convalescence, Strauss visited Egypt, Sicily and Corfu.

61 During the 1893–4 season, Strauss conducted Weber's *Der Freischütz* (three performances) and *Preciosa* (one performance), Lortzing's *Der Waffenschmied* (one performance) and *Zar und Zimmermann* (two performances), Flotow's *Alessandro Stradella* (one performance), Mozart's *Don Giovanni* (four performances), *Bastien und Bastienne* (three performances) and *Die Zauberflöte* (two performances), Metzdorff's *Hagbart und Signe* (three performances), Wagner's *Die Meistersinger von Nürnberg* (one performance), *Tannhäuser* (five performances), *Lohengrin* (four performances) and *Tristan und Isolde* (three performances), Humperdinck's *Hänsel und Gretel* (eight performances), Mottl's *Fürst und Sänger* (two performances), Fiebach's *Bei frommen Hirten* (two performances) and his own *Guntram* (four performances).

62 Strauss directed the world première of *Guntram* on 10 May 1894.

63 Franz Strauss's letter to Richard Strauss, dated 16 March 1893. Strauss, *Briefe an die Eltern*, pp. 167–9.

64 The figure of 272 performances includes Strauss's performances of Beethoven's overture *Leonore* No. 2 and Act 2 of *Fidelio* on 20 April 1898 to mark the silver wedding anniversary of Prince Leopold of Bavaria. Strauss also conducted the first part of a performance at the Hofoper on 31 January 1897 to mark the 100th anniversary of Schubert's birth, but that performance is not included in the above tally.

Between 7 October 1894 and 18 October 1898, Strauss conducted Mozart's *Die Zauberflöte* (14 performances), *Le nozze di Figaro* (one performance), *Don Giovanni* (32 performances), *Die Entführung aus dem Serail* (19 performances) and *Così fan tutte* (18 performances), Lortzing's *Der Waffenschmied* (six performances), Weber's *Oberon* (three performances) and *Der Freischütz* (one performance), Wagner's *Die Meistersinger von Nürnberg* (16 performances), *Tristan und Isolde* (24 performances), *Tannhäuser* (30 performances), *Rienzi* (13 performances) and *Der fliegende Holländer* (two performances), Humperdinck's *Hänsel und Gretel* (nine performances), Liszt's *Die Legende von der heiligen Elisabeth* (five performances), Brüll's *Das goldene Kreuz* (five performances), Maillart's *Les Dragons de Villars* (three performances), Flotow's *Martha* (seven performances), Bizet's *Carmen* (six performances), Nicolai's *Die lustigen Weiber von Windsor* (six performances), Verdi's *Il trovatore* (three performances) and *Un ballo in maschera* (one performance), Kreutzer's *Das Nachtlager in Granada* (six performances), Zöllner's *Der Überfall* (four performances), Beethoven's *Fidelio* (eight performances), Rossini's *Il barbiere di Siviglia* (three performances), Gluck's *Iphigénie en Aulide* (three performances) and *Orfeo ed Euridice* (one performance), Adam's *La Poupée de Nuremberg* (seven performances), Cornelius's *Der Barbier von Bagdad* (four performances), Thuille's *Theuerdank* (four performances), Smetana's *The Bartered Bride* (two performances), Schilling's

Ingwelde (three performances), Hausegger's *Zinnober* (two performances) and his own *Guntram* (one performance).

65 R. Strauss, 'Erinnerungen an die ersten Aufführungen meiner Opern', *Betrachtungen und Erinnerungen*, ed. W. Schuh (Zürich, 1949), p. 178.

66 K. Wilhelm, trans. M. Whittall, *Richard Strauss: An Intimate Portrait*, (London, 1989), p. 56.

67 Ernst von Possart (1841–1921): German actor and theatre manager. Possart was manager of the Munich Theatre from 1875 and Intendant of the Royal Theatres from 1895 to 1905. For him, Strauss composed the melodramas *Enoch Arden* and *Das Schloss am Meere*, which they premièred at Munich and Berlin on 24 March 1897 and 23 March 1899 respectively.

68 At the summer seasons, Strauss conducted four performances of *Rienzi* and three each of *Tannhäuser*, *Tristan und Isolde* and *Die Meistersinger von Nürnberg* in 1895, four performances of *Tannhäuser*, three each of *Tristan und Isolde* and *Die Meistersinger von Nürnberg* and two of *Rienzi* in 1896, eight performances of *Tristan und Isolde* and five of *Tannhäuser* in 1897 and two performances each of *Tristan und Isolde* and *Tannhäuser* in 1898.

69 Strauss conducted the première of the new production of *Don Giovanni* on 29 May 1896. He had conducted two performances of an earlier production on 12 and 26 December 1895. He had conducted the new productions of *Die Entführung aus dem Serail*, *Così fan tutte* and *Die Zauberflöte* on 3 February 1897, 25 June 1897 and 30 April 1898 respectively. Strauss conducted four performances of an earlier production of *Die Zauberflöte* at Munich on 7 October and 13 December 1894, 7 October 1895 and 27 January 1896.

70 R. Holden, *Richard Strauss: The Origin, Dissemination and Reception of His Mozart Renaissance*, Ph.D. dissertation, University of London, 1995.

71 The basis for these reforms was set out in Possart's article *Ueber die Neueinstudierung und Neuinszenierung des Mozart'schen Don Giovanni (Don Juan) auf dem kgl. Residenztheater zu München* (Munich, 1896).

72 By performing the Prague version of *Don Giovanni*, Strauss and Possart reinstated the epilogue, which had fallen from favour during the nineteenth century.

73 Strauss's approach to continuo playing was inimitable and often involved quotes from his own works. The conductor Wolfgang Sawallisch heard Strauss in the theatre and recalled in his autobiography: 'What he [Strauss] played on the cembalo during the recitatives could not be repeated today. From the outset, Strauss's Mozart was a total surprise, but then, after a few moments, I grasped that every theme that he charmingly interwove had an exact reference to the action somewhere on the stage. When there was a joke, witticism or some other form of humour on stage, there suddenly appeared a touch of *Till Eulenspiegel*, or when there was a romantic exchange between Fiordiligi and Ferrando, a touch of *Don Juan* would ring out! But one knew exactly that each of the situations was correctly represented. Eventually, one waited for what would come next! So, suddenly, one was confronted with a completely different style which made Mozart live, a topical style of Mozart interpretation, even though Strauss was at least seventy years old.' W. Sawallisch, *Im Interesse der Deutlichkeit: Mein Leben mit der Musik* (Hamburg, 1988), pp. 29–30 [trans. present author].

74 R. Strauss, 'Die Münchener Oper', *Betrachtungen und Erinnerungen*, p. 97.

75 With the Berlin Philharmonic, Strauss conducted Beethoven's Symphony No. 7 on 15 October 1894, overture *Leonore* No. 3 on 12 November 1894, Symphony No. 2 on 26 November 1894, Symphony No. 3 on 14 January 1895, the overture to *Egmont* on 28 January 1895, Symphony No. 5 on 18 February 1895 and the overture to *Coriolan* on 18 March 1895.

76 At the Philharmonic Concerts, Strauss programmed Saint-Saëns's Introduction

and Rondo capriccioso (Pablo de Sarasate, violin) on 12 November 1894 and Piano Concerto No. 4 (Josef Hofmann, piano) on 4 March 1895, Schillings's Prelude to Act 2 from *Ingwelde* on 15 October 1894, Rubinstein's Piano Concerto in D minor (Fannie Bloomfield-Zeisler, piano) on 29 October 1894, d'Albert's Prelude to *Der Rubin* on 10 December 1894, Ritter's *Olafs Hochzeitsreigen* on 26 November 1894, Gernsheim's Violin Concerto (Emile Sauret, violin) on 14 January 1895, Stenhammar's Piano Concerto Op. 1 (Wilhelm Stenhammar, piano) on 10 December 1894, Sauret's Elégie and Rondo (Emile Sauret, violin) on 14 January 1895 and three movements from Mahler's Symphony No. 2 ('Resurrection') with Mahler conducting on 4 March 1895.

77 On 18 March 1895, Strauss conducted the Preludes to Acts 1 and 2, 'Friedenserzählung' (Heinrich Zeller, tenor) and the Conclusion to Act 3 from *Guntram*. The remainder of the programme included Beethoven's overture to *Coriolan*, vocal scenes by Spohr (Heinrich Zeller, tenor), Schumann's overture to *Manfred* and violin solos played by Leopold Auer.

78 See Chapter 2.

79 The programme that Strauss conducted on 16 November 1894 included Berlioz's overture *Le Roi Lear*, Schillings's Prelude to Act 2 from *Ingwelde*, Mozart's Violin Concerto No. 4 (Joseph Miroslav Weber, violin), violin solos by Paganini (Joseph Miroslav Weber, violin) and Beethoven's Symphony No. 7.

80 The works that Strauss conducted at both Munich and Berlin included Beethoven's Symphonies Nos. 2 and 7, Schillings's Prelude to Act 2 from *Ingwelde* and extracts from his own *Guntram*.

81 Among the works by contemporary composers that Strauss programmed with the Hofkapelle during the 1894–5 season were Schillings's Prelude to Act 2 from *Ingwelde* (16 November 1894), Rubinstein's Piano Concerto in D minor (Fannie Bloomfield-Zeisler, piano) (30 November 1894) and 'Ocean' Symphony (9 February 1895), Rheinberger's Concerto for Organ (soloist unknown) (14 December 1894), Gilson's *La Mer* (14 December 1894), extracts from his own *Guntram* (25 December 1894) and the world première of Bussmeyer's Concert Overture in C minor (22 February 1895).

82 The works by living or recently deceased composers that Strauss programmed in the Hofkapelle's 1895–6 season included his own *Till Eulenspiegel* (29 November 1895), Schillings's *Meergruss* and *Seemorgan* (7 February 1896), Ritter's *Sursum corda* (6 March 1896) and Brahms's Symphony No. 4 (20 March 1896).

83 Strauss conducted Beethoven's Symphony No. 1 on 15 November 1895, Symphony No. 2 on 29 November 1895, Symphony No. 3 ('Eroica') on 10 December 1895, Symphony No. 4 on 25 December 1895, Symphony No. 5 on 7 February 1896, Symphony No. 6 on 24 February 1896, Symphony No. 7 on 6 March 1896, Symphony No. 8 on 20 March 1896 and Symphony No. 9 ('Choral') on 27 April 1896. Symphony No. 9 was performed outside the Abonnement series and was given at a concert at which Strauss replaced an indisposed Franz Fischer.

84 At Berlin, Strauss conducted Wagner's *Der Ring des Nibelungen* for the first time. He performed *Das Rheingold* on 19 June 1899, *Die Walküre* on 20 June 1899, *Siegfried* on 22 June 1899 and *Götterdämmerung* on 24 June 1899.

85 J. Kapp, *Richard Strauss und die Berliner Oper* (Berlin-Halensee, 1939), p. 39.

86 Ibid.

87 Strauss conducted *Guntram* at Weimar on 10, 15 and 24 May and 1 June 1894 and at Munich on 16 November 1895.

88 Some years later, Strauss erected a memorial to *Guntram* in his garden. The inscription leaves no doubt that the opera was, at least in Strauss's mind, 'horribly slain', by his own 'symphony orchestra'.

89 After the fall of Kaiser Wilhelm II at the end of World War I, the Berlin Hofkapelle became known as the Berlin Staatskapelle.

90 This figure excludes the performances in which Strauss programmed his tone poems in the same evening as either *Elektra* or *Salome* but includes the Sonderkonzerte.

91 Strauss's tenure with the Berlin Hofkapelle was from 1908 to 1919. He conducted Mahler's Symphony No. 1 on 13 December 1909 and 22 March 1918, Symphony No. 2 on 25 November 1914, Symphony No. 3 on 11 December 1911, Symphony No. 4 on 15 January 1909 and *Das Lied von der Erde* on 7 November 1913.

Strauss conducted Hochberg's Symphony No. 3 on 17 December 1909, Boehe's *Die Klage der Nausikaa* on 23 March 1911, Hausegger's *Natursinfonie* on 15 February 1912 and *Barbarossa* on 21 January 1916, Rüfer's Symphony No. 1 on 28 February 1912, Taubert's Suite for string orchestra in D major on 22 March 1912 and Symphony in G minor on 6 December 1918, Reznicek's Prelude and Figure on 14 February 1913, Scrontino's *Romantische Sinfonie* on 9 March 1914, Georg Schumann's Bach Variations on 22 March 1914 and *Im Ringen nach dem Ideal* on 22 April 1916, Koch's *Halali* on 22 March 1915, Mandl's *Ouvertüre zu einem Gascogner Ritterspiel* on 9 March 1916, Szell's Variations on an Original Theme on 8 December 1916, Müller-Herrmann's *Sinfonische Ouvertüre* on 22 March 1917, Weingartner's Symphony No. 4 on 6 November 1917 and Strässer's *Drei Frühlingsbilder* on 30 November 1917.

92 When Strauss accepted the direction of the Berliner Tonkünstler-Orchester in 1901, he made it clear to the ensemble's administration from the outset that he intended to pursue his interest in modern music. At the two seasons of six concerts each that he performed with the orchestra, he conducted, among others, works by Sgambati, d'Indy, Hausegger, Mahler, Rösch, Elgar, Thuille, Blech, Nietzel, Bruneau, Pfitzner, Schillings, Ritter, Reznicek, Sauer, Bischoff, Stanford, Brecher and Rüfer. See K. Birkin '". . . wollen sehen, ob's gelingt" Richard Strauss and the Berlin Tonkünstler-Orchester', *Richard Strauss-Blätter* 46 (December 2001), pp. 3–60.

93 Franz Schalk (1863–1931): Austrian conductor. After engagements at Reichenberg (1888), Graz (1890–5), Prague (1895–8) and Berlin (1898–1900), Schalk joined the staff of the Vienna Hofoper in 1900, being promoted to Leiter in 1919. In recent years, his influence over Bruckner and his editing of the composer's symphonies have been the subject of lively academic debate.

94 Letter from Hugo von Hofmannsthal to Richard Strauss, dated 1 August 1918. As found in *The Correspondence between Richard Strauss and Hugo von Hofmannsthal*, ed. F. and A. Strauss, arr. W. Schuh, trans. H. Hammelmann and E. Osers (Cambridge, 1980), pp. 307–9.

95 Ibid.

96 Letter from Richard Strauss to Hugo von Hofmannsthal, dated 5 August 1918. Ibid., pp. 309–11.

97 Ibid.

98 Ibid.

99 *Salome* received its première at Dresden on 9 December 1905.

100 Player pianos could reproduce the duration of the notes with relative accuracy but could not replicate the player's articulation and dynamics fully.

101 Strauss was in the recording studio on 5, 6, 13, 15 and 20 December 1916. Franz Trenner, ed. Florian Trenner, *Richard Strauss: Chronik zu Leben und Werk* (Vienna, 2003), pp. 379–80.

102 R. Wimbush, 'Here and There', *The Gramophone*, May 1968, p. 585.

103 Written in response to a request for verification by Yale Collection of Historical

Sound Recordings. P. Morse, 'Richard Strauss' Recordings: A Complete Discography', *Journal of the Association for Recorded Sound Collections* 9:1 (1977), p. 12.

104 On the labels of the 1921 gramophone recordings, the orchestra is anonymous, but because the recordings were made in November that year, it is likely that it is the Chicago Symphony Orchestra. Strauss's 1921–2 tour of the USA was the third of his four visits to that country. His other tours of North America were in 1904, 1920 and 1923.

In 1921, Strauss also made his first recordings as an accompanist. In Berlin, he recorded some of his songs with the tenor Robert Hutt and the baritone Heinrich Schlusnus, for Deutsche Grammophon. During his 1921–2 tour of the USA, Strauss recorded the accompaniments to *Zueignung*, *Allerseelen* and *Traum durch die Dämmerung* in December 1921 on piano rolls for the Ampico company. The accompaniments were intended for amateur singers whose desire to be accompanied by the composer could be fulfilled in the comfort of their parlour. Each accompaniment was recorded twice in different keys.

105 As guest conductor, Strauss performed in Britain between 1897 and 1947. See R. Holden, 'Richard Strauss in London', *Richard Strauss-Blätter* 37 (June 1997), pp. 18–53.

106 At the concert on 17 January 1922, Strauss conducted a selection of songs with orchestra (Ethel Frank, soprano) and the tone poems *Don Juan*, *Till Eulenspiegel* and *Tod und Verklärung*.

107 In the 1922 recording of *Don Juan*, Strauss cuts from bar 208 to bar 232. On 19 January 1922, Strauss was again in the studio with the London Symphony Orchestra. At that session, he recorded the waltzes from Act 2 of *Der Rosenkavalier* and the 'Tanz' (Dance of the Seven Veils) from *Salome*.

108 *The Times*, 14 January 1922.

109 The film of *Der Rosenkavalier* was shot in 1925 and directed by Robert Wiene; Wiene also made *The Cabinet of Dr Caligari*.

110 Strauss conducted another performance of the film music at the Stadttheater in Zürich on 16 July 1926.

111 Strauss recorded Beethoven's Symphonies Nos. 5 and 7 with the Berlin Staatskapelle in 1928 and 1926 respectively.

112 From the matrix numbers, *Till Eulenspiegel* seems to have been recorded in advance of *Don Juan*. As the matrices for the two tone poems are non-consecutive, it is possible that these recordings were made on separate occasions, but that possibility is remote in view of the conductor's and the orchestra's complex schedules.

113 Strauss had recorded *Ein Heldenleben* and *Tod und Verklärung* with the Berlin Staatskapelle in 1926.

114 Strauss's performing version of *Idomeneo* was given its première in Vienna on 16 April 1931. See R. Holden, 'Richard Strauss' Performing Version of Idomeneo', *Richard Strauss-Blätter* 36 (December 1996), pp. 83–131.

115 The recording of Strauss's 1941 performance of *Idomeneo* was released by Koch Schwann (3–1453–2).

116 Strauss conducted *Salome* at the Vienna Staatsoper on 15 February, 5 March, 23 March and 6 May 1942.

117 May recorded Paul Schöffler and Hans Hotter singing the role of Jochanaan on 15 February 1942 and 6 May 1942 respectively.

118 Between 1942 and 1943, Austrian Radio also recorded Strauss accompanying some forty of his songs with leading singers from the Vienna Staatsoper.

119 Strauss and his cousin, the violinist Benno Walter, gave the première of Strauss's

Violin Concerto at the Bösendorfersaal, Vienna, on 5 December 1882. For that performance, Strauss accompanied Walter at the piano.

120 Strauss conducted the Vienna Philharmonic on 16 December 1906, 3 March and 1 December 1907 and 8 March 1908.

121 In advance of the 1944 recordings, Strauss documented *Also sprach Zarathustra* (10 March 1942), some Lieder (12 March 1942), *Till Eulenspiegel* (12 March 1942) and the *Symphonia domestica* (17 February 1943) with the Vienna Philharmonic for Austrian Radio.

122 As Strauss's daughter-in-law was Jewish, the Nazis also considered his two grandsons ethnic Jews.

123 Strauss was appointed President of the Reichsmusikkammer in 1933 but he was removed from office in 1935.

124 R. Strauss and S. Zweig, trans. M. Knight, *A Confidential Matter: The Letters of Richard Strauss and Stefan Zweig, 1931–1935* (London, 1977), pp. 99–100. Strauss's letter never reached Zweig, who committed suicide in Brazil in 1942. The letter was found in the Gestapo's files in 1948.

125 A communiqué issued on 24 January 1944 by the Partei-Kanzlei (party headquarters) of the Nationalsozialistische Deutsche Arbeiterpartei.

126 In an interview with the present author, Wolfgang Sawallisch was asked whether he felt Strauss showed little interest as a participant. Sawallisch replied: 'That is certainly not true. One thing is absolutely true, that his conducting always retained a certain distance between himself and the symphonies. Some people have said that his conducting was too cold and with a certain reservation but I feel it wasn't true. He was too great a musician to make too many personal influences in the music. Perhaps [it was] for this reason and because he was an active composer that he had such respect and kept a certain distance.' Interview with Wolfgang Sawallisch, Henry Wood Hall (London), 12 December 1991.

127 Letter from Franz Strauss to his son, dated 26 October 1885. Strauss, *Briefe an die Eltern*, p. 64.

128 R. Strauss, 'On Conducting Classical Masterpieces', *Recollections and Reflections*, p. 44.

129 Ibid.

130 Ibid.

131 As found in Strauss, *Recollections and Reflections*, p. 38.

132 The present author has written extensively on Strauss's activities as a performer and much of that research has been published in the *Richard Strauss-Blätter*, the journal of the Internationale Richard Strauss-Gesellschaft (Vienna).

Chapter 6. 'That greasy rascal Bruno Walter'

1 Richard Strauss's letter to Stefan Zweig, dated 17 June 1935. See Chapter 5 note 124.

2 Walter's daughter, Gretel, was murdered by her husband in 1939 after his discovery that she had been having an affair with the Italian bass Ezio Pinza.

3 Although Walter was known as Schlesinger until his move to Breslau in 1876, his adopted name, Walter, will be used throughout the chapter to avoid confusion.

4 B. Walter, trans. J. A. Galston, *Theme and Variations: An Autobiography* (London, 1947), p. 2.

5 Walter's father, Joseph, was a bookkeeper, and his mother, Johanna, was a musician who had studied at the Stern Conservatory. His siblings were Leo and Emma Schlesinger.

6 According to Walter, Radecke wrote a testimonial at the end of the interview that 'conclud[ed] with the words: "Every inch of him is music"'. Ibid., p. 10.

7 The concert was an Öffentliche Prüfung (public examination) held by the Stern Conservatory. Along with the choir of the conservatory, sixteen other young musicians and speakers performed at that examination. The performance was conducted by Robert Radecke.

8 At that concert, Walter also played piano solos by Bach and Chopin. The concert also included the Berlin Philharmonic première of Goldmark's overture *Im Frühling*. The conductor was Gustav F. Kogel.

9 During the first decade of the twentieth century, some of Walter's works were performed at leading venues by artists and organizations of renown, including the Rosé Quartet, who performed his String Quartet in D major in 1903 and his Piano Trio in 1907, the Tonkünstler-Versammlung, which performed his Symphonic Fantasy at Frankfurt in 1904 and the Konzertverein Orchestra of Vienna, which performed his Symphony No. 1 under his direction at the Musikverein in 1909.

10 Walter heard Mozart's *Le nozze di Figaro* and *Don Giovanni*, Rossini's *Il barbiere di Siviglia* and Verdi's *Rigoletto* and *Un ballo in maschera* at the Kroll Theatre, and Lortzing's *Undine* and Mozart's *Die Zauberflöte* at the Hofoper. Walter, *Theme and Variations*, p. 31.

11 Ibid., pp. 40–1.

12 The performance of *Tristan und Isolde* that Walter attended at the Hofoper was conducted by the eminent Wagnerian Josef Sucher. Ibid., p. 43.

13 Ibid., p. 42.

14 F. Weingartner trans. M. Wolff, *Buffets and Rewards* (London, 1937), p. 52.

15 Walter, *Theme and Variations*, p. 56.

16 Walter's *Meerestille und glückliche Fahrt* was composed for chorus and orchestra.

17 The concert of 18 March 1893 was an Öffentliche Prüfung (public examination) held by the Stern Conservatory. Walter was one of seven young artists performing at that concert. Along with Radecke and Walter, Alberto Nepomuceno also conducted.

18 Hofmann offered Walter a one-year contract as a vocal coach starting on 1 September 1893 with a monthly salary of 100 marks. Walter, *Theme and Variations*, p. 59.

19 Ibid., p. 69.

20 Ibid., p. 70.

21 Walter described his senior colleagues at Cologne thus: 'Wilhelm Karl Mühldorfer . . . [was] a capable *routinier*, and Josef Grossman, a young, gifted, and temperamental Viennese who, however, seemed to be lacking in seriousness and weight.' Ibid.

22 Ibid., p. 75.

23 Ibid.

24 Ibid., p. 76.

25 *Kölner-Tageblatt*, 21 March 1894, as found in E. Ryding and R. Pechefsky, *Bruno Walter: A World Elsewhere* (New Haven and London, 2001), p. 13.

26 Walter, *Theme and Variations*, p. 83.

27 The operas that Walter conducted as chorus master included Mascagni's *Cavalleria rusticana*, Lortzing's *Zar und Zimmermann*, *Undine* and *Die beiden Schützen*, Flotow's *Martha* and Verdi's *La traviata*.

28 Mahler wrote: 'The fact that the end of the aria did not go according to *our* plan is entirely Walter's fault for taking the whole preceding aria too fast, *rushing* it, so that you never had time to *breathe*.' Undated letter from Gustav Mahler to Anna von Mildenburg. *Selected Letters of Gustav Mahler* trans. E. Wilkins, E. Kaiser, and B. Hopkins, ed. K. Martner (London, 1979), p. 170.

29 Walter, *Theme and Variations*, p. 97.
30 Ibid.
31 Ryding and Pechefsky, *Bruno Walter*, p. 25.
32 Walter, *Theme and Variations*, p. 106.
33 Ryding and Pechefsky describe Walter's reading of *Die Zauberflöte* as 'a new production'. Ryding and Pechefsky, *Bruno Walter*, p. 25.
34 Walter, *Theme and Variations*, p. 106.
35 Ibid., p. 107.
36 Ibid., p. 110.
37 Walter was a deeply religious and spiritual man. Although he took a profound interest in anthroposophy in later life, his ashes were interred at the Catholic cemetery of Sant' Abbondio, Montagnola, near Lugano. For further information about Walter's thoughts on anthroposophy, see B. Walter, trans. P. Hamburger, 'Epilogue', *Of Music and Music-making* (London, 1961), pp. 212–13.
38 Walter recalled that some of the German community guaranteed the theatre against loss, and that its director was responsible financially to a committee of German speakers. Walter, *Theme and Variations*, p. 120.
39 At Riga, Walter also conducted orchestral and choral concerts, including a performance of Mendelssohn's *Elijah*. He continued to perform as a pianist, giving chamber music recitals at the Schwarzhäupterhaus, and taught piano at the Gyzicki Music School during his second season.
40 Works that Walter conducted during his two seasons at Riga included Beethoven's *Fidelio*, Bizet's *Carmen*, Glinka's *A Life for the Tsar*, Goldmark's *Die Königin von Saba*, Gounod's *Roméo et Juliette*, Humperdinck's *Hänsel und Gretel*, Marschner's *Hans Heiling*, Massenet's *Werther*, Mozart's *Die Zauberflöte*, *Don Giovanni* and *Le nozze di Figaro*, Nessler's *Der Rattenfänger von Hameln*, Spinelli's *A basso porto*, Rubinstein's *Der Makkabäer*, Wagner's *Der fliegende Holländer*, *Lohengrin* and *Tannhäuser*, Siegfried Wagner's *Der Bärenhäuter*, Tchaikovsky's *Eugene Onegin* and Verdi's *Rigoletto*.
41 Walter, *Theme and Variations*, p. 118.
42 Along with Strauss and Muck, Weingartner continued to be associated with the Hofoper. Although he no longer performed operas there, he was the conductor of the Hofkapelle's subscription concerts. Walter was particularly impressed by Strauss's reading of Wagner's *Tristan und Isolde*, but considered his rubato excessive by comparison with that of Mahler in Vienna, a strange notion considering the personalities involved. Walter was also impressed by Muck's interpretation of Wagner's *Götterdämmerung*. Ibid., p. 140.
43 The British conductor Sir John Pritchard once described *Carmen* as the 'graveyard of inexperienced conductors'. Conversation with the author, Cologne 1978.
44 At the Berlin Hofoper, the operas that Walter conducted included Weber's *Der Freischütz*, Mozart's *Der Zauberflöte*, Wagner's *Lohengrin*, Siegfried Wagner's *Der Bärenhäuter*, Auber's *Fra Diavolo* and Lortzing's *Zar und Zimmermann*.
45 Walter conducted the first Berlin performance of Pfitzner's *Der arme Heinrich* on 19 December 1900.
46 The Berlin Tonkünstler-Orchestra was conducted later by Richard Strauss. For a detailed account of the orchestra, K. Birkin, '"... wollen sehen, ob's gelingt" Richard Strauss and the Berlin Tonkünstler-Orchester', *Richard Strauss-Blätter* 46 (December 2001), pp. 3–60.
47 Karl Kampf, *Allgemeine Deutsche Musik-Zeitung*, 23 November 1900, p. 706, as found ibid.
48 Walter, *Theme and Variations*, p. 147.
49 Of Walter's Vienna début, Mahler's friend Natalie Bauer-Lechner wrote: 'Mahler really enjoys Bruno Walter. The first opera he conducted [at the Vienna Hofoper]

was *Aida*, and Mahler, who was listening to the performance in his box, was so delighted with it that he declared that from now on he could let Walter conduct in his place with complete confidence, and turn everything over to him.' N. Bauer-Lechner, trans. D. Newlin, ed. P. Franklin, *Recollections of Gustav Mahler* (London, 1980), p. 175.

50 Walter's cast included Anna von Mildenburg (Aida), Edyth Walker (Amneris) and Leo Slezak (Radamès).

51 Bauer-Lechner, *Recollections of Gustav Mahler*, p. 175.

52 The operas that Walter conducted at the Vienna Hofoper included Bizet's *Carmen*, Gluck's *Orfeo ed Euridice*, Grisar's *Bonsoir, Monsieur, Pantalon!* Nicolai's *Die lustigen Weiber von Windsor*, Meyerbeer's *L'Africaine*, Offenbach's *Les Contes d'Hoffmann*, Verdi's *Un ballo in maschera*, Wagner's *Der fliegende Holländer* and *Tannhäuser* and Weber's *Der Freischütz*.

53 At the Vienna Hofoper, Walter conducted the local premières of Mozart's *Zaide* on 4 October 1902 in a double bill with Bizet's *Djamileh* conducted by Mahler, Delibes's *Lakmé* on 14 November 1904, Erlanger's *Der polnische Jude* on 4 October 1906 and Saint-Saëns's *Samson et Dalila* on 11 May 1907.

54 Francesco Spetrino conducted the house première of Puccini's *La Bohème* on 25 November 1903 and a new production of Rossini's *Guillaume Tell* on 11 May 1905. Franz Schalk conducted a new production of Wagner's *Lohengrin* on 27 February 1906 and the house première of d'Albert's *Flauto solo* on 28 November 1906.

55 As a chamber musician, Walter worked regularly with Arnold Rosé, Marie Soldat-Röger, the Rosé Quartet and the Soldat-Röger Quartet. He was also still active as a composer and some of his chamber performances featured his music.

56 Given Walter's doubts about Schumann as an orchestrator, it is possible that he employed some of Mahler's amendments to the score when performing the work in Vienna and elsewhere. The other works on the programme were Robert Fuchs's Serenade No. 2, an aria from Rossini's *Semiramide* (Selma Kurz, soprano) and Strauss's *Till Eulenspiegel*. See Chapter 2 note 54.

57 Walter, *Theme and Variations*, pp. 195–6.

58 Between 2 January 1908 and 6 February 1912, a period that also includes the first months of Hans Gregor's tenure as Director of the Hofoper, Walter conducted the house premières of Debussy's *Pelléas et Mélisande* (23 May 1911), Bittner's *Der Musikant* (12 April 1910) and d'Albert's *Die verschenkte Frau* (6 February 1912) and the world premières of Goldmark's *Ein Wintermärchen* (2 January 1908) and Bittner's *Der Bergsee* (9 November 1911).

59 Caruso sang in *Rigoletto* and *Carmen* at the Vienna Hofoper on 23 and 25 September 1911 respectively.

60 The concert also included performances by Emil Sauer of Liszt's *Ricordanza* and Chopin's *Allegro de concert* in A major. Walter's début with the Philharmonic Society took place nearly a month after the première of his Symphony No. 1 with the Konzertverein Orchestra at Vienna on 6 February 1909. Mahler was less than impressed by the work and expressed his despair about Walter as a composer to his wife, Alma, in a letter from September 1907. See H.-L. de La Grange and G. Weiss, *Ein Glück ohne Ruh': Die Briefe Gustav Mahlers an Alma* (Munich, 1997), p. 334.

61 See Royal Philharmonic Society Letters Vol. 35 (Vi–Wh), British Library, RPS MS 367.

62 On 25 November 1909, Walter repeated Smyth's overture to *The Wreckers*, and on 8 December 1909, Smyth conducted her songs *Chrysilla* and *Anacreontic Ode* (Frederic Austin, baritone). The other works performed at Walter's concert with the Society on 4 December 1924 were Weber's overture to *Der Freischütz*,

Mozart's Symphony No. 35 ('Haffner') and Wagner's Prelude to *Der Meistersinger von Nürnberg*. Walter's programme on 18 November 1926 resembled strongly that of his début with the Society and included Smyth's Prelude to Act 2 of *The Wreckers*, Schumann's Symphony No. 1, Mozart's Piano Concerto No. 20 (Myra Hess, piano), Prokofiev's Suite from *The Love for Three Oranges* and Beethoven's overture *Leonore* No. 3. See M. B. Foster, *The History of the Philharmonic Society of London 1813–1912* (London, 1912), R. Elkin, *Royal Philharmonic: The Annals of the Royal Philharmonic Society* (London, 1946) and C. Ehrlich, *First Philharmonic: A History of the Royal Philharmonic Society* (Oxford, 1995).

63 Walter's cast for Wagner's *Tristan und Isolde* at Covent Garden included Zdenka Fassbender as Isolde, later replaced by Anna Bahr-Mildenburg, Jacques Urlus as Tristan and Hermann Weidemann as Kurwenal.

64 The cast for Smyth's *The Wreckers* included Edyth Walker and Hermann Weidemann.

65 With the fall of the monarchies at the end of World War I, this agreement no longer applied and Walter continued in post at Munich past the stipulated date.

66 Walter's salary at Vienna was equivalent to 24,000 marks.

67 Along with the first performance of *Das Lied von der Erde* on 20 November 1911, Walter conducted a performance of Mahler's Symphony No. 2 ('Resurrection'). The previous night, 19 November 1911, Walter accompanied Madame Charles Cahier in a recital of Mahler songs at Munich. He later conducted the Munich première of Bittner's *Das höllisch Gold* on 3 March 1917.

68 Letter from Hugo von Hofmannsthal to Richard Strauss dated 2 December 1912. *The Correspondence between Richard Strauss and von Hofmannsthal*, ed. F. and A. Strauss, arr. W. Schuh, trans. H. Hammelmann and E. Osers (Cambridge, 1980), p. 146.

69 Ibid., pp. 157–8.

70 Ibid.

71 Despite their strained relations, Walter later conducted the first Munich performance of *Die Frau ohne Schatten* on 9 November 1919.

72 Walter conducted Klenau's *Sulamith* on 16 November 1913, Korngold's *Der Ring des Polykrates* and *Violanta* on 28 March 1916, Pfitzner's *Palestrina* on 12 June 1917, Courvoisier's *Lanzelot und Elaine* on 3 November 1917, Schreker's *Das Spielwerk* on 30 October 1920 and Braunfels's *Die Vögel* on 30 November 1920. Walter also conducted the first Munich performance of Klenau's ballet *Klein Idas Blumen* on 3 March 1917 and Schreker's *Die Gezeichneten* on 15 February 1919, as well as new productions of Pfitzner's *Der Rose vom Liebesgarten* and *Das Christelflein* on 19 December 1915 and 7 December 1918 and Schreker's *Der ferne Klang* on 28 February 1914.

73 Walter, *Theme and Variations*, p. 219.

74 Walter later conducted a new production of Verdi's *Otello* on 20 May 1916.

75 Walter later conducted new productions of *Parsifal* on 22 May 1914 and *Der Ring des Nibelungen* on 20 November 1921 (*Die Walküre*), 5 January 1922 (*Siegfried*), 30 April 1922 (*Götterdämmerung*) and 14 June 1922 (*Das Rheingold*). The tetralogy was produced by the soprano Anna Bahr-Mildenburg.

76 Walter, *Theme and Variations*, p. 187.

77 Walter, like Strauss some twenty-four years earlier, bade farewell to Munich with a performance of Beethoven's *Fidelio* on 3 October 1922.

78 Walter, *Theme and Variations*, p. 269.

79 Walter's programme at the Aeolian Hall included Mozart's Serenade in D major ('Haffner'), Mendelssohn's overture to *Ein Sommernachtstraum*, Schumann's Symphony No. 1 and Wagner's Prelude to *Die Meistersinger von Nürnberg*. After

his two New York concerts, Walter travelled to Detroit, Minneapolis and Boston. He made a positive impression wherever he performed and he was invited to return to the New York, Detroit and Minneapolis orchestras the following year.

80 Ryding and Pechefsky, *Bruno Walter*, p. 154.

81 Walter's programme with the Berlin Philharmonic included Brahms's Symphony No. 2, Mozart's *Per pietà ricercare* (John McCormack, tenor), Strauss's *Don Juan*, an aria from Beethoven's *Christus am Ölberge* (John McCormack, tenor) and Wagner's Prelude to *Die Meistersinger von Nürnberg*.

82 With the Gewandhaus Orchestra, Walter conducted Brahms's Symphony No. 2, Schubert's Entr'acte from *Rosamunde* and Weber's overture to *Euryanthe* and accompanied Bruch's 'Aus der Tiefe des Grames' from *Achilleus* and Brahms's *Nicht mehr zu dir, O wüsst ich doch, Sapphische Ode* and *Mein Mädel hat einen Rosenmund*. With the Concertgebouw Orchestra, he performed Mahler's Symphony No. 1 ('Titan') and Pfitzner's Piano Concerto in E flat (Walter Gieseking, piano).

83 Covent Garden's Grand Opera Season usually ran from late spring to early summer. For details of casting see H. Rosenthal, *Two Centuries of Opera at Covent Garden* (London, 1958).

84 Between the two World Wars, Walter also conducted six concerts with the London Symphony Orchestra and five with the London Philharmonic Orchestra. The repertoire performed was overwhelmingly Austro-German. Information gleaned from the records of the London Symphony and the London Philharmonic Orchestras.

85 Karl Alwin shared the conducting of *Die Walküre* and *Götterdämmerung* with Walter in 1924 and Robert Heger shared the conducting of some of the German repertoire with him between 1925 and 1931.

86 Along with Wagner's *Der Ring des Nibelungen*, Walter performed Johann Strauss's *Die Fledermaus* (1930, 1931), Wagner's *Die Meistersinger von Nürnberg* (1925, 1926, 1928, 1929, 1930), *Der fliegende Holländer* (1925) and *Tristan und Isolde* (1924, 1925, 1926, 1929, 1931), Richard Strauss's *Der Rosenkavalier* (1924, 1925, 1927, 1929, 1931) and *Elektra* (1925), Beethoven's *Fidelio* (1927) and Mozart's *Don Giovanni* (1926), *Die Entführung aus dem Serail* (1927) and *Die Zauberflöte* (1931) at Covent Garden.

87 Erich Kleiber (1890–1956): Austrian conductor. After leaving Germany in 1935, Kleiber worked mainly in South America and Cuba. He returned to Europe when the hostilities had ceased. His son was the renowned conductor Carlos Kleiber (1930–2004).

88 Walter, *Theme and Variations*, p. 296.

89 At the Städtische Oper, Walter conducted Pfitzner's *Der arme Heinrich* in March 1927, Debussy's *Pelléas et Mélisande* in December 1927, the Berlin première of Korngold's *Das Wunder der Heliane* in April 1928 and the world première of Bittner's *Mondnacht* in November 1928.

90 As in Munich some seven years earlier, Walter conducted Beethoven's *Fidelio* for his farewell performance.

91 Walter conducted fifty-one 'Bruno Walter Concerts' between 1924 and 1933. His activities with the Berlin Philharmonic were not restricted to that series, however, and during the period in question he conducted the orchestra regularly at other concerts.

92 At the 'Bruno Walter Concerts', Walter conducted Mahler's Symphony No. 1 (1926–7), Symphony No. 3 (1928–9), Symphony No. 4 (1925–6, 1929–30), Symphony No. 5 (1924–5, 1930–1), *Das Lied von der Erde* (1925–6, 1927–8, 1931–2) and *Lieder eines fahrenden Gesellen* (1930–1).

93 The twelve world, local or Berlin premières that Walter conducted at the 'Bruno

Walter Concerts' included Prokofiev's Symphony No. 1 (13 December 1926), *The Prodigal Son* (23 November 1931) and Violin Concerto No. 1 (Joseph Szigeti, violin) (1 December 1924), Shostakovich's Symphony No. 1 (6 February 1928), Janáček's *Taras Bulba* (28 January 1929), Krenek's *Der Triumph der Empfindsamkeit* (14 March 1932), Rachmaninoff's Piano Concerto No. 4 (Sergei Rachmaninoff, piano) (8 December 1930), Lopatnikoff's Symphony No. 1 (16 February 1931), Thomas's Serenade for small orchestra (17 February 1930) and Strauss's *Panathenaeenzug* for piano left hand and orchestra (Paul Wittgenstein, piano) (16 January 1928).

The works from music's cutting edge that Walter conducted in Berlin included Stravinsky's Suite from *Pulcinella* (1 November 1926) and *Chant du rossignol* (16 December 1929), Bartók's Rhapsody for piano and orchestra Op. 1 (Béla Bartók, piano) (18 January 1926), Schreker's *Der Geburtstag der Infantin* (4 October 1926) and Bloch's Concerto Grosso (10 December 1928).

94 At his eponymous series with the Berlin Philharmonic, Walter conducted four all-Beethoven concerts, three all-Mozart concerts, two all-Brahms concerts and one all-Schubert concert. He performed eight of the nine Beethoven symphonies (the exception being Symphony No. 2) and gave two performances each of Symphonies Nos. 3 ('Eroica'), 5, 8, 7 and 9 ('Choral') and the Missa solemnis. He did not programme Brahms's Symphony No. 3 or Piano Concerto No. 2 and restricted his readings of Schubert's symphonies to Nos. 7 in B minor ('Unfinished') and 8 in C major ('Great').

95 Walter, *Theme and Variations*, p. 318.

96 Ibid.

97 Some of the new works that Walter conducted at the Leipzig Gewandhaus Orchestra's Subscription Series included Shostakovich's Symphony No.1 (14 November 1929), Ravel's *Shéhérazade* (17 October 1929), Krenek's *Kleine Sinfonie* Op. 58 (28 November 1929), Sekles's Symphony No. 1 (6 November 1930), Goetz's Violin Concerto (Charles Münch, violin) (6 November 1930), Erdmann's Piano Concerto Op. 15 (Eduard Erdmann, piano) (4 December 1930), Hindemith's Overture to *Neues vom Tage* (17 December 1931), Schmidt's Variations on a Hussar's Song (1 January 1931), Trapp's Symphony No. 4 (7 April 1932), Grabner's Variations and Figure on a Theme by Bach (27 October 1932), Graener's *Sinfonia breve* (3 November 1932) and Prokofiev's *Der Spieler* (10 November 1932).

98 With the Leipzig Gewandhaus Orchestra, Walter performed Mahler's *Das Lied von der Erde* (1929–30), Symphony No. 5 (1930–1), Symphony No. 2 (1931–2) and *Lieder eines fahrenden Gesellen* and Symphony No. 1 (1932–3).

99 Walter performed the following Bruckner symphonies with the Gewandhaus Orchestra: Symphony No. 5 (1929–30), Symphony No. 8 (1930–1), Symphony No. 6 (1931–2) and Symphony No. 9 (1932–3).

100 Walter conducted all nine symphonies by Beethoven at Leipzig and gave multiple performances of Symphony No. 5 (14 November 1929, 25 November 1931), Symphony No. 6 (16 October 1930, 8 December 1932) and Symphony No. 9 (13 March 1930, 19 March 1931, 17 March 1932). His performances of Symphony No. 9 at Leipzig were the only concerts devoted solely to the music of one composer, and their programmes contained no other works.

101 Richard Strauss replaced Walter as conductor of the concert on 20 March 1933. According to Walter, the substitution was made at the suggestion of the Nazis: 'What was our surprise when we were told that it was considered desirable to have the concert take place, but under Richard Strauss's guidance instead of mine. . . . The composer of *Ein Heldenleben* actually declared himself ready to conduct in place of a colleague who had been forcibly removed. This made him

especially popular with the upper ranks of Nazism. Later, to be sure, for reasons unknown to me, Strauss was said to have fallen out with the government.' Walter, *Theme and Variations*, p. 329. Strauss's recollection of the incident differs sharply from that of Walter. He maintained that he performed as a favour to the orchestra and that he donated his fee to the ensemble. Because of the history of acrimony between the two artists, the truth may never be known fully.

102 The new productions under Walter at the Vienna Staatsoper were Verdi's *Don Carlos* (1 January 1937), Donizetti's *Don Pasquale* (13 January 1937), Weber's *Oberon* (arr. Mahler) (19 May 1937) and *Euryanthe* (23 September 1937), Pfitzner's *Palestrina* (14 October 1937) and Bizet's *Carmen* (22 December 1937) and Smetana's *Dalibor* (26 February 1938).

103 Walter learned of Austria's fate in Amsterdam, where he had just conducted the world première of Krenek's Piano Concerto No. 2 (Ernst Krenek, piano) with the Concertgebouw Orchestra on 17 March 1938.

104 Ryding and Pechefsky, *Bruno Walter*, p. 268. Walter gives the date as 31 October [1939]. Walter, *Theme and Variations*, p. 372.

105 For the Metropolitan Opera, New York, Walter revisited repertoire that had become his stock-in-trade, and after making his house début with Beethoven's *Fidelio* on 14 February 1941 he conducted Mozart's *Don Giovanni*, *Die Zauberflöte* and *Le nozze di Figaro*, Gluck's *Orfeo e Euridice*, Smetana's *The Bartered Bride* and Verdi's *Un ballo in maschera*, *La forza del destino* and *Requiem*. For the New York Philharmonic, where he was later invited to act as Music Advisor between 1947 and 1949, his work was again dominated by music from the Austro-German tradition.

106 With the Los Angeles Philharmonic Orchestra, Walter conducted John Alden Carpenter's Symphony on 5 and 6 December 1940, David Stanley Smith's *Credo* on 5 and 6 February 1942, Rachmaninoff's *Rhapsody on a Theme of Paganini* on 12 and 13 February 1942, Vaughan Williams's *Dives and Lazarus* on 19 and 20 February 1942 and Mahler's *Kindertotenlieder* on 19 and 20 February 1942. Information provided kindly by the Los Angeles Philharmonic Orchestra. In addition to the works listed and those from the Austro-German canon, Walter performed compositions by Tchaikovsky, d'Indy, Debussy, Smetana, Vaughan Williams and Dvořák with the Los Angeles Philharmonic Orchestra. Information provided kindly by the Los Angeles Philharmonic Orchestra.

107 Since Walter's death, many private recordings with him have appeared, some of which document his wider interests. For comprehensive discographies of Walter, see: D. A. Pickett, rev. R. Warren, *A Bruno Walter Discography, Part One: Commercial Recordings: Issued Discs Only*, Bruno Walter Society, 1973; U. Masini, pref., 'Discografia di Bruno Walter', *Musica* 8 (June 1984), pp. 32–9; R. C. Marsh, 'The Heritage of Bruno Walter', *High Fidelity* 14 (1964), pp. 44–8, 103–9; R. Louis, 'Bruno Walter au disque', *Diapason 415*, supplement (May 1995), pp. xiv–xviii; F. F. Clough and G. J. Cuming, 'Diskography', *Gramophone Record Review*, August and September 1959, pp. 718–19, 824, and J. Altena, S. Reveyoso and E. Ryding, *Recorded Performances of Bruno Walter (1876–1962)*, on-line publication <www.geocities.com/walteriana76/B WrecordsB. htm>.

108 Walter recorded Barber's Symphony No. 1 with the New York Philharmonic Orchestra on 23 January 1945 (Columbia X252 and MX252), Berlioz's 'Danse des Sylphes' from *La Damnation de Faust* with the Orchestra of the Royal Philharmonic Society on 5 December 1924 (Columbia 67075–D(b); L 1623b), *Symphonie fantastique* with the Orchestre de la Société des Concerts du Conservatoire de Paris on 19 and 20 May 1939 (VM 662, Victor 12692/7; DB 3852/7; DB 8704/9), overture *Le Carnaval romain* with the Berlin Philharmonic

in 1923 (Polydor 65929) and the overture to *Benvenuto Cellini* with the Berlin Staatskapelle in 1924 (Polydor 66075/6a), Bizet's Preludes to Acts 3 and 4 of *Carmen* with the Berlin Philharmonic in 1923 (Polydor 65954 and 69596b), Cherubini's overture to *Les Deux Journées, ou Le Porteur d'eau* with the Berlin Philharmonic in 1925 (Polydor 66073), Dvořák's Slavonic Dance in C major Op. 6 No. 1 with the New York Philharmonic Orchestra on 4 February 1941 (Columbia CX-211), Symphony No. 8 with the New York Philharmonic Orchestra on 28 November 1947 (Columbia M-770) and the Columbia Symphony Orchestra on 8 and 12 February 1961 (Columbia ML 5761) and Symphony No. 9 ('From the New World') with the Columbia Symphony Orchestra on 14, 16 and 20 February 1959 (Columbia ML 5384), Smetana's 'Moldau' from *Ma vlast* with the New York Philharmonic Orchestra on 4 February 1941 (Columbia MX 211) and the overture to *The Bartered Bride* with the London Symphony Orchestra on 12 September 1938 (HMV DB 3652) and Tchaikovsky's Symphony No. 6 ('Pathétique') with the Berlin Staatskapelle in 1925 (Polydor 69771–5).

109 Live recordings of Walter conducting Beethoven's *Fidelio*, Mozart's *Don Giovanni, Le nozze di Figaro* and *Die Zauberflöte*, and Verdi's *Un ballo in maschera* and *La forza del destino* have been released by independent companies.

110 The soloists were Kirstin Thorborg, contralto, and Charles Kullmann, tenor.

111 Walter, *Of Music and Music-making*, p. 80.

112 Ibid., pp. 136–8.

113 Ibid., p. 140.

114 Ibid., p. 85.

115 Ibid., p. 87.

116 Ibid., p. 88.

117 Ibid., p. 132.

118 See Note 37.

119 Walter, *Of Music and Music-Making*, p. 213.

Chapter 7. A Troubled Mind: Otto Klemperer

1 Klemperer suffered from bouts of wild euphoria alternating with periods of deep gloom from maturity until death.

2 Klemperer was accepted into the Catholic faith in 1919 and left the church in 1967.

3 Klemperer's sisters, Regina and Marianne, were born in 1885 and 1889 respectively.

4 P. Heyworth, ed., *Conversations with Klemperer* (London, 1985), p. 21.

5 P. Heyworth, *Otto Klemperer: His Life and Times*, Vol. 1: *1885–1933* (Cambridge, 1996), p. 10.

6 Heyworth, *Conversations*, p. 21.

7 Ibid.

8 Ibid.

9 Ibid., p.22.

10 Klemperer left school without any formal qualifications.

11 Heyworth, *Otto Klemperer*, Vol. 1, p. 14.

12 O. Klemperer, trans. J. Maxwell Brownjohn, *Minor Recollections* (London, 1964), p. 62.

13 Ibid.

14 See Chapter 5.

15 Heyworth, *Conversations*, p. 47.

16 Ibid., p.115.
17 Klemperer was unimpressed by Mahler's Symphony No. 5, which received its Berlin première with the Berlin Philharmonic under Arthur Nikisch. The programme also included the Prelude and Liebestod from Wagner's *Tristan und Isolde* and the Berlin première of scenes from Cornelius's *Gunlöd*.
18 Oskar Fried (1871–1941) had a curious career. He trained as a horn player and violinist, studied composition with Engelbert Humperdinck and worked as a conductor and as a breeder of dogs. With the rise of the Nazis, Fried left Germany and moved to the Soviet Union, where he died. His discography is diverse and includes symphonies by Beethoven and Berlioz and works by Rimsky-Korsakov, Stravinsky, Saint-Saëns, Mozart and Liszt. In 1924, he recorded Mahler's Symphony No. 2, the first recording of a symphony by the composer.
    Fried conducted Mahler's Symphony No. 2 with the Berlin Philharmonic on 8 November 1905. The programme also included Reger's *O Haupt voll Blut und Wunden* and two Lieder by Liszt.
19 Heyworth, *Otto Klemperer*, Vol. 1, p. 25.
20 Klemperer, *Minor Recollections*, p. 53.
21 Heyworth, *Otto Klemperer*, Vol. 1, p. 25.
22 Klemperer, *Minor Recollections*, p. 16.
23 Heyworth, *Conversations*, p. 40.
24 Ibid., p. 41.
25 Klemperer, *Minor Recollections*, pp. 70–1.
26 Arthur Bodansky (1877–1939): Austrian conductor. Klemperer was already familiar with Bodansky through having acted as his assistant at the Lortzing Theatre in Berlin.
27 Heyworth, *Conversations*, p. 41.
28 Klemperer, *Minor Recollections*, p. 17.
29 During his second season at Prague, Klemperer's repertoire included Thomas's *Mignon*, Lortzing's *Der Waffenschmied*, Kienzl's *Der Evangelimann* and Nessler's *Der Trompeter von Säkkingen*. Heyworth, *Otto Klemperer*, Vol. 1, p. 39.
30 Ibid., pp. 39–40.
31 Enigmatically, Klemperer later recalled: 'So I gave up my position, or rather, I was given up.' Heyworth, *Conversations*, p. 42.
32 Heyworth, *Otto Klemperer*, Vol. 1, p. 44.
33 Heyworth, *Conversations*, p. 34.
34 Klemperer, *Minor Recollections*, p. 26.
35 Ibid.
36 Ibid.
37 Heyworth, *Conversations*, p. 35.
38 Ibid., p. 34.
39 Ibid.
40 Gustav Brecher (1879–1940): German conductor.
41 Klemperer conducted Gounod's *Faust*, Bizet's *Carmen* and Weber's *Der Freischütz* on 4, 5 and 9 September 1910 respectively. During the 1910–11 season he also conducted new productions of Offenbach's *Fortunios Lied*, Künnecke's *Robins Ende* and Delibes's *Lakmé*.
42 Klemperer, *Minor Recollections*, p. 80.
43 Heyworth, *Otto Klemperer*, Vol. 1, p. 54. Klemperer's depression was made worse by the death of Gustav Mahler on 18 May 1911.
44 Heyworth, *Conversations*, p. 36.
45 Weingartner opened the 1912–13 season at the Hamburg Stadttheater with Verdi's *Aida* on 30 August 1912. Klemperer's performances of *Le nozze di Figaro* during the 1912–13 season were his first of an opera by Mozart.

46 Klemperer's performance of Wagner's *Der Ring des Nibelungen* was the first of his career. Heyworth, *Otto Klemperer*, Vol. 1, p. 71.

47 After learning of the affair, Schumann's husband attacked Klemperer with a riding crop during a performance of Wagner's *Lohengrin*. Ibid., pp. 76–7.

48 The repertoire that Klemperer conducted at Barmen included d'Albert's *Tiefland*, Verdi's *Il trovatore*, Halévy's *La Juive*, Mozart's *Così fan tutte* and Wagner's *Tannhäuser, Tristan und Isolde, Parsifal* and *Der Ring des Nibelungen*.

49 In later life, Klemperer argued vigorously against the practice of conducting from memory and wrote, 'Some conductors say that they feel better and freer without score. This is vanity. Naturally, every conductor must know the score by memory. But is it necessary to show his knowledge to the audience? Vanity, nothing but vanity. Mahler and Strauss, who were not only great composers but great conductors, never conducted without score. They were strict opponents to that method.' Klemperer, *Minor Recollections*, p. 62.

50 Performances of Wagner's *Parsifal* had already been given in the USA, Holland and South America between 1903 and 1913.

51 Heyworth, *Otto Klemperer*, Vol. 1, p. 83.

52 *Barmen Zeitung*, 16 March 1914, as found in *Klemperer on Music: Shavings from a Musician's Workbench*, ed. M. Anderson (London, 1986), pp. 158–61.

53 *Stilbühne* is a series of curtains arranged in a manner that allows easy scene changes.

54 Heyworth, *Conversations*, p. 49.

55 Ibid.

56 Ibid., p. 109.

57 Ibid.

58 In the period following his début at Strasbourg, Klemperer also conducted Wagner's *Tannhäuser, Die Meistersinger von Nürnberg* and *Tristan und Isolde*.

59 Heyworth, *Otto Klemperer*, Vol. 1, p. 96.

60 Klemperer made his début as a concert conductor with the Hamburg Philharmonic at the Hamburg Musikhalle on 30 January 1912. At that concert, he performed Beethoven's overture *Die Weihe des Hauses*, Bach's Piano Concerto in D minor (Ilse Fromm, piano) and Mahler's Symphony No. 4, a local première. Klemperer hired both the orchestra and the hall.

61 Klemperer's concert at Frankfurt in December 1915 also contained vocal music by Mozart and Strauss.

62 Klemperer performed Wagner's *Die Meistersinger von Nürnberg, Der fliegende Holländer, Die Walküre* and *Tannhäuser*, Mozart's *Die Entführung aus dem Serail* and *Don Giovanni*, Strauss's *Ariadne auf Naxos*, Pfitzner's *Die Rose vom Liebesgarten*, Gluck's *Orfeo ed Euridice* and the local premières of Korngold's *Violanta* and *Der Ring des Polykrates* during the period under discussion.

63 For his farewell performance at the Strasbourg Sängerhaus on 19 April 1917, Klemperer performed Pfitzner's overture to *Christelflein*, Liszt's *Totentanz* (Otto Neitzel, piano), Neitzel's Capriccio for piano and orchestra, some of his own songs, his incidental music to Goethe's *Faust* and his *Geistliches Kampflied*. Heyworth, *Otto Klemperer*, Vol. 1, p. 117.

Klemperer's successor at Strasbourg was the 19-year-old George Szell, who had been recommended to him by Richard Strauss.

64 Heyworth, *Conversations*, p. 50.

65 Among the operas performed by Klemperer at Cologne were Bizet's *Carmen*, Wagner's *Der Ring des Nibelungen*, Rossini's *Il barbiere di Siviglia*, Cherubini's *Les Deux Journées*, Weber's *Euryanthe* (arr. Mahler) and Mozart's *Die Entführung aus dem Serail, Così fan tutte* and *Don Giovanni*.

66 At Cologne, Klemperer conducted Mussorgsky's *Boris Godunov*, Janáček's

Jenůfa and *Kát'a Kabanová*, Busoni's *Turandot* and *Arlecchino*, Strauss's *Der Rosenkavalier*, *Die Frau ohne Schatten*, *Ariadne auf Naxos* and *Salome*, Pfitzner's *Palestrina*, Korngold's *Die tote Stadt*, Schreker's *Der Schatzgräber*, *Der ferne Klang* and *Irrelohe*, Zemlinsky's *Der Zwerg* and Stravinsky's *Petrushka*. *Die tote Stadt*, *Irrelohe* and *Der Zwerg* were world premières. *Die tote Stadt* was given simultaneous world premières at Hamburg and Cologne on 4 December 1920, while *Der Zwerg* was first heard at Cologne on 28 May 1922 and *Irrelohe* on 27 March 1924.

67 *Klemperer on Music*, p. 203.

68 Of Schreker's operas, for example, Klemperer argued that at first they seemed important but with the appearance of each successive work the quality declined and, of Pfitzner's *Palestrina*, he felt that the libretto was of a higher standard than the music.

69 Herman Abendroth (1883–1956) was Wilhelm Furtwängler's successor at Lübeck (see Chapter 8) and was Gewandhauskapellmeister in Leipzig between 1934 and 1946. Like Klemperer, Abendroth championed the music of Anton Bruckner, and his performances of that composer's symphonies were held in high regard.

70 At his first concert with the Gürzenich Orchestra on 26 March 1922, Klemperer shared a programme of works by Strauss and Wagner with Abendroth; at his second, on 13 March 1923, he performed his own Mass in C major and Abendroth conducted Reger's 'Hiller' Variations and Mozart's Violin Concerto K. 219 (Anna Hegner, violin).

71 Heyworth, *Conversations*, p. 50.

72 Ibid., pp. 32–3.

73 Ibid., p. 33.

74 The programme for the concert on 11 December 1920 included Symphonies Nos. 2 and 5.

75 Klemperer was also invited to conduct opera as a guest conductor during the 1920s, performing works by Wagner, Strauss and Beethoven in Barcelona and Wagner in Rome.

76 Klemperer's wife, the soprano Johanna Geissler, was one of the soloists for his performance of Mahler's Symphony No. 2. They had married in Cologne in 1919.

77 During the 1920–1 season with the Berlin Philharmonic, Heinz Unger conducted *Kindertotenlieder* and Symphony No. 5 on 9 September 1920, Gustav Brecher conducted Symphony No. 1 on 15 October 1920, Arthur Nikisch conducted the Berlin Philharmonic première of Symphony No. 7 on 8 November 1920, Oskar Fried conducted *Das Lied von der Erde* on 15 November and 18 December 1920, Karl Muck conducted three songs with orchestra on 22 November 1920, Hanns W. David conducted some songs with orchestra on 28 January 1921, Heinz Unger performed Symphony No. 7 on 11 February 1921 and Carl Schuricht conducted Symphony No. 6 on 2 May 1921.

The frequency with which Mahler's music was performed in Berlin during the second decade of the twentieth century might seem surprising. Modern commentators frequently state that music was largely neglected before the 1960s, but its inclusion at eight per cent of the Berlin Philharmonic's concerts during the 1920–1 season suggests that further research is needed before any conclusions can be drawn.

78 Konrad Adenauer was later elected Chancellor of Germany (1949–64).

79 Heyworth, *Conversations*, p. 64.

80 The annual series of concerts that Klemperer led at Wiesbaden was again a vehicle for his wide-ranging interests. Along with works by Haydn, Beethoven and

Bruckner, Klemperer's Wiesbaden concerts contained Stravinsky's Piano Concerto (Igor Stravinsky, piano) and *Pulcinella* Suite, Schoenberg's arrangements of Bach's chorale preludes, Tchaikovsky's Symphony No. 6 ('Pathétique'), Berg's Three Pieces from *Wozzeck*, Debussy's 'Fêtes' from *Nocturnes*, Ravel's *Alborada del gracioso* and the German premières of Janáček's Sinfonietta and Sibelius's Symphony No. 7.

81 Heyworth, *Otto Klemperer*, Vol. 1, p. 194.

82 C. Hagemann, *Bühne und Welt: Erlebnisse und Betrachtungen eines Theaterleiters* (Wiesbaden, 1948), p. 255.

83 Ibid., pp. 102–3.

84 The repertoire performed by Klemperer at Wiesbaden included Stravinsky's *Histoire du soldat*, Wagner's *Lohengrin* and *Die Meistersinger von Nürnberg*, Mozart's *Le nozze di Figaro* and *Don Giovanni*, Strauss's *Elektra*, Weber's *Der Freischütz*, Ravel's *L'Heure espagnole*, Busoni's *Arlecchino* and Hindemith's *Cardillac*.

85 Hans Curjel (1896–1974): German art historian and Dramaturg. *Klemperer on Music*, p. 54.

86 Alexander von Zemlinsky (1871–1942): Austrian composer and conductor. Fritz Zweig (1893–1984): Czech-born conductor.

87 *Klemperer on Music*, p. 192.

88 Heyworth, *Conversations*, p. 68.

89 Ibid., p. 69.

90 Ibid., p. 70.

91 The section of the Berlin Staatsoper that performed in the theatre on Unter den Linden was commonly known as the Linden Opera.

92 Heyworth, *Conversations*, p. 71.

93 F. Hadamowsky, *Die Wiener Hoftheater (Staatstheater)*, Vol. 2: *1811–1974* (Vienna, 1975), p. 331.

94 Heyworth, *Conversations*, p. 74.

95 Klemperer's salary was reduced from 55,000 to 45,000 marks. Heyworth, *Otto Klemperer*, Vol. 1, p. 265. Ernst Legal (1881–1955): German theatre administrator.

96 *Klemperer on Music*, p. 203.

97 Ibid., p. 186.

98 Ibid., p. 188.

99 Ibid.

100 Ibid.

101 The statistic of twenty-six concerts applies only to Klemperer's discrete series with the Staatskapelle at the Kroll Theatre and not to his other engagements with the orchestra

102 Heyworth, *Conversations*, p. 76. Klemperer conducted Hindemith's Kammermusik No. 5 for viola and chamber orchestra (Paul Hindemith, viola) on 3 November 1928, the Konzertmusik for wind ensemble on 11 May 1928, Kammermusik No. 4 for violin and large chamber orchestra on 7 February 1929, Concerto for Orchestra on 25 April 1929, Kammermusik for cello and 10 solo instruments on 5 December 1929, Konzertmusik for viola and large orchestra (Paul Hindemith, viola) on 27 November 1930 and Konzertmusik for piano, brass and two harps (Walter Gieseking, piano) on 24 April 1931.

103 Klemperer conducted *Apollon Musagète* on 1 November 1928 and 17 June 1929, *Pulcinella* Suite on 7 February 1929, the Piano Concerto (Igor Stravinsky, piano) on 17 June 1929, *Les Noces* on 17 June and 5 December 1929, *The Fairy's Kiss* and *Capriccio* (Igor Stravinsky, piano) on 23 January 1930, and the *Firebird* Suite and *Symphony of Psalms* on 19 February 1931.

104 Schoenberg's arrangement of Bach's Prelude and Fugue in E flat major and the world première of *Begleitmusik zu einer Lichtspielszene* were performed on 6 November 1930.

105 Klemperer, *Minor Recollections*, p. 44.

106 Ibid., p. 46.

107 Heyworth, *Conversations*, p. 79.

108 Klemperer conducted Janáček's Sinfonietta on 29 September 1927, Ravel's *Alborado del gracioso* on 11 May 1928, Krenek's *Kleine Sinfonie* on 1 November 1928, Hauer's Sinfonietta and *Wandlungen* on 13 December 1928 and 14 June 1930 respectively and Weill's *Der Lindberghflug* on 5 December 1929. Also new to Klemperer's repertoire was Weill's *Kleine Dreigroschenmusik*, which he performed on 7 February 1929.

109 The all-Stravinsky concert on 17 June 1929 was the only concert at the Kroll that Klemperer devoted to a living composer. The works performed at the concert were *Apollon Musagète*, the Piano Concerto (Igor Stravinsky, piano) and *Les Noces*. The pianists in *Les Noces* were Fritz Zweig, Julius Bürger, Paul Gergely and Georg Szell, a conductor at the Berlin Staatsoper between 1924 and 1929.

110 Klemperer performed Beethoven's Symphonies Nos. 1 on 15 June 1928, 3 on 8 and 19 October 1930, 5 on 15 June 1928, 6 on 1 December 1927, 7 on 1 December 1927 and 9 on 24 April 1931. He also conducted Piano Concertos Nos. 1 (Edwin Fischer, piano) on 25 April 1929 and 5 ('Emperor') (Artur Schnabel, piano) on 21 February 1929, the *Grosse Fuge* on 25 April 1929 and the overture *Leonore* No. 3 on 8 and 19 October 1930. The Violin Concerto was performed on 15 June 1928 (Adolf Busch, violin) and 8 and 19 October 1930 (Joseph Wolfsthal, violin).

111 When Beethoven's Symphony No. 9 was performed by Klemperer on 24 April 1931, it was not an expression of hope for the future but a celebration of the past, because it was the last work to be performed at the Kroll's moribund concert series.

112 At the Kroll, Klemperer conducted Bach's Orchestral Suites Nos. 1, 2 and 3 on 27 March 1930, 14 November 1929 and 29 September 1927 respectively; Brandenburg Concertos Nos. 1, 4, 5 and 6 on 14 November 1929, 25 April 1929, 19 February 1931 and 7 February 1929 respectively and the Violin Concerto in E major (Joseph Wolfsthal, violin) on 14 November 1929.

113 Klemperer conducted Mozart's Symphonies Nos. 40 and 38 ('Prague') on 23 January 1930 and 5 March 1931 respectively. The other works by Mozart that he conducted at the Kroll were Piano Concertos Nos. 20 (Arthur Schnabel, piano) and 23 (Walter Gieseking, piano) on 29 September 1927 and 11 May 1928 respectively and Violin Concertos Nos. 4 (Adolf Busch, violin) and 5 (Max Strub, violin) on 1 November 1928 and 19 February 1931 respectively.

114 Klemperer conducted Mahler's *Kindertotenlieder* on 18 October 1928, *Das Lied von der Erde* on 13 December 1928, *Lieder eines fahrenden Gesellen* on 6 November 1930, Symphony No. 2 on 14 June 1930, Symphony No. 4 on 6 November 1930 and Symphony No. 9 on 18 October. Klemperer performed no music by Mahler during the 1927–8 season.

115 Klemperer conducted Brahms's Symphony No. 1 on 13 January 1928, Symphony No. 2 on 27 November 1930, *Academic Festival Overture* on 13 January 1928, Violin Concerto (Joseph Wolfsthal, violin) on 13 January 1928 and Piano Concerto No. 2 (Edwin Fischer, piano) on 5 March 1931.

116 Klemperer conducted Bruckner's Symphonies Nos. 7 and 9 on 3 November 1927 and 3 October 1929 respectively

117 Klemperer conducted premières of the new productions of Offenbach's *Les*

Contes d'Hoffmann on 19 February 1929, Hindemith's *Neues vom Tage* on 8 June 1929 and *Hin und züruck* on 29 November 1930, Mozart's *Die Zauberflöte* on 10 November 1929 and *Le nozze di Figaro* on 25 January 1931, Krenek's *Leben des Orest* on 4 March 1930 and Schoenberg's *Die glückliche Hand* on 7 June 1930. Klemperer's reading of Hindemith's *Neues vom Tage* was the world première.

118 During the early 1930s, Berlin supported the Staatsoper, the Theater am Platz der Republik (the Kroll Opera) and the Städtische Oper.

119 At the time of the Kroll Opera's closure Klemperer was not in Berlin but in South America, where he had accepted engagements as a guest conductor.

120 Leo Blech (1871–1958): German conductor.

121 On 15 December 1932 Klemperer conducted Hindemith's *Konzertmusik* for brass and strings, and on 12 January 1933 he gave Busoni's *Berceuse élégiaque*, Janáček's Sinfonietta and the world première of Krenek's Theme and Thirteen Variations for orchestra.

122 Siegfried Ochs (1858–1929): German conductor. Klemperer conducted Ochs's memorial concert with the Berlin Philharmonic and the Philharmonischer Chor on 21 February 1929. The concert was devoted to the music of Bach and included an organ chorale (Fritz Kleiner, organ), the Kyrie from the B minor Mass, the cantata *Christ lag in Todesbanden* and the final chorus from the *St Matthew Passion*.

123 The period instruments that Klemperer used on 18 December 1929 included the viola d'amore, viola da gamba and harpsichord played by Josef Wolfsthal, Eva Heinitz and Günther Ramin respectively.

124 Günther Ramin (1898–1956): German organist, harpsichordist and conductor.

125 Klemperer conducted Beethoven's Missa solemnis on 15 March 1930 and 4 March 1933, Verdi's Requiem on 18 December 1930, Bach's *St John Passion* on 26 March 1931, *St Matthew-Passion* on 13 March 1932 and Mass in B minor on 5 December 1932, and the world première of Hindemith's *Das Unaufhörliche* on 21 November 1931.

126 Heyworth, *Otto Klemperer*, Vol. 1, p. 410.

127 Information concerning Klemperer's activities with the Vienna Philharmonic was provided kindly by Dr Clemens Hellsberg.

128 *Klemperer on Music*, p. 200.

129 That figure includes performances and open rehearsals in Vienna and Salzburg. After World War II, Klemperer returned to the Vienna Philharmonic to conduct eight performances between 24 August 1947 and 16 June 1968.

130 At the Vienna Philharmonic's Abonnement Concerts that Klemperer conducted on 1 and 2 October 1933, he included Beethoven's Symphony No. 3 and Bach's cantata *Ich hatte viel Bekümmernis*, and at the open rehearsal and Abonnement Concert on 12 and 13 May 1934 respectively, he conducted Berlioz's overture *Carnaval romain*, Debussy's *Nocturnes*, Stravinsky's *Petrushka* Suite and Mendelssohn's *Ein Sommernachtstraum*.

131 On 11 October 1936, Klemperer conducted the slow movement of Bruckner's Symphony No. 7 and the original version of Symphony No. 5, and on 25 October 1936 he conducted the world première of Alban Berg's Violin Concerto with Louis Krasner as soloist.

132 *Klemperer on Music*, p. 117.

133 Klemperer's first programme with the Los Angeles Philharmonic included Bach's Toccata and Fugue in C major, Stravinsky's *Petrushka* Suite and Beethoven's Symphony No. 5.

134 Information concerning Klemperer's Los Angeles period is based on data kindly provided by Orrin Howard, Archives Advisor of the Los Angeles Philharmonic.

135 Artur Rodzinski (1892–1958) conducted the Los Angeles Philharmonic between 1929 and 1933. He was later the conductor of the Cleveland (1933–43), the New York Philharmonic (1943–7) and the Chicago Symphony (1947–8) Orchestras.

136 On 8 December 1934, Klemperer conducted a concert of excerpts from *Tannhäuser*, *Lohengrin*, *Tristan und Isolde* and *Die Meistersinger von Nürnberg* and, on 28 August 1936, he gave a programme that consisted of the Overture to *Tannhäuser*, Preludes to Acts 1 and 3 from *Lohengrin*, the Prelude to Act 1 of *Die Meistersinger von Nürnberg* and the 'Grail Scene' from *Parsifal*.

137 Of the twenty-two performances of Beethoven's Symphony No. 5 that Klemperer gave with the Los Angeles Philharmonic, eight were heard during his first year with the orchestra.

138 Klemperer conducted Bruckner's Symphony No. 4 on 30 November and 1 December 1933, Bruckner's Symphony No. 7 on 19 and 20 March 1936, Mahler's *Das Lied von der Erde* on 18 and 19 March 1937 and Mahler's Symphony No. 2 on 24 and 26 November 1938.

139 Klemperer conducted Hindemith's symphony *Mathis der Maler* on 29 and 30 November 1934, *Trauermusik* on 3 and 4 February 1938, *Symphonic Dances* on 14 and 15 April 1938 and *Der Schwanendreher* and *Nobilissima visione* on 23 and 24 March 1939.

140 Although Schoenberg had a notoriously prickly personality, he was on relatively good terms with Klemperer, who was instrumental in securing teaching work for him at the University of California at Los Angeles. While Klemperer had serious doubts about Schoenberg's later works, he admired his ability in general and had a series of composition lessons with him during his Los Angeles period.

141 Klemperer conducted Schoenberg's Suite for Strings on 18 May 1935, *Verklärte Nacht* on 13 and 14 December 1934 and the 'Lied der Waldtraube' from *Gurrelieder* 18 April 1936.

142 Klemperer conducted Schoenberg's Cello Concerto (Emanuel Feuermann, cello) on 2 and 3 April 1936 and the composer's arrangement of Brahms's Piano Quartet in G minor on 8 May 1938, 9 and 10 March 1939 and 1 September 1939.

143 Along with Hindemith, Schoenberg and Weill, Klemperer also conducted works by Richard Strauss during his Los Angeles period, but these were mainly compositions written before the end of the first decade of the twentieth century.

144 P. Heyworth, *Otto Klemperer: His Life and Times*, Vol. 2: *1933–1973* (Cambridge, 1996), p. 27.

145 Klemperer conducted Shostakovich's Symphony No. 1 on 20 and 21 February and 18 April 1936 and Piano Concerto No. 1 on 23 and 24 January 1936.

146 Klemperer conducted Shostakovich's Symphony No. 1 again on 9, 10 and 14 February 1939.

147 Although Louis Gruenberg (1884–1964) was born in Brest-Litovsk, Russia, he came to America as an infant and gained most of his professional experience there.

148 Klemperer conducted Barber's Adagio for strings and *Essay* No. 1 on 3 and 4 March 1939, Carpenter's *Danza* on 4 and 5 March 1937 and Violin Concerto on 20 and 21 January and 8 February 1938, Gruenberg's *Serenade to a Beauteous Lady* on 20 November 1937, Harris's *When Johnny Comes Marching Home* on 10 (twice) and 11 May 1935, 11 and 12 November 1937 and 24 November 1938, Hill's Symphony No. 1 on 23, 24 and 28 February 1939, MacDowell's 'Dirge' from *Indian Suite* on 27 January 1938, Mason's *A Lincoln Symphony* on 17 and 18 November and 6 December 1938, McDonald's *Rhumba* on 20 and 21 January 1939, Sessions's *The Black Maskers* Suite on 8 and 9 March 1934, Still's *Kaintuck* on 17 and 18 February 1939, Strang's *Intermezzo*

on 9 and 10 February 1939 and Taylor's *Through the Looking Glass* on 15 and 16 April 1937 and Ballet Music from *Casanova* on 11, 12 and 30 November 1937.

149 Of the American compositions performed, very few impressed Klemperer positively and none was heard regularly in his concerts after he left California.

150 Heyworth, *Otto Klemperer*, Vol. 2, p. 110.

151 *Klemperer on Music*, p. 209.

152 Heyworth, *Conversations*, p. 110.

153 Ibid., p. 113.

154 *Klemperer on Music*, p. 84.

155 When Klemperer returned to Europe in 1947, he was also engaged by the London Symphony Orchestra, the Concertgebouw Orchestra and the Vienna Philharmonic.

156 At the Hungarian State Opera, Klemperer conducted Beethoven's *Fidelio* (11 times), Mozart's *Così fan tutte* (seven times), *Die Entführung aus dem Serail* (eight times), *Don Giovanni* (12 times), *Le nozze di Figaro* (nine times) and *Die Zauberflöte* (16 times), Mussorgsky's *Sorochintsy Fair* (three times), Offenbach's *Les Contes d'Hoffmann* (nine times), Johann Strauss's *Die Fledermaus* (seven times), Richard Strauss's *Der Rosenkavalier* (once), Wagner's *Lohengrin* (six times), *Tannhäuser* (three times) and *Die Meistersinger von Nürnberg* (11 times) and Verdi's *Otello* (once) and *La Traviata* (six times). Along with his work at the State Opera, Klemperer conducted twenty-two performances of Mendelssohn's incidental music to Shakespeare's *A Midsummer Night's Dream* at the National Theatre and two further performances of *Die Fledermaus* at the Budapest zoological gardens on 28 August and 3 September 1948. The information concerning Klemperer's activities in Budapest was kindly provided by Nóra Wellman, archivist at the Hungarian State Opera.

157 Because Hungary's finances were in a perilous state in the immediate post-war period, the State Opera's management was able to offer Klemperer only two new productions: Mussorgsky's *Sorochintsy Fair* and Verdi's *La traviata*.

158 At Budapest, Klemperer also conducted six performances of Beethoven's Symphony No. 5, four of Symphony No. 7, three each of Symphonies Nos. 3, 4, 6 8 and one of Symphony No. 2. Klemperer also performed the Choral Fantasy and the Missa solemnis on 22 January and 10 March 1950 respectively.

159 At Budapest, Klemperer conducted three performances each of Symphonies Nos. 39 and 41 ('Jupiter'), two each of Symphonies Nos. 38 and 40 and one each of Symphonies Nos. 35 ('Haffner') and 36 ('Linz').

160 At Budapest, Klemperer conducted a single performance of Stravinsky's *Jeu de cartes* on 12 March 1948.

161 Klemperer conducted Strauss's *Metamorphosen* with the Orchestra of the Hungarian Radio on 12 March 1948 and the Budapest Philharmonic on 21 November 1949.

162 Heyworth, *Conversations*, p. 45.

163 P. Boulez, 'Preface' to *Klemperer on Music*, p. 12.

164 Klemperer's first concert with the Philharmonia Orchestra was an all-Beethoven programme and his second contained Walton's overture *Scapino* and Mozart's Symphony No. 41.

165 Elisabeth Schwarzkopf (b. 1915): German soprano.

166 See Chapter 9.

167 Klemperer conducted Bartók's Divertimento for Strings in November 1960 and February 1964, Stravinsky's *Pulcinella* Suite in February 1964 and his own Symphony No. 1 in May 1962.

168 Statistics concerning Klemperer's work with the Philharmonia and New Philharmonia Orchestras are based on the information kindly provided by the archivist of the Philharmonia Orchestra, Martyn Jones.

169 With the Philharmonia Orchestra, Klemperer conducted Beethoven's Symphony No. 1 three times, Symphony No. 2 twice, Symphony No. 3 five times, Symphony No. 4 twice, Symphony No. 5 three times, Symphony No. 6 four times, Symphony No. 7 three times, Symphony No. 8 three times and Symphony No. 9 four times. In keeping with his programme policy in Budapest, he juxtaposed Symphonies Nos. 1 and 9 in the same concert on three occasions. Klemperer also gave three performances of the Missa solemnis.

170 With the exception of Symphony No. 29, which he gave once only, the symphonies by Mozart that Klemperer conducted in London were Nos. 35, 38, 39, 40 and 41. Of these, Symphony No. 35 was given on three occasions, Symphonies Nos. 39 and 40 were heard twice each and Symphonies Nos. 38 and 41 were given once only. Klemperer also conducted two concert performances of *Die Zauberflöte* at the Royal Festival Hall on 1 and 3 May 1961. After his successful performances of Beethoven's *Fidelio* at the Royal Opera House, Covent Garden, in February 1961, Klemperer also conducted *Die Zauberflöte* there in 1962.

171 With the Philharmonia at the Royal Festival Hall, Klemperer gave Brahms's Symphonies Nos. 1 and 2 twice each and Symphony No. 4 and *Ein deutsches Requiem* once each.

172 In London, Klemperer's interpretations of Bach had a mixed reception. His heavy use of rubato, his refusal to employ decorations that were not the composer's own and his juxtaposition of period and modern instruments were all criticized heavily.

173 Klemperer restricted his performances of Mahler's music to one each of *Das Lied von der Erde* and Symphony No. 4 and two of Symphony No. 2.

174 With the Philharmonia at the Royal Festival Hall, Klemperer gave two performances of Symphony No. 7 and one each of Symphonies Nos. 8 and 9.

175 Klemperer recorded Beethoven's Symphonies Nos. 1 and 8, the Adagio from Bruckner's Symphony No. 8 and Schubert's Symphony No. 7 ('Unfinished') in 1924. Klemperer made electrical recordings of Beethoven's Symphony No. 8 in 1926 and Brahms's Symphony No. 1 in 1928. All the recordings were made with the Berlin Staatskapelle.

176 Klemperer recorded Beethoven's *Coriolan*, *Egmont* and *Leonore* No. 3 overtures, Mendelssohn's overture to *Ein Sommernachtstraum*, Weber's overture to *Euryanthe* and Brahms's *Academic Festival Overture* in 1927. In 1929, he recorded the overtures to Auber's *Fra Diavolo* and Offenbach's *La Belle Hélène*. All the recordings were made with the Berlin Staatskapelle.

177 Klemperer recorded Strauss's 'Tanz' (Dance of the Seven Veils) from *Salome* in 1928 and *Till Eulenspiegel* and *Don Juan* in 1929 with the Berlin Staatskapelle.

178 Klemperer recorded Wagner's *Siegfried Idyll* and the Prelude to Act 1 of *Tristan und Isolde* in 1927 with the Berlin Staatskapelle.

179 For Vox, Klemperer recorded Bach's Brandenburg Concertos, 'Nun komm' der Heiden Heiland' (arr. Klemperer) and 'Bist du bei mir' (arr. Klemperer) and Mozart's *Eine kleine Nachtmusik* with the Pro Musica Orchestra, Paris, in 1946. In 1950, he recorded Mozart's Symphonies Nos. 25 and 36 with the same orchestra and Schubert's Symphony No. 4 ('Tragic') with the Lamoureux Orchestra. In 1951, he recorded Beethoven's Symphonies Nos. 5 and 6, Missa solemnis and Piano Concerto No. 4 (Guiomar Novaes, piano), Bruckner's Symphony No. 4, Mahler's *Das Lied von der Erde* and Symphony No. 2, Mendelssohn's Symphonies Nos. 3 ('Scottish') (movements 1 and 2 only) and 4

('Italian'), Chopin's Piano Concerto No. 2 (Guiomar Novaes, piano) and Schumann's Piano Concerto (Guiomar Novaes, piano) with the Wiener Symphoniker.
180 Decca 425 970–2.
181 Heyworth, *Otto Klemperer,* Vol. 2, p. 310.
182 Legge later sold the library to the Bournemouth Symphony Orchestra for £300. Ibid.

Chapter 8. The Transcendental Furtwängler

1 Szymon Goldberg, the leader of the Berlin Philharmonic from 1929 to 1934, once commented rightly that Furtwängler 'knew exactly what he did. His way of music-making created the impression that he would permanently improvise, but it really was not so. He conducted according to a very definite plan, and what was generally supposed to be improvisation was just imaginative planning.' As found in H.-H. Schönzeler, *Furtwängler* (London, 1990), p. 155.
2 Furtwängler's siblings were Walter (1887–1967), Marthe Edith (1891–1971) and Anna (1900–74).
3 Furtwängler's first composition was *Ein Stückche* [*sic*] *von den Tieren* (*A Little Piece about Animals*), dated 30 June 1893 and labelled 'Opus 1'. A facsimile is reproduced in F. Herzfeld, *Wilhelm Furtwängler: Weg und Wesen* (Leipzig, 1942), p. 25.
4 W. Furtwängler, trans. S. Whiteside, ed. M. Tanner, *Notebooks 1924–54* (London, 1995), p. 81.
5 *Münchner Neueste Nachrichten,* 24 February 1906.
6 W. Furtwängler, 'Bruckner', as found in *Furtwängler on Music: Essays and Addresses,* trans. and ed. R. Taylor (Aldershot, 1991), p. 107.
7 Letter from Furtwängler to Max Auer, President of the International Bruckner Society, dated 12 November 1952. As found in Schönzeler, *Furtwängler,* p. 135.
8 On 10 January 1950, Furtwängler conducted the Munich Philharmonic in a programme that included Handel's Concerto grosso Op. 6 No. 5 and his own Symphony No. 2 in E minor.
9 Furtwängler performed the overture to Berlioz's *Benvenuto Cellini* with the Munich Philharmonic on 26 January 1921. The programme also included Bach's Brandenburg Concerto No. 5 (W. Furtwängler, piano; A. Reichel, violin; P. Stammann, flute) and Schumann's Symphony No. 4.
10 Furtwängler performed Tchaikovsky's Symphony No. 6 with the Munich Philharmonic on 26 and 30 January 1949. The programme also included Beethoven's Symphony No. 4.
11 With the Munich Philharmonic, Furtwängler performed Beethoven's overtures *Die Weihe des Hauses* and *Leonore* No. 2 and Symphonies Nos. 1, 4, 5, 6 ('Pastoral') and 9 ('Choral').
12 Felix Mottl conducted the world première of Beer-Walbrunn's *Don Quijote, der sinnreiche Junker von Mancha* on 1 January 1908 and the first Munich performance of Schillings's *Moloch* on 3 June 1908.
13 In 1936, Furtwängler wrote: 'But whether the artificially-produced performances by ambitious directors and conductors (Pfitzner) are better [than trivial performances left to chance] is a major question.' Furtwängler, *Notebooks,* p. 82.
14 Ibid., p. 112.
15 Along with Maillart's *Les Dragons de Villars,* with which he made his Strasbourg début, Furtwängler conducted Donizetti's *L'elisir d'amore,* Flotow's *Martha* and Verdi's *Rigoletto* at the Stadttheater.

16 Herzfeld, *Wilhelm Furtwängler*, p. 39.
17 W. Furtwängler, 'The Tools of the Conductor's Trade', as found in *Furtwängler on Music*, pp. 16–22.
18 Furtwängler, *Notebooks*, p. 42.
19 Ibid., p. 44.
20 Herzfeld, *Wilhelm Furtwängler*, p. 41.
21 Two of Furtwängler's Lübeck subscription concerts each season were with the Philharmonischer Chor.
22 Herzfeld, *Wilhelm Furtwängler*, p. 46.
23 Ibid., p. 47.
24 Bruno Walter's letter to Ernst von Possart, dated 26 June 1914, as found in E. Ryding and R. Pechefsky, *Bruno Walter: A World Elsewhere* (New Haven and London, 2001), p. 116.
25 B. Geissmar, *The Baton and the Jackboot* (London, 1988), pp. 12–13.
26 Furtwängler, *Notebooks*, p. 81.
27 Ibid.
28 At Mannheim, Furtwängler began to build and to consolidate his operatic repertoire with performances of Bizet's *Carmen*, Mozart's *Die Zauberflöte*, *Die Entführung aus dem Serail* and *Le nozze di Figaro*, Johann Strauss's *Die Fledermaus*, Richard Strauss's *Salome* and *Ariadne auf Naxos*, Sekles's *Scheherazade*, Rossini's *Il barbiere di Siviglia*, Wagner's *Die Meistersinger von Nürnberg*, Verdi's *Otello* and *Aida*, Gluck's *Orfeo ed Euridice* and Siegel's *Herr Dandolo*.
29 C. Hagemann, *Bühne und Welt: Erlebnisse und Betrachtungen eines Theaterleiters* (Wiesbaden, 1948), p. 99.
30 For his Berlin Philharmonic début, Furtwängler conducted excerpts from Wagner's *Tannhäuser*, *Parsifal*, *Die Meistersinger von Nürnberg* and *Die Walküre* and Strauss's *Feuersnot* (excerpts), three songs with orchestra and *Don Juan*.
31 On 13 December 1917, Leopold Schmidt conducted the Berlin Philharmonic in a programme that included excerpts from operas by Mozart, Verdi, Weber and Wagner, Beethoven's overture *Leonore* No. 3 and Strauss's *Don Juan*.
32 On 25 January 1918, Furtwängler conducted Beethoven's overture *Leonore* No. 3, Schumann's Piano Concerto (Max Pauer, piano) and Bruckner's Symphony No. 4 ('Romantic'); on 8 March 1918, he conducted Beethoven's overture to *Coriolan* and Piano Concerto No. 5 ('Emperor') (Edwin Fischer, piano) and Brahms's Symphony No. 1.
33 The Vienna Tonkünstler Orchestra later became the Vienna Symphony Orchestra.
34 On 2 April 1920, Furtwängler conducted Wagner's Prelude to *Parsifal*, Bach's Orchestral Suite No. 3 in D major and Beethoven's Symphony No. 3 ('Eroica'). The concert was a Sonderkonzert and not part of the Abonnement series.
35 Of the concerts conducted by Furtwängler with the Berlin Staatskapelle, nineteen were subscription concerts, one was a Sonderkonzert and one was a charity concert.
36 With the Berlin Staatskapelle, Furtwängler conducted Bruckner's Symphonies Nos. 7 and 8 on 27 October 1920 and 4 November 1921 respectively and Mahler's Symphony No. 2 ('Resurrection') on 19 November 1920.
37 Furtwängler conducted Kaun's Symphony No. 3 on 4 May 1920, Schillings's Violin Concerto (Leopold Premyslaw, violin) on 9 February 1921, Busoni's *Zwei Studien zu 'Faust'* on 22 February 1922, Koch's *Romantic Suite* on 17 March 1922, Reger's 'Mozart' Variations on 17 March 1922, Schoenberg's *Verklärte Nacht* on 25 February 1921, Hausegger's *Aufklänge* on 11 March 1921, Rezniček's Variations for Orchestra on 7 December 1921 and Braunfels's Symphonic Variations on 3 February 1922.
38 Furtwängler conducted Nikisch's memorial concerts with the Gewandhaus Orchestra and the Berlin Philharmonic on 26 January and 6 February 1922

respectively. At Leipzig, the programme included Beethoven's overture to *Coriolan*, Brahms's Four Serious Songs (Sigrid Onegin, contralto; Günther Ramin, piano) and the slow movement from Beethoven's Symphony No. 3; in Berlin, it included Brahms's *Nänie* (Bruno Kittel, conductor) and Four Serious Songs (Julius von Raatz-Brockmann, baritone; Wilhelm Furtwängler, piano) and Beethoven's Symphony No. 3.

39 Fritz Busch and the Sächsische Staatskapelle also undertook some of the subscription concerts during the 1925–6 season.

40 Furtwängler conducted Schoenberg's Five Orchestral Pieces on 7 December 1922 (first performance of the new version), Graener's *Waldmusik* on 1 February 1923 and Divertimento Op. 67 on 6 November 1924, Kempff's Symphony No. 2 on 6 March 1924, Trapp's Symphony No. 3 on 23 October 1924, Braunfels's *Don Juan* on 13 November 1924 and Concerto for Organ, Orchestra and Choir on 23 February 1928, Georg Schumann's Variations and Gigue on a Theme by Handel on 19 February 1925, Raphael's Symphony No. 1 on 14 October 1926, Jarnach's *Morgenklangspiele* on 4 November 1926 and Toch's *Komödie* on 10 November 1927.

41 Furtwängler conducted Strauss's *Till Eulenspiegel* on 2 November 1922 and 13 October 1927, 'Grossmächtige Prinzessin' from *Ariadne auf Naxos* (Irene Eden, soprano) on 7 December 1922, *Symphonia domestica* on 11 October 1923, *Ein Heldenleben* on 17 January 1924 and 4 November 1926, *Also sprach Zarathustra* on 24 January 1924, 29 October 1925 and 15 December 1927, *Festliches Präludium* on 16 October 1924, *Drei Hymnen von Hölderlin* on 16 October 1924, *Eine Alpensinfonie* on 16 October 1924, *Tod und Verklärung* on 6 November 1924, *Don Juan* on 8 October 1925, *Parergon zur Symphonia domestica* (Paul Wittgenstein, piano) on 29 October 1925 and *Morgen, Cäcilie* and *Meinem Kinde* (Elisabeth Rethberg, soprano) on 13 October 1927, Pfitzner's overture to *Käthchen von Heilbronn* on 15 February 1923, Piano Concerto (Frieda Kwast-Hodapp, piano) on 25 October 1923, *Herr Oluf* on 17 January 1924 and Violin Concerto (Alma Moodie) on 27 November 1924, Respighi's *Fontane di Roma* on 25 January 1923, *Antiche arie e danze* (Suite No. 1) on 29 November 1923 and *Pini di Rom* on 8 October 1925, Sibelius's *En Saga* on 1 March 1923, Korngold's *Viel Lärm um nichts* on 7 February 1924, Stravinsky's *Le Sacre du printemps* on 1 November 1923, *Petrushka* on 24 January 1924 and 3 November 1927, Piano Concerto (Igor Stravinsky, piano) on 4 December 1924 and *Fireworks* on 4 November 1926, Prokofiev's Violin Concerto (Carl Münch [Charles Munch], violin) on 28 October 1926 and the Suite from *Chout* on 6 October 1927, Hindemith's Kammermusik No. 1 on 11 January 1923 and Concerto for Orchestra on 17 December 1925, Busoni's Violin Concerto (Adolf Busch, violin) on 10 November 1927, Schoeck's *Gaselen* on 25 November 1926, Casella's Partita for piano and orchestra (Alfredo Casella, piano) on 16 December 1926, Vaughan Williams's *Fantasia on a Theme by Thomas Tallis* on 20 October 1927, Ravel's *Daphnis et Chloé* (Suite No. 2) on 6 January 1927, Nielsen's Symphony No. 5 on 27 October 1927 and Honegger's *Chant de joie* on 7 October 1926.

42 Furtwängler conducted Stravinsky's *Le Sacre du printemps* on 1 November 1923. The programme also included Brahms's 'Haydn' Variations and Beethoven's Piano Concerto No. 5 (Edwin Fischer, piano).

43 The symphony by Beethoven that Furtwängler performed most at Leipzig was No. 9, which he gave on 22 March 1923, 20 March 1924, 19 March 1925, 22 April 1926, 28 April 1927 and 29 March 1928. In keeping with local practice, the symphony was performed at the last concert of each season and was the only work in the programme.

44 Furtwängler conducted Mahler's Symphony No. 1 ('Titan') on 26 February 1925, Symphony No. 3 on 14 February 1924, *Kindertotenlieder* on 19 October 1922 (Lula Mysz-Gmeiner, contralto) and *Lieder eines fahrenden Gesellen* on 11 October 1923 (Rosette Anday, contralto).
   Furtwängler conducted Bruckner's Symphony No. 4 on 1 January 1924, Symphony No. 5 on 9 October 1924, Symphony No. 7 on 12 October 1922 and 1 January 1928, Symphony No. 8 on 1 January 1924 and Symphony No. 9 on 30 October 1924 and 21 October 1926.

45 Otto Klemperer conducted the Berlin Philharmonic on 26 January 1925, the only Philharmonic Concert that Furtwängler did not conduct during his tenure. The programme included Mozart's Symphony No. 40, Brahms's Piano Concerto No. 1 (Frieda Kwast-Hodapp, piano) and Stravinsky's Suite from *Pulcinella*.

46 The figure of 124 concerts excludes Furtwängler's general rehearsals and other activities with the Berlin Philharmonic – specifically, the pension fund concerts and the foreign and domestic tours.

47 Of the premières that Furtwängler gave with the Berlin Philharmonic, most were of works by living composers. The statistic also includes local premières of some works from the eighteenth century.

48 Of the concerts given by Furtwängler at Berlin between the beginning of the 1922–3 season and the end of the 1927–8 season, more than eighty-six per cent contained a work that was also performed by him at Leipzig during the same period.

49 Furtwängler conducted Schoenberg's Variations for Orchestra on 3 December 1928, Prokofiev's Piano Concerto No. 5 (Serge Prokofiev, piano) on 31 October 1932 and Hindemith's symphony *Mathis der Maler* on 12 March 1934.

50 Furtwängler, *Notebooks*, p. 53.

51 With the exception of the 1925–6 season, where Brahms's Symphony No. 1 followed Beethoven's Symphony No. 4, the Philharmonic Concerts concluded with a performance of either Beethoven's Symphony No. 3 or Symphony No. 5. Symphony No. 3 concluded four of the seasons between 1922–3 and 1933–4 while Symphony No. 5 concluded seven.

52 Furtwängler conducted all-Beethoven concerts on 19 December 1923 (overture *Leonore* No. 3, Choral Fantasy (Frieda Kwast-Hodapp, piano; Bruno Kittel'scher Chor, chorus), Symphony No. 7), 23 March 1925 (Symphonies Nos. 6 and 5), 24 January 1927 (overture to *Coriolan*, Piano Concerto No. 4 (Edwin Fischer, piano), Symphony No. 7), 14 April 1930 (Symphonies Nos. 6 and 5), 30 March 1931 (overture *Die Geschöpfe des Prometheus*, Grosse Fuge, overture *Leonore* No. 2, Symphony No. 3) and 26 March 1934 (Symphony No. 2, overture to *Coriolan*, Symphony No. 5).
   Furtwängler conducted all-Brahms concerts on 11 February 1924 ('Haydn' Variations, *Alto Rhapsody* (Emmi Leisner, contralto; Berliner Liedertafel, chorus), *Zigeunerlieder* (Emmi Leisner, contralto; Wilhelm Furtwängler, piano), Symphony No. 3) and 27 February 1933 (*Tragic Overture*, Violin Concerto (Carl Flesch, violin), Symphony No. 4).

53 Furtwängler conducted Vaughan's Williams *Fantasia on a Theme by Thomas Tallis* at Leipzig on 20 October 1927 and *Norfolk Rhapsody* at Vienna on 17 November 1929.

54 C. Ehrlich, *First Philharmonic: A History of The Royal Philharmonic Society* (Oxford, 1995), p. 198.

55 Furtwängler conducted again for the Royal Philharmonic Society on 20 November 1924. The programme included Smetana's overture to *The Bartered Bride*, Strauss's *Tod und Verklärung*, Brahms's Piano Concerto No. 1 (Katharine Goodson, piano) and Beethoven's Symphony No. 7.

56 For the Royal Philharmonic Society, Goossens conducted Honegger's *Pacific 231* on 29 January 1925, Ansermet performed Prokofiev's Violin Concerto No. 1 (Josef Szigeti, violin) on 26 February 1925 and Sargent gave Howells's Piano Concerto No. 2 (Harold Samuel, piano) on 27 April 1925.

57 Furtwängler was impressed immediately by the playing of the New York Philharmonic. He maintained that the way in which it was funded had a positive effect on the standard of playing and that 'thanks to the money behind it . . . [the] technical virtuosity, lightness, elegance and natural beauty of tone of [the orchestra are] extraordinary'. Furtwängler, *Notebooks*, p. 33.

58 Furtwängler's first programme with the New York Philharmonic also included Haydn's Cello Concerto in D major with Pablo Casals as soloist.

59 Furtwängler recorded Beethoven's Symphony No. 5 in 1926 and 1937, Bach's Brandenburg Concerto No. 3 in 1929, Strauss *Till Eulenspiegel* in 1930, Mozart's *Eine kleine Nachtmusik* in 1936–7 and Tchaikovsky's Symphony No. 6 ('Pathétique') in 1938.

60 Although Furtwängler documented little new music, he did record Bartók's Violin Concerto No. 2 with Yehudi Menuhin and the Philharmonia Orchestra in 1953 for HMV.

61 Furtwängler, *Notebooks*, p. 197.

62 O. Strasser, trans. J. Williamson, 'Beethoven's Ninth and the Vienna Philharmonic', disc notes, Deutsche Grammophon CD 435 325–2, pp. 3–6.

63 Ibid.

64 The figure of eighty-four concerts includes five concerts, five open rehearsals in Vienna and two concerts in Budapest with the Vienna Philharmonic, fifty-seven concerts with the Berlin Philharmonic in Berlin and on tour, and fifteen concerts with the Leipzig Gewandhaus Orchestra.

65 Furtwängler conducted Prohaska's Passacaglia, Theme, Variation and Fugue for large orchestra on 9 February 1930 and Weigl's *Phantastiches Intermezzo* for orchestra on 16 February 1930.

66 Furtwängler did not conduct Beethoven's Symphonies Nos. 2, 4 and 6 with the Philharmonic in Vienna. He did, however, conduct two all-Beethoven programmes that included Symphony No. 9 on 14 April 1929 and 23 March 1930. The programmes were also heard at the general rehearsals that preceded the concerts. The only other concert devoted to a single composer was an all-Schubert concert, given presumably to mark the centenary of the composer's death containing Symphonies Nos. 7 in B minor and 8 in C major on 21 October 1928. The programme was also heard at the general rehearsal the previous day.

67 At Vienna, Furtwängler conducted Bruckner's Symphony No. 7 on 15 April 1928, Symphony No. 4 on 9 December 1928 and Symphony No. 8 on 27 October 1929. The symphonies were also performed at the general rehearsal that preceded each concert.

68 Lothar Wallerstein was the producer and Alfred Roller the designer.

69 Toscanini was the first non-Central European conductor to perform at the festival.

70 Furtwängler conducted three performances of *Tristan und Isolde* at the 1931 festival.

71 Furtwängler returned to the Bayreuth Festival in 1936, 1937, 1943, 1944, 1951 and 1954. At the 1951 and 1954 festivals, he conducted performances of Beethoven's Symphony No. 9.

72 Furtwängler belatedly signed his contract with the Staatsoper on 16 January 1934. It was to run for a period of five years with an annual salary of 36,000 Reichsmark. F. K. Prieberg, trans. C. Dolan, *Trial of Strength: Wilhelm Furtwängler and the Third Reich* (London, 1991), p. 117.

73 Pfitzner's *Das Herz* had the distinction of having two world premières on the same day: in Berlin under Furtwängler and in Munich under Hans Knappertsbusch. Pfitzner attended the Munich performance.

74 Hitler became Chancellor of Germany on 30 January 1933.

75 Furtwängler, 'Open Letter to Dr. Joseph Goebbels', *Furtwängler on Music*, p. 138.

76 Furtwängler conducted Hindemith's Kammermusik No. 1 (11 January 1923) and Concerto for Orchestra (17 December 1925) with the Leipzig Gewandhaus, Concerto for Orchestra (21 December 1925), dances from *Das Nusch-Nuschi* (29 October 1928), Concerto for Organ and Chamber Orchestra (25 February 1929), Viola Concerto (Paul Hindemith, viola) (31 March 1930), overture to *Neues vom Tage* (20 October 1930) and symphony *Mathis der Maler* (12 March 1934) with the Berlin Philharmonic, and Concerto for Orchestra (11 December 1927) with the Vienna Philharmonic.

77 Otto Klemperer conducted the première of Hindemith's *Neues vom Tage* at the Kroll Opera on 8 June 1929.

78 At the time of the confrontation, Furtwängler was Director of the Berlin Staatsoper and conductor of the Berlin Philharmonic. He was also Vice-President of the Reichsmusikkammer – Richard Strauss was President – and Prussian Staatsrat. He was told that he could not resign as Prussian Staatsrat, because the post was honorary, but he was informed in a letter dated 5 December 1934 that his resignation from the Berlin Philharmonic and the Reichsmusikkammer had been accepted and, in a letter dated 10 December 1934, that his resignation from the Berlin Staatsoper had also been accepted. Prieberg, *Trial of Strength*, pp. 142, 144.

79 Furtwängler's first concert under the new deal was with the Vienna Philharmonic at Budapest on 12 April 1935.

80 Furtwängler conducted the Berlin Philharmonic in Britain in 1927, 1928, 1929, 1931 and 1932. After the Nazis were elected to power, they returned in 1933, 1934, 1935, 1937 and 1938.

81 Furtwängler conducted the Vienna Philharmonic at Budapest on 12 April 1935, 7 January 1936 and 20 December 1937, at Salzburg on 27 August 1937, 23 July 1938, 10 August 1938, 19 August 1938, 28 and 29 August 1938, at Berlin on 22 and 23 April 1938, at Nürnberg on 5 September 1938, at Pressburg (Bratislava) on 16 December 1938 and at Munich on 19 December 1938.

82 D. Gillis, *Furtwängler and America* (Woodhaven, NY, 1970), p. 55.

83 Ibid., pp. 55–6.

84 J. Hunt, *The Furtwängler Sound* (London, 1992), p. 145.

85 Furtwängler accompanied the soprano Elisabeth Schwarzkopf at the piano for a recital of Wolf's Lieder at Salzburg on 12 August 1953.

86 At the Salzburg Festival, Furtwängler conducted Mozart's *Don Giovanni* fifteen times between 27 July 1950 and 13 August 1954, *Die Zauberflöte* fourteen times between 27 July 1949 and 29 August 1951 and *Le nozze di Figaro* four times in 1953.

87 At the Salzburg Festival, Furtwängler conducted thirteen performances of Beethoven's *Fidelio* between 1948 and 1950, four performances of Wagner's *Die Meistersinger von Nürnberg* in 1938, five performances of Weber's *Der Freischütz* in 1954 and five performances of Verdi's *Otello* in 1951.

88 In his notebooks, Furtwängler wrote: 'Bach, Beethoven, Schubert, Brahms, finally Bruckner, Wagner, Hugo Wolf, Richard Strauss, Pfitzner, etc. all adhere to the same laws – they form a world. Not the nineteenth century, not the eighteenth century, not an "historical" world, but a common concept of music.' It is interesting that Furtwängler, whether consciously or unconsciously, omitted Mozart

from the list of composers who formed 'a common concept of music'. Furtwängler, *Notebooks*, p. 93.

89 As well as conducting the Berlin Philharmonic's subscription concerts in Hamburg in 1939, 1940 and 1941, Furtwängler toured with the orchestra in Germany and Holland in January 1940, performed with them at major German cities between October 1939 and March 1940, toured with them in Germany, Prague and Vienna in May 1940, performed with them in Leipzig and Italy in 1941, toured with them in Sweden, Denmark and Switzerland in 1942 and conducted them at Prague in 1944. With the Vienna Philharmonic, Furtwängler performed in Munich in 1939 and 1941, Salzburg in 1940 and 1944 and Budapest in 1941 and 1944.

90 In Berlin, Furtwängler conducted fifteen of the twenty-six performances given at the Philharmonic Concerts during the 1940–1 season. Carl Schuricht, Willem Mengelberg and Clemens Krauss conducted the remainder of the series. The figure of twenty-six performances includes open rehearsals, concerts and repeat concerts.

91 At Berlin during the 1940–1 season, Furtwängler conducted Pfitzner's Symphony in C major on 13, 14 and 15 October 1940, Rezniček's 'Chamisso' Variations on 3, 4 and 5 November 1940, Berger's *Rondino giocoso* on 15, 16 and 17 December 1940 and Zilcher's Violin Concerto (Eric Röhn, violin) on 2, 3 and 4 February 1941. These dates represent the general rehearsal, the performance and the repeat performance.

92 At Vienna during the 1940–1 season, Furtwängler conducted Rezniček's 'Chamisso' Variations on 26 and 27 October 1940, Pfitzner's Symphony in C on 23 and 24 November 1940 and Berger's *Rondino giocoso* on 21 and 22 December 1940. These dates include both the general rehearsal and the concert.

93 Furtwängler performed Beethoven's Symphony No. 6 in Berlin on 3, 4 and 5 November 1940 and in Vienna on 23 and 24 November 1940. These dates include the general rehearsals, performance and/or repeat performance.

94 Furtwängler conducted L'Orchestre de la Suisse Romande at Geneva and Lausanne on 12 and 14 February 1945 respectively.

95 Schönzeler, *Furtwängler*, p. 103.

96 Gillis, *Furtwängler and America*, p. 88.

97 As the Philharmonie in Berlin had been destroyed, the concerts on 25, 26 and 29 May were given at the Titania-Palast, while the performance on 27 May was given at the Haus des Rundfunks. At those concerts, Furtwängler conducted Beethoven's overture to *Egmont* and Symphonies Nos. 6 and 5.

98 On 8 September 1953, Karajan conducted Bartók's Concerto for Orchestra and Beethoven's Symphony No. 3 with the Berlin Philharmonic, and on 23 September 1954 he performed Mozart's Symphony No. 39, Bartók's Piano Concerto No. 3 (Géza Anda, piano) and Brahms's Symphony No. 1 with the orchestra. Although Furtwängler did conduct the orchestra regularly after the war, the bulk of its concerts were undertaken by the young Romanian conductor Sergiu Celibidache. See Chapter 9 note 104.

99 Statistic based on the information kindly provided by Dr Clemens Hellsberg of the Vienna Philharmonic.

100 For his recording of Wagner's *Die Walküre*, Furtwängler conducted the Vienna Philharmonic.

101 At the time of his recording of Wagner's *Die Walküre* in Vienna, Furtwängler was living at Clarens in Switzerland.

102 Schönzeler, *Furtwängler*, p. 118.

103 D. Barenboim, *A Life in Music* (London, 1991), pp. 31–2.

Chapter 9. 'Das Wunder Karajan'

1 Karajan began to use the name 'Herbert' from the late 1920s but continued to use 'Heribert' sporadically until the early 1930s. Similarly, he abandoned the noble 'von' after World War I because it was illegal in Austria but re-adopted it when he joined the staff of the Ulm Stadttheater in 1929.

2 Georg was ennobled by Friedrich August, Duke of Saxony, on 1 June 1792. R. Osborne, *Herbert von Karajan: A Life in Music* (London, 1998), p. 8.

3 Karajan played a Mozart rondo at a charity event in a Salzburg restaurant in 1912. Ibid., p. 5.

4 Bernhard Paumgartner (1887–1971) Austrian composer, musicologist and conductor.

5 Karajan played the Rondo K. 485 on 27 January 1917, the Fantasy in D minor K. 397 on 26 January 1918 and the Rondo for piano and orchestra K. 382 on 26 January 1919.

6 At the Mozarteum, Karajan performed Beethoven's Rondo in C major Op. 51 No. 1 on 22 June 1918, Liszt's Consolations in E major, D flat major and G major on 14 April 1920, Piano Concerto No. 1 on 5 March 1925 and 12 May 1926 and Hungarian Rhapsody No. 12 on 24 March 1926, Brahms's Piano Sonata in F minor Op. 5 on 6 February 1924, Franck's Sonata for piano and violin in A major (Josef Schmalwieser, violin) on 17 December 1925, Corelli's *La Folia* (arr. piano and violin) (Norbert Hofmann, violin) on 10 October 1925 and Vladigerov's Two Pieces for violin and piano Op. 12 (Josef Schmalwieser, violin) on 17 December 1925 and Piano Concerto No. 1 in A minor Op. 6 on 25 June 1926.

7 In 1923, Molière's play *Der eingebildete Kranke (Le Malade imaginaire)*, produced by Max Reinhardt, was the only work performed and no festival was held in 1924. H. Jaklitsch, *Die Salzburger Festspiele*, Vol. 3: *Verzeichnis der Werke und der Künstler 1920–1990* (Salzburg, 1991), p. 3.

8 H. von Karajan (as told to F. Endler), trans. S. Spencer, *My Autobiography* (London, 1989), p. 11.

9 Josef Hofmann (1865–?): Austrian pianist and teacher, not to be confused with his more famous Polish namesake.

10 E. Haeusserman, *Herbert von Karajan* (Vienna, 1978), p. 30.

11 Ibid., p. 32.

12 R. Osborne, *Conversations with Karajan* (Oxford, 1989), p. 40.

13 Haeusserman, *Herbert von Karajan*, p. 32.

14 G. K. Kende, 'Was Richard Strauss in Wien dirigierte', *Richard Strauss-Blätter*, 19 (June 1988), pp. 29–40.

15 F. Hadamowsky, *Die Wiener Hoftheater (Staatstheater)*, Vol. 2: *1811–1974* (Vienna, 1975), p. 642.

16 Osborne, *Conversations*, p. 41.

17 Osborne, *Herbert von Karajan*, p. 34.

18 Karajan orchestrated the first movement of Beethoven's Piano Sonata in C major Op. 2 No. 3. Ibid., p. 38.

19 Reinhardt's production of *Ein Sommernachtstraum* was given eight performances between 6 and 27 August 1927. Bernhard Paumgartner conducted Mendelssohn's incidental music.

20 Osborne, *Conversations*, p. 45.

21 According to Richard Osborne, Karajan's monthly salary of 80 Reichsmark compared poorly with that of an orchestral player at Ulm, who earned approximately 240 Reichsmark a month. Osborne, *Herbert von Karajan*, p. 50.

22 Ibid., p. 52.

23 Handel's *Giulio Cesare* and d'Albert's *Tiefland* are included in the Austro-German statistic.
24 The operas that Karajan conducted at Ulm included Mozart's *Le nozze di Figaro* and *Don Giovanni*, Weinberger's *Schwanda the Bagpiper*, Verdi's *Rigoletto*, *Il trovatore* and *La traviata*, Flotow's *Martha*, Leoncavallo's *Cavalleria rusticana*, Rossini's *Il barbiere di Siviglia*, Bizet's *Carmen*, Puccini's *La Bohème* and *Madama Butterfly*, Donizetti's *Don Pasquale*, d'Albert's *Tiefland*, Wagner's *Die Meistersinger von Nürnberg*, *Tannhäuser* and *Lohengrin*, Beethoven's *Fidelio*, Strauss's *Der Rosenkavalier* and *Arabella*, Lortzing's *Undine* and *Der Wildschütz*, Nicolai's *Die lustigen Weiber von Windsor* and Handel's *Giulio Cesare*.
25 Karajan conducted *Arabella* on 9, 15 and 20 February 1934. Those were the only performances of the opera that he conducted during his career.
26 With the exception of a single performance of Weinberger's *Schwanda the Bagpiper* on 18 March 1929, Karajan conducted, for example, eight consecutive performances of *Le nozze di Figaro* between 2 and 31 March 1929, then six consecutive performances of Verdi's *Rigoletto* between 9 and 26 October 1929, followed by eight consecutive performances of Flotow's *Martha* between 24 November and 28 December 1929.
27 The second piano was played by Otto Schulmann.
28 At the concert on 22 July 1931, Karajan conducted Wagner's Prelude to *Die Meistersinger von Nürnberg*, Schumann's Piano Concerto (Ralph Lawton, piano), Tchaikovsky's Piano Concerto No. 1 (Ralph Lawton, piano) and Strauss's *Till Eulenspiegel*.
29 The programme for 21 August 1934 included Debussy's *Fantaisie* for piano and orchestra (Ralph Lawton, piano) and *Prélude à l'après-midi d'un faune* and Ravel's *La Valse*.
30 The other performances of *Faust* were given on 21, 25 and 31 August 1933.
31 Toscanini conducted the following repertoire at Salzburg in 1934: Mozart's Symphony No. 35 ('Haffner'), Brahms's 'Haydn' Variations and Beethoven's Symphony No. 7 on 23 August; Wagner's *Faust Overture*, Preludes to Acts 1 and 3 from *Lohengrin*, the 'Hallenarie' from *Tannhäuser* (Lotte Lehmann, soprano), Siegfried's Rhine Journey from *Götterdämmerung*, three songs from the 'Wesendonck' Lieder (Lotte Lehmann, soprano), Siegfried's Death and Funeral March from *Götterdämmerung* and the Prelude to *Die Meistersinger von Nürnberg* on 26 August, and Cherubini's overture *Anacreon*, Brahms's Symphony No. 3, Debussy's *Prélude à l'après-midi d'un faune*, Berlioz's 'Queen Mab' Scherzo from *Roméo et Juliette* and Bach's Passacaglia (arr. Respighi) on 30 August.
32 Karajan attended Toscanini's performances with the La Scala company at the Vienna Staatsoper in 1929, with the New York Philharmonic at Vienna in May 1930 and at the Bayreuth Festival in July 1930.
33 Haeusserman, *Herbert von Karajan*, p. 103.
34 Osborne, *Conversations*, pp. 68-9.
35 Erich Leinsdorf (1912–93): Austrian-born American conductor. After leaving Europe before World War II, Leinsdorf made his American début at the Metropolitan Opera, New York, in 1938. He was appointed Music Director of the Cleveland Orchestra in 1943 and Music Director of the Boston Symphony Orchestra between 1962 and 1969.
36 *Erich Leinsdorf on Music* (Portland, OR, 1997), p. 216.
37 Karajan/Endler, *My Autobiography*, p. 31.
38 In later life, Karajan maintained that he was 'thrown out' by Dieterich. Ibid.
39 Ibid., p. 33.
40 Osborne, *Herbert von Karajan*, p. 75.
41 Haeusserman, *Herbert von Karajan*, p. 55.

42 The operas that Karajan conducted at Aachen included d'Albert's *Tiefland*, Beethoven's *Fidelio*, Bizet's *Carmen*, Handel's *Giulio Cesare*, Mozart's *Die Entführung aus dem Serail*, *Don Giovanni*, *Così fan tutte* and *Die Zauberflöte*, Puccini's *Tosca*, J. Strauss's *Die Fledermaus*, Strauss's *Elektra*, *Der Rosenkavalier*, *Die Frau ohne Schatten* and *Friedenstag*, Verdi's *Aida*, *Un ballo in maschera*, *Otello*, *Il trovatore* and *Falstaff* and Wagner's *Der fliegende Holländer*, *Tannhäuser*, *Lohengrin*, *Tristan und Isolde*, *Die Meistersinger von Nürnberg*, *Das Rheingold*, *Die Walküre*, *Siegfried*, *Götterdämmerung* and *Parsifal*.

43 The operas that Karajan had conducted previously included d'Albert's *Tiefland*, Beethoven's *Fidelio*, Bizet's *Carmen*, Handel's *Giulio Cesare*, Mozart's *Don Giovanni*, Puccini's *Tosca*, Strauss's *Der Rosenkavalier* and Wagner's *Tannhäuser*, *Lohengrin* and *Die Meistersinger von Nürnberg*.

44 Karajan's Aachen cycle of *Der Ring des Nibelungen* was heard on the following dates: 21 November 1937 (*Das Rheingold*), 24 November 1937 (*Die Walküre*), 26 November 1937 (*Siegfried*) and 28 November 1937 (*Götterdämmerung*).

45 The first performance of Karajan's new production of *Die Meistersinger von Nürnberg* was on 21 September 1940.

46 Karajan/Endler, *My Autobiography*, p. 39.

47 Ibid, p. 40.

48 Karajan conducted *Friedenstag* on 4 and 9 May 1939. The opera was premièred at the Bavarian Staatsoper on 24 July 1938 by Clemens Krauss.

49 At Karlsruhe, Karajan conducted Wagner's *Tannhäuser* and Mozart's *Le nozze di Figaro* at the Badisches Staatstheater on 31 January and 12 March 1935 respectively.

50 Karajan's contract allowed for a salary of 14,000 marks in the first year, 15,000 marks in the second and 16,000 marks in the third. He also had the ability to hire and to fire the musicians and singers under his direction. Osborne, *Herbert von Karajan*, pp. 82–3.

51 Haeusserman, *Herbert von Karajan*, pp. 58–9.

52 Apparently, Karajan's initial membership of the Nazi Party had lapsed.

53 Karajan/Endler, *My Autobiography*, p. 37.

54 Haeusserman, *Herbert von Karajan*, p. 58.

55 Before being promoted to Generalmusikdirektor, Karajan conducted a concert with the Städtisches Orchester on 8 December 1934. The programme included Weber's overture to *Euryanthe*, Tchaikovsky's Violin Concerto (Sigmund Bleier, violin) and Brahms's Symphony No. 1.

56 The programme for Karajan's contemporary concert on 13 May 1936 was Wunsch's *Fest auf Monbijou*, Frommel's Suite for small orchestra, Waertisch's Rondo for large orchestra, Pepping's Partita and Atterberg's *Älvin*. On 14 May 1936, Karajan conducted Pepping's Partita for orchestra, Georg Schumann's Variations on *Gestern Abend war Vetter Michel da*, Palmgren's Piano Concerto No. 2 and Ravel's *La Valse*.

57 For Karajan's first concert as Generalmusikdirektor at Aachen, he conducted Beethoven's overture to *Egmont*, Piano Concerto No. 5 ('Emperor') (Walter Gieseking, piano) and Symphony No. 5.

58 Karajan also conducted Symphonies No. 7 and No. 9 during the 1938–9 and 1937–8 seasons respectively.

59 The statistics pertaining to the choral works exclude Beethoven's Symphony No. 9 and the performances that Karajan gave on tour.

60 The choral works that Karajan conducted on tour with the Städtisches Orchester and the Städtischer Gesangsverein included Bach's Mass in B minor (Brussels, 26 April 1936; Paris, 17, 18 and 19 December 1940) and *St Matthew Passion* (with the Knabenchor des Domchores, Aachen) (Brussels, 20 February 1938), Brahms's

Ein deutsches Requiem (Brussels, 9 May 1937; Berlin, 8 May 1939), Bruckner's Te Deum (Brussels, 9 May 1937) and Beethoven's Missa solemnis (Brussels, 15 January 1939). The Aachen choir also performed the Missa solemnis with the Berlin Staatskapelle and Karajan at Berlin on 19 January 1942 and at an open rehearsal the day before.

61 Karajan/Endler, *My Autobiography*, p. 44.

62 The only rehearsal that Karajan had for that performance of *Tristan und Isolde* was with the singers.

63 For his début with the Berlin Philharmonic Karajan conducted Mozart's Symphony No. 33, Ravel's *Daphnis et Chloé* Suite No. 2 and Brahms's Symphony No. 4. The concert was one of the orchestra's Sonderkonzerte and not part of the subscription series.

64 Victor de Sabata (1892–1967): Italian conductor.

65 Karajan/Endler, *My Autobiography*, p. 47.

66 Ibid., p. 48.

67 Karajan conducted the world première of *Die Bürger von Calais* on 28 January 1939.

68 Karajan/Endler, *My Autobiography*, p. 48.

69 Ibid., p. 49.

70 Ibid., p. 50.

71 Osborne, *Herbert von Karajan*, p. 136.

72 Strauss meticulous sense of rhythm and phrasing, restrained approach on the podium, understanding of stagecraft and adherence to the printed text in Mozart all influenced Karajan's mature performance style.

73 At Karajan's concerts with the Staatskapelle on 4 and 5 October 1944, Bruckner's Symphony No. 8 was the only work on the programme.

74 The all-Strauss programme that Karajan gave on 14 and 15 May 1944 was part of the composer's eightieth birthday celebrations and contained *Tanzsuite nach Couperin*, *Die heiligen drei Könige* and *Allerseelen* (Erna Berger, soprano) and *Ein Heldenleben*.

75 Karajan performed Rasch's Toccata for large orchestra on 10 November 1941, Berger's *Legende vom Prinzen Eugen* on 24 January and 25 October 1943 and the world première of von Einem's Concerto for Orchestra on 3 April 1944. The von Einem work was repeated on the following day.

76 Karajan performed Borck's *Sinfonisches Vorspiel* at Aachen and Berlin on 25 October 1940 and 8 and 9 December 1940 respectively, Knaak's *Sinfonisches Vorspiel* at Aachen and Berlin 3 October 1941 and 13 October 1941 respectively and Viski's *Enigma* at Aachen and Berlin on 13 February 1942 and 23 February 1942 respectively.

77 Karajan performed Sibelius's Symphony No. 6 with the Stockholm Radio Orchestra and the Berlin Philharmonic on 7 February and 27 September 1938 respectively and *En Saga* with the Aachen Städtisches Orchester on 9 March 1939.

78 Karajan conducted Geminiani's Concerto grosso Op. 3 No. 2 at Aachen on 6 January 1937 and 12 December 1941 and at Berlin on 23 February 1942, Locatelli's Concerto grosso Op. 1 No. 10 (arr. Marinucci) at Berlin on 9 and 10 February 1941 and Concerto grosso Op. 4 No. 10 at Aachen on 24 November 1940 and Respighi's *Fontane di Roma* and *Pini di Roma* at Aachen on 24 November 1940 and at Berlin on 5 and 6 January 1941 respectively.

79 For the performance of Bach's Concerto for Four Keyboard Instruments at Berlin on 30 November 1942, Karajan was one of the solo pianists; the others were Conrad Hansen, Ferry Gebhardt and Pál Kiss. For the performance of Brandenburg Concerto No. 2 at Berlin on 10 May 1943, Karajan was the continuo player.

Karajan conducted Bach's Concerto for Two Violins (Detlef Grümmer, Franz Neander, violins) and Orchestral Suite No. 2 at Aachen on 6 January 1937 and Orchestral Suite No. 3 at Berlin on 7 and 8 November 1943. He conducted Handel's Concerto grosso Op. 6 No. 12 at Berlin on 10 and 11 November 1940 and Op. 6 No. 5 at Aachen on 21 September 1941.

80 At Aachen, Walter Gieseking played Beethoven's Piano Concerto No. 5 on 10 October 1935, Edwin Fischer played Mozart's Piano Concerto No. 20 on 15 April 1937, Wilhelm Backhaus played Beethoven's Piano Concerto No. 4 on 6 January 1938, Ely Ney played Mozart's Piano Concerto No. 21, Beethoven's Piano Concerto No. 5 and Liszt's Piano Concerto No. 1 in a triple bill on 3 November 1938, Georg Kulenkampff played Brahms's Violin Concerto on 12 December 1935, Brahms's Double Concerto (with Tibor de Machula, cello) on 16 December 1937 and Tchaikovsky's Violin Concerto on 9 March 1939, Gaspar Cassadó played Dvořák's Cello Concerto on 5 March 1936, and Enrico Mainardi played Casella's Notturno e Tarantella for cello and orchestra on 5 January 1939 and Haydn's Cello Concerto in D major on 4 October 1940.

81 At Berlin, Georg Kulenkampff played Dvořák's Violin Concerto on 10 and 11 November 1940, Walter Gieseking played Rachmaninoff's Piano Concerto No. 3 on 9 and 10 February 1941 and Schumann's Piano Concerto on 1 and 2 November 1944, Enrico Mainardi played Strauss's *Don Quixote* on 10 November 1941 and Edwin Fischer played Mozart's Piano Concerto No. 20 on 24 November 1941. Among the soloists with whom Karajan performed in Berlin was the Italian pianist Arturo Benedetti Michelangeli, who played Grieg's Piano Concerto on 8 and 9 December 1940.

82 Karajan/Endler, *My Autobiography*, p. 52.

83 Karajan's replacement at Aachen was the Dutch conductor Paul van Kempen (1893–1955).

84 Osborne, *Conversations*, p. 59.

85 Karajan/Endler, *My Autobiography*, p. 51.

86 After the closure of German theatres by the Minister of Propaganda, Joseph Goebbels, in 1944, the Berlin Staatskapelle began to give concerts devoted to operatic excerpts. Of the sixty-four concerts in that format, nearly all were conducted by either Robert Heger or Johannes Schüler. An exception, however, was the concert on 29 October 1944, when Wilhelm Furtwängler conducted excerpts from *Götterdämmerung*. Karajan conducted none of the sixty-four concerts.

87 Osborne, *Herbert von Karajan*, p. 178.

88 Karajan's last wartime concert with the Berlin Staatskapelle was on 18 February 1945. The programme included Weber's overture to *Der Freischütz*, Schumann's Symphony No. 4, Mozart's Symphony No. 35 and Strauss's *Till Eulenspiegel*.

89 Karajan/Endler, *My Autobiography*, pp. 56–9.

90 Karajan conducted three concerts at Trieste shortly after the end of the war. The programmes included Haydn's Symphony No. 104 ('London'), Strauss's *Tod und Verklärung*, Beethoven's Symphony No. 5, Tchaikovsky's Symphony No. 6 ('Pathétique'), Sibelius's *Finlandia*, a concerto grosso by Locatelli, Wagner's *Siegfried Idyll* and Brahms's Symphony No. 1. Osborne, *Herbert von Karajan*, p. 184.

91 Karajan argued that although he was a member of the Nazi Party, he was not an activist. The American tribunal accepted his argument and cleared him in November 1945.

92 Osborne, *Herbert von Karajan*, pp. 189–206.

93 Karajan also performed at the Bayreuth Festival in 1951 and 1952. The works that he conducted there included *Die Meistersinger von Nürnberg* and *Der Ring des Nibelungen* in 1951 and *Tristan und Isolde* in 1952.

The operas that Karajan conducted with the La Scala company either at Milan or on tour included Wagner's *Tannhäuser* (1951), *Lohengrin* (1953), *Die Walküre* (1958) and *Tristan und Isolde* (1959), Mozart's *Don Giovanni* (1951, 1953), *Le nozze di Figaro* (1954, 1960) and *Die Zauberflöte* (1955), Beethoven's *Fidelio* (1952, 1961), Strauss's *Der Rosenkavalier* (1952) and *Salome* (1956), Donizetti's *Lucia di Lammermoor* (1954, 1956) Bizet's *Carmen* (1955), Verdi's *Falstaff* (1957) and *La traviata* (1964), Puccini's *La Bohème* *(1964)* and Mascagni's *Cavalleria rusticana* (1968). Karajan also conducted Verdi's Requiem with the La Scala company at Milan and on tour in 1963, 1964, 1966 and 1967 and Mozart's Requiem in 1965. He also appeared with the orchestra of the La Scala, Milan, as a concert conductor.

94 Karajan included Strauss's *Don Juan* at his first concert with the Vienna Philharmonic after World War II, on 12 January 1946; also in the programme were Haydn's Symphony No. 104 and Brahms' Symphony No. 1. Karajan gave no fewer than ninety performances of *Don Juan* during his career.

95 E. Schwarzkopf, *On and Off the Record: A Memoir of Walter Legge* (London, 1982), p. 222.

96 Ibid., p. 223.

97 The statistics for Karajan's films apply to the number of works recorded and not the number of performances. The statistics in this section are based on information found in John Hunt's discography of Karajan, *Philharmonic Autocrat* (London, 1993).

98 The composers who were still active after Karajan's début at Salzburg in 1929 and whom he recorded included Bartók, Berg, Britten, Cilea, Giordano, Hindemith, Holst, Honegger, Kodály, Lehár, Leimer, Mascagni, Martin (unpublished 1958 recording of Etude for Strings with the Berlin Philharmonic), Nielsen, Orff, Prokofiev, Rachmaninoff, Ravel, Respighi, Reznišek, Roussel, Franz Schmidt, Schoenberg, Shostakovich, Sibelius, Strauss, Stravinsky, Vaughan Williams, Webern, Weinberger and Wolf-Ferrari.

99 With the Berlin Philharmonic, Karajan recorded for DGG Berg's Three Orchestral Pieces Op. 6 and *Lyric Suite*, Schoenberg's *Pelleas und Melisande*, Variations for Orchestra and *Verklärte Nacht*, and Webern's Passacaglia Op. 1, Symphony Op. 21, Five Movements for string orchestra Op. 5 and Six Pieces Op. 6.

100 Like many of the works mentioned in this section, some of the symphonies of Haydn and Mozart were recorded by Karajan more than once.

101 Karajan made only one recording each of Tchaikovsky's Symphonies Nos. 1 ('Winter Daydreams'), 2 ('Little Russian') and 3 ('Polish') and multiple recordings of Symphonies Nos. 4, 5 and 6.

102 The operas, operettas and stage works that Karajan recorded commercially and complete included Beethoven's *Fidelio*, Bizet's *Carmen*, Debussy's *Pelléas et Mélisande*, Humperdinck's *Hänsel und Gretel*, Lehár's *Die lustige Witwe*, Leoncavallo's *Pagliacci*, Mascagni's *Cavalleria rusticana*, Mozart's *Così fan tutte*, *Don Giovanni*, *Le nozze di Figaro* and *Die Zauberflöte*, Mussorgsky's *Boris Godunov*, Orff's *De temporum fine comoedia*, Puccini's *La Bohème*, *Madama Butterfly*, *Tosca* and *Turandot*, Johann Strauss's *Die Fledermaus*, Richard Strauss's *Ariadne auf Naxos*, *Der Rosenkavalier* and *Salome*, Verdi's *Aida*, *Un ballo in maschera*, *Don Carlos*, *Falstaff*, *Otello* and *Il trovatore* and Wagner's *Der fliegende Holländer*, *Lohengrin*, *Tristan und Isolde*, *Die Meistersinger von Nürnberg*, *Das Rheingold*, *Die Walküre*, *Siegfried*, *Götterdämmerung* and *Parsifal*. Karajan recorded some of these more than once.

103 A performance of *Elektra* recorded at the 1964 Salzburg Festival is now available widely on CD.

104 Sergiu Celibidache (1912–96): Romanian conductor. Of Karajan, Celibidache

once remarked: 'I know, he excited the masses. So does Coca Cola' [trans. present author]. S. Piendl and T. Otto, eds., *Stenographische Umarmung* (Regensburg, 2002), p. 40.

105 Karajan/Endler, *My Autobiography*, p. 73

106 Osborne, *Herbert von Karajan*, p. 372.

107 Ibid.

108 During the 1955 North American tour, Karajan conducted at Washington (27 February and 27 March), Philadelphia (28 February), New York (1 and 30 March, 1 April), Harrisburg (2 March), Pittsburgh (3 March), Cleveland (4 March), Cincinnati (5 March), Lexington (7 March), Bloomington (8 March), Milwaukee (10 March), Chicago (11, 12 and 13 March), Ann Arbor (15 March), Columbus (16 March), Detroit (17 March), Toronto (18 March), Rochester (20 March), Montreal (21 March), Syracuse (22 March), Boston (24 March), Hartford (25 March), Baltimore (26 March) and Newark (29 March).

109 Osborne, *Herbert von Karajan*, p. 379.

110 Ibid.

111 K. Lang, trans. S. Spencer, *The Karajan Dossier* (London, 1992).

112 Osborne, *Herbert von Karajan*, p. 383.

113 Ibid., p. 372.

114 The Philharmonic Concerts were renamed Abonnement Series P from the 1970–1 season and were no longer under the general direction of Karajan. From that year, Karajan began to conduct across the various Abonnement Series of the Berlin Philharmonic.

115 Besides conducting non-subscription concerts with the Berlin Philharmonic, Karajan also performed regularly at its youth concerts and its concerts for the Berlin Festwochen.

116 From the 1970–1 season Karajan usually performed one concert annually at the Berlin Philharmonic's series devoted to twentieth-century music.

117 At the Philharmonic and Abonnement Series, Karajan performed Schoenberg's Variations for Orchestra six times, *Gurrelieder* twice, *Verklärte Nacht* four times and *Pelleas und Melisande* once, Berg's Three Orchestral Pieces Op. 6 eleven times, Three Movements from the *Lyric Suite* nine times and the Violin Concerto five times, and Webern's Five Movements for string orchestra Op. 5 fourteen times, Six Pieces Op. 6 three times and the Passacaglia Op. 1 and the Symphony Op. 21 once each. Those figures exclude performances that Karajan gave with the Berlin Philharmonic outside the subscription series.

118 Osborne, *Conversations*, p. 123.

119 Symphony No. 9 was heard on 31 December 1967 and repeated on 1 January 1968. The soloists were Gundula Janowitz, Christa Ludwig, Jess Thomas and Walter Berry. The choir was the chorus of the Deutsche Oper, Berlin.

120 Karajan conducted cycles of Beethoven's symphonies in Paris in April 1960, London in April 1961, New York in January 1965, Tokyo in April 1966 and Osaka in May 1970.

121 The figure of twelve all-Brahms concerts includes those devoted to *Ein deutsches Requiem*.

122 At the Royal Festival Hall, London, Karajan performed Brahms's Piano Concerto No. 2 (Géza Anda, piano) and Symphony No. 4 on 31 January 1964, Symphonies Nos. 2 and 3 on 1 February 1964, the Violin Concerto (Christian Ferras, violin) and Symphony No. 1 on 3 February 1964, Symphonies Nos. 2 and 4 on 17 June 1974 and Nos. 3 and 1 on 18 June 1974. At the Berlin Festwochen, he performed the Violin Concerto (Christian Ferras, violin) and Symphony No. 1 on 25 September 1968, Piano Concerto No. 2 (Géza Anda, piano) and Symphony No. 4 on 28 September 1968, Symphonies Nos. 2 and 3 on 30 September 1968 and *Ein deutsches Requiem* on 1 October 1968.

123 Osborne, *Conversations*, p. 117.
124 Between 12 March 1955 and 31 October 1982, Karajan conducted at least two performances of *Lieder eines fahrenden Gesellen*, ten of *Das Lied von der Erde*, ten of Symphony No. 4, nine of Symphony No. 5, thirteen of Symphony No. 6 and nine of Symphony No. 9 with the Berlin Philharmonic either in Berlin or on tour. He also conducted three performances of *Das Lied von der Erde* with the Vienna Philharmonic in Vienna on 18, 19 and 26 June 1960. When performing *Das Lied von der Erde* and Symphonies Nos. 5, 6 and 9, Karajan generally programmed them alone. Exceptions to that policy occurred, however, on 28 and 29 February and 1 March 1960 when he programmed *Das Lied von der Erde* with Mozart's Symphony No. 29 at concerts with the Berlin Philharmonic.
125 Karajan conducted *Das Lied von der Erde* from 1960 and Symphonies Nos. 4, 5, 6 and 9 from 1980, 1973, 1977 and 1982 respectively with the Berlin Philharmonic at its subscription, non-subscription and tour concerts.
126 Osborne, *Herbert von Karajan*, p. 696.
127 Karajan/Endler, *My Autobiography*, p. 75.
128 Karajan's choral conducting technique can be seen clearly in his video recording of Bruckner's Te Deum with the Wiener Singverein and the Vienna Philharmonic for DGG. DGG 072 137–3 GH PAL.
129 The works that Karajan conducted with the Singverein included Bach's *St Matthew Passion*, Beethoven's Missa solemnis and Symphony No. 9, Brahms's *Ein deutsches Requiem*, Haydn's *Die Schöpfung*, Mozart's *Ave verum corpus*, *Die Zauberflöte* and Requiem and Verdi's *Aida* and Requiem.
130 Karajan married Eliette Mouret on 6 October 1958.
131 Osborne, *Herbert von Karajan*, p. 567.
132 Karl Böhm was born at Graz on 28 August 1894 and died at Salzburg on 14 August 1981.
133 Karajan/Endler, *My Autobiography*, p. 147.
134 Ibid., p. 86.
135 The operas that Karajan conducted as Director of the Staatsoper included Beethoven's *Fidelio*, Bizet's *Carmen*, Debussy's *Pelléas et Mélisande*, Gluck's *Orfeo ed Euridice*, Monteverdi's *L'incoronazione di Poppea*, Mozart's *Le nozze di Figaro*, *Die Zauberflöte* and *Don Giovanni*, Pizzetti's *Assassinio nella cattedrale*, Puccini's *Madama Butterfly*, *La Bohème* and *Tosca*, Johann Strauss's *Die Fledermaus*, Richard Strauss's *Die Frau ohne Schatten* and *Der Rosenkavalier*, Stravinsky's *Oedipus Rex*, Verdi's *Il trovatore*, *Otello*, *Aida*, *Falstaff* and *La traviata*, and Wagner's *Tristan und Isolde*, *Die Meistersinger von Nürnberg*, *Parsifal*, *Tannhäuser*, *Das Rheingold*, *Die Walküre*, *Siegfried* and *Götterdämmerung*.
136 Karajan conducted *L'incoronazione di Poppea* and *Assassinio nella cattedrale* at Vienna in the 1962–3 and the 1959–60 seasons respectively.
137 Karajan conducted Mozart's *Die Zauberflöte* and *Don Giovanni* during the 1961–2 and the 1962–3 seasons respectively.
138 Osborne, *Conversations*, p. 43.
139 Karajan/Endler, *My Autobiography*, p. 150.
140 Karajan did perform at two Salzburg Festivals in the immediate post-war years, directing performances of Mozart's *Le nozze di Figaro* in 1948 and Verdi's Requiem and Beethoven's Symphony No. 9 in 1949.
141 The Salzburg Festival's Orchestral Concerts were instituted in 1925. The only other orchestras that performed in the series after that date were the Budapest Philharmonic (two concerts) under Ernst von Dohnányi at the 1931 Festival, the Mozarteum Orchestra (one concert) under Willem van Hoogstraten at the 1941 Festival and the Mozarteum Orchestra (five concerts) under Bertil Wetzelsberger, Robert F. Denzler, Eugen Jochum, Bernhard Paumgartner and Felix Prohaska at the 1945 Festival.

Besides the Orchestral Concerts, other series that were given annually or regularly as part of the Salzburg Festival's programme were Dramatic Theatre, Opera, Ballet, Serenades, Matinées, Chamber Concerts, Lieder Evenings, Solo Concerts, Concerts of Spiritual Music and Church Concerts.

142 Osborne, *Herbert von Karajan*, p. 402. The new Festspielhaus was opened in 1960.

143 The Berlin Philharmonic gave five concerts in 1957, under Herbert von Karajan (29 July), Rafael Kubelik (1 August), George Szell (3 August), Wolfgang Sawallisch (6 August) and Eduard van Beinum (9 August); the Concertgebouw Orchestra gave five concerts in 1958, under Wolfgang Sawallisch (2 August), George Szell (6 and 8 August), Dimitri Mitropoulos (10 August) and Eugen Jochum (12 August); the Orchestre National de la Radiodiffusion-Télévision Française gave five concerts in 1959, under Georg Solti (1 August), George Szell (3 August), Manuel Rosenthal (6 August), Joseph Keilberth (9 August) and Rudolf Kempe (11 August); the New York Philharmonic gave one concert in 1959 under Leonard Bernstein (16 August); the Berlin Philharmonic gave three concerts in 1960, under Herbert von Karajan (7 August), Joseph Keilberth (17 August) and Dimitri Mitropoulos (21 August); the Staatskapelle Dresden gave five concerts in 1961, under Franz Konwitschny (4 August), George Szell (6 August), Joseph Keilberth (9 August), Miltiades Caridis (11 August) and Karl Böhm (13 August); the Berlin Philharmonic gave five concerts in 1962, under Herbert von Karajan (9 August), István Kertész (11 August), William Steinberg (15 August), Rudolf Kempe (16 August) and Karl Böhm (19 August); the Czech Philharmonic gave five concerts in 1963, under Karl Ančerl (30 July), George Szell (4 August), Wolfgang Sawallisch (6 August), Lorin Maazel (9 August) and George Georgescu (12 August), and the Berlin Philharmonic gave five concerts in 1964, under Zubin Mehta (3 August), Carl Schuricht (5 August), Wolfgang Sawallisch (8 August), George Szell (10 August) and Herbert von Karajan (15 August).

144 As Artistic Director, Karajan conducted five performances of Beethoven's *Fidelio* and four of Verdi's *Falstaff* in 1957, five performances of Verdi's *Don Carlos* and four of *Fidelio* in 1958, five performances of Gluck's *Orfeo ed Euridice* in 1959, six performances of Strauss's *Der Rosenkavalier* and five of Mozart's *Don Giovanni* in 1960, five performances of *Don Giovanni* in 1961, six performances of Verdi's *Il trovatore* in 1962, three performances of *Der Rosenkavalier* and four of *Il trovatore* in 1963 and three performances each of Strauss's *Elektra* and *Der Rosenkavalier* in 1964. Karajan also acted as producer for *Fidelio, Falstaff, Il trovatore* and *Elektra*.

145 Karajan/Endler, *My Autobiography*, p. 150.

146 At the first Salzburg Easter Festival in 1967, Karajan conducted Wagner's *Die Walküre* on 19, 23 and 27 March, Beethoven's Missa solemnis on 22 and 25 March, Bach's Brandenburg Concertos Nos. 1 and 3 and the Violin Concerto in E major (Christian Ferras, violin) on 20 and 26 (matinée) March and Bruckner's Symphony No. 8 on 21 and 26 March.

147 At the first Salzburg Whitsun Festival in 1973, Karajan devoted all the concerts to the music of his fellow countrymen Mozart and Bruckner. He conducted Bruckner's Symphony No. 5 on 9 June, Mozart's Requiem and Bruckner's Te Deum at a matinée on 10 June, Mozart's Concerto for Three Pianos K. 242 (Christoph Eschenbach, Justus Franz and Herbert von Karajan, pianos) and Symphony No. 4 on the evening of 10 June and Bruckner's Symphony No. 8 on 11 June.

148 Karajan resigned as a member of the Salzburg Festival's management committee in 1988 and as conductor of the Berlin Philharmonic in the spring of 1989.

149 Karajan's last public performance, at which he conducted Bruckner's Symphony No. 7, was with the Vienna Philharmonic at the Musikverein, Vienna, on 23 April 1989. He died of a heart attack at his home at Anif, an elegant dormer town near Salzburg.
150 Sir Georg Solti replaced Karajan as conductor of *Un ballo in maschera* at the 1989 Salzburg Festival.
151 Riccardo Muti conducted Mozart's Requiem at Salzburg Cathedral on 23 July 1989.
152 A. Previn, ed., *Orchestra* (London, 1979), p. 162.

Conclusion

1 Richard Wagner, Act 3, *Die Meistersinger von Nürnberg*.

Bibliography

Altena, J., S. Reveyoso, and E. Ryding, *Recorded Performances of Bruno Walter (1876–1962)*, on-line publication <www.geocities.com/walteriana76/BWrecordsB.htm>

Baker-Carr, J., *Evening at Symphony: A Portrait of the Boston Symphony Orchestra* (Boston: Houghton Mifflin, 1977)

Bamberger, C., ed., *The Conductor's Art* (New York: Columbia University Press, 1965)

Barea, I., *Vienna* (London: Pimlico, 1992)

Barenboim, D., *A Life in Music* (London:Weidenfeld & Nicolson, 1991)

Bauer, W. A., and O. E. Deutsch, ed., *Mozart: Briefe und Aufzeichnungen, Gesamtausgabe*, Vol. 2 (Kassel: Bärenreiter, 1962–3)

Bauer-Lechner, N., *Erinnerungen an Gustav Mahler* (Leipzig: E. P. Tal, 1923) [for trans., see following]

——, *Recollections of Gustav Mahler*, trans. D. Newlin, ed. P. Franklin, (London: Faber Music, 1980)

Beecham, T., *A Mingled Chime* (London: Columbus Books, 1987)

Berlioz, H., trans. J. Broadhouse, *The Conductor: The Theory of His Art* (London, 1917)

Bernstein, L., *The Unanswered Question* (Cambridge, MA: Harvard University Press, 1976)

Birkin, K., 'Richard Strauss in Weimar', *Richard Strauss-Blätter* 33 (June 1995), pp. 3–36; 34 (December 1995), pp.3–56

——,'". . . wollen sehen, ob's gelingt" Richard Strauss and the Berlin Tonkünstler-Orchester', *Richard Strauss-Blätter* 46 (December 2001), pp. 3–60

Blackwood, A., *Sir Thomas Beecham: The Man and the Music* (London: Ebury Press, 1994)

Blaukopf, H., ed., *Gustav Mahler/Richard Strauss: Correspondence 1888–1911*, trans. E. Jephcott (London: Faber & Faber, 1984)

Blaukopf, K., trans. I. Goodwin, *Mahler* (London: Arts Book Club, 1973)

Blaukopf, K. and H., trans. P. Baker and others, *Mahler: His Life, Work and World* (London: Thames & Hudson, 2000)

Böhm, K., *Begegnung mit Richard Strauss* (Vienna: Doblinger, 1964)

——, *Ich erinnere mich ganz genau* (Vienna: Fritz Molden, 1970)

——, *A Life Remembered: Memoirs*, trans. J. Kehoe (London and New York: Marion Boyars, 1992)

Boult, A., *My Own Trumpet* (London: Hamish Hamilton, 1973)

——, *Boult on Music* (London: Toccata Press, 1983)

Brockhaus Riemann Musiklexikon (Mainz: Schott, 1979)

Brown, C., 'Bowing Styles, Vibrato and Portamento in Nineteenth-Century Violin Playing', *Journal of the Royal Musical Association*: 1 113 (1988), pp. 97–128

Letters of Hans von Bülow to Richard Wagner and Others, ed. Richard Count du Moulin Eckart, trans. H. Walter, ed. S. Goddard (New York: Da Capo Press, 1979).

Bülow, M. von, *Hans von Bülow: Briefe*, Vol. 1: *1841–1853* (Leipzig, 1899)

Busch, F., *Aus dem Leben eines Musikers* (Frankfurt: Fischer, 1949)

Busch, G., *Fritz Busch, Dirigent* (Frankfurt: Fischer, 1985)

——, and T. Mayer, *Fritz Busch: Der Dirigent* (Frankfurt: Fischer, 1990)

Cardus on Music ed. D. Wright (London: Hamish Hamilton, 1988)

Chasins, A., *Leopold Stokowski: A Profile* (London: Robert Hale, 1979)

Chesterman, R., *Conversations with Conductors* (London: Robson Books, 1976)

Chevalley, H., ed., *Arthur Nikisch: Leben und Wirken* (Berlin: Bote & Bock, 1922)

Clément, F., and P. Larousse, *Dictionnaire des opéras (Dictionnaire lyrique)*, ed. A. Pougin (Paris: Librairie Larousse, 1905)

Clough, F. F., and G. J. Cuming, 'Diskography', *Gramophone Record Review* (August and September 1959), pp. 718–19, 824

Cox, D., *The Henry Wood Proms* (London: BBC, 1980)

Daniel, O., *Stokowski: A Counterpoint of View* (New York: Dodd, Mead, 1982)

Del Mar, N., *Richard Strauss: A Critical Commentary on His Life and Works*, 3 vols. (London: Faber & Faber, 1986)

Dent, E. J., *Mozart's Operas: A Critical Study* (London: Chatto & Windus, 1913); rev. edn (Oxford: Clarendon Press, 1991)

De Wolfe Howe, M. A., *The Boston Symphony Orchestra: An Historical Sketch* (Boston: Atlantic Monthly Press, 1914)

Doráti, A., *Notes of Seven Decades* (London:Hodder & Stoughton, 1979)

Dupêchez, C., *Histoire de l'Opéra de Paris* (Paris: Librairie Académique Perrin, 1984)

Dyment, C., 'Felix Weingartner', *Musica* 17 (Milan, April 1980), pp. 142–52

Eaton, Q., *The Boston Opera Company* (New York: Appleton-Century, 1965)

Ehrlich, C., *First Philharmonic: A History of the Royal Philharmonic Society* (Oxford:University Press, 1995)

Elkin, R., *Queen's Hall 1893–1941* (London: Rider, 1942)

——, *Royal Philharmonic: The Annals of the Royal Philharmonic Society* (London: Rider, 1946)

Fifield, C., *True Artist and True Friend: A Biography of Hans Richter* (Oxford: Clarendon Press, 1993)

Flesch, C., trans. H. Keller, *The Memoirs of Carl Flesch* (London: Rockliff, 1957)

Forner, J., ed., *Die Gewandhaus-Konzerte zu Leipzig* (Leipzig: Deutscher Verlag für Musik, 1981)

Foster, M. B., *The History of the Philharmonic Society of London 1813–1912* (London:Bodley Head, 1912)

Franklin, P., *The Life of Mahler* (Cambridge: University Press, 2001)

Furtwängler on Music: Essays and Addresses, trans. and ed. R. Taylor (Aldershot: Scolar Press, 1991)

Furtwängler, W., trans. S. Whiteside, ed. M. Tanner, *Notebooks 1924–54* (London: Quartet Books, 1995)

Gaisberg, F. W., *Music on Record* (London: Robert Hale, 1946)

Galkin, E. W., *A History of Orchestral Conducting in Theory and Practice* (Stuyvesant, NY: Pendragon Press, 1988)

Gay, P., *Pleasure Wars* (London: Fontana, 1998)

Geissmar, B., *The Baton and the Jackboot* (London: Columbus Books, 1988)

Gilliam, B., ed., *Richard Strauss and His World* (Princeton: University Press, 1992)
——, *Richard Strauss: New Perspectives on the Composer and His Work* (Durham and London: Duke University Press, 1992)
Gillis, D., *Furtwängler and America* (Woodhaven, NY: Manyland Books, 1970)
Goossens, E., *Overture and Beginners: A Musical Autobiography* (London: Methuen, 1951)
Glenn Gould: Selected Letters, ed. J. P. L. Roberts and G. Guertin (Toronto: Oxford University Press, 1992)
Gregor, J., *Richard Strauss, der Meister der Oper* (Munich: Piper, 1939)
Gruber, G., *Mozart & Posterity*, trans. R.S. Furness (London: Quartet Books, 1991)
Haas, F., *Hans von Bülow: Leben und Wirken: Wegbereiter für Wagner, Liszt und Brahms* (Wilhelmshaven: Florian Noetzel, 2002)
Hadamowsky, F., *Die Wiener Hoftheater (Staatstheater)*, Vol. 2: *1811–1974* (Vienna: Hollinek, 1975)
Haeusserman, E., *Herbert von Karajan* (Vienna: Fritz Molden, 1978)
Hagemann, C., *Bühne und Welt: Erlebnisse und Betrachtungen eines Theaterleiters* (Wiesbaden: Der Greif, Walther Gericke, 1948)
Hagen, G., *Die Cölner Oper seit ihrem Einzug in das Opernhaus 1902/03–1911/12* (Cologne: Paul Neubner, 2001)
Hanslick, E., *Vom Musikalisch-Schönen* (Leipzig: Barth, 1854); trans. G. Cohen, *The Beautiful in Music* (NewYork: Da Capo, 1974)
Harnoncourt, N., trans. M. O'Neill, *The Musical Dialogue* (London: Christopher Helm, 1989)
Hartmann, R., trans. G. Davies, *Richard Strauss: The Staging of His Operas and Ballets* (Oxford: University Press, 1982)
Hennenberg, F., *The Leipzig Gewandhaus Orchestra* (Leipzig: VEB, 1962)
Herzfeld, F., *Wilhelm Furtwängler: Weg und Wesen* (Leipzig: Wilhelm Goldmann, 1942)
Heyworth, P., *Conversations with Klemperer* (London: Faber & Faber, 1985)
——, *Otto Klemperer: His Life and Times*, Vol. 1: *1885–1933*, Vol. 2: *1933–1973* (Cambridge: University Press, 1996)
Higgins, J., *The Making of an Opera* (London: Secker & Warburg, 1978)
——, ed., *Glyndebourne: A Celebration* (London: Jonathan Cape, 1984)
Hinrichsen, H.-J., *Musikalische Interpretation: Hans von Bülow* (Stuttgart: Franz Steiner, 1999)
Hirsch, F., *Das grosse Wörterbuch der Musik* (Wilhelmshaven: Heinrichshofen, 1984)
Hirsh, H. J., and J. Saul, 'A George Szell Discography', *Le Grand Baton* 9: 1–2 (1972), p. 88
Hofmann, J., *Piano Playing with Piano Questions Answered* (New York: Doubleday, Page, 1909)
Holden, R., *Richard Strauss: The Origin, Dissemination and Reception of His Mozart Renaissance*, Ph.D. dissertation, University of London, 1995
——, 'Richard Strauss: The Mozart & Beethoven Recordings', *Richard Strauss-Blätter* 35 (June 1996)
——, 'Richard Strauss' Performing Version of Idomeneo', *Richard Strauss-Blätter* 36 (December 1996)
——, 'Richard Strauss in London', *Richard Strauss-Blätter* 37 (June 1997)
——, 'Richard Strauss: The *Don Juan* recordings', *Performance Practice Review* 10: 1 (Spring 1997)
——, 'Percy Pitt: Richard Strauss' English Correspondent', *Richard Strauss-Blätter* 38 (June 1998)

Holden, R., 'Recording *Don Juan*: The Composer's Perspective', *Richard Strauss-Blätter* 40 (December 1998)

——, 'Richard Strauss & the Philharmonic Society, London', *Richard Strauss-Blätter* 44 (December 2000)

——, 'Richard Strauss: An Organised Mozartian', *Richard Strauss-Blätter* 46 (December 2001)

Horowitz, J., *Understanding Toscanini* (London: Faber & Faber, 1987)

Hoyer, H., *Chronik der Wiener Staatsoper 1945 bis 1995* (Vienna and Munich: Anton Schroll, 1995)

Hughes, S., *Glyndebourne* (London: Methuen, 1965)

Hunt, J., *More 20th Century Conductors* (London: John Hunt, 1993)

——, *Philharmonic Autocrat* (London: John Hunt, 1993)

——, *Leopold Stokowski Discography and Concert Register* (London: John Hunt/ Leopold Stokowski Society, 1996)

Jacobs, A., *Henry J. Wood: Maker of the Proms* (London: Methuen, 1995)

Jaklitsch, H., *Die Salzburger Festspiele*, Vol. 3: *Verzeichnis der Werke und der Künstler 1920–1990* (Salzburg: Residenz Verlag, 1991)

Jefferson, A., *The Life of Richard Strauss* (Newton Abbot: David & Charles, 1973)

Johnson, E., ed., *Stokowski: Essays in Analysis of His Art* (London: Triad Press, 1973)

Kapp, J., *Richard Strauss und die Berliner Oper* (Berlin-Halensee: Max Hesses Verlag, 1939)

Karajan, H. von, as told to F. Endler, trans. S. Spencer, *Herbert von Karajan: My Autobiography* (London: Sidgwick & Jackson, 1989)

Kende, G. K., 'Was Richard Strauss in Wien dirigierte', *Richard Strauss-Blätter* 19 (June 1988) (Hans Scheider Verlag)

Kennedy, M., *The Hallé Tradition: A Century of Music* (Manchester: University Press, 1960)

——, *Barbirolli: Conductor Laureate* (London: MacGibbon & Kee, 1971)

——, *Strauss Tone Poems* (London: BBC, 1984)

——, *Adrian Boult* (London: Hamish Hamilton, 1987)

——, *Richard Strauss* (London: Dent, 1988)

King, A. H., *Musical Pursuits* (London: British Library, 1987)

Kipnis, I., 'Molto improvvisato', *Classic Record Collector*, Winter 2000

Klemperer, O., trans. J. Maxwell Brownjohn, *Minor Recollections* (London: Dobson Books , 1964)

Klemperer on Music: Shavings from a Musician's Workbench, ed. M. Anderson (London: Toccata Press, 1986)

Kobbé's Complete Opera Book, 10th edn, ed. Harewood (London: Bodley Head, 1987)

Köhler, J., trans. S. Spencer, *Richard Wagner: The Last of the Titans* (New Haven and London: Yale University Press, 2004)

Kraus, H., and K. Schreinzer, *Wiener Philharmoniker 1842–1942* (Vienna: Universal Edition, 1942)

Kropfinger, K., trans. P. Palmer, *Wagner and Beethoven: Richard Wagner's Reception of Beethoven* (Cambridge: University Press, 1991)

Kuret, P., *Mahler in Laibach: Ljubljana 1881–2* (Vienna, Cologne and Weimar: Böhlau, 2001)

Kučerová, D., 'Gustav Mahler v Olomouci', *Hudební věda* 4 (1968), Eng., Ger. résumés, pp. 649–51, 653–5

La Grange, H.-L. de, *Mahler*, Vol. 1 (London: Gollancz, 1974)

——, *Gustav Mahler*, Vol. 3 *Vienna: Triumph and Disillusion (1904–1907)*, (Oxford: University Press, 1999)

——, and G. Weiss, *Ein Glück ohne Ruh': Die Briefe Gustav Mahlers an Alma* (Munich: BTB, 1997)

Landon, H. C. Robbins, ed., *The Mozart Compendium: A Guide to Mozart's Life and Music* (London: Thames & Hudson, 1990)

Lang, K., trans. S. Spencer, *The Karajan Dossier* (London: Faber & Faber, 1992)

Lang, P. H., *Music in Western Civilization* (London: Dent, 1963)

Lebrecht, N., *Mahler Remembered* (London: Faber & Faber, 1987)

——, *The Maestro Myth* (London: Simon & Schuster, 1991)

Lehmann, L., *My Path through Life* (New York: Putnams, 1914)

Leinsdorf, E., *On Music* (Portland: Amadeus Press, 1997)

Louis, R., 'Bruno Walter au disque', *Diapason 415* Supplement (May 1995), pp. xiv–xviii

Lyser, F. P., 'Zweier Meister Söhne (Schluß)', *Neue Zeitschrift für Musik* 44 (1844)

——, 'Mozart's eigene Verdeutschung des Textes "Don Giovanni", nebst zwei Proben daraus', *Neue Zeitschrift für Musik* 32 (1845)

MacClintock, C., *Readings in the History of Music in Performance* (Bloomington: Indiana University Press, 1979)

Mahler, A., trans. B. Creighton, ed. D. Mitchell and K. Martner, *Gustav Mahler Memories and Letters* (London: Cardinal, 1990)

Selected Letters of Gustav Mahler, trans. E. Wilkins and B. Hopkins, ed. K. Martner (London: Faber & Faber, 1979)

Alma Mahler-Werfel: Diaries 1898–1902, trans. and ed. A. Beaumont (London: Faber & Faber, 1998)

Mann, W., *Richard Strauss: A Critical Study of the Operas* (London: Cassell, 1964)

Marek, G. R., *Richard Strauss: The Life of a Non-Hero* (London: Gollancz, 1967)

Marsh, R. C., 'The Heritage of Bruno Walter', *High Fidelity* 14 (1964), pp. 44–8, 103–9

——, *Dialogues & Discoveries: James Levine, His Life and His Music* (New York: Scribner, 1998)

Martner, K., *Gustav Mahler im Konzertsaal: Eine Dokumentation seiner Konzerttätigkeit 1870–1911* (Copenhagen: K-M Privatdruck, 1985)

Masini, U., pref., 'Discografia di Bruno Walter', *Musica* 8 (June 1984), pp. 32–9

Meyer, G. E., *100 Jahre Münchner Philharmoniker* (Munich: Alois Knürr, 1994)

Meyers Taschen-Lexikon Musik (Mannheim: Taschen, 1984)

Millington, B., and S. Spencer, eds., *Wagner in Performance* (New Haven and London: Yale University Press , 1992)

Moberly, R., and C. Raeburn, 'Mozart's "Figaro": The Plan of Act III', *Music and Letters* 46 (1965), pp. 134–6

Morse, P., 'Richard Strauss' Recordings: A Complete Discography', *Journal of the Association for Recorded Sound Collections* 9: 1 (1977)

Moulin-Eckart, R., *Hans von Bülow* (Munich: Rösl, 1921)

Müller, H., and V. Gerasch, eds., *Beiträge zum Kolloquium Hans von Bülow: Leben, Wirken und Vermächtnis [. . .] zum 100. Todestag Hans von Bülows*, Südthüringer Forschungen 28 (Meiningen: Staatliche Museen Meiningen, 1995)

Müller, H., and V. Kern, eds., *Die Meininger kommen!* (Meiningen: Staatliche Museen Meiningen, 1999)

Myers, R., ed., *Richard Strauss & Romain Rolland: Correspondence and Diary Fragments* (London: Calder & Boyars, 1968)

Newlin, D., *Bruckner–Mahler–Schoenberg* (London: Marion Boyars, 1979)

Osborne, R., *Conversations with Karajan* (Oxford: University Press, 1989)

——, *Herbert von Karajan: A Life in Music* (London: Chatto & Windus, 1998)

Ott, A., ed., *Die Münchner Philharmoniker 1893–1968: Ein Kapitel Kulturgeschichte* (Munich: Peter Winkler, 1968)

Paumgartner, B., *Gustav Mahlers Bearbeitung von Mozarts 'Così fan tutte' für seine Aufführungen an der Wiener Hofoper* (Kassel: Bärenreiter, 1968)

Pearton, M., *The LSO at 70: A History of the Orchestra* (London: Gollancz, 1974)

Philip, R., *Early Recordings and Musical Style: Changing Tastes in Instrumental Performance 1900–1950* (Cambridge: University Press, 1994)

Pickett, D. A., rev. R. Warren, *A Bruno Walter Discography, Part One: Commercial Recordings: Issued Discs Only*, Bruno Walter Society, 1973

Pickett, D. A., *Gustav Mahler as an Interpreter: A Study of his Textural Alterations and Performance Practice in the Symphonic Repertoire*, Ph.D. dissertation, University of Surrey (1988)

Piendl, S., and T. Otto, eds., *Stenographische Umarmung* (Regensburg: ConBrio, 2002)

Pitou, S., *The Paris Opéra: An Encyclopaedia of Opera, Ballets, Composers and Performers: 'Growth and Grandeur 1815–1914'*, Volume M–Z (Westport, CT: Greenwood, 1990)

Possart, E. von, *Ueber die Neueinstudierung und Neuinszenierung des Mozart'schen Don Giovanni (Don Juan) auf dem kgl. Residenztheater zu München* (Munich: A. Bruckmann, 1896)

Praeger, F., *Wagner as I Knew Him* (New York: Longmans, 1893)

Prawy, M., *Die Wiener Oper* (Vienna: Molden, 1969)

Previn, A., ed., *Orchestra* (London: Macdonald & Janes, 1979)

Prieberg, F. K., trans. C. Dolan, *Trial of Strength: Wilhelm Furtwängler and the Third Reich* (London: Quartet Books, 1991)

Pritchard, J., 'Conducting Mozart', *Opera Annual* 2 (1956)

Quander, G., *Klangbilder: Portrait der Staatskapelle Berlin* (Frankfurt: Ullstein, Berlin: Propyläen, 1995)

Rees, C. B., *100 Years of the Hallé* (London: MacGibbon & Kee, 1957)

Reilly, E. R., *Gustav Mahler and Guido Adler: Records of a Friendship* (Cambridge: University Press, 1982)

Reid, C., *John Barbirolli* (London: Hamish Hamilton, 1971)

Rigby, C., *John Barbirolli: A Biographical Sketch* (Altrincham: John Sherratt, 1948)

Robinson, P., *Karajan* (London: Macdonald & Janes, 1975)

Roman, Z., *Gustav Mahler's American Years 1907–1911: A Documentary History* (Stuyvesant, NY: Pendragon, 1989)

——, *Gustav Mahler and Hungary* (Budapest:Akadémiai Kiadó, 1991)

Rosenthal, H., *Two Centuries of Opera at Covent Garden* (London: Putnam, 1958)

Rösler, W., M. Haedler, and M. von Marcard, *Das 'Zauberschloss' Unter den Linden: Die Berliner Staatsoper: Geschichte und Geschichten von den Anfängen bis heute* (Berlin: Edition Q, 1997)

Rushton, J., ed., *W. A. Mozart: Idomeneo* (Cambridge: University Press, 1993)

Ryding, E., and R. Pechefsky, *Bruno Walter: A World Elsewhere* (New Haven and London:Yale University Press, 2001)

Sachs, H., *Toscanini* (London: Robson Books, 1993)

Sadie, S., ed., *The New Grove Dictionary of Music and Musicians* (London: Macmillan, 1980)

Saul, J., 'A Personal Account of George Szell', *Le Grand Baton* 9: 1–2 (1972)

Sawallisch, W., *Im Interesse der Deutlichkeit: Mein Leben mit der Musik* (Hamburg: Hoffmann & Campe, 1988)

Schabas, E., *Theodore Thomas, America's Conductor and Builder of Orchestras, 1835–1905* (Urbana and Chicago: University of Illinois Press, 1989)

Schaefer, H.-J., 'Gustav Mahlers Wirken in Kassel', *Musica* 14: 6 (1960), p. 350

Schlötterer-Traimer, R., *Richard Strauss und die Musikalische Akademie in München* (Munich: Hypo-Vereinsbank Kulturgesellschaft, 1999)

Schmoll gen. Eisenwerth, R., ed., *Die Münchener Philharmoniker von der Gründung bis heute* (Munich: Wolf & Sohn, 1985)

Schnabel, A., *My Life and Music* (New York: Dover and Colin Smythe, 1988)

Schonberg, H., *The Great Conductors* (London: Gollancz, 1977)

Schönzeler, H.-H., *Furtwängler* (London: Duckworth, 1990)

Schuh, W., trans. M. Whittall, *Richard Strauss: A Chronicle of the Early Years, 1864–1898* (Cambridge: University Press, 1982)

Schuller, G., *The Compleat Conductor* (Oxford: University Press, 1997)

Schwarzkopf, E., *On and Off the Record: A Memoir of Walter Legge* (London: Faber & Faber, 1982)

Shanet, H., *Philharmonic: A History of New York's Orchestra* (New York: Doubleday, 1975)

Shirakawa, S. H., *The Devil's Music Master* (Oxford: University Press, 1992)

Shore, B., *The Orchestra Speaks* (London: Longmans Green, 1938)

Testimony: the Memoirs of Dmitri Shostakovich, ed. S. Volkov (London: Faber & Faber, 1979)

Simek, U., ed, *100 Jahre Wiener Volksoper* (Vienna, Cologne and Weimar: Böhlau, 1998)

Slonimsky, N., rev., *Baker's Biographical Dictionary of Musicians*, 8th edn (New York: Schirmer Books, 1992)

Snyder, L., *Community of Sound: Boston Symphony and its World of Players* (Boston: Beacon Press, 1979)

Stewart, A., *The LSO at 90: From Queen's Hall to the Barbican Centre* (London: Symphony Orchestra, 1994)

Stokowski, L., *Music for All of Us* (New York: Simon & Schuster, 1943)

Strasser, O., trans. J. Williamson, 'Beethoven's Ninth and the Vienna Philharmonic', disc notes, Deutsche Grammophon CD 435 325–2

Strauss, R., ed. W. Schuh, *Betrachtungen und Erinnerungen* (Zürich: Atlantis, 1949); trans. L. J. Lawrence, *Recollections and Reflections* (London: Boosey & Hawkes, 1953)

Richard Strauss: Briefe an die Eltern 1882–1906, ed. W. Schuh (Zürich: Atlantis, 1954)

Richard Strauss: Briefwechsel mit Josef Gregor, ed. R. Tenschert (Salzburg: Otto Müller, 1955)

Hans von Bülow and Richard Strauss: Correspondence, ed. W. Schuh and F. Trenner, trans. A. Gishford (London: Boosey & Hawkes, 1955)

Richard Strauss: Briefwechsel mit Willi Schuh, ed. W. Schuh (Zürich, 1969)

A Confidential Matter: The Letters of Richard Strauss and Stefan Zweig, 1931–1935, trans. M. Knight (London: University of California Press, 1977)

The Correspondence between Richard Strauss and von Hofmannsthal, ed. F. and A. Strauss, arr. W. Schuh, trans. H. Hammelmann and E. Osers (Cambridge: University Press , 1980)

Richard Strauss: Briefwechsel mit Clemens Krauss, ed. G. Brosche (Vienna: Institut für Österreichische Musikdokumentation, 1997)

Stroff, S. M., 'Albert Coates', *Le Grand Baton* 45/17: 1 (March 1980)

Trenner, F., 'Anmerkungen zur Aufführung von Beethovens Symphonien', *Neue Zeitschrift für Musik* 125 (June 1964)

——, 'Richard Strauss and Munich', trans. G. Simon, *Tempo* 69 (Summer 1964), pp. 5–14

——, *Richard Strauss: Werkverzeichnis* (Vienna: Doblinger, 1985)

——, 'Richard Strauss am Pult der Münchner Oper', *Richard Strauss-Blätter* 25 (June 1991)

Trenner, Franz, ed., Florian Trenner, *Richard Strauss: Chronik zu Leben und Werk* (Vienna: Verlag Richard Strauss, 2003)

Trotter, W. R., *Priest of Music: The Life of Dimitri Mitropoulos* (Portland, OR: Amadeus Press, 1995)

Tschulik, N., *Musiktheater in Österreich: Die Oper im 20. Jahrhundert* (Vienna: Österreichischer Bundesverlag, 1984)

Turnbull, R., *The Opera Gazetteer* (New York: Rizzoli, 1988)

Vaughan, R., *Herbert von Karajan: A Biographical Portrait* (London: Weidenfeld & Nicolson, 1990)

Vermeil, J., trans. C. Naish, *Conversations with Boulez: Thoughts on Conducting* (Portland, OR: Amadeus Press, 1996)

Wagner, R., *Über das Dirigieren* (Leipzig, 1869); trans. E. Dannreuther, *On Conducting* (London, 1919)

——, trans. M. Whittall, ed. A. Gray, *My Life* (Cambridge: University Press, 1983)

——, *My Life* (London: Constable, 1994)

——, trans. W. Ashton Ellis, *Pilgrimage to Beethoven and Other Essays* (Lincoln and London: University of Nebraska Press (Bison Books), 1994)

——, trans. W. Ashton Ellis, *Actors and Singers* (Lincoln and London: University of Nebraska Press (Bison Books), 1995)

——, trans. W. Ashton Ellis, *Art and Politics* (Lincoln and London: University of Nebraska Press (Bison Books), 1995)

——, trans. W. Ashton Ellis, W., *Jesus of Nazareth and Other Writings* (Lincoln and London: University of Nebraska Press (Bison Books), 1995)

Walter, B., trans. J. A. Galston, *Theme and Variations: An Autobiography* (London: Hamish Hamilton, 1947)

——, trans. P. Hamburger, *Of Music and Music-making* (London: Faber & Faber, 1961)

——, trans. L W. Lindt, *Gustav Mahler* (London: Quartet Books, 1990)

Walton, C., 'Richard Wagner als Dirigent in Zürich', *Tribschener Blätter* 55–6, (September 1998)

Warfield, S., 'Friedrich Wilhelm Meyer: Some Biographical Notes on Richard Strauss's Composition Teacher', *Richard Strauss-Blätter* 37 (June 1997)

Warrack, J., and E. West, *The Oxford Dictionary of Opera* (Oxford: University Press, 1992)

Weingartner, F., *Über das Dirigieren* (Leipzig: Breitkopf & Härtel, 1895); trans. E. Newman, *On Conducting* (London: Breitkopf & Härtel, 1906)

——, *Die Symphonie nach Beethoven* (Leipzig: Breitkopf & Härtel, 1897); trans. A. Bles, *The Post-Beethoven Symphonists: Symphony Writers since Beethoven* (London: W. Reeves, n.d.)

——, *Ratschläge für Aufführung der Symphonien Beethovens* (Leipzig: Breitkopf & Härtel, 1906); trans. J. Crosland, *On the Performance of Beethoven's Symphonies* (London: Breitkopf & Härtel, 1907)

——, *Ratschläge für Aufführungen Klassischer Symphonien*, Vol. III, *Mozart* (Leipzig: Breitkopf & Härtel, 1923)

——, trans. M. Wolff, *Buffets and Rewards: A Musician's Reminiscences* (London: Hutchinson, 1937)

Westernhagen, C. von, 'Wagner', *The New Grove Dictionary of Music and Musicians*, ed. S. Sadie (London: Macmillan, 1980)

——, trans. M. Whittall, *Wagner: A Biography*, Vol. 1: *1813–64* (Cambridge: University Press, 1978)

Wilhelm, K., trans. M. Whittall, *Richard Strauss: An Intimate Portrait* (London: Thames & Hudson, 1989)

Williamson, J., *Strauss: Also sprach Zarathustra* (Cambridge University Press, 1993)

Willnauer, F., *Gustav Mahler und die Wiener Oper* (Vienna: Löcker Verlag, 1993)

Wolff, K., *Schnabel's Interpretation of Piano Music* (London: Faber Music, 1972)

Wurmser, L., 'Richard Strauss as an Opera Conductor', *Music and Letters* 45 (1964), pp. 4–15

Young, K., *Music's Great Days in the Spas and Watering Places* (London: Macmillan, 1968)

Zaslaw, N., *Mozart's Symphonies: Context, Performance Practice, Reception* (Oxford: University Press, 1989)

Zimdars, R. L., trans. and ed., *The Piano Master Classes of Hans von Bülow: Two Participants' Accounts* (Bloomington and Indianapolis: Indiana University Press, 1993)

Zehetmair, H., and J. Schläder, eds., *Nationaltheater: Die Bayerische Staatsoper* (Munich: Bruckmann, 1992)

Index